Gankutsuou

The Count of Monte Cristo

1

Manga by Mahiro Maeda
Scenario by Yura Ariwara

Planning by Mahiro Maeda and GONZO

Translated and adapted by Gemma Collinge
Lettered by North Market Street Graphics

BALLANTINE BOOKS • NEW YORK

A Del Rey Manga/Kodansha Trade Paperback Original

Gankutsuou: The Count of Monte Cristo volume 1 copyright © 2005 Mahiro Maeda · GONZO/MEDIA FACTORY · GDH © 2005 Mahiro Maeda/Yura Ariwara English translation copyright © 2008 by Mahiro Maeda/Yura Ariwara

Published in the United States by Del Rey Books, an imprint of The Random House Publishing Group, a division of Random House, Inc., New York.

DEL REY is a registered trademark and the Del Rey colophon is a trademark of Random House, Inc.

Publication rights arranged through Kodansha Ltd.

First published in Japan in 2005 by Kodansha Ltd., Tokyo

ISBN 978-0-345-50520-0

Printed in the United States of America

www.delreymanga.com

9 8 7 6 5 4 3 2 1

Translator/Adapter—Gemma Collinge
Lettering—North Market Street Graphics

Gankutsuo 1

CONTENTS

← strange

Mahiro Maeda
I'm so happy and embarrassed. Please enjoy.

Little cat

Yura Ariwara
We've worked for a year to bring you
a slightly different perspective on the anime...

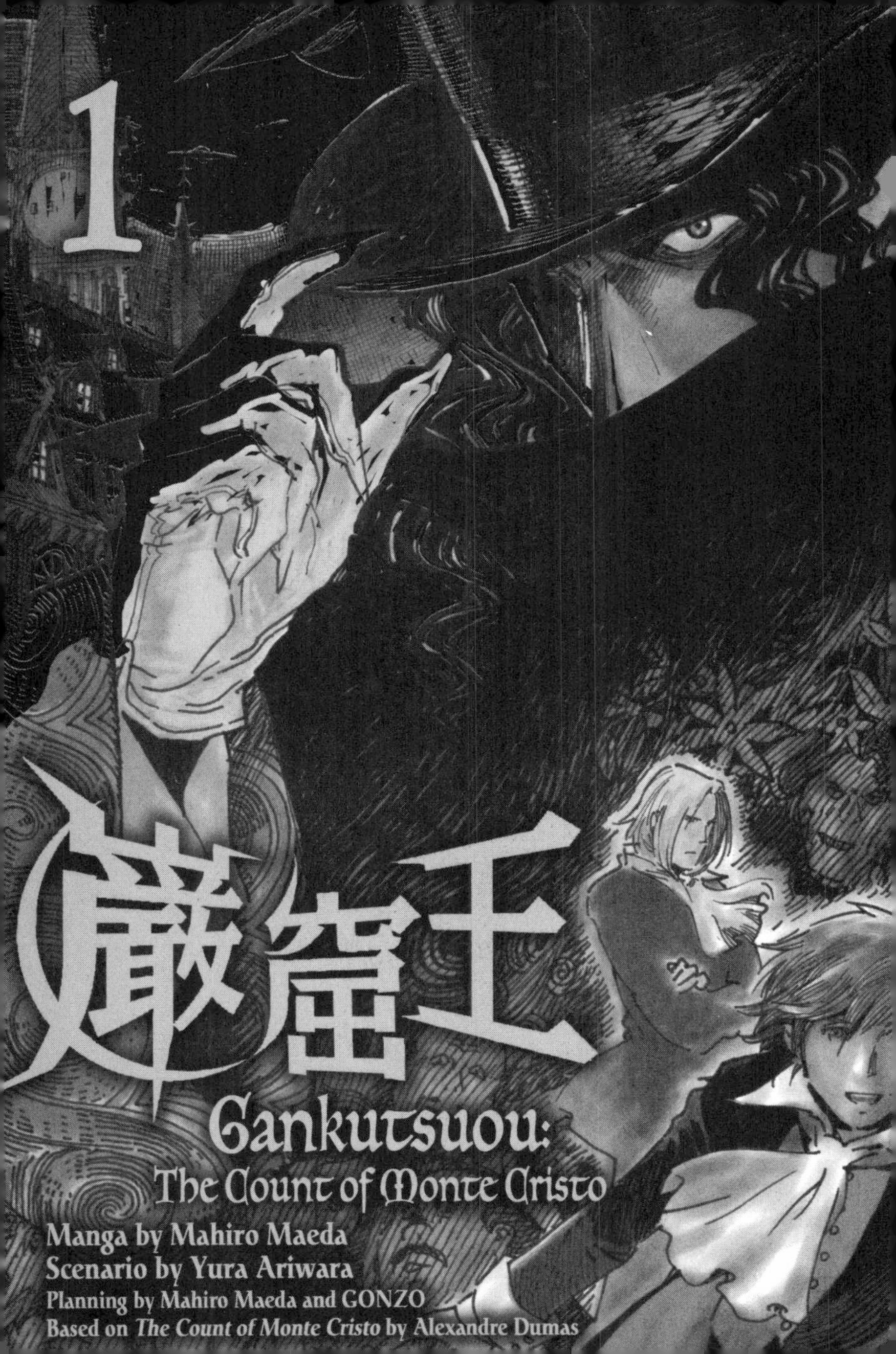
1
巌窟王
Gankutsuou:
The Count of Monte Cristo
Manga by Mahiro Maeda
Scenario by Yura Ariwara
Planning by Mahiro Maeda and GONZO
Based on *The Count of Monte Cristo* by Alexandre Dumas

SOMMAIRE
CONTENTS

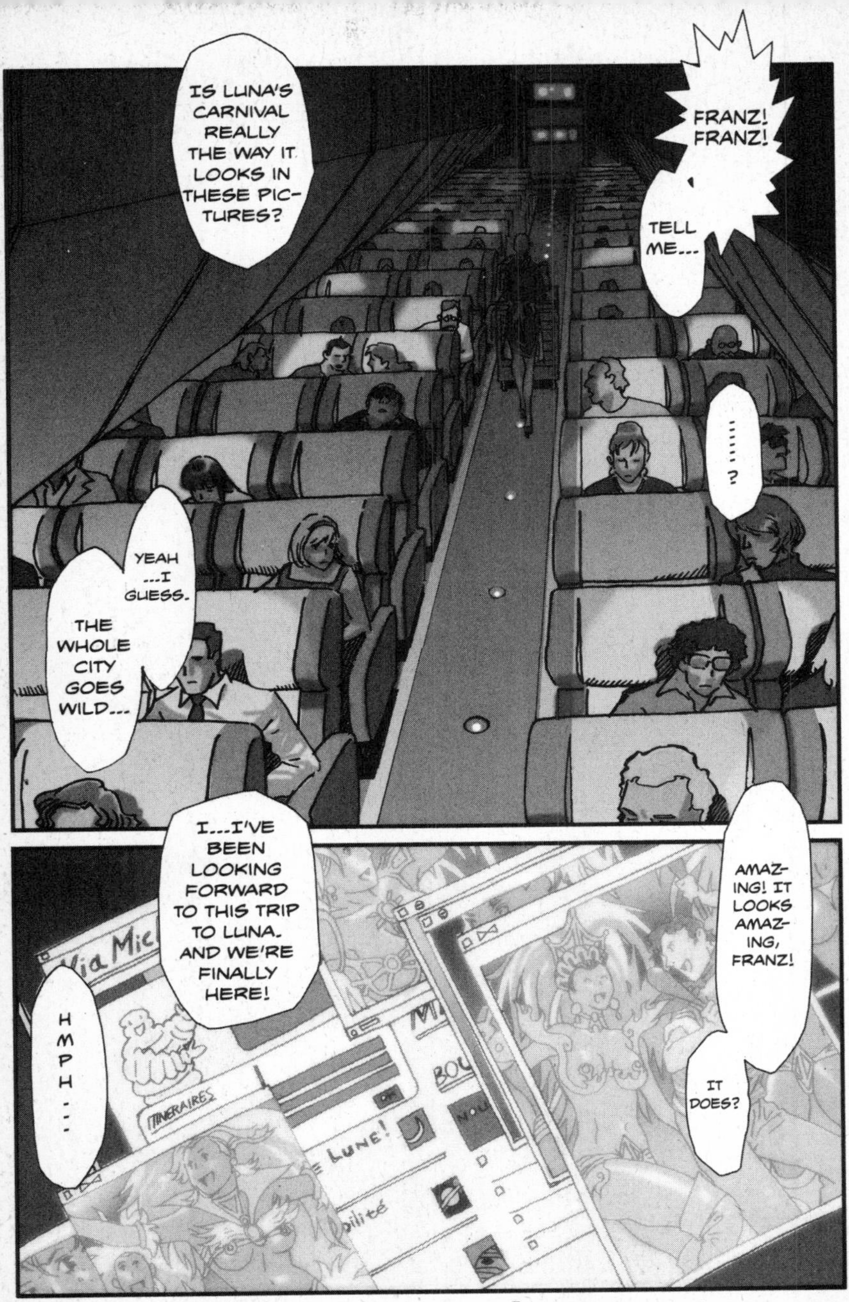
FRANZ! FRANZ!
TELL ME...
IS LUNA'S CARNIVAL REALLY THE WAY IT LOOKS IN THESE PICTURES?
......?
YEAH ...I GUESS.
THE WHOLE CITY GOES WILD...
AMAZING! IT LOOKS AMAZING, FRANZ!
IT DOES?
I...I'VE BEEN LOOKING FORWARD TO THIS TRIP TO LUNA. AND WE'RE FINALLY HERE!
HMPH...

Chapitre 1: At Journey's End, We Meet

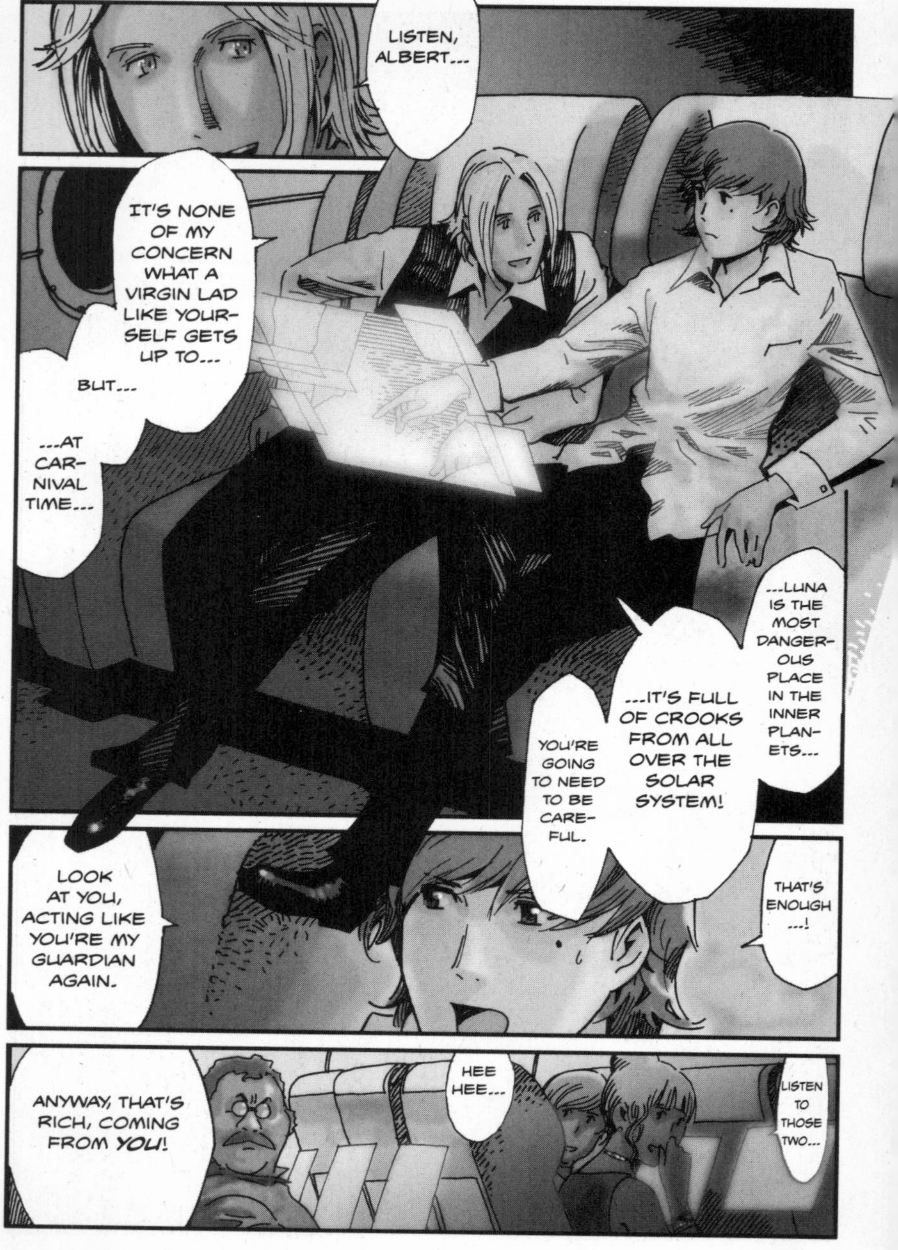
LISTEN, ALBERT...
IT'S NONE OF MY CONCERN WHAT A VIRGIN LAD LIKE YOURSELF GETS UP TO...
BUT...
...AT CARNIVAL TIME...
...LUNA IS THE MOST DANGEROUS PLACE IN THE INNER PLANETS...
...IT'S FULL OF CROOKS FROM ALL OVER THE SOLAR SYSTEM!
YOU'RE GOING TO NEED TO BE CAREFUL.
LOOK AT YOU, ACTING LIKE YOU'RE MY GUARDIAN AGAIN.
THAT'S ENOUGH...!
ANYWAY, THAT'S RICH, COMING FROM *YOU*!
HEE HEE...
LISTEN TO THOSE TWO...

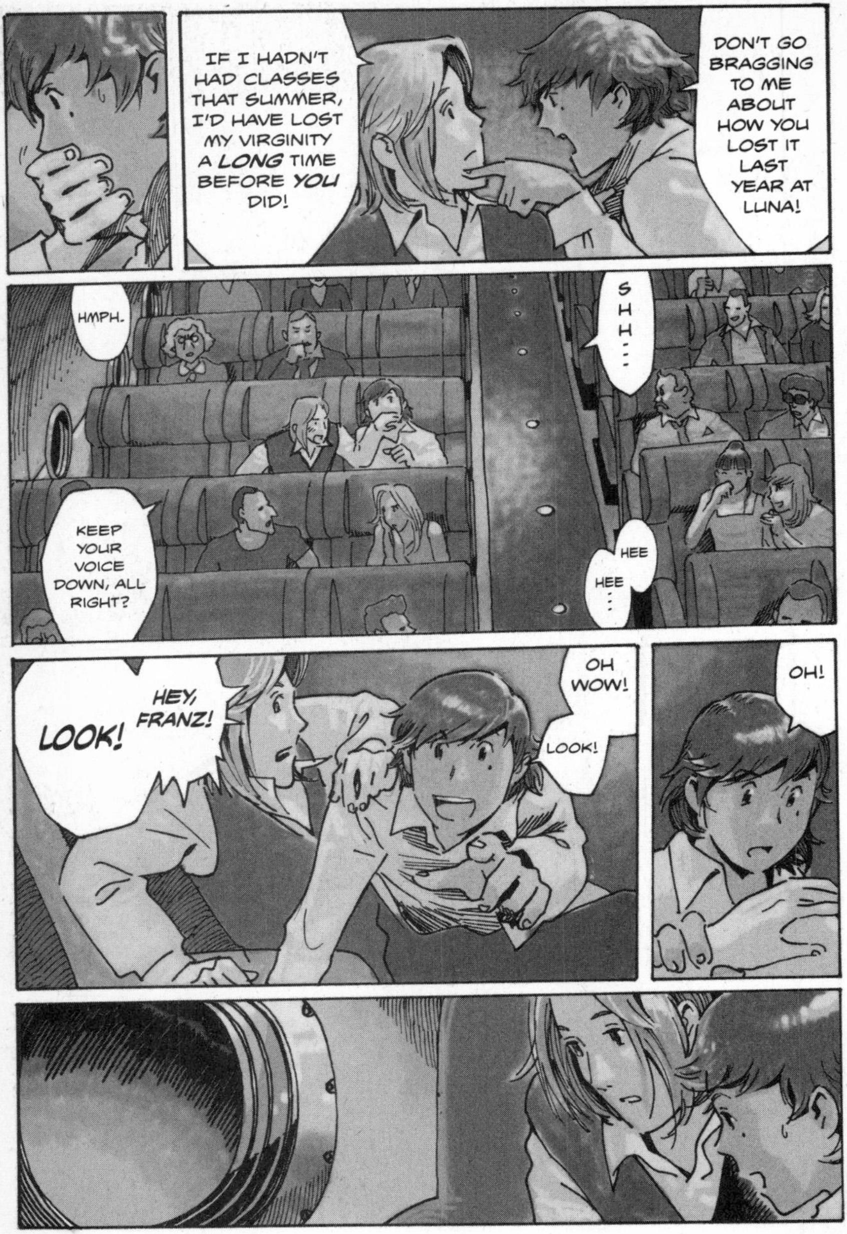
DON'T GO BRAGGING TO ME ABOUT HOW YOU LOST IT LAST YEAR AT LUNA!
IF I HADN'T HAD CLASSES THAT SUMMER, I'D HAVE LOST MY VIRGINITY A **LONG** TIME BEFORE **YOU** DID!
SHH...
HMPH.
HEE HEE...
KEEP YOUR VOICE DOWN, ALL RIGHT?
OH!
OH WOW!
LOOK!
HEY, FRANZ!
LOOK!

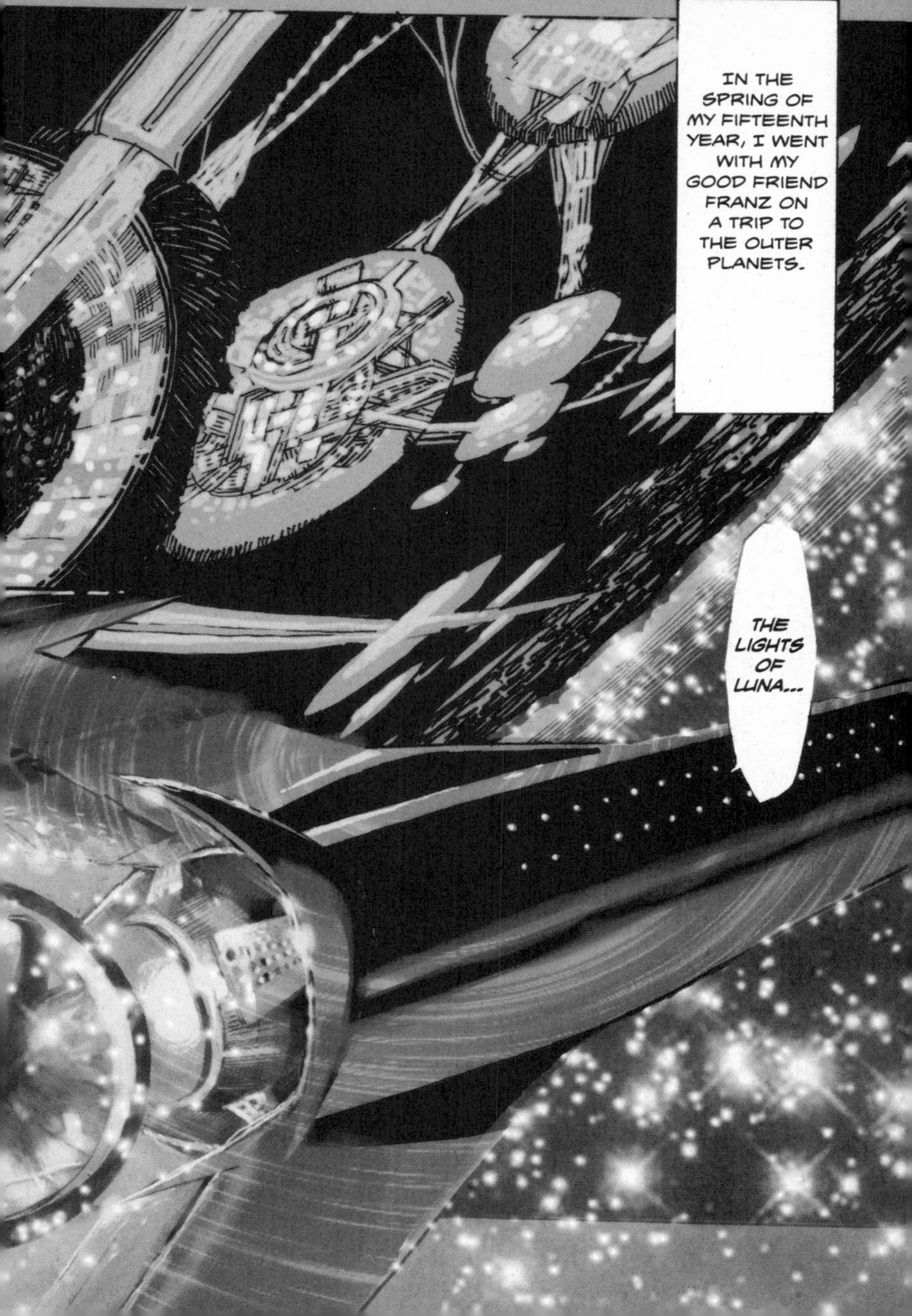
IN THE SPRING OF MY FIFTEENTH YEAR, I WENT WITH MY GOOD FRIEND FRANZ ON A TRIP TO THE OUTER PLANETS.
THE LIGHTS OF LUNA...

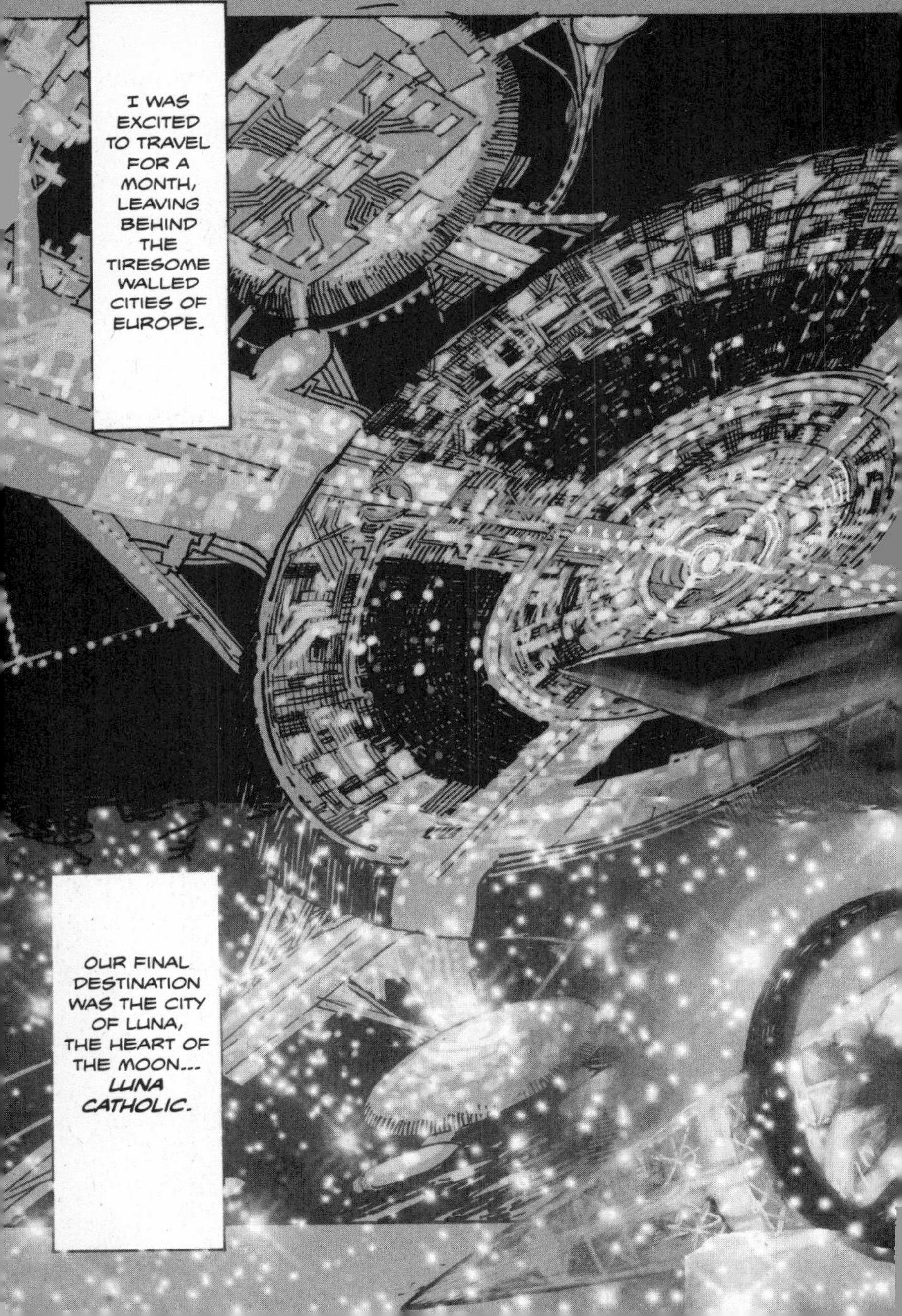
I WAS EXCITED TO TRAVEL FOR A MONTH, LEAVING BEHIND THE TIRESOME WALLED CITIES OF EUROPE.
OUR FINAL DESTINATION WAS THE CITY OF LUNA, THE HEART OF THE MOON... *LUNA CATHOLIC*.

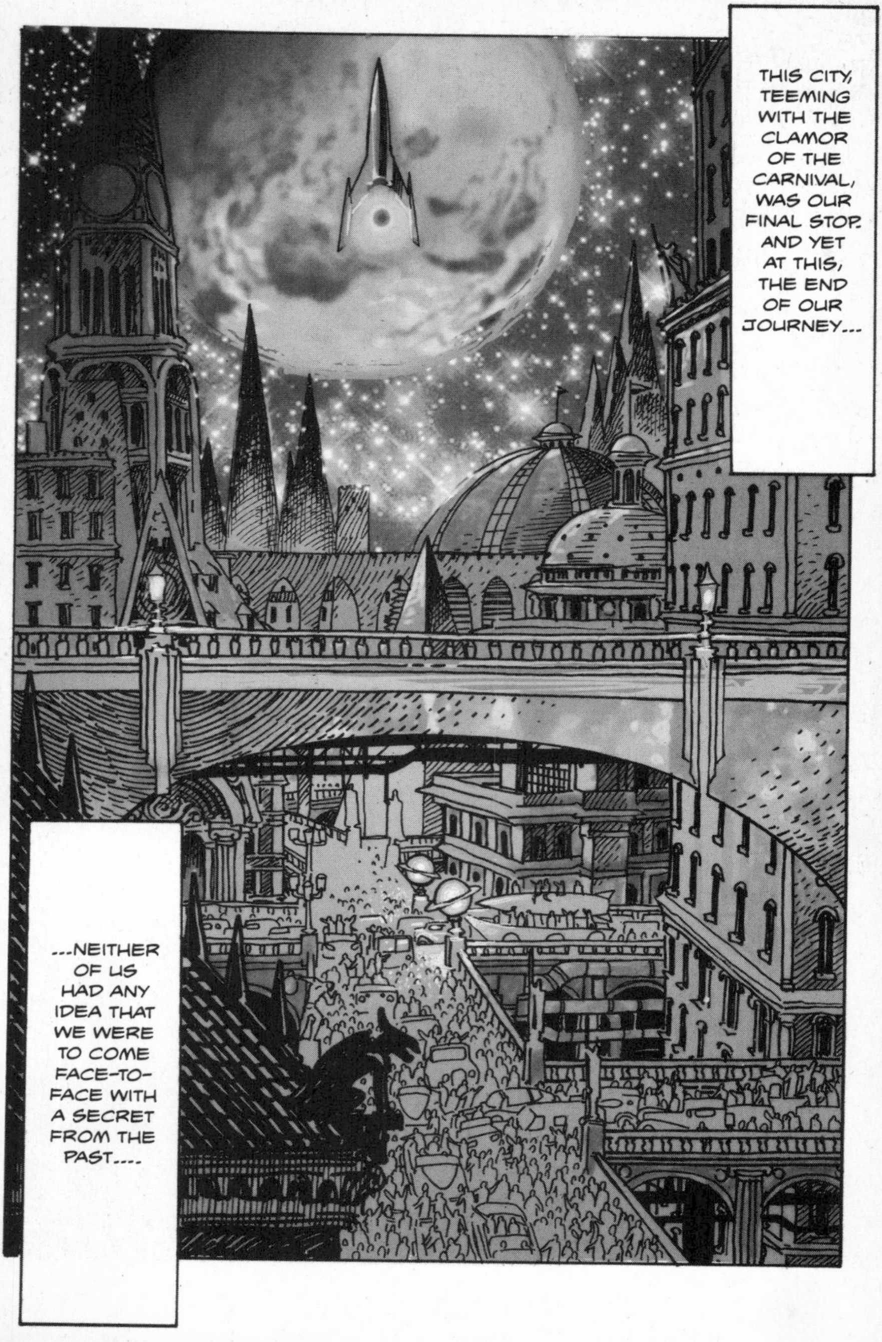
THIS CITY, TEEMING WITH THE CLAMOR OF THE CARNIVAL, WAS OUR FINAL STOP. AND YET AT THIS, THE END OF OUR JOURNEY...
...NEITHER OF US HAD ANY IDEA THAT WE WERE TO COME FACE-TO-FACE WITH A SECRET FROM THE PAST....

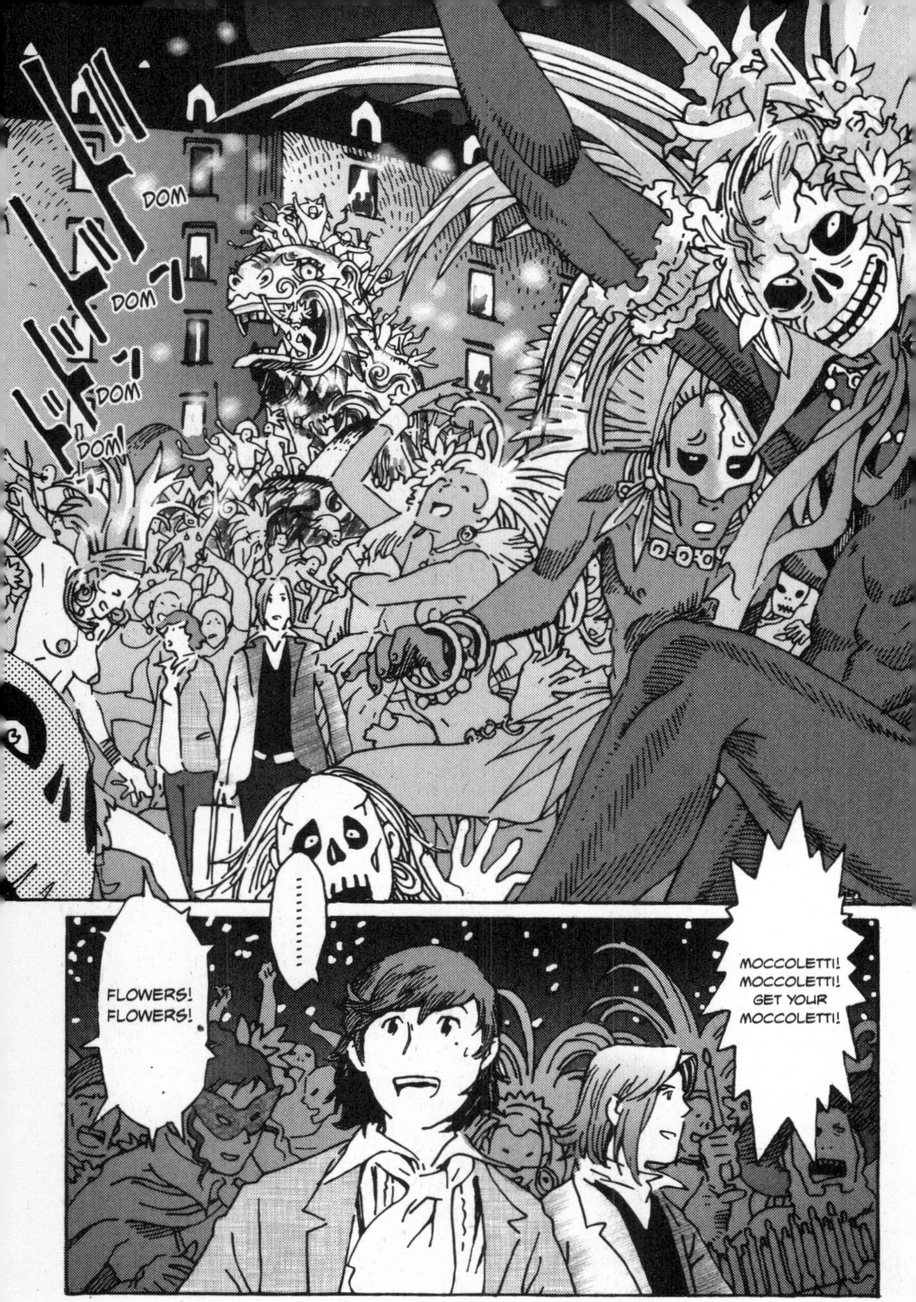
DOM
DOM
DOM
DOM!
MOCCOLETTI! MOCCOLETTI! GET YOUR MOCCOLETTI!
FLOWERS! FLOWERS!

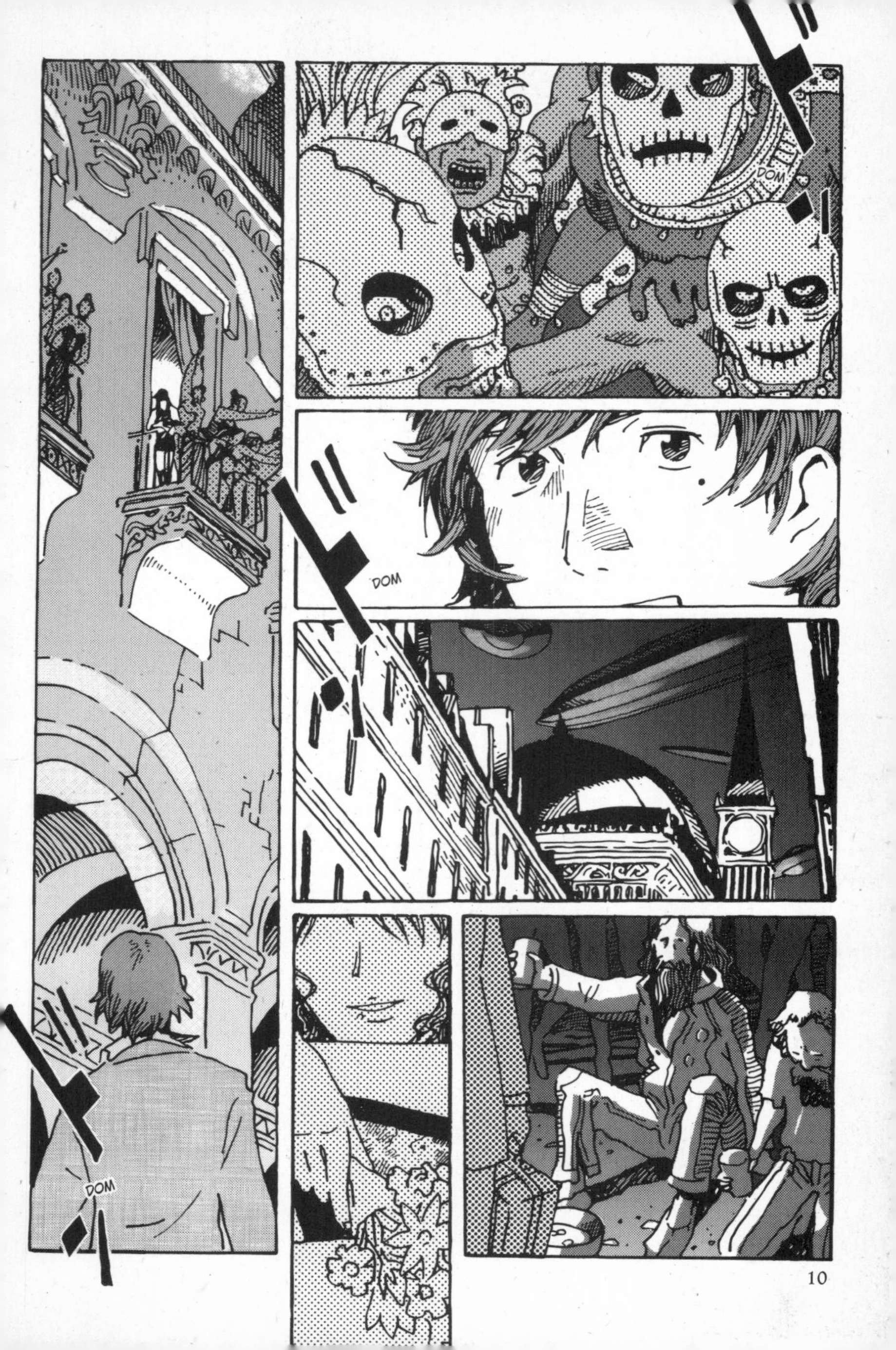
DOM
DOM
DOM

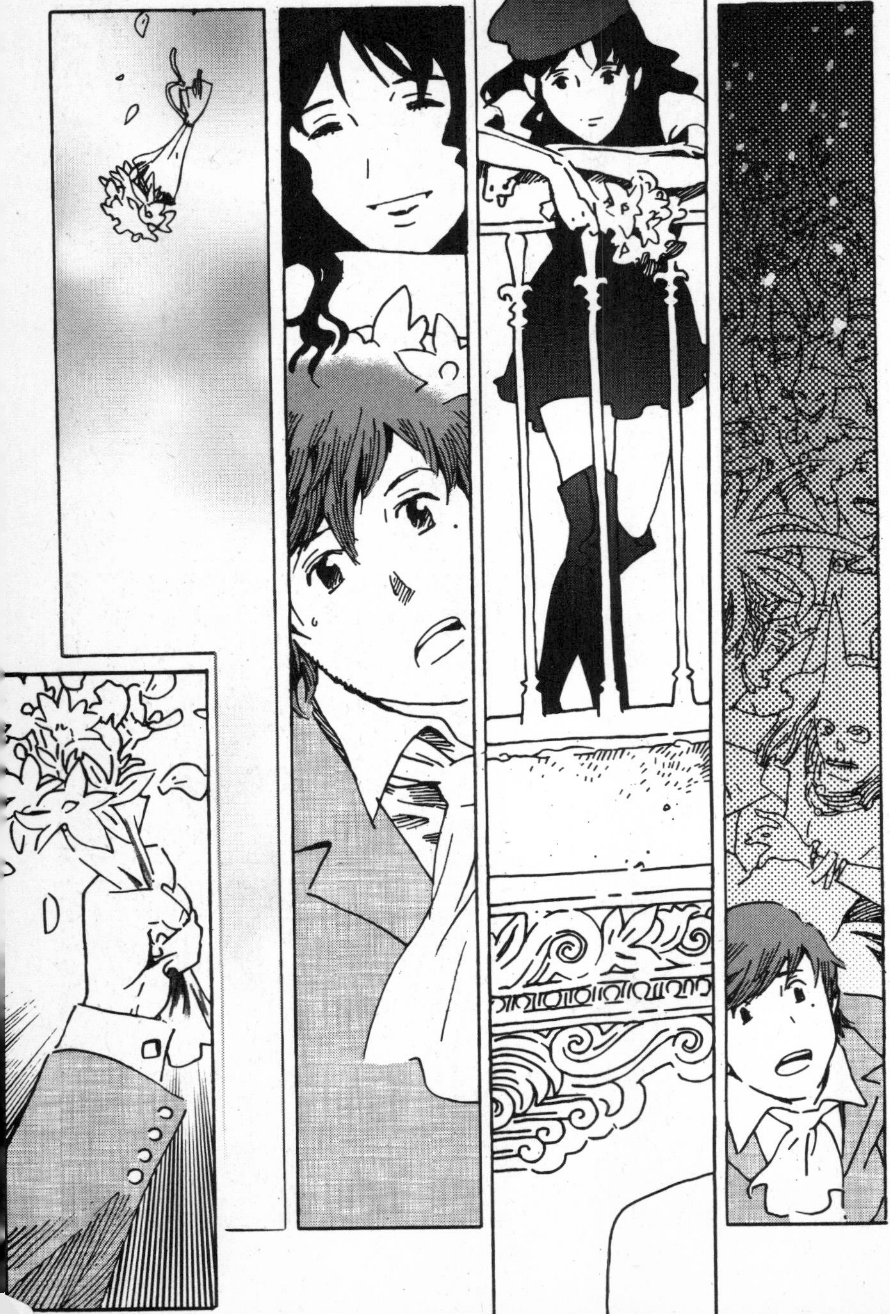

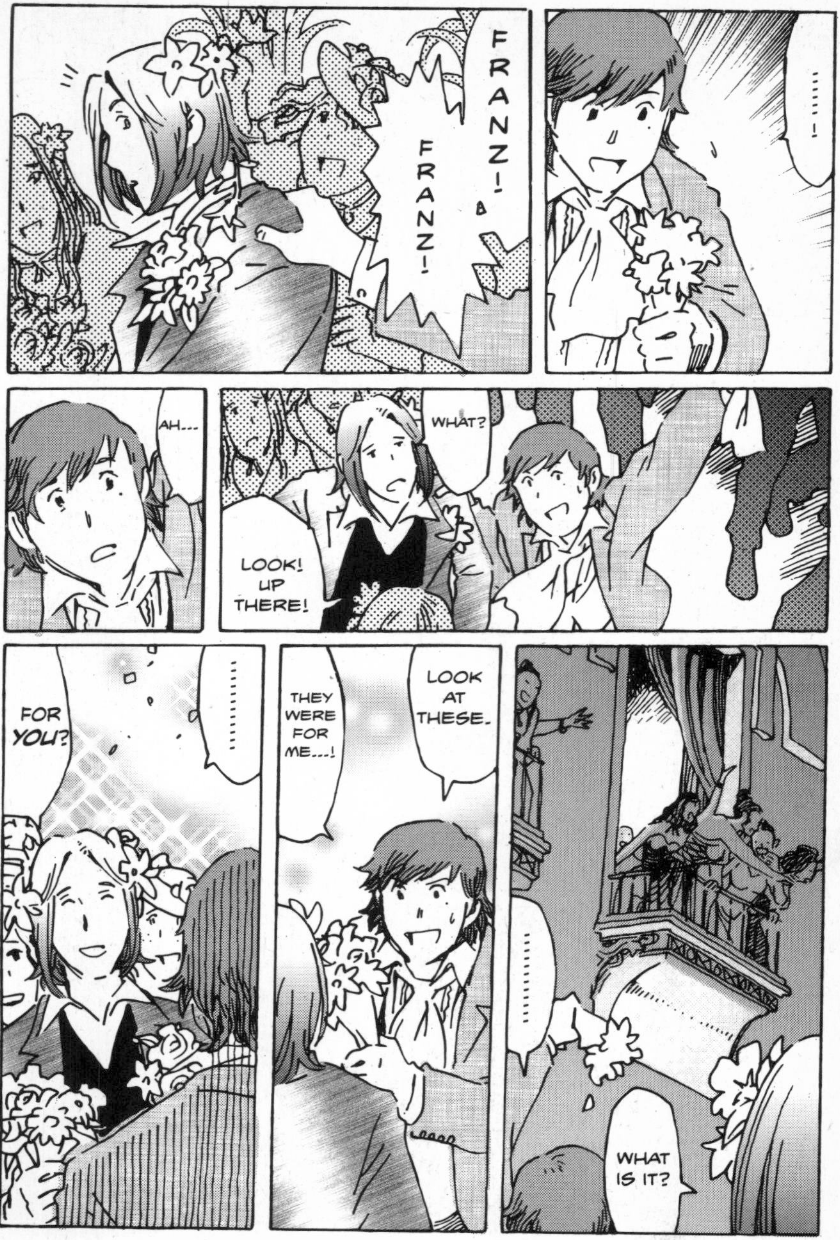
......!
FRANZ!
FRANZ!
WHAT?
LOOK! UP THERE!
AH...
......
WHAT IS IT?
LOOK AT THESE.
THEY WERE FOR ME...!
......
FOR YOU?

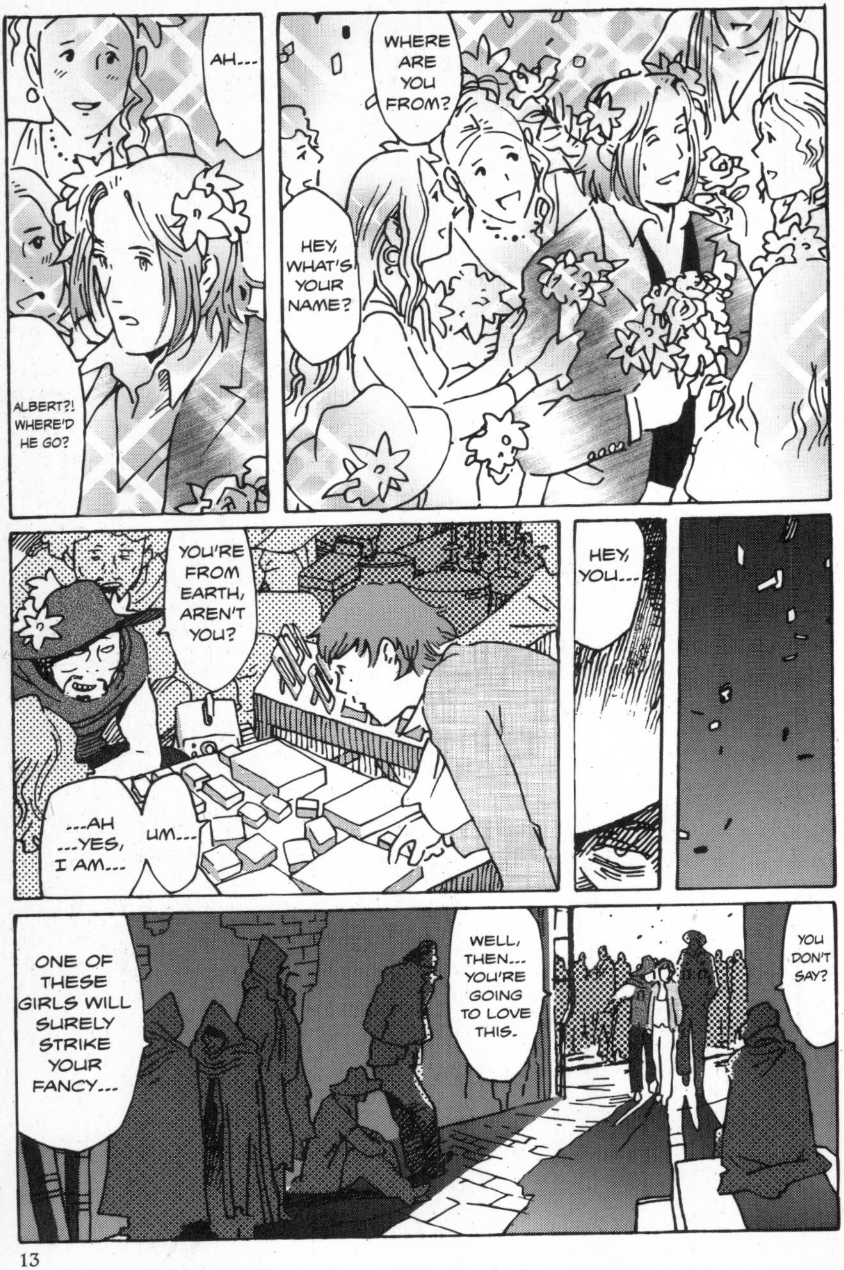
WHERE ARE YOU FROM?
HEY, WHAT'S YOUR NAME?
AH...
ALBERT?! WHERE'D HE GO?
HEY, YOU...
YOU'RE FROM EARTH, AREN'T YOU?
UM...
...AH ...YES, I AM...
YOU DON'T SAY?
WELL, THEN... YOU'RE GOING TO LOVE THIS.
ONE OF THESE GIRLS WILL SURELY STRIKE YOUR FANCY...

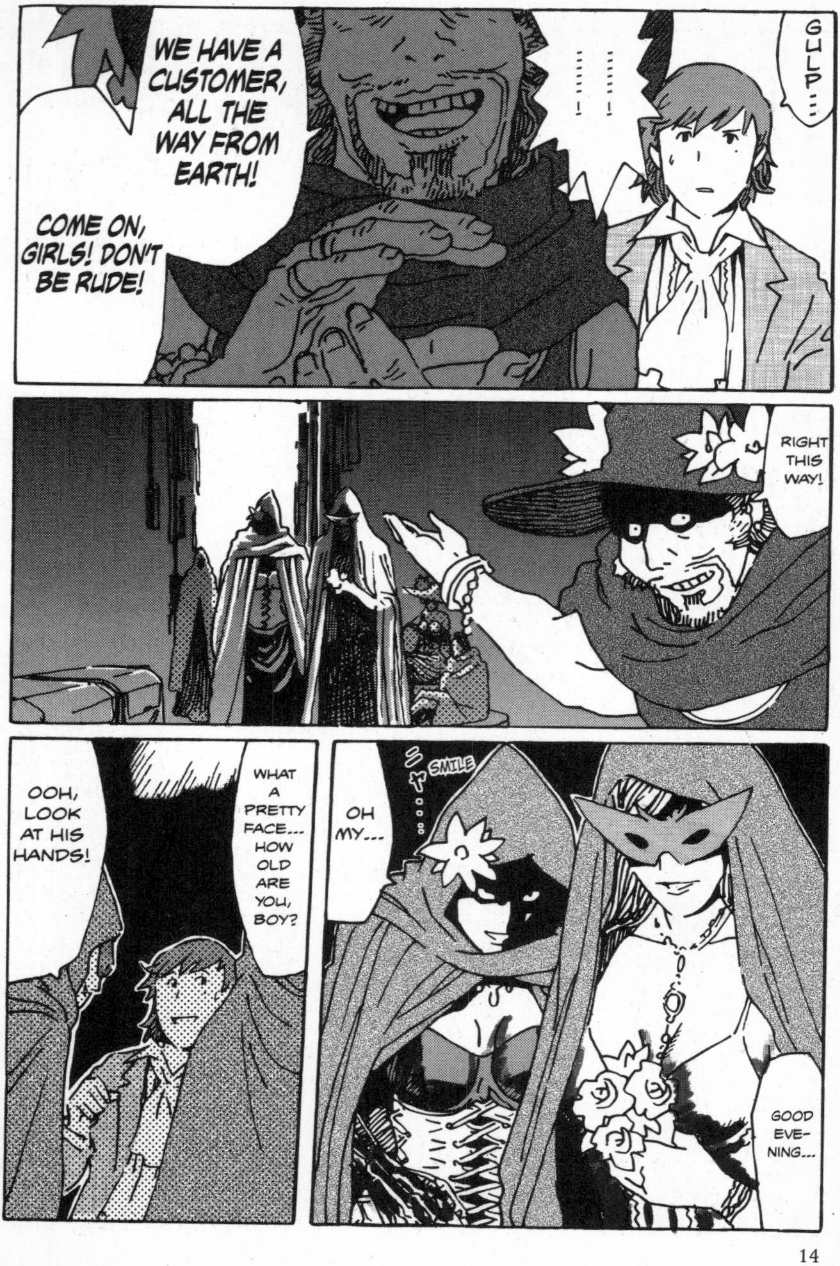
GULP...
......!
......!
WE HAVE A CUSTOMER, ALL THE WAY FROM EARTH!
COME ON, GIRLS! DON'T BE RUDE!
RIGHT THIS WAY!
ニヤ...
SMILE
OH MY...
GOOD EVE-NING...
WHAT A PRETTY FACE... HOW OLD ARE YOU, BOY?
OOH, LOOK AT HIS HANDS!

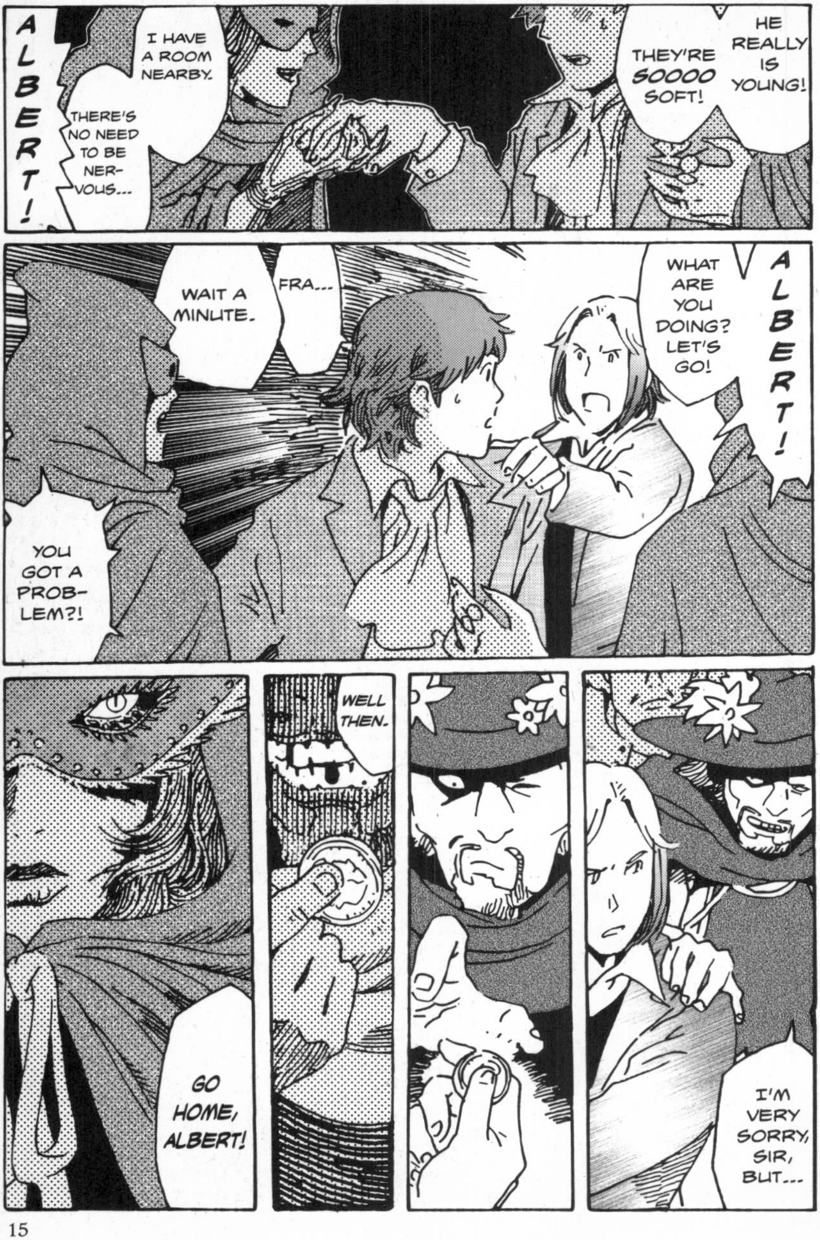
HE REALLY IS YOUNG!
THEY'RE SOOOO SOFT!
I HAVE A ROOM NEARBY.
THERE'S NO NEED TO BE NER-VOUS...
ALBERT!
ALBERT!
WHAT ARE YOU DOING? LET'S GO!
FRA...
WAIT A MINUTE.
YOU GOT A PROB-LEM?!
I'M VERY SORRY, SIR, BUT...
WELL THEN.
GO HOME, ALBERT!

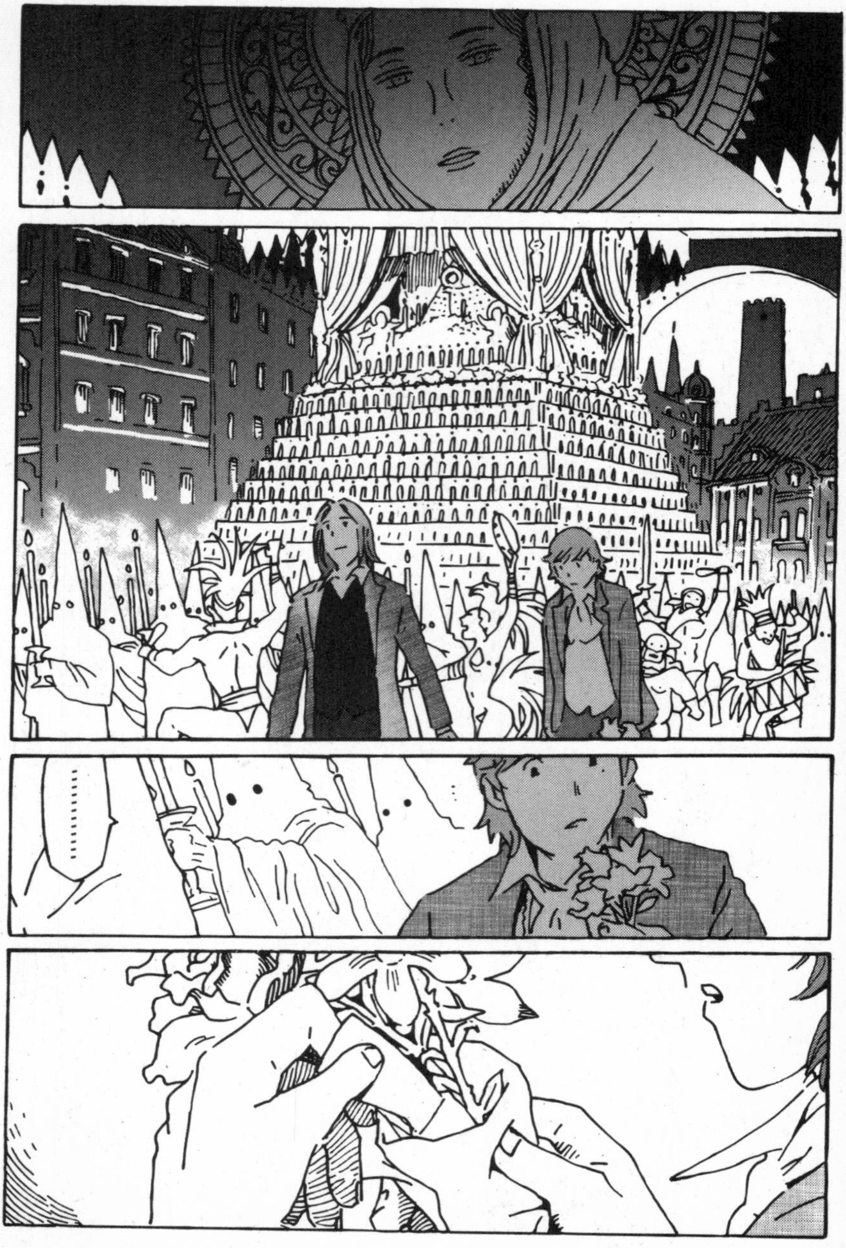

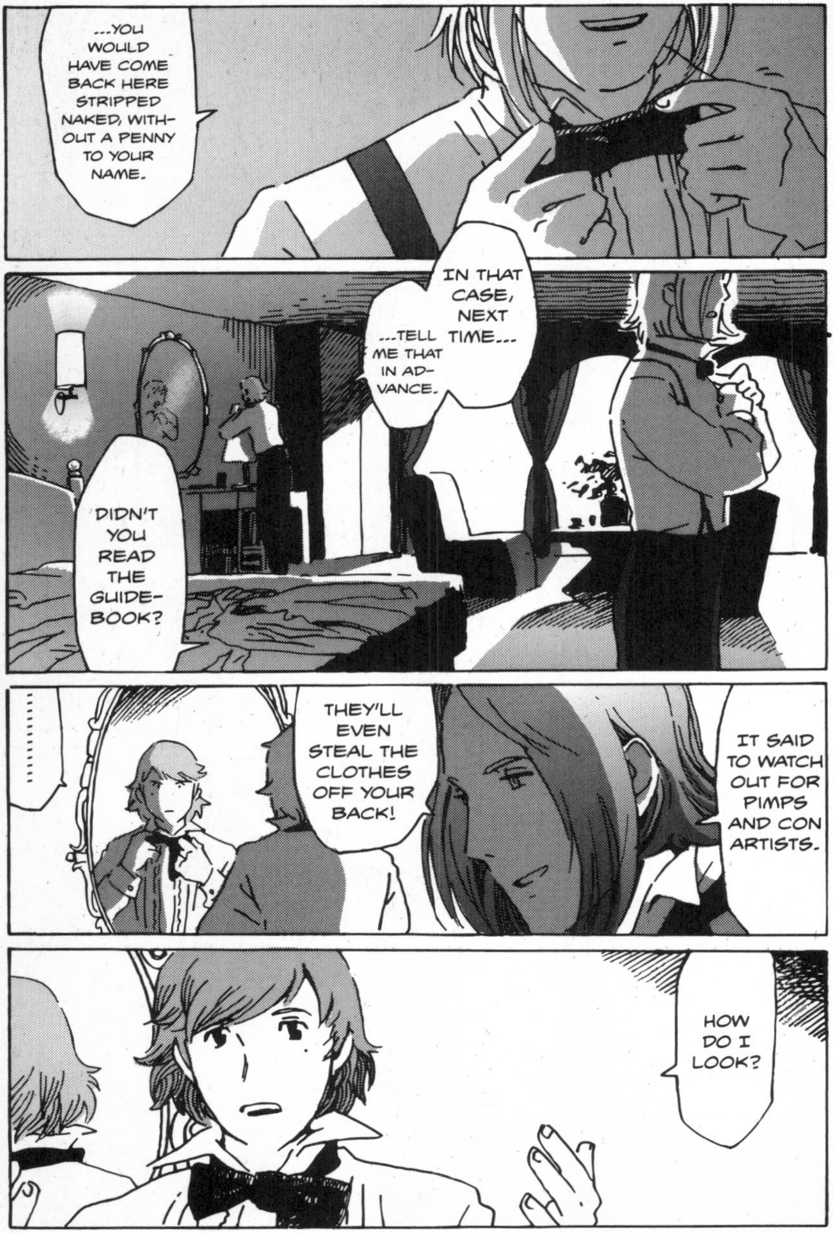
...YOU WOULD HAVE COME BACK HERE STRIPPED NAKED, WITHOUT A PENNY TO YOUR NAME.
IN THAT CASE, NEXT TIME...
...TELL ME THAT IN ADVANCE.
DIDN'T YOU READ THE GUIDEBOOK?
IT SAID TO WATCH OUT FOR PIMPS AND CON ARTISTS.
THEY'LL EVEN STEAL THE CLOTHES OFF YOUR BACK!
....
HOW DO I LOOK?

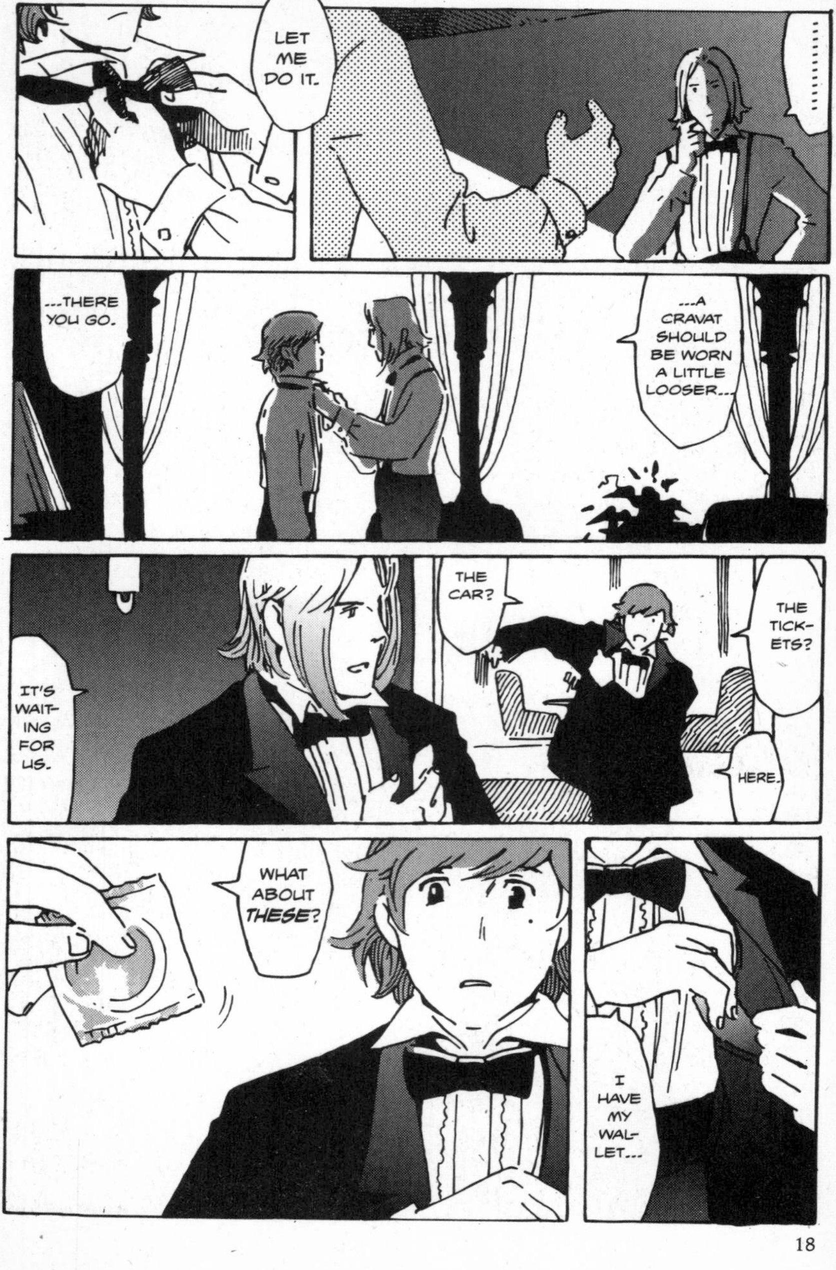
......
LET ME DO IT.
...A CRAVAT SHOULD BE WORN A LITTLE LOOSER...
...THERE YOU GO.
THE TICK-ETS?
HERE.
THE CAR?
IT'S WAIT-ING FOR US.
I HAVE MY WAL-LET...
WHAT ABOUT *THESE*?

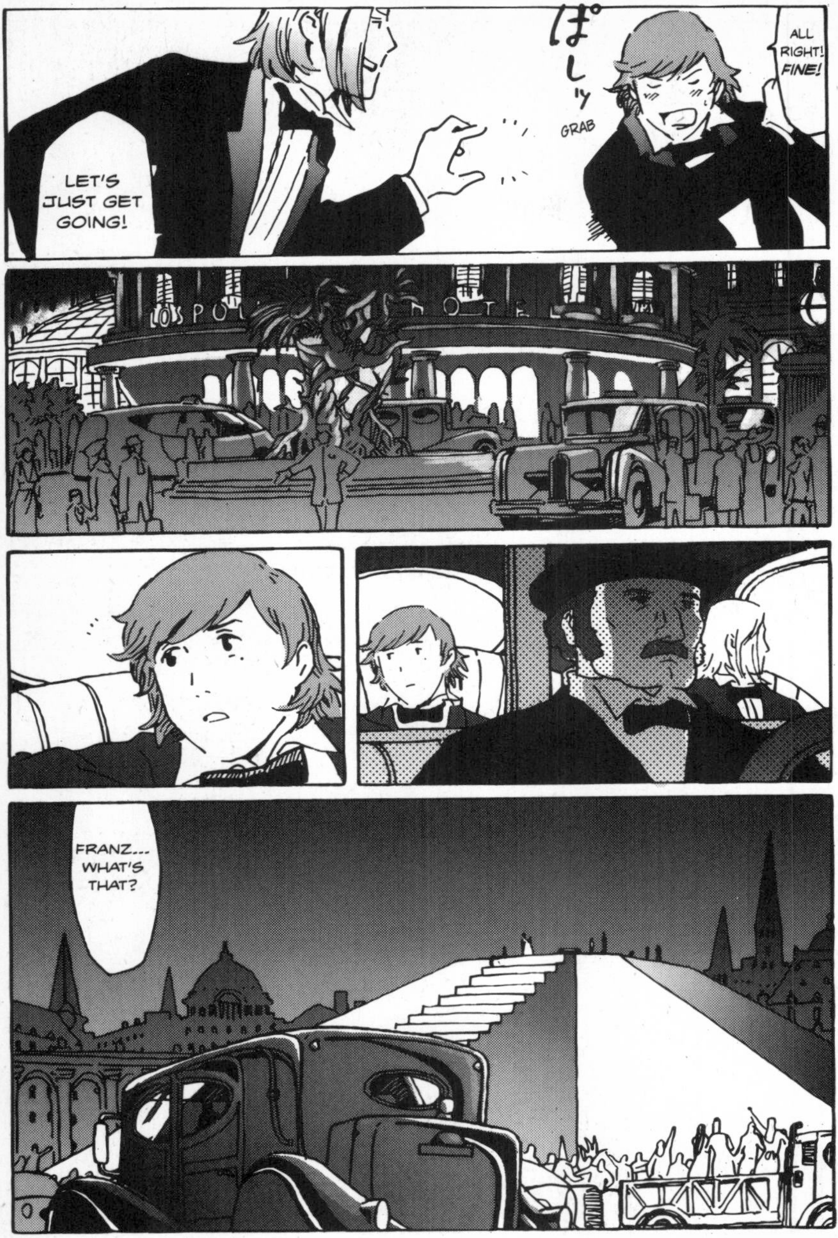
ALL RIGHT! FINE!
ぱしッ
GRAB
LET'S JUST GET GOING!
FRANZ... WHAT'S THAT?

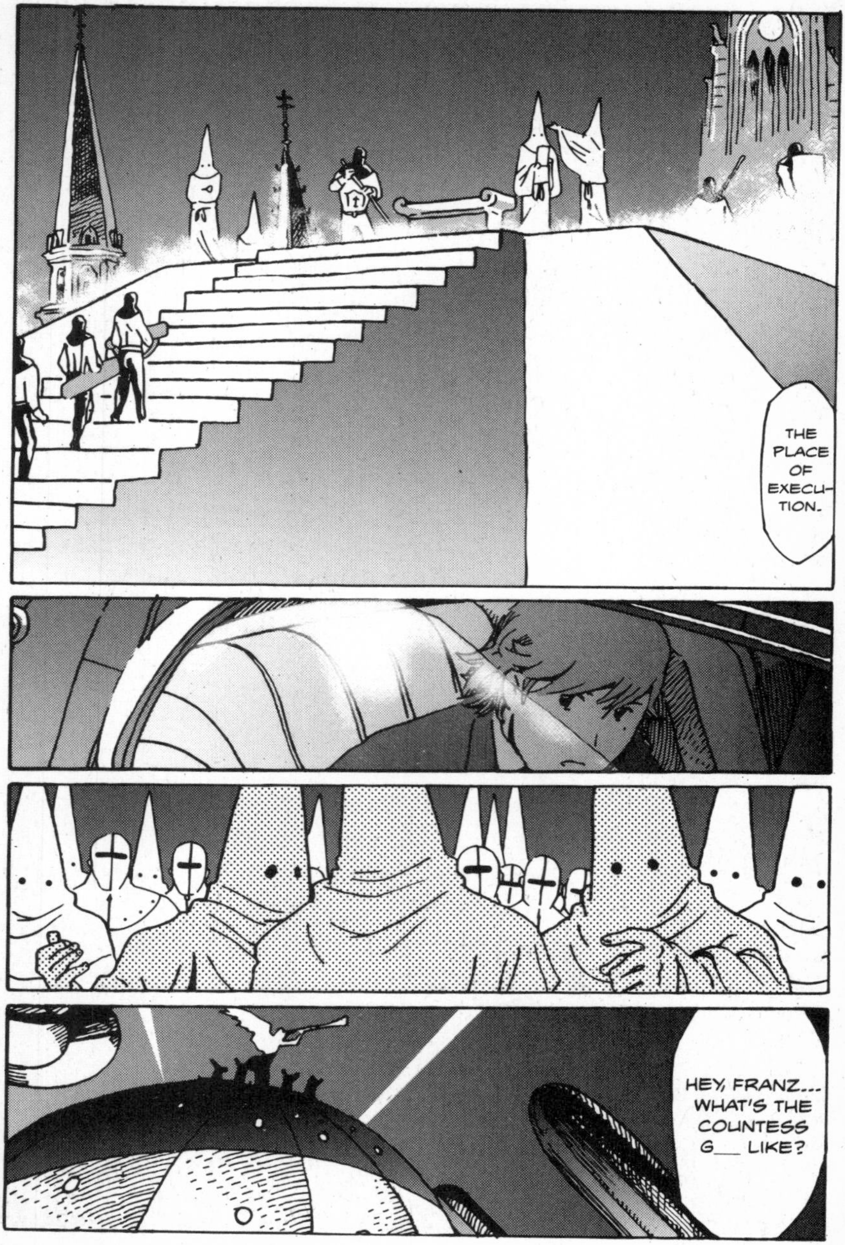
THE PLACE OF EXECU-TION.
HEY, FRANZ... WHAT'S THE COUNTESS G__ LIKE?

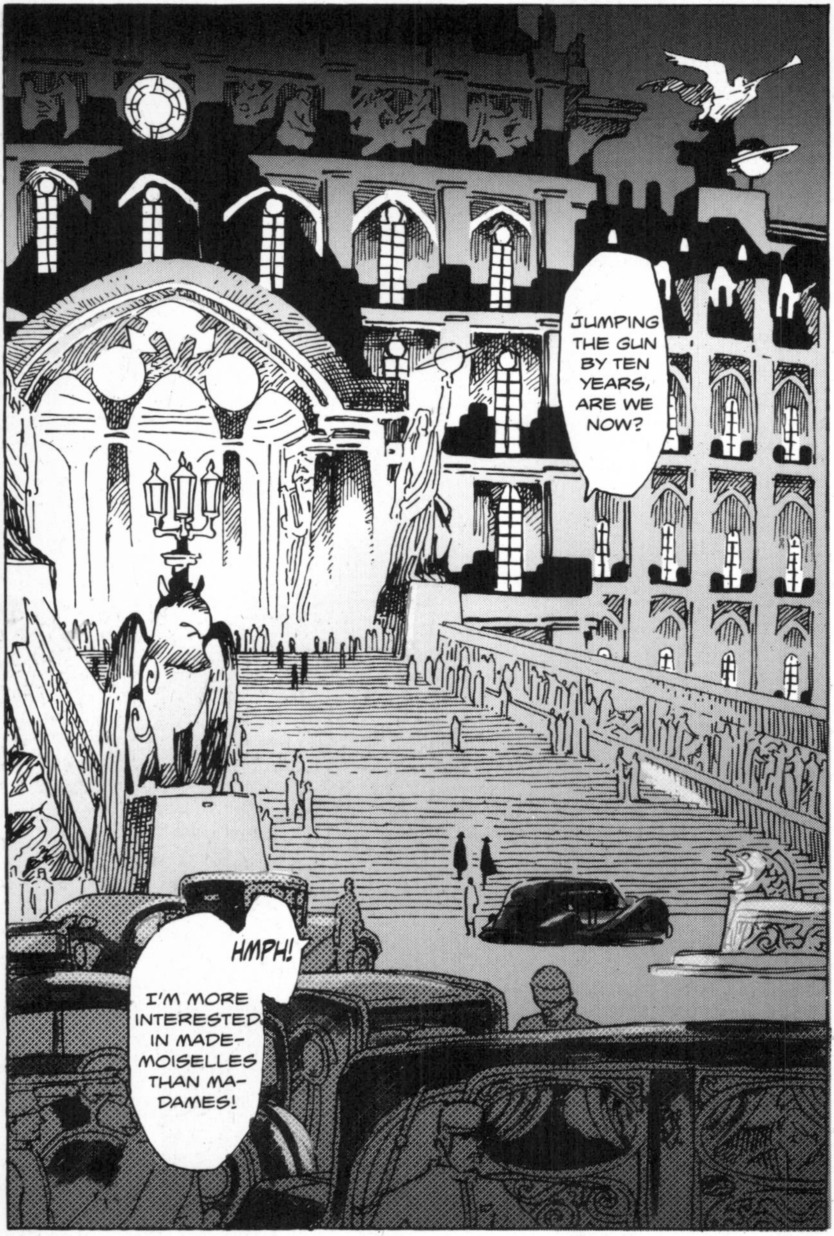
JUMPING THE GUN BY TEN YEARS, ARE WE NOW?
HMPH!
I'M MORE INTERESTED IN MADE-MOISELLES THAN MA-DAMES!

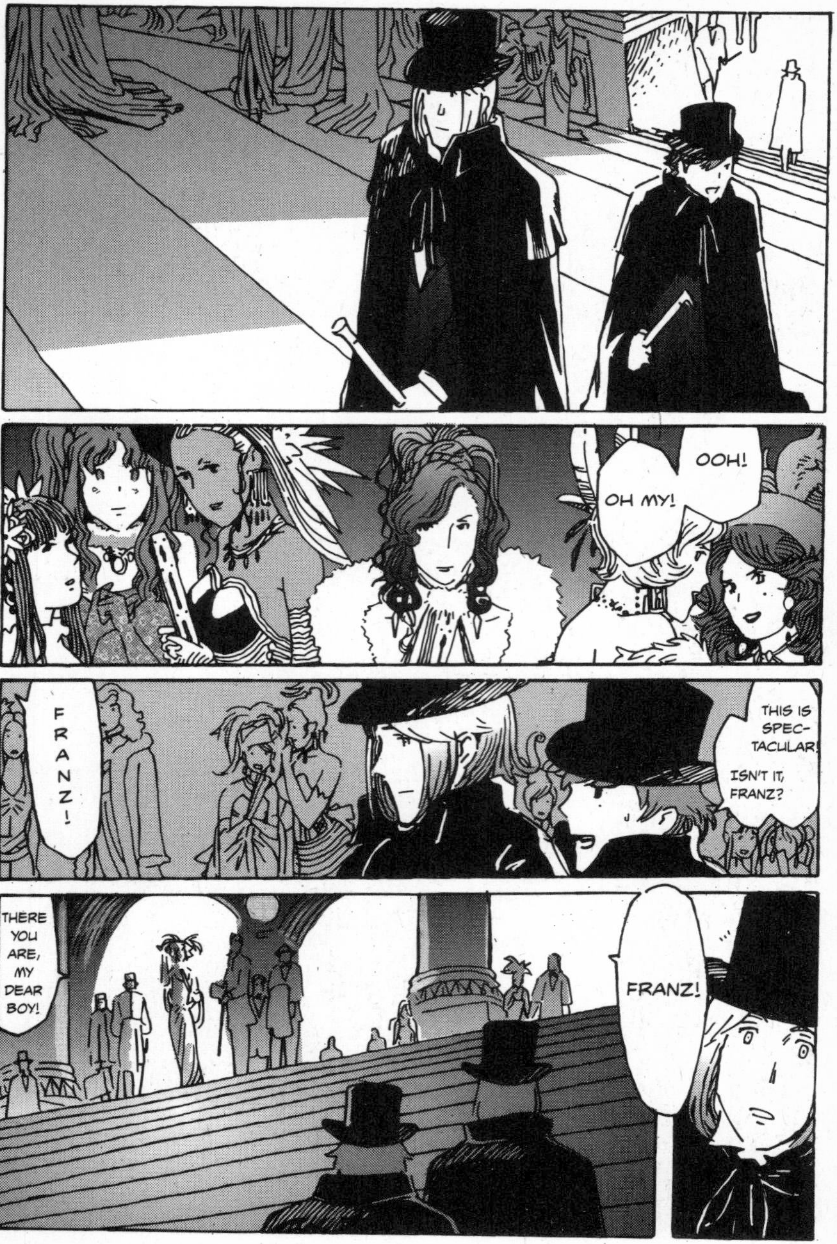
OOH!
OH MY!
THIS IS SPECTACULAR!
ISN'T IT, FRANZ?
FRANZ!
...
FRANZ!
THERE YOU ARE, MY DEAR BOY!

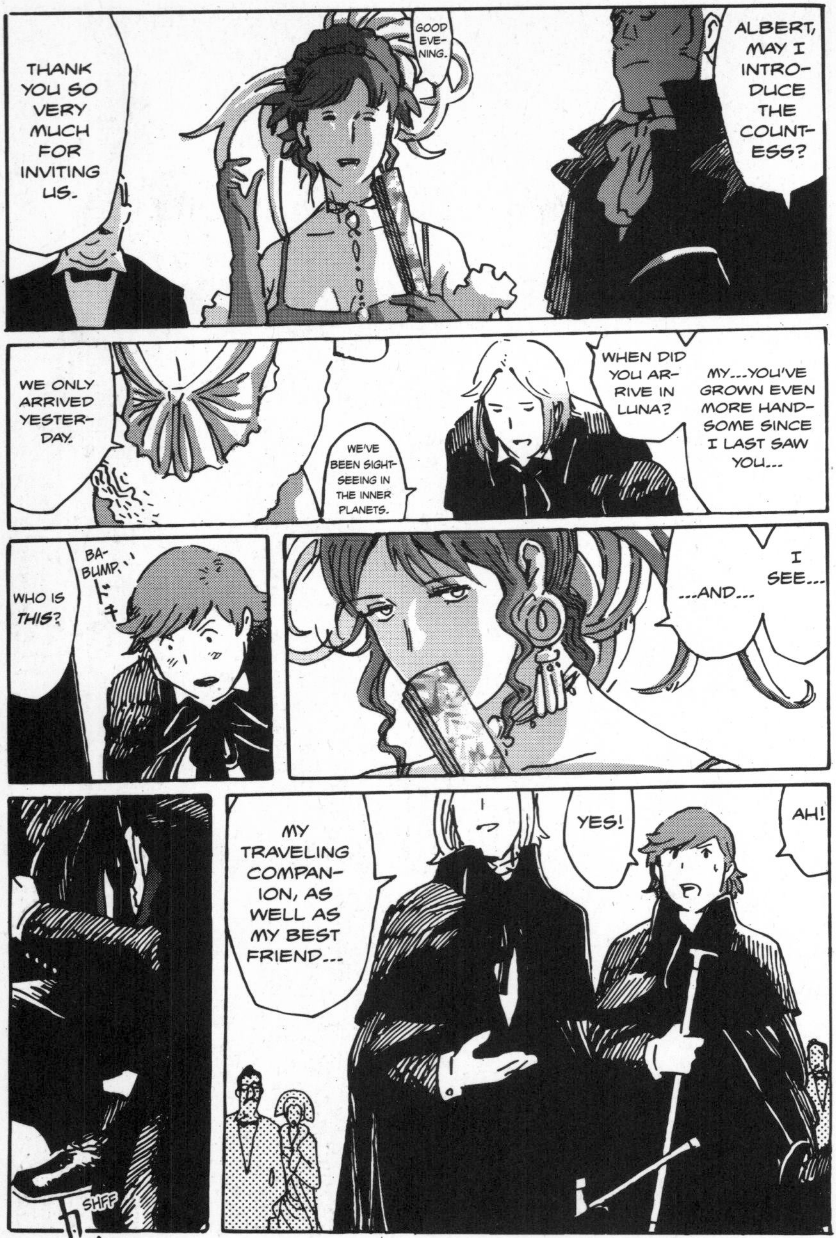
ALBERT, MAY I INTRODUCE THE COUNTESS?
GOOD EVENING.
THANK YOU SO VERY MUCH FOR INVITING US.
MY...YOU'VE GROWN EVEN MORE HANDSOME SINCE I LAST SAW YOU...
WHEN DID YOU ARRIVE IN LUNA?
WE'VE BEEN SIGHTSEEING IN THE INNER PLANETS.
WE ONLY ARRIVED YESTERDAY.
I SEE...
...AND...
BA-BUMP
ドキ
WHO IS *THIS*?
AH!
YES!
MY TRAVELING COMPANION, AS WELL AS MY BEST FRIEND...
SHFF
カツ

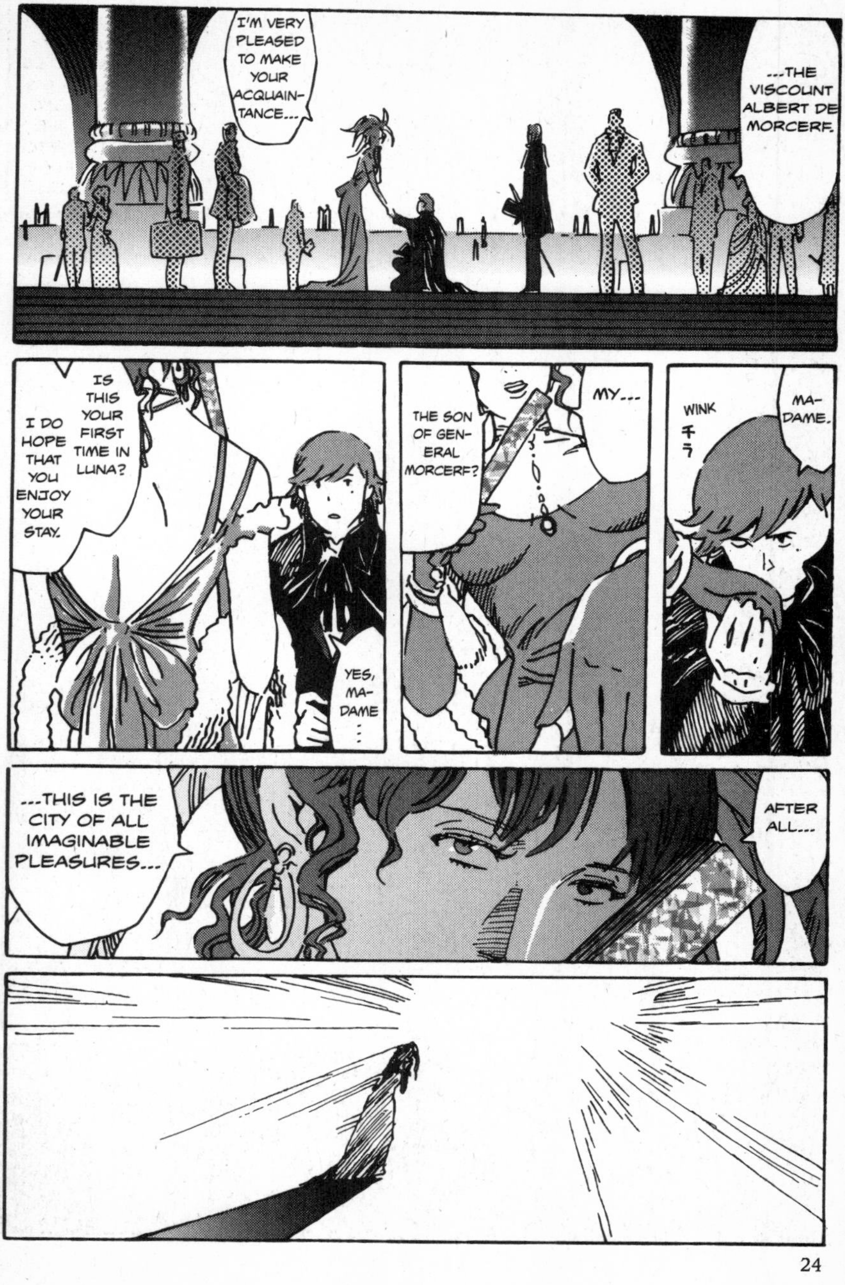
...THE VISCOUNT ALBERT DE MORCERF.
I'M VERY PLEASED TO MAKE YOUR ACQUAIN-TANCE...
MA-DAME.
WINK
チラ
MY...
THE SON OF GEN-ERAL MORCERF?
IS THIS YOUR FIRST TIME IN LUNA?
I DO HOPE THAT YOU ENJOY YOUR STAY.
YES, MA-DAME ...
AFTER ALL...
...THIS IS THE CITY OF ALL IMAGINABLE PLEASURES...

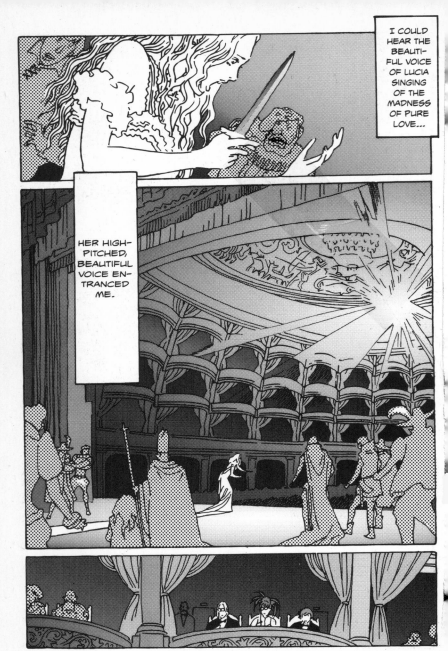

I COULD HEAR THE BEAUTIFUL VOICE OF LUCIA SINGING OF THE MADNESS OF PURE LOVE...

HER HIGH-PITCHED, BEAUTIFUL VOICE ENTRANCED ME.

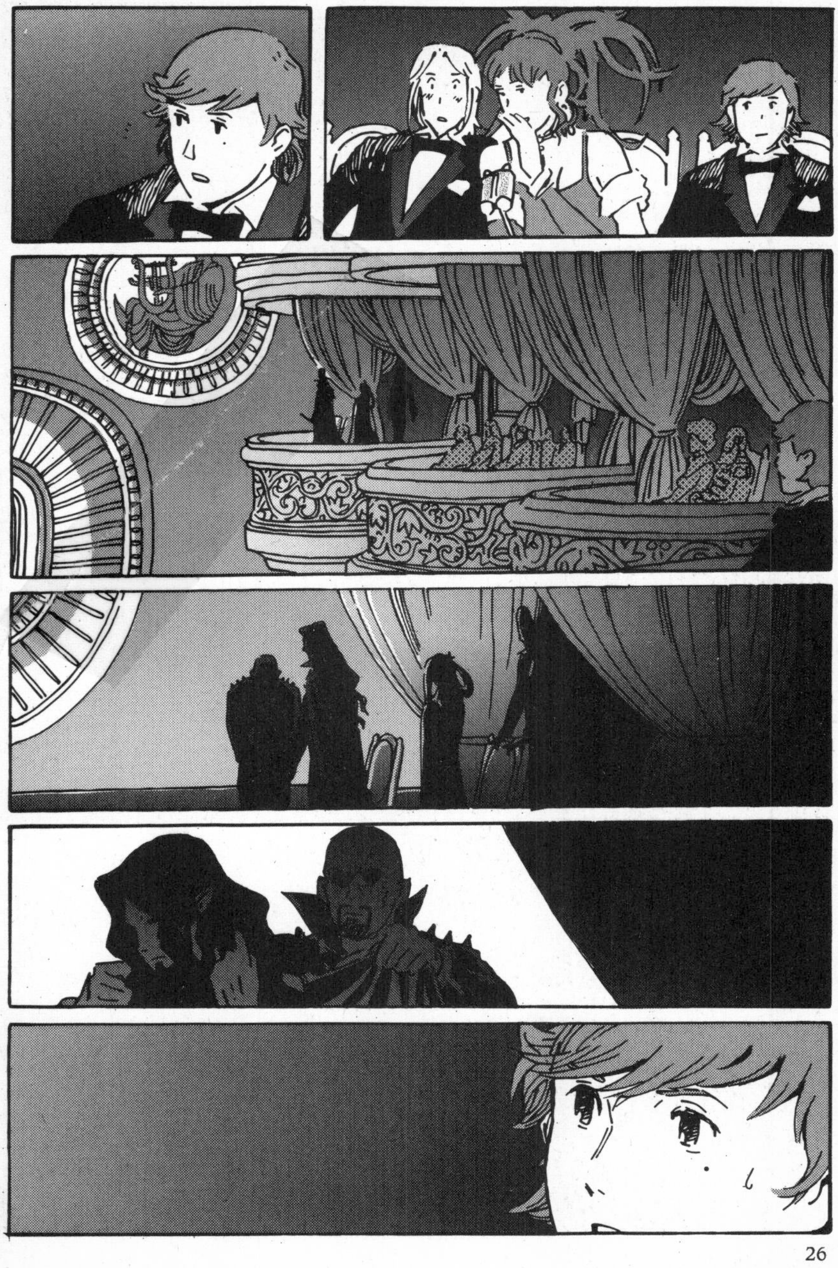

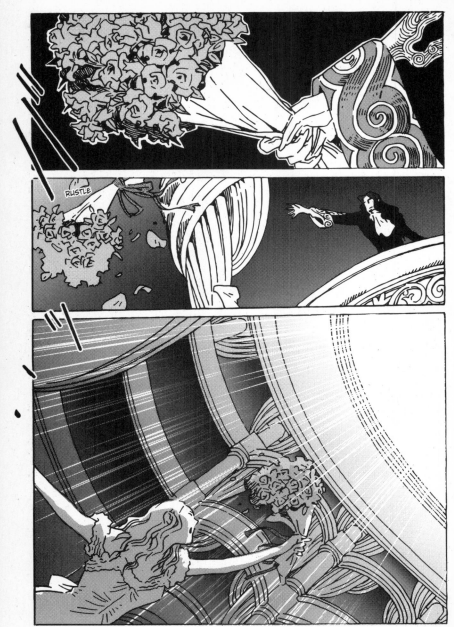

RUSTLE

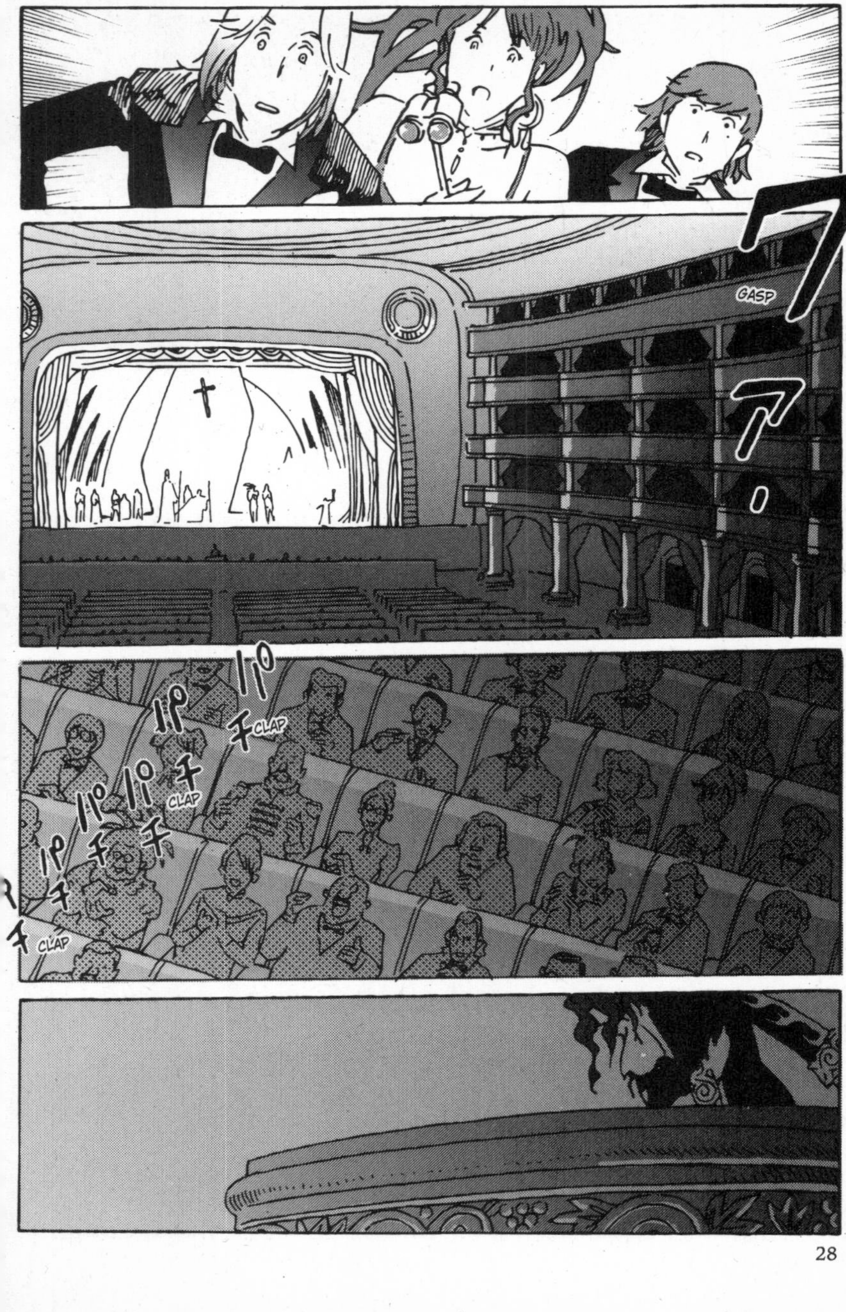

ワァ…
GASP
パチ
CLAP
パチ
CLAP
パチ
パチ
パチ
CLAP

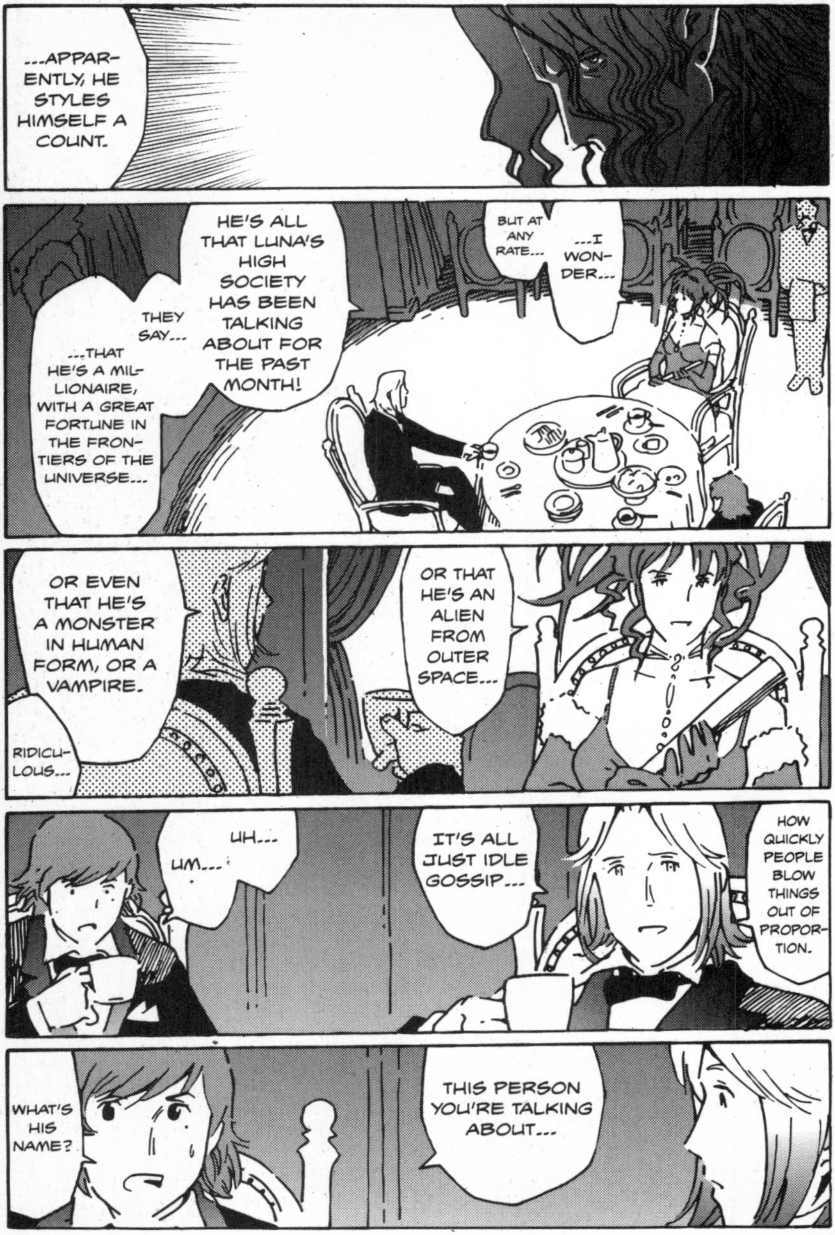
...APPARENTLY, HE STYLES HIMSELF A COUNT.
...I WONDER...
BUT AT ANY RATE...
HE'S ALL THAT LUNA'S HIGH SOCIETY HAS BEEN TALKING ABOUT FOR THE PAST MONTH!
THEY SAY...
...THAT HE'S A MILLIONAIRE, WITH A GREAT FORTUNE IN THE FRONTIERS OF THE UNIVERSE...
OR THAT HE'S AN ALIEN FROM OUTER SPACE...
OR EVEN THAT HE'S A MONSTER IN HUMAN FORM, OR A VAMPIRE.
RIDICULOUS...
HOW QUICKLY PEOPLE BLOW THINGS OUT OF PROPORTION.
IT'S ALL JUST IDLE GOSSIP...
UH...
UM...
THIS PERSON YOU'RE TALKING ABOUT...
WHAT'S HIS NAME?

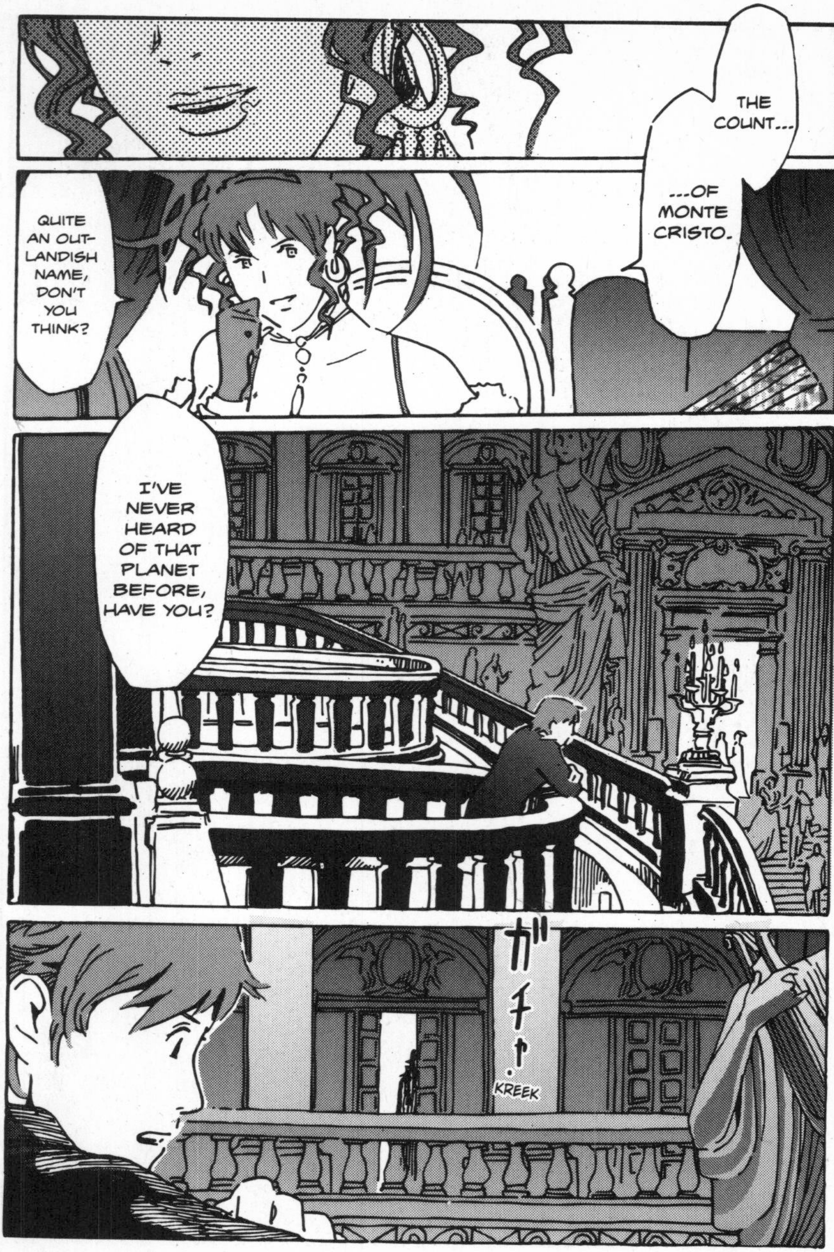
THE COUNT...
...OF MONTE CRISTO.
QUITE AN OUT-LANDISH NAME, DON'T YOU THINK?
I'VE NEVER HEARD OF THAT PLANET BEFORE, HAVE YOU?
ガチャ
KREEK

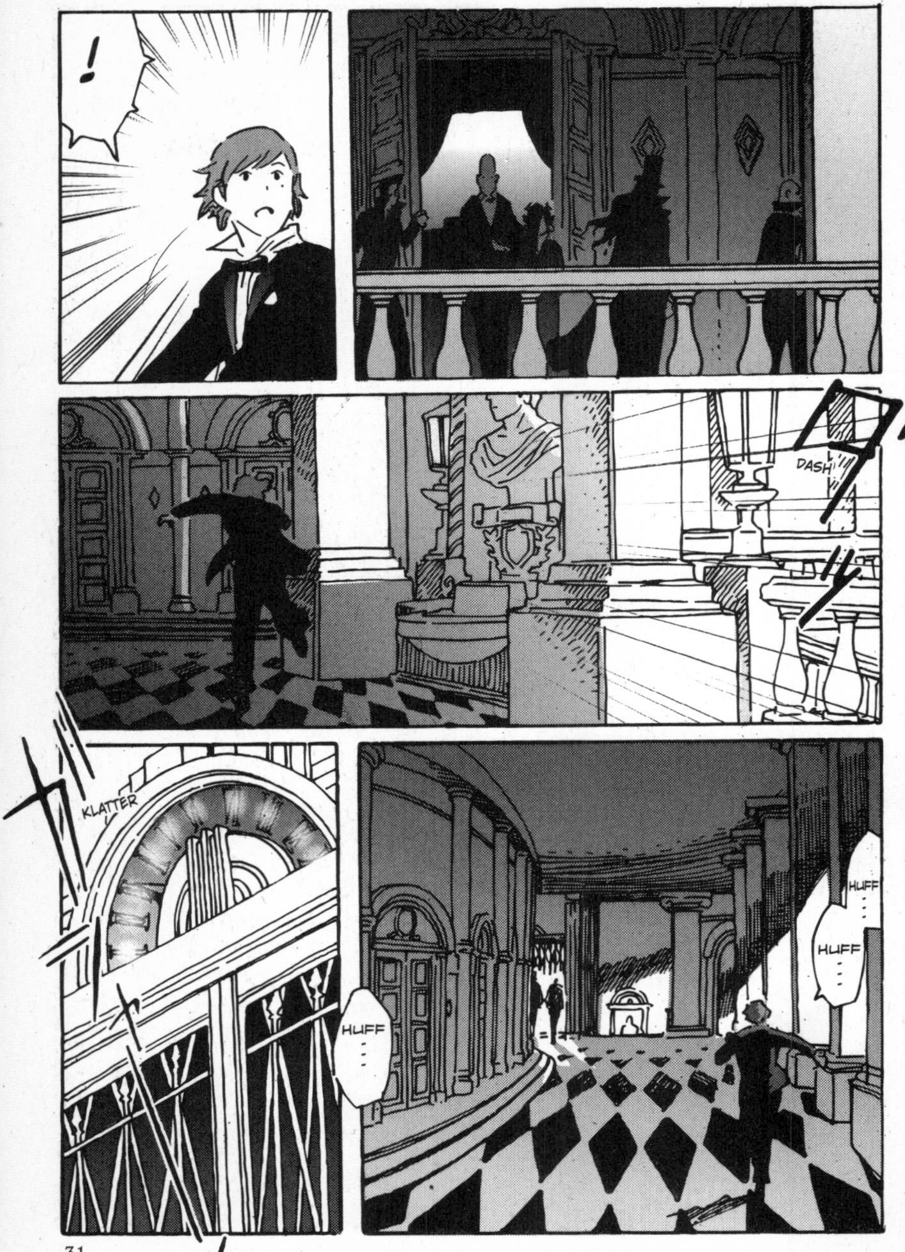
!
DASH
HUFF...
HUFF...
HUFF...
KLATTER

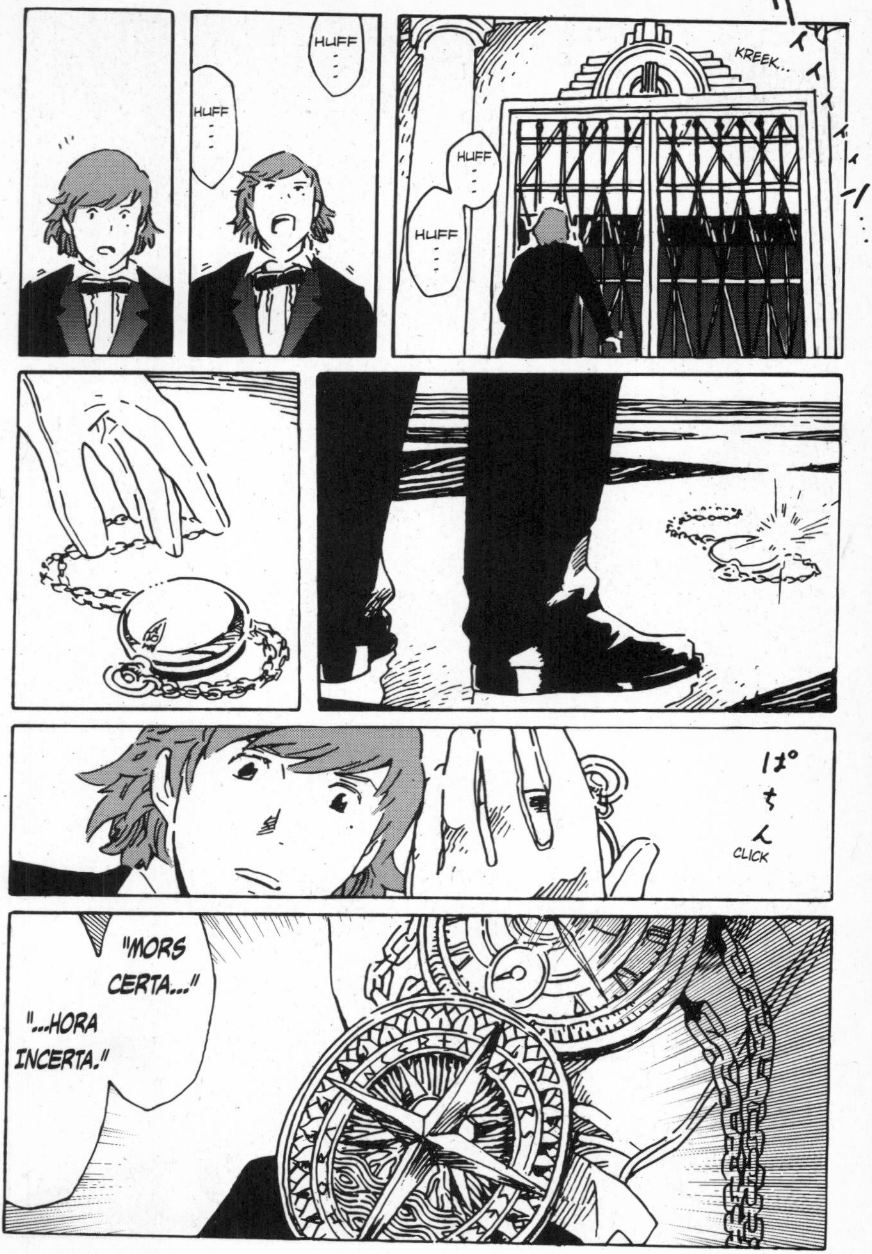

グイイイィィー
KREEK...
HUFF...
HUFF...
HUFF...
HUFF...
ぱちん
CLICK
"MORS CERTA..."
"...HORA INCERTA."

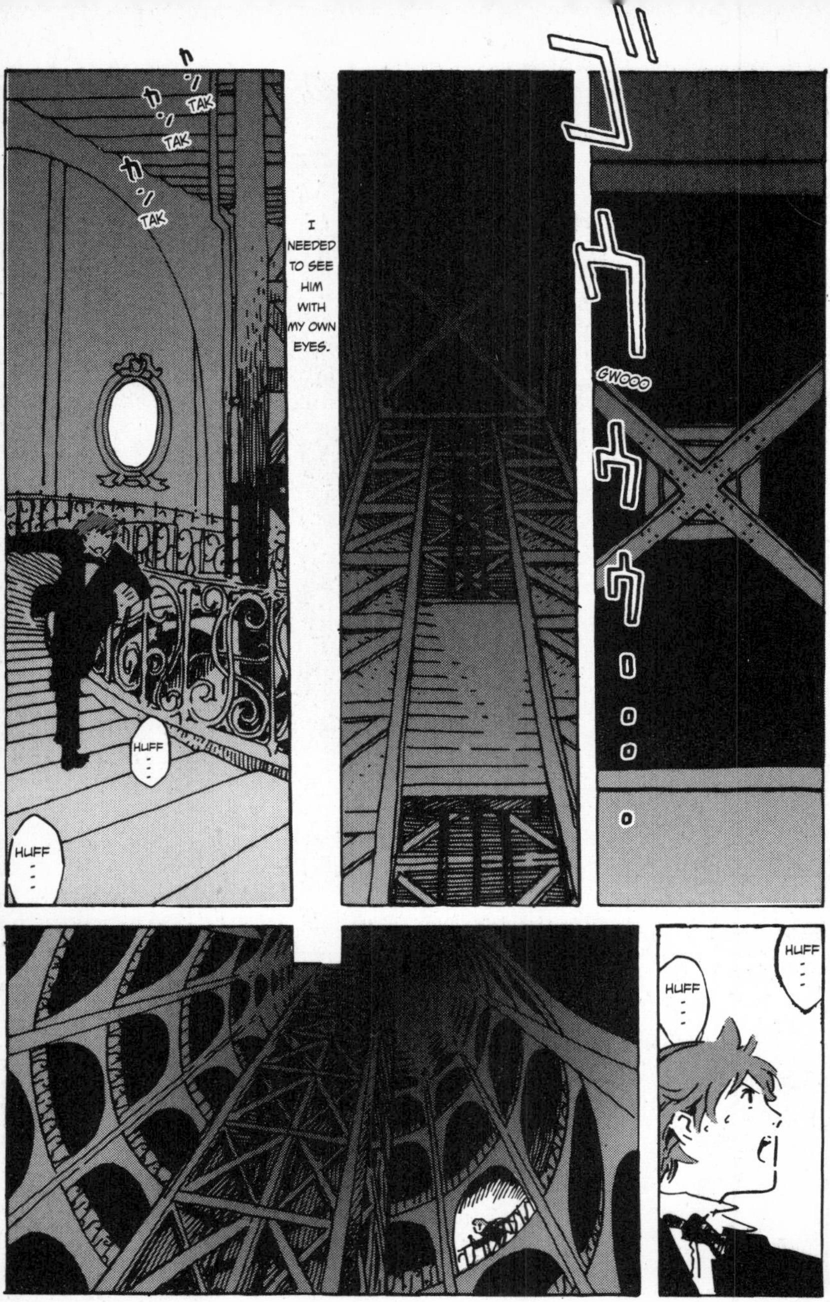
GWOOO
I NEEDED TO SEE HIM WITH MY OWN EYES.
TAK
TAK
TAK
HUFF...
HUFF...
HUFF...
HUFF...

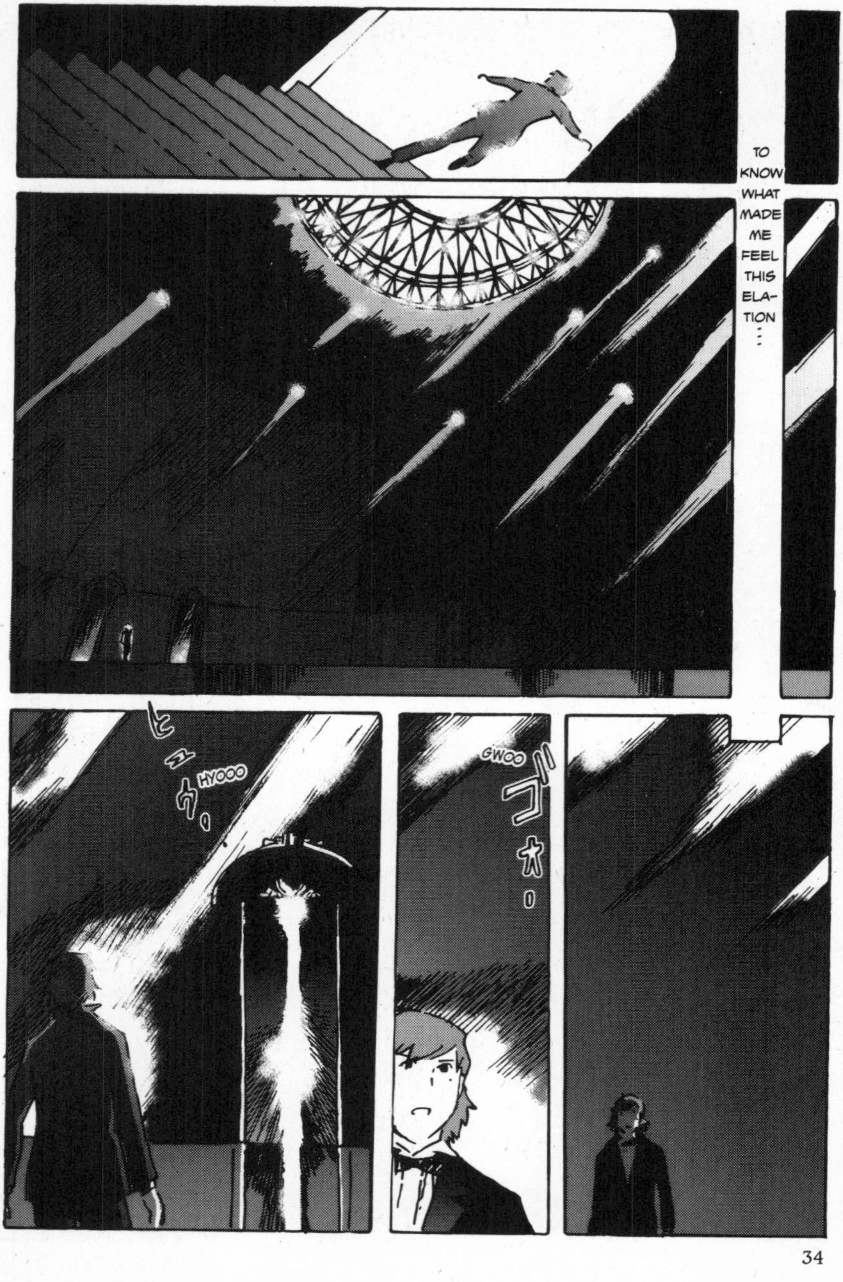
TO KNOW WHAT MADE ME FEEL THIS ELA-TION...
GWOO
HYOOO

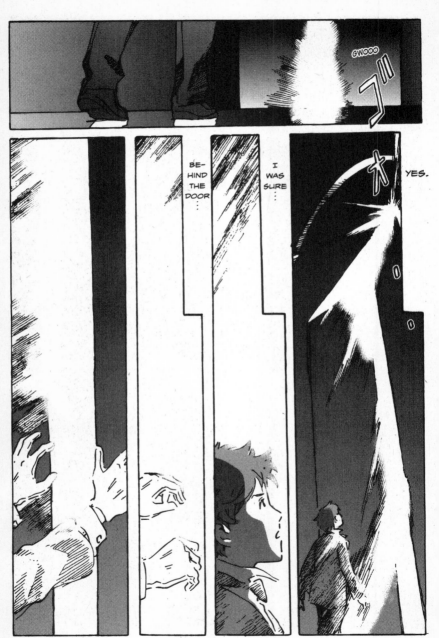

GWOOO

BE-
HIND
THE
DOOR
...

I
WAS
SURE
...

YES.

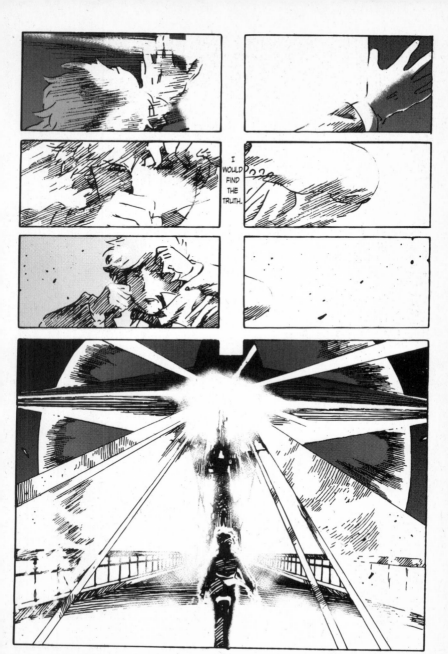

I WOULD FIND THE TRUTH.

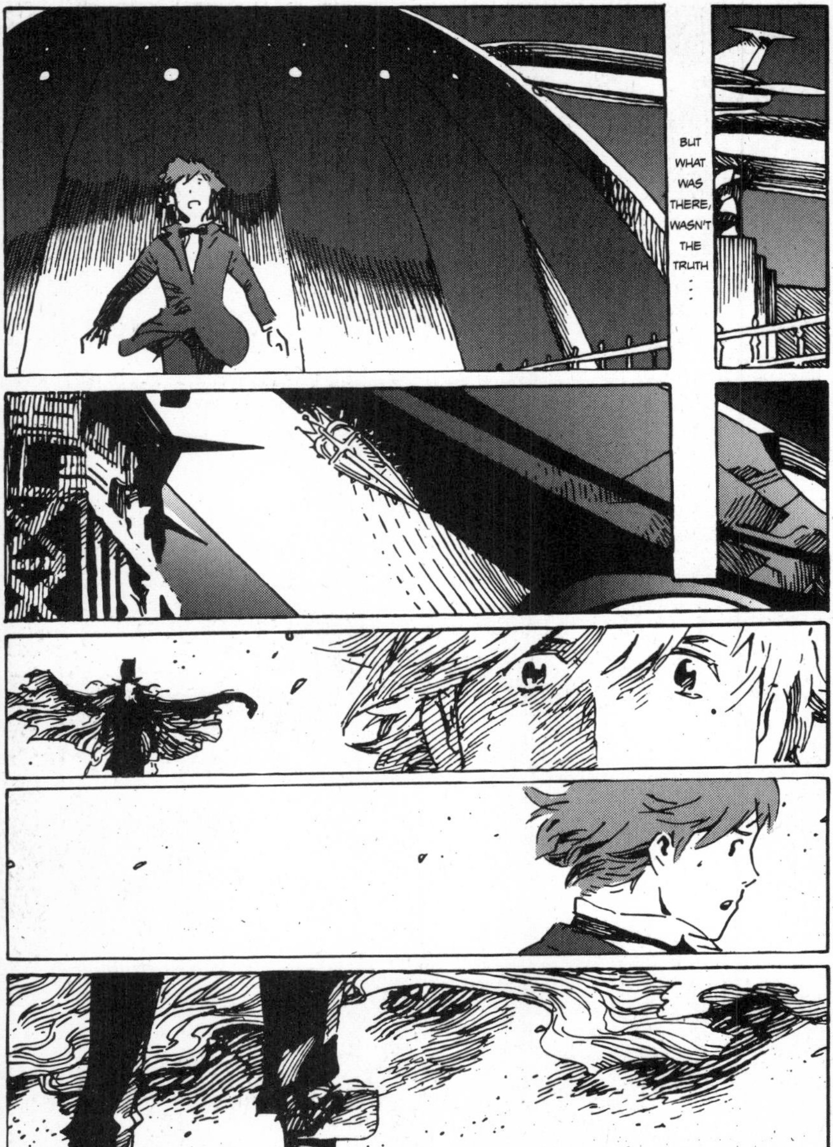
BUT WHAT WAS THERE, WASN'T THE TRUTH . . .

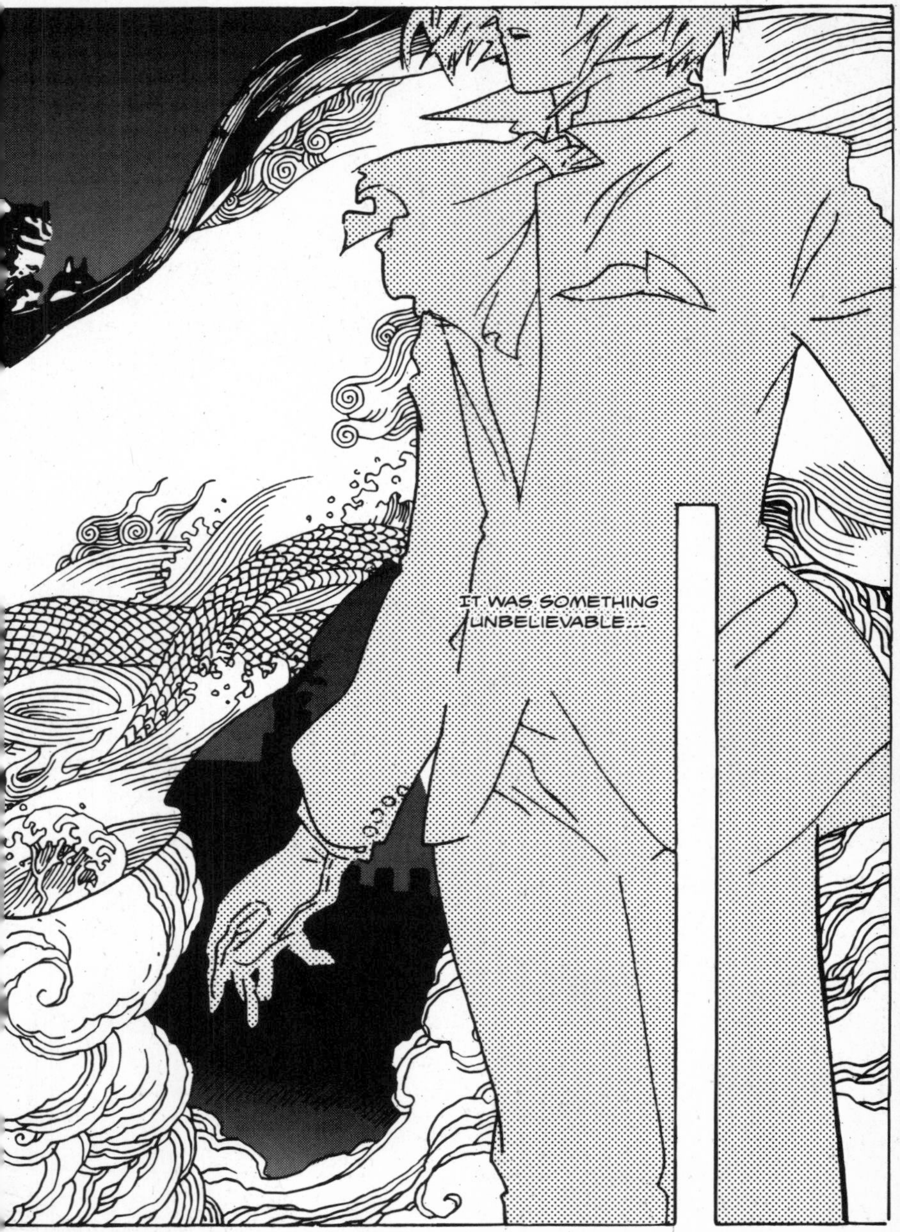
IT WAS SOMETHING UNBELIEVABLE...

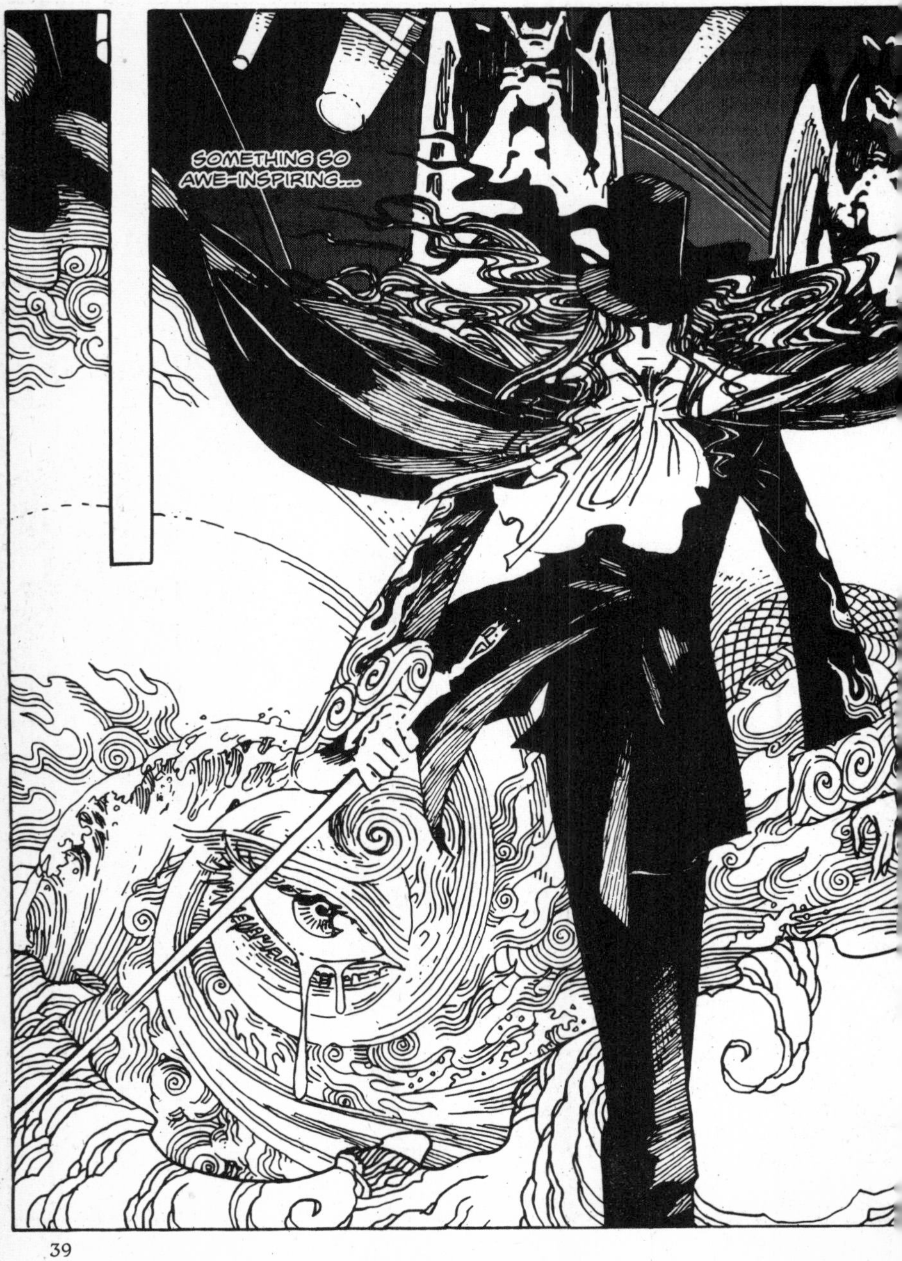
SOMETHING SO AWE-INSPIRING...

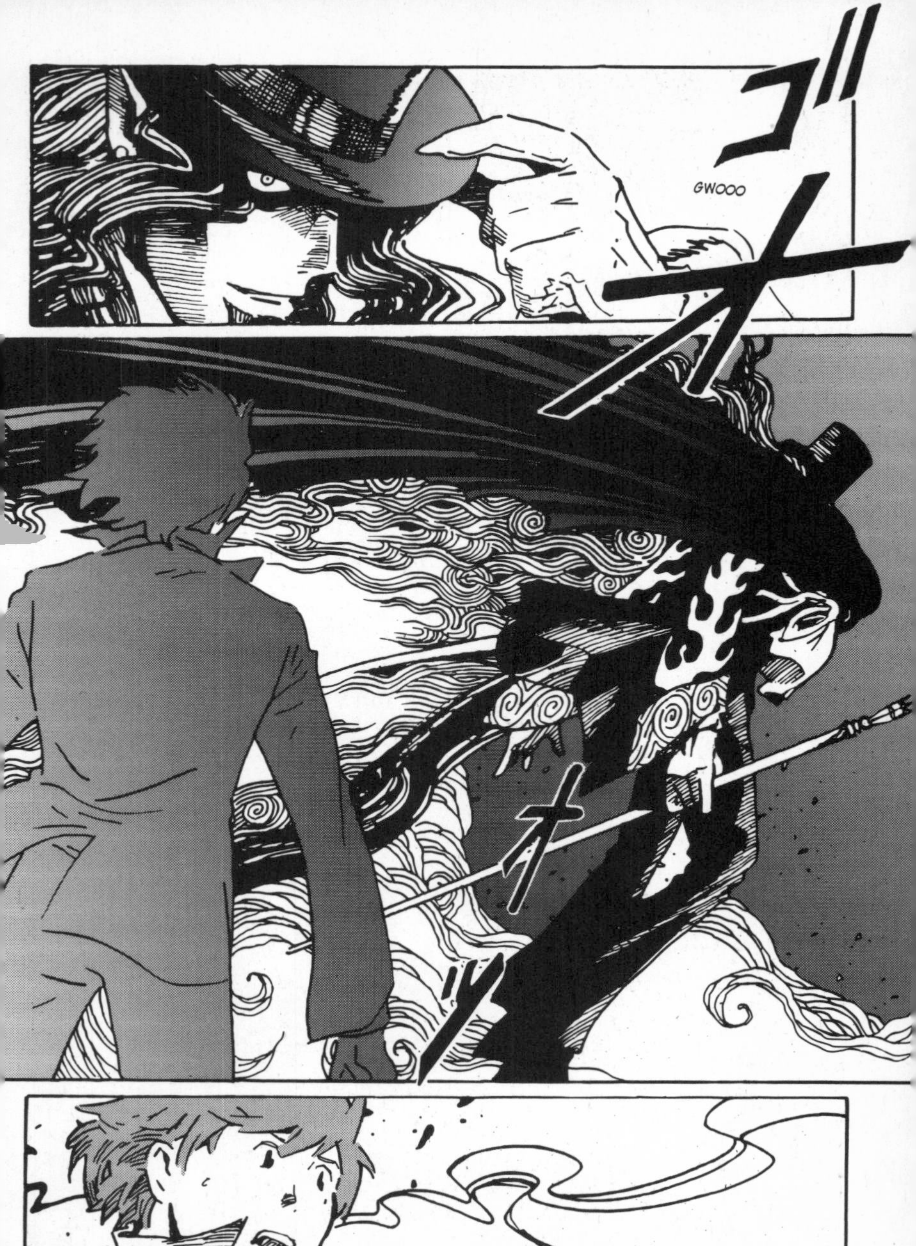
ゴオ
GWOOO

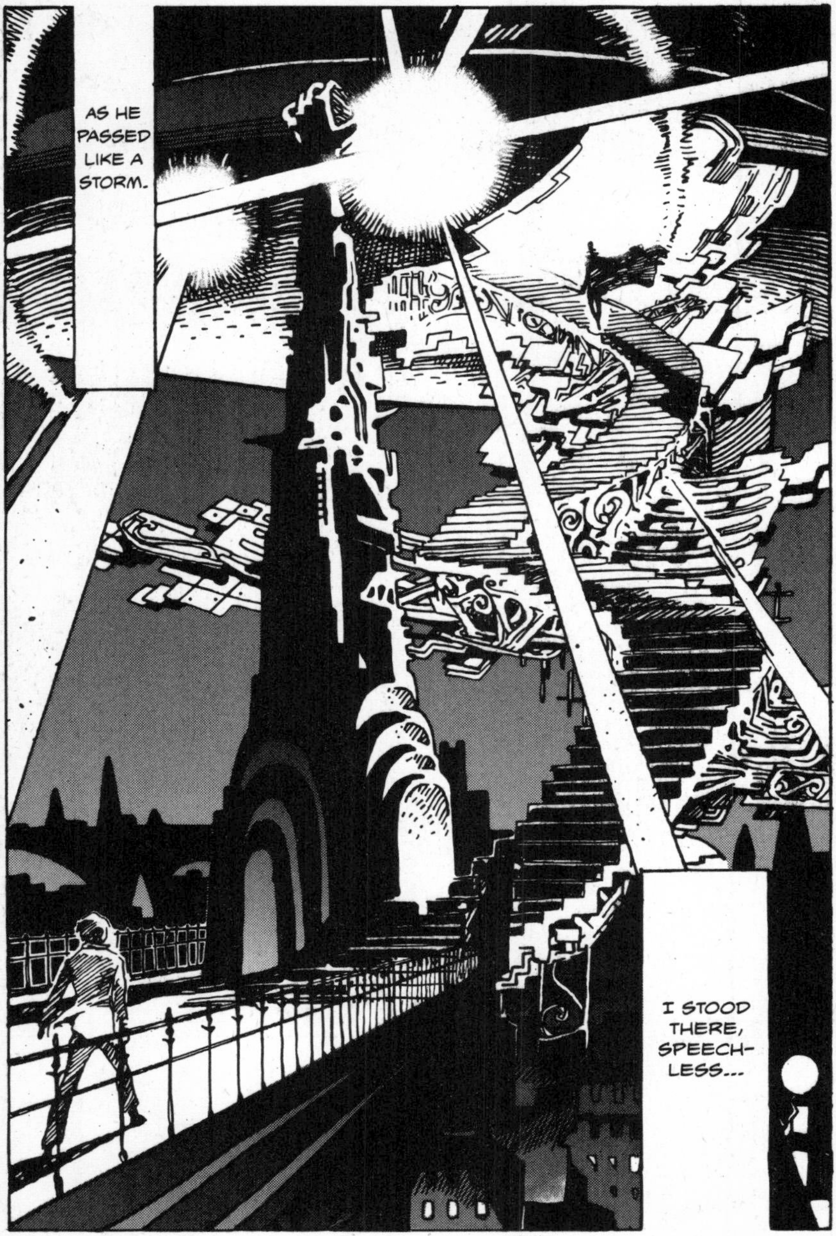
AS HE PASSED LIKE A STORM.
I STOOD THERE, SPEECH-LESS...

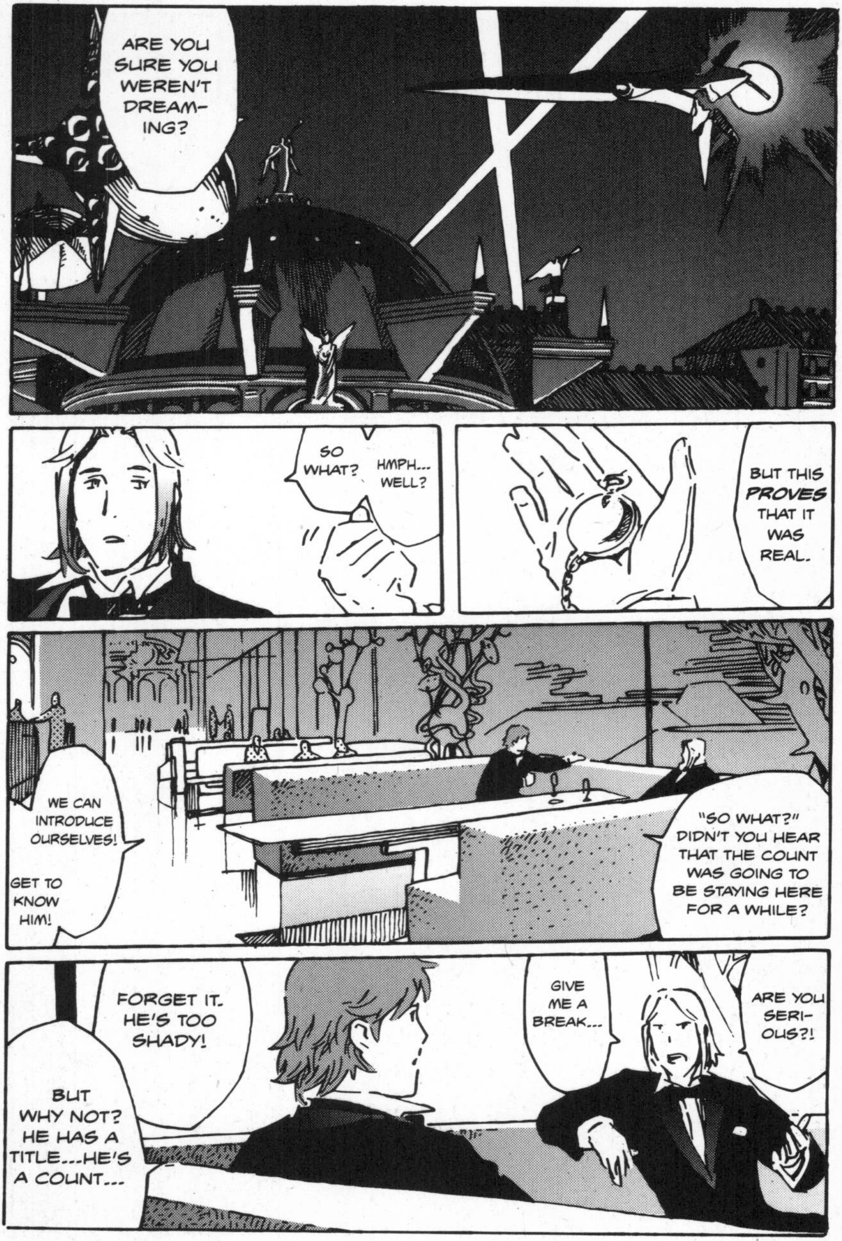
ARE YOU SURE YOU WEREN'T DREAM-ING?
BUT THIS ***PROVES*** THAT IT WAS REAL.
HMPH... WELL?
SO WHAT?
"SO WHAT?" DIDN'T YOU HEAR THAT THE COUNT WAS GOING TO BE STAYING HERE FOR A WHILE?
WE CAN INTRODUCE OURSELVES!
GET TO KNOW HIM!
ARE YOU SERI-OUS?!
GIVE ME A BREAK...
FORGET IT. HE'S TOO SHADY!
BUT WHY NOT? HE HAS A TITLE...HE'S A COUNT...

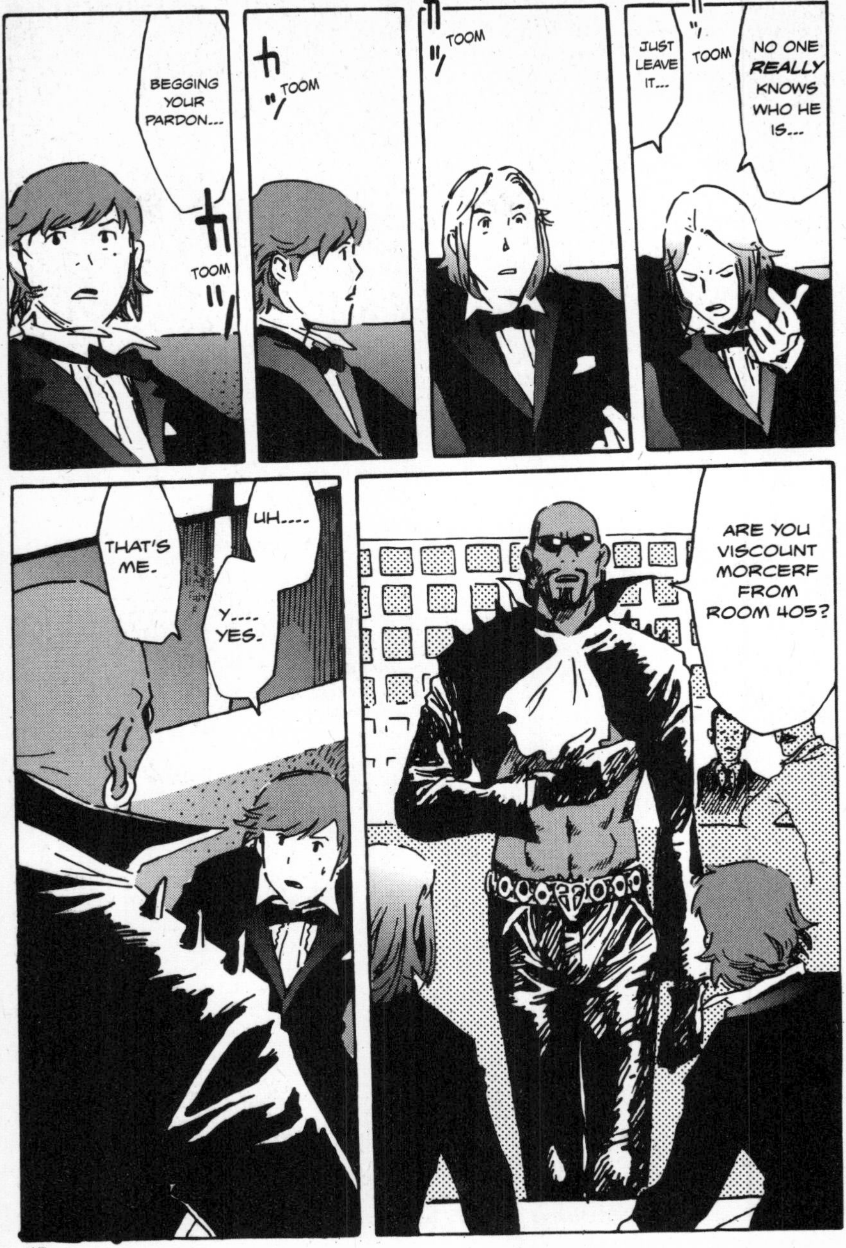
NO ONE *REALLY* KNOWS WHO HE IS...
JUST LEAVE IT...
TOOM
TOOM
TOOM
BEGGING YOUR PARDON...
TOOM
ARE YOU VISCOUNT MORCERF FROM ROOM 405?
UH.... Y.... YES.
THAT'S ME.

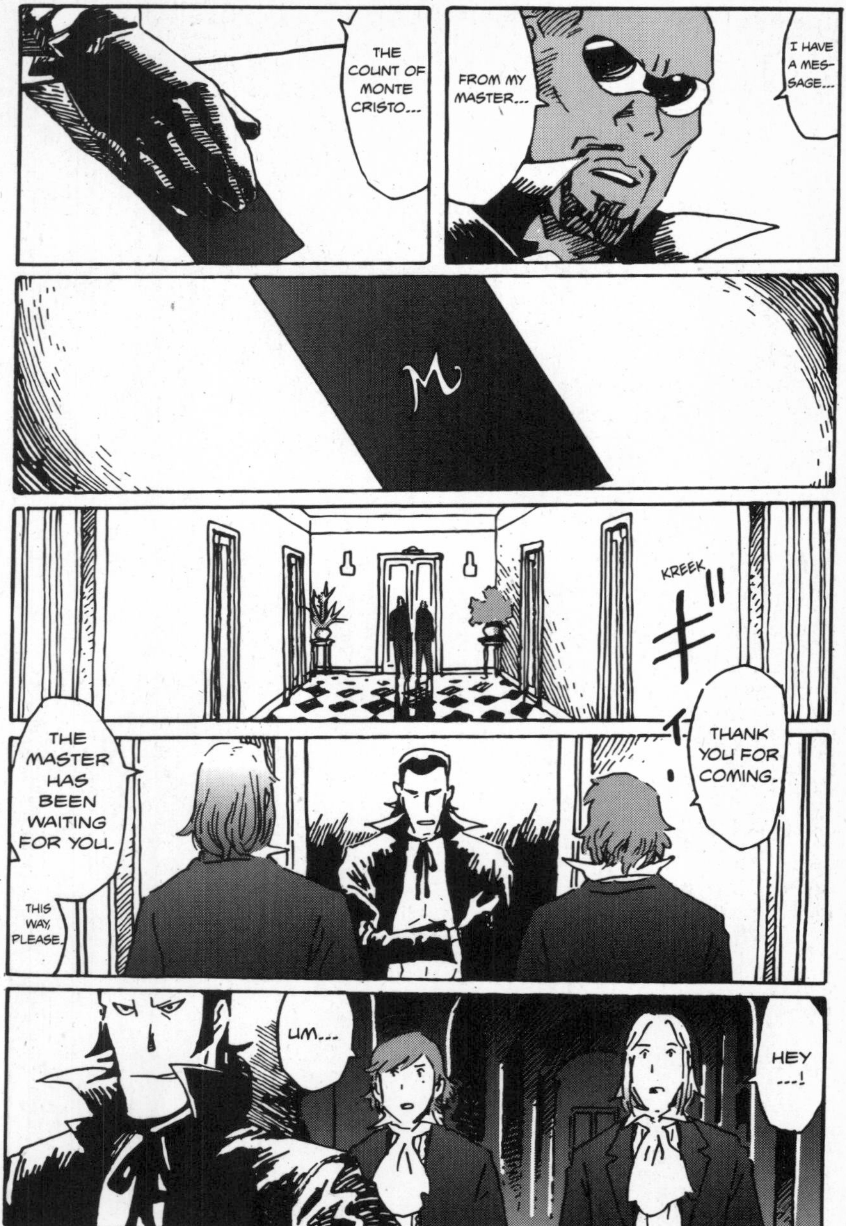
I HAVE A MES-SAGE...
FROM MY MASTER...
THE COUNT OF MONTE CRISTO...
KREEK
THANK YOU FOR COMING.
THE MASTER HAS BEEN WAITING FOR YOU.
THIS WAY, PLEASE.
HEY---!
UM...

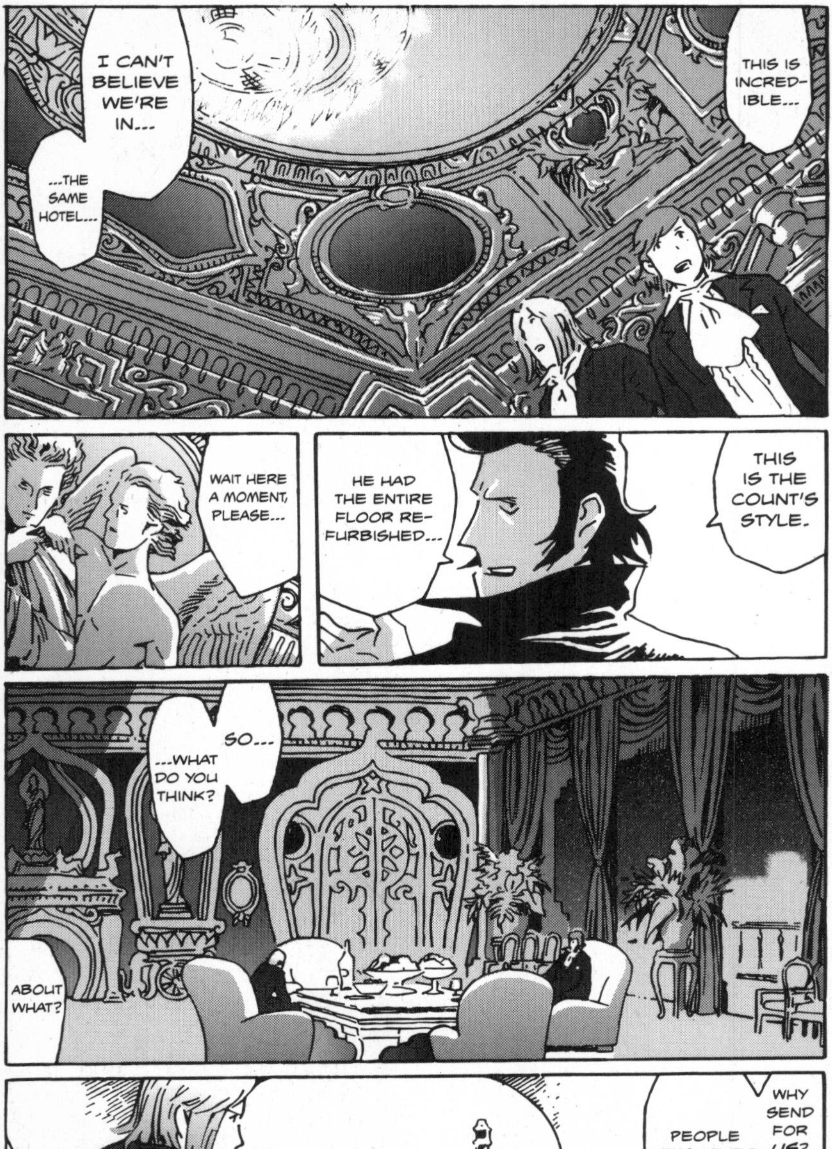
THIS IS INCREDIBLE...
I CAN'T BELIEVE WE'RE IN...
...THE SAME HOTEL...
THIS IS THE COUNT'S STYLE.
HE HAD THE ENTIRE FLOOR REFURBISHED...
WAIT HERE A MOMENT, PLEASE...
SO...
...WHAT DO YOU THINK?
ABOUT WHAT?
WHY SEND FOR *US*?
PEOPLE HE'S NEVER EVEN SEEN BEFORE?

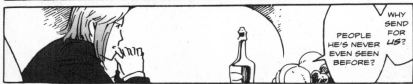

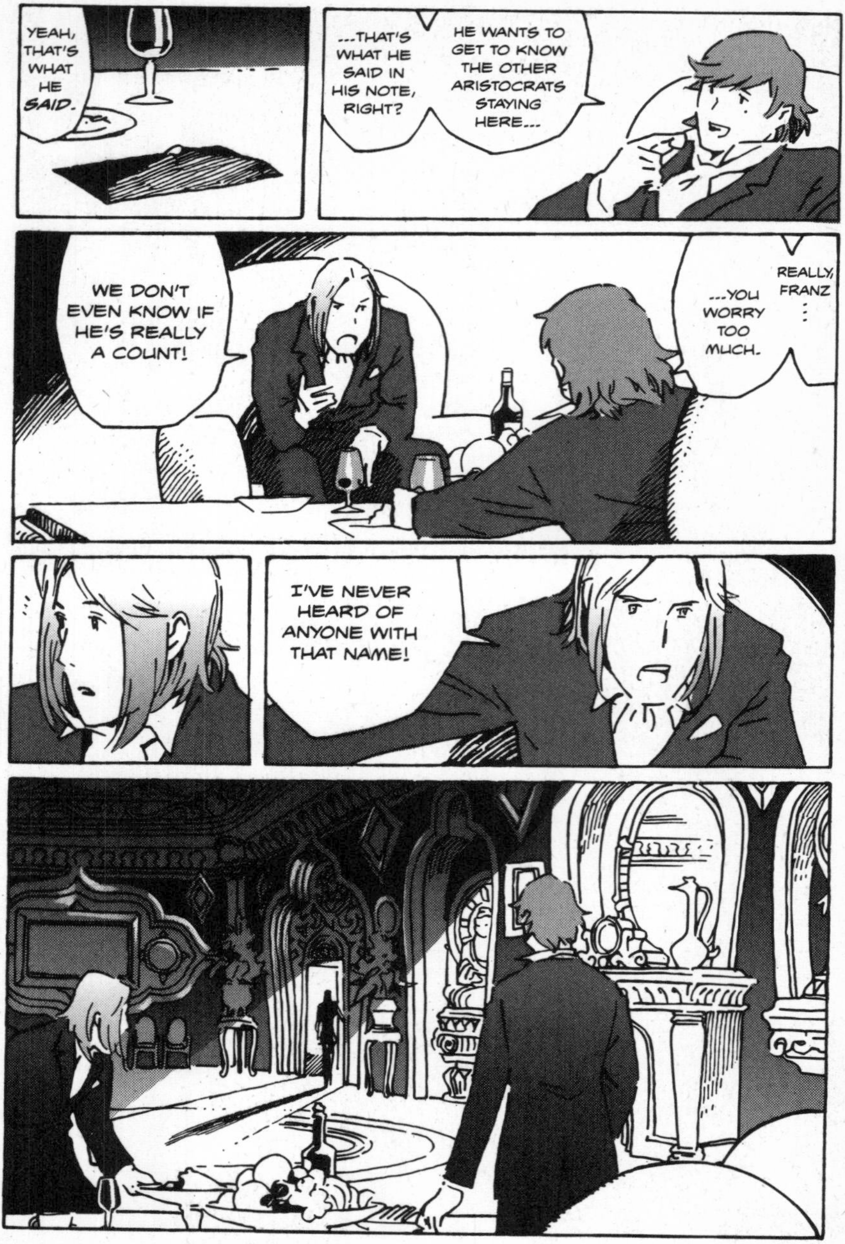
HE WANTS TO GET TO KNOW THE OTHER ARISTOCRATS STAYING HERE...
...THAT'S WHAT HE SAID IN HIS NOTE, RIGHT?
YEAH, THAT'S WHAT HE *SAID*.
REALLY, FRANZ...
...YOU WORRY TOO MUCH.
WE DON'T EVEN KNOW IF HE'S REALLY A COUNT!
I'VE NEVER HEARD OF ANYONE WITH THAT NAME!

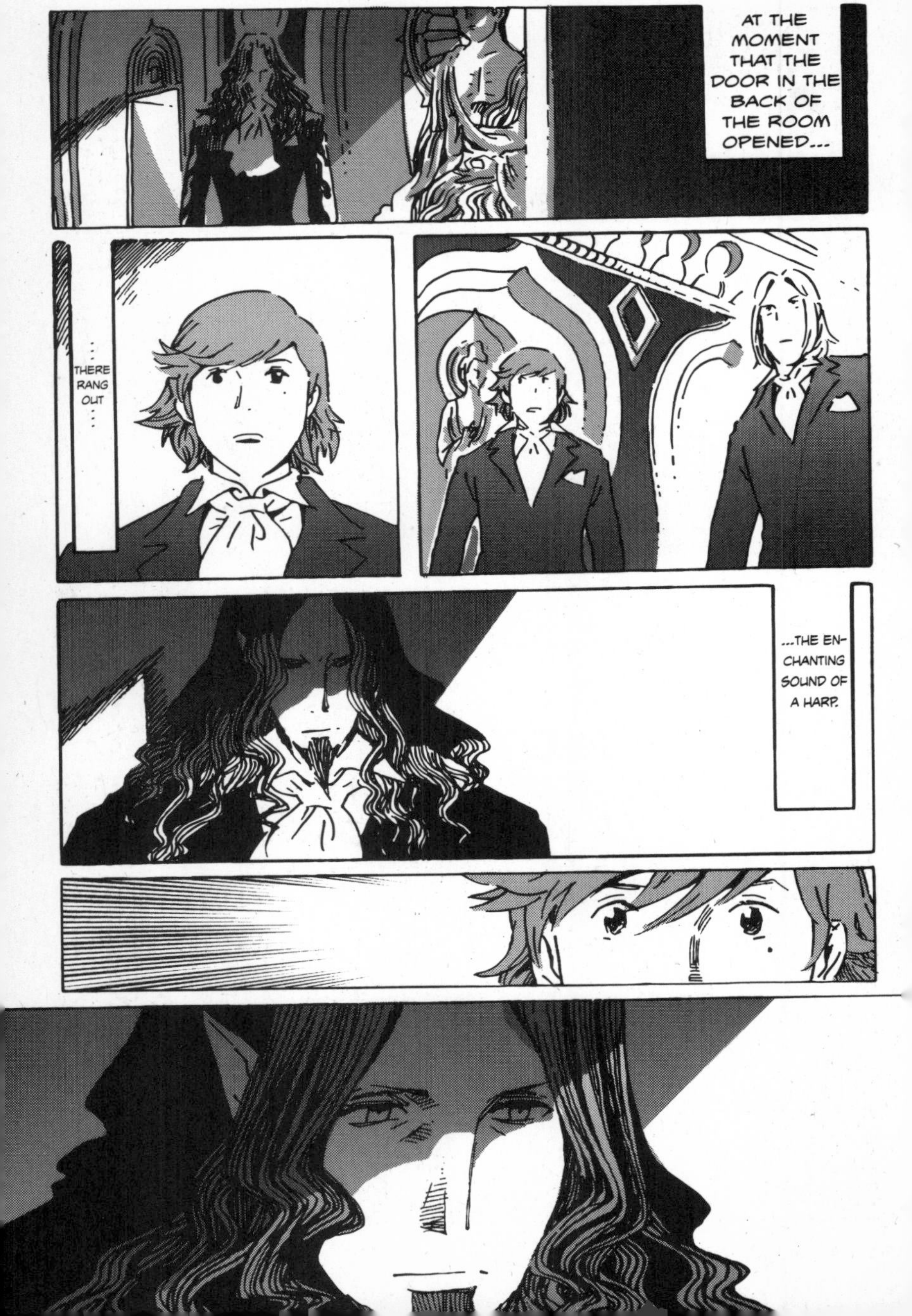
AT THE MOMENT THAT THE DOOR IN THE BACK OF THE ROOM OPENED...
...THERE RANG OUT...
...THE EN-CHANTING SOUND OF A HARP.

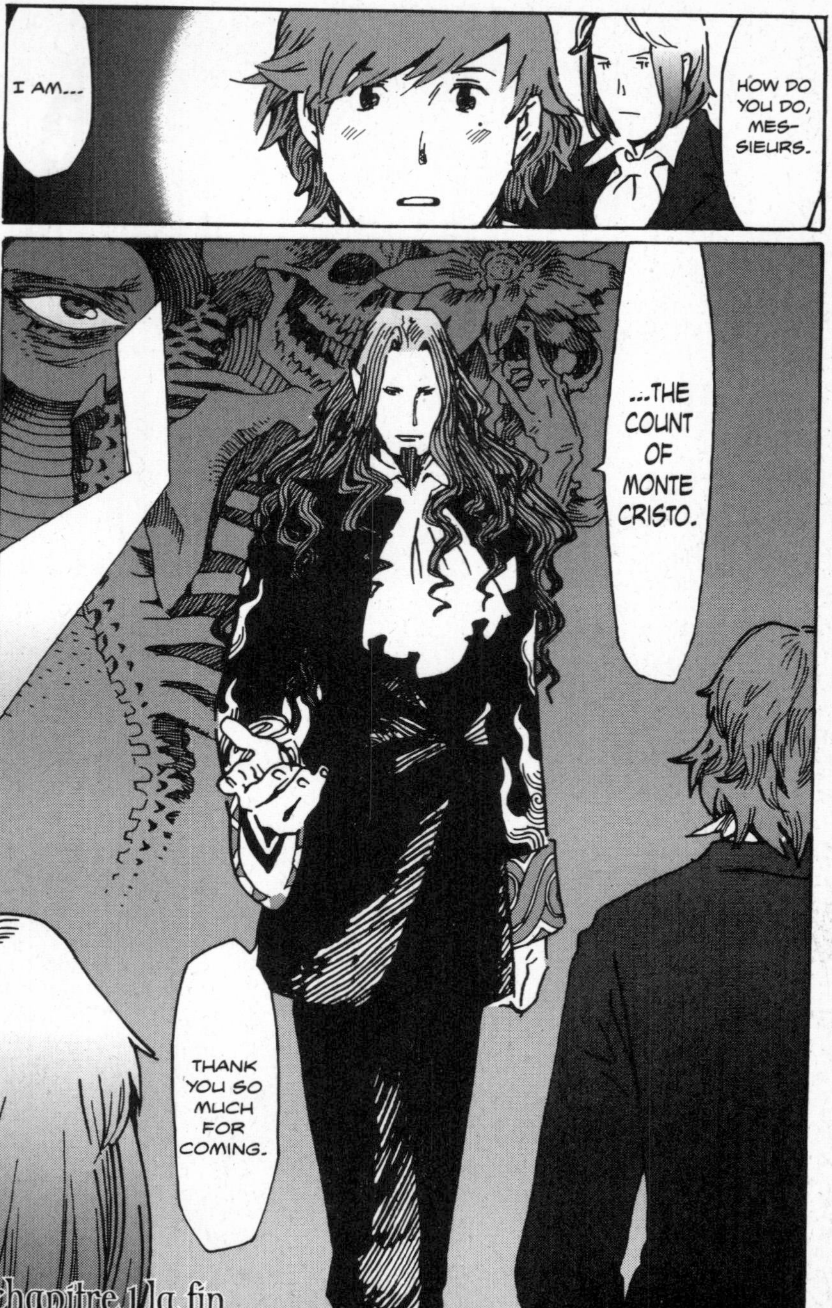
HOW DO YOU DO, MES-SIEURS.
I AM...
...THE COUNT OF MONTE CRISTO.
THANK YOU SO MUCH FOR COMING.
chapitre 1 la fin

Chapitre 2: The Public Execution

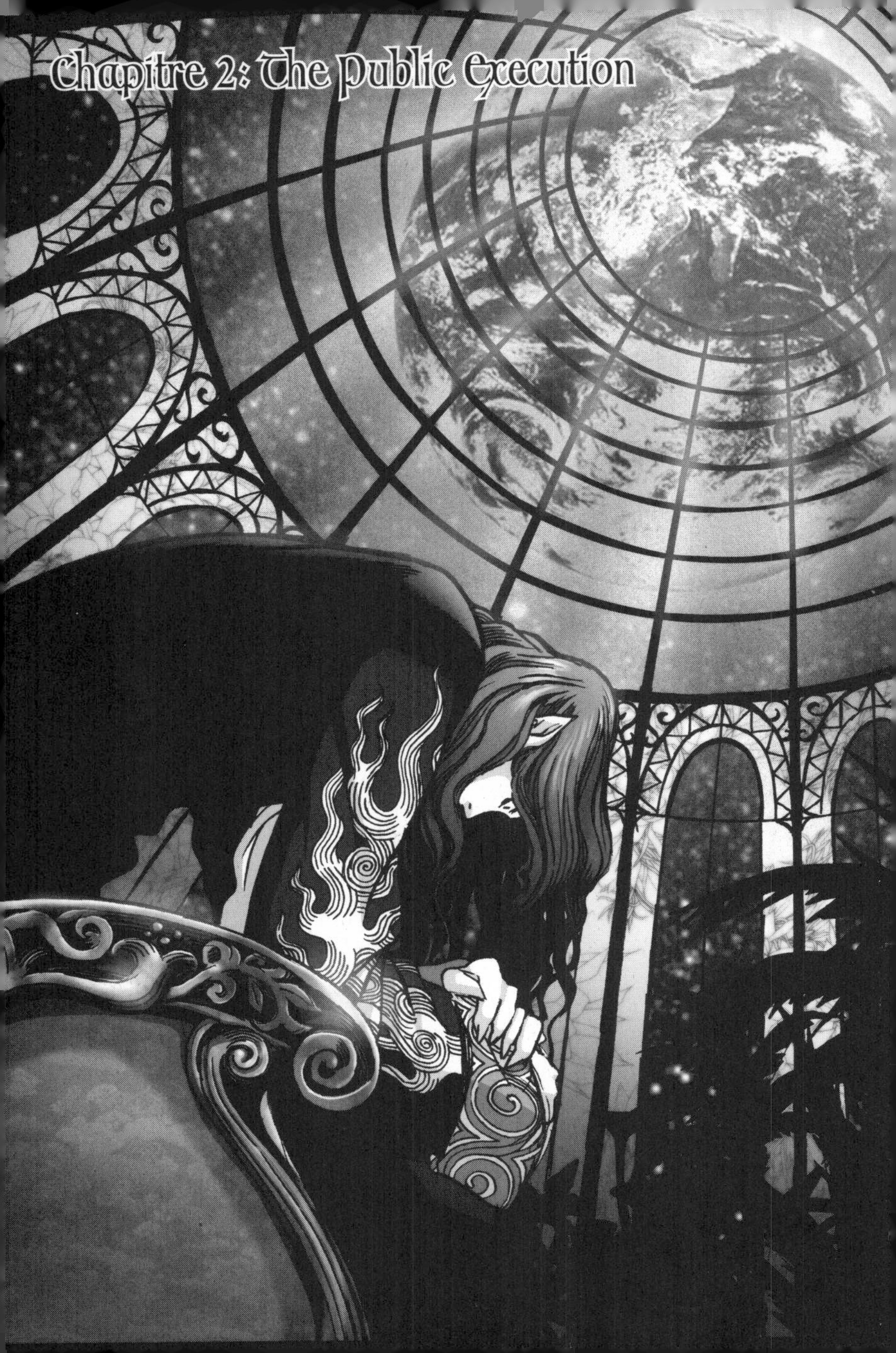

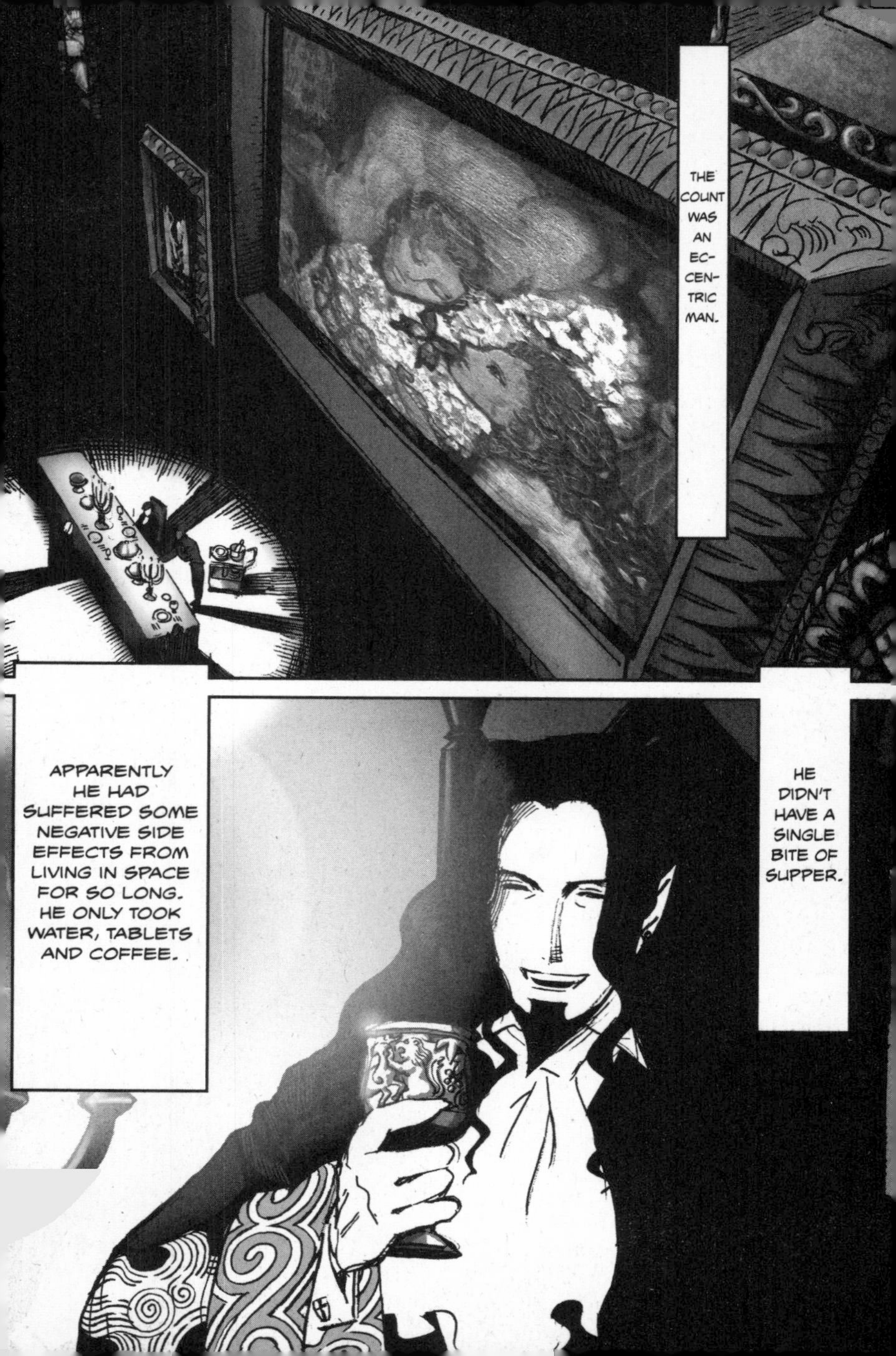
THE COUNT WAS AN EC-CEN-TRIC MAN.
HE DIDN'T HAVE A SINGLE BITE OF SUPPER.
APPARENTLY HE HAD SUFFERED SOME NEGATIVE SIDE EFFECTS FROM LIVING IN SPACE FOR SO LONG. HE ONLY TOOK WATER, TABLETS AND COFFEE.

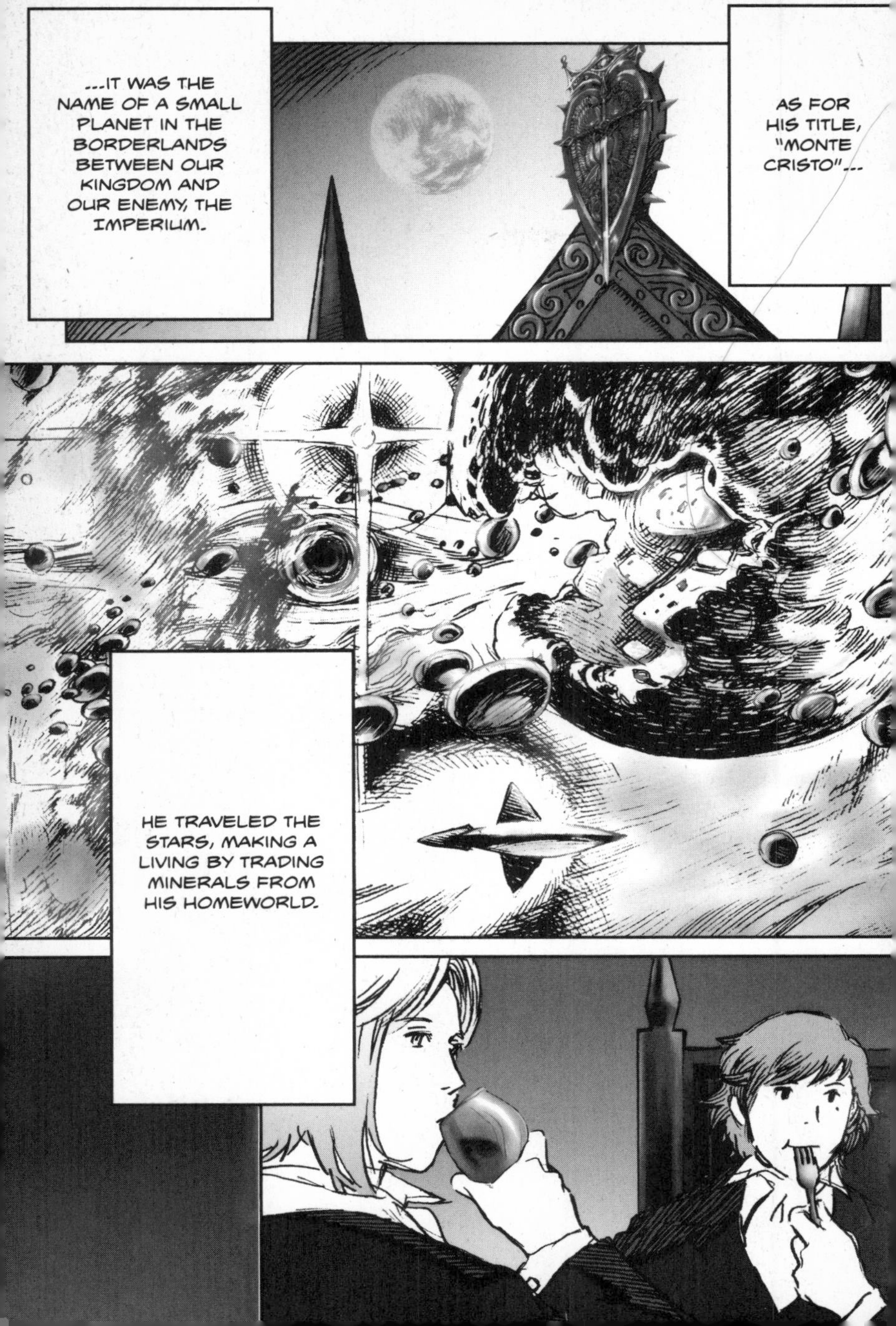
AS FOR HIS TITLE, "MONTE CRISTO"...
...IT WAS THE NAME OF A SMALL PLANET IN THE BORDERLANDS BETWEEN OUR KINGDOM AND OUR ENEMY, THE IMPERIUM.
HE TRAVELED THE STARS, MAKING A LIVING BY TRADING MINERALS FROM HIS HOMEWORLD.

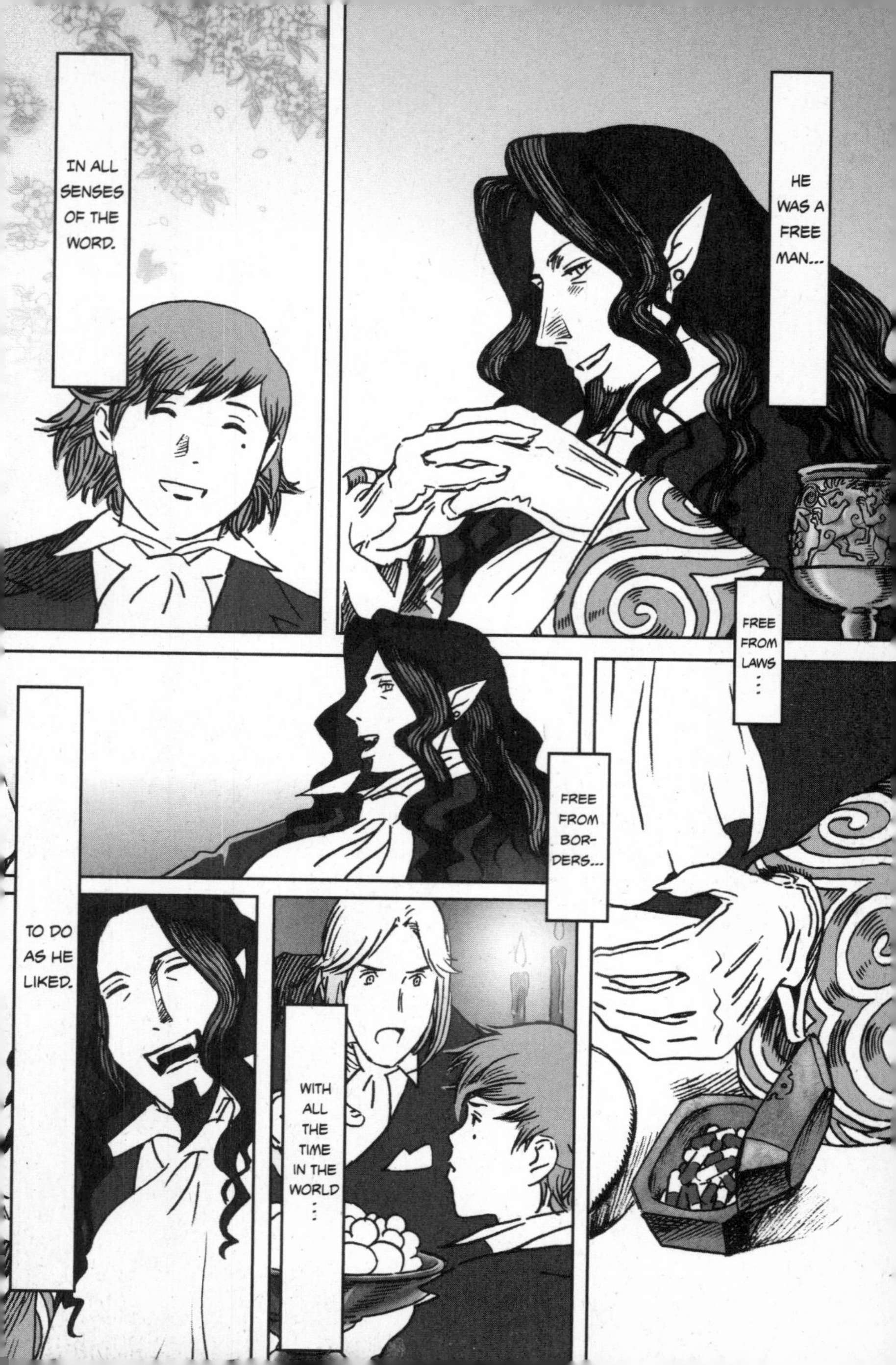
HE WAS A FREE MAN...
IN ALL SENSES OF THE WORD.
FREE FROM LAWS...
FREE FROM BOR-DERS...
WITH ALL THE TIME IN THE WORLD...
TO DO AS HE LIKED.

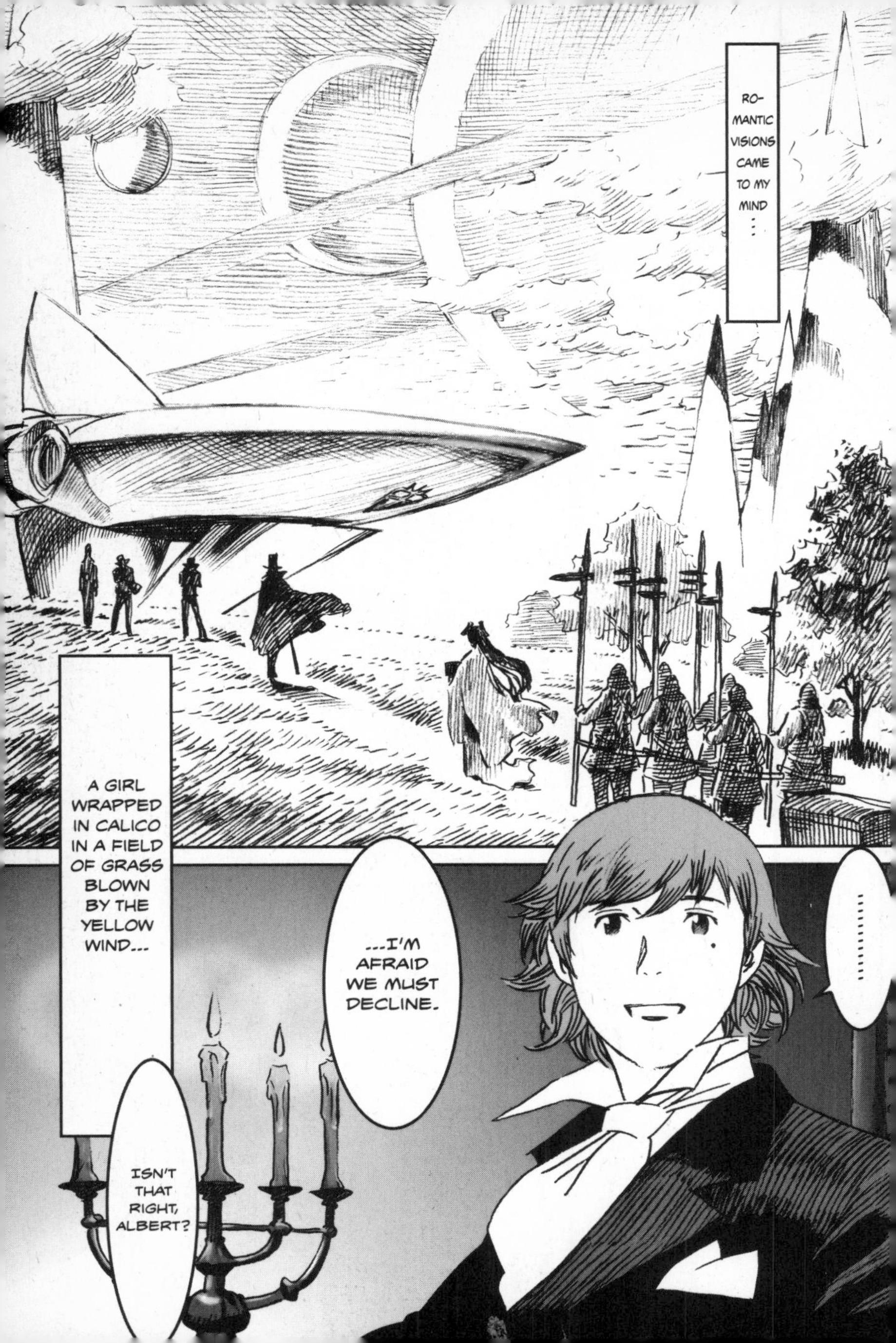

RO-MANTIC VISIONS CAME TO MY MIND...
A GIRL WRAPPED IN CALICO IN A FIELD OF GRASS BLOWN BY THE YELLOW WIND...
......
...I'M AFRAID WE MUST DECLINE.
ISN'T THAT RIGHT, ALBERT?

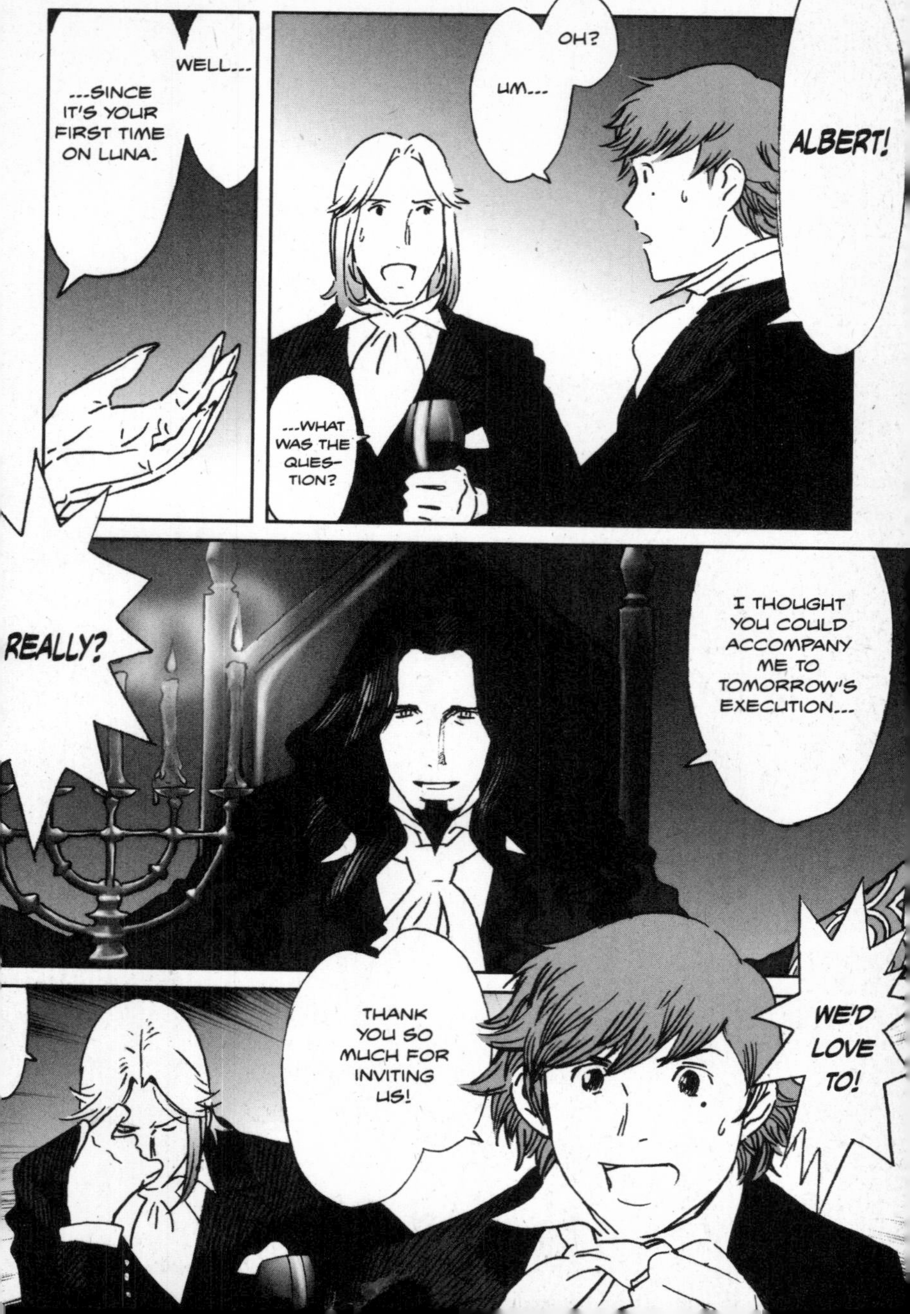
ALBERT!
OH?
UM...
...WHAT WAS THE QUES-TION?
WELL...
...SINCE IT'S YOUR FIRST TIME ON LUNA.
I THOUGHT YOU COULD ACCOMPANY ME TO TOMORROW'S EXECUTION...
REALLY?
WE'D LOVE TO!
THANK YOU SO MUCH FOR INVITING US!

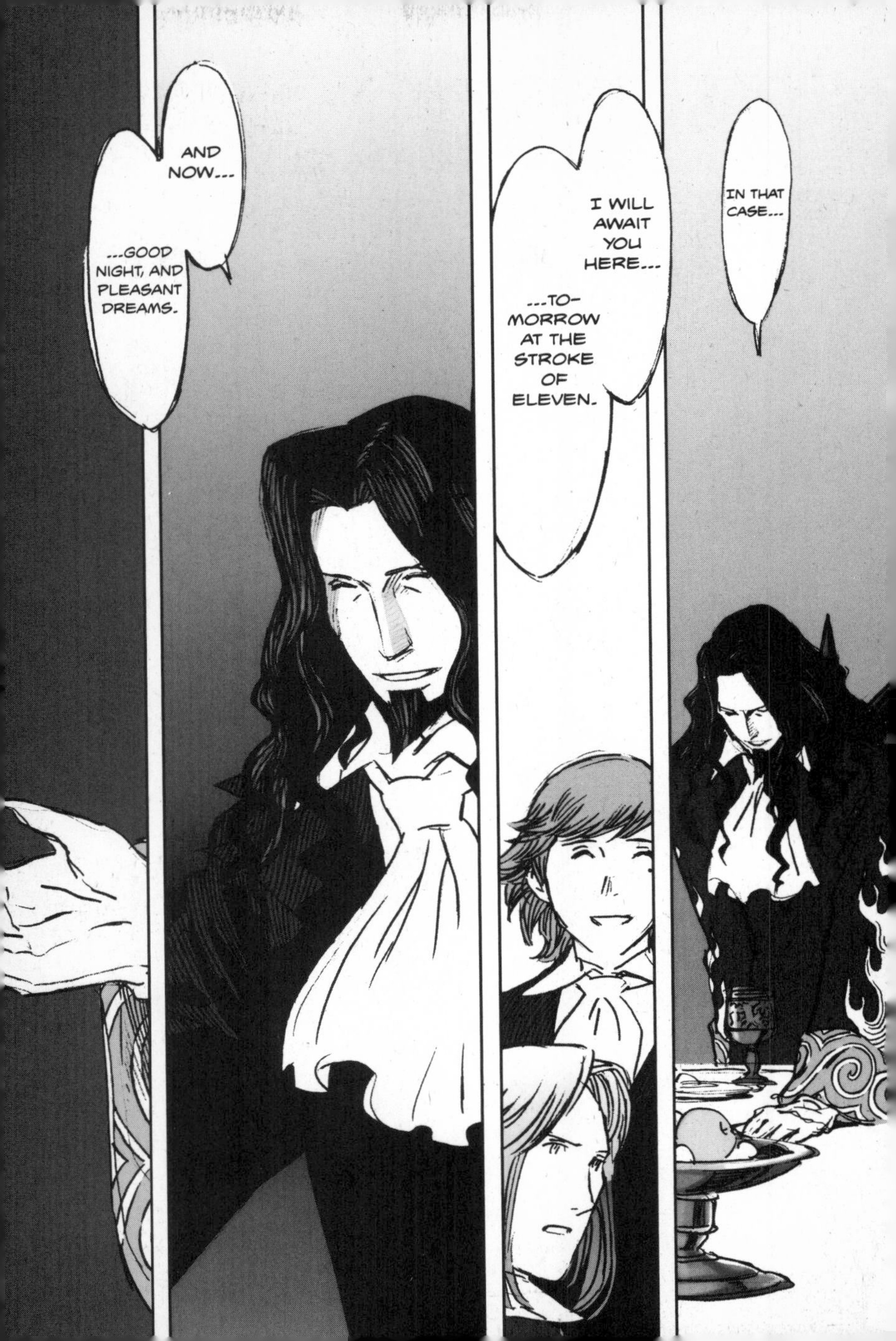
IN THAT CASE...
I WILL AWAIT YOU HERE...
...TO-MORROW AT THE STROKE OF ELEVEN.
AND NOW...
...GOOD NIGHT, AND PLEASANT DREAMS.

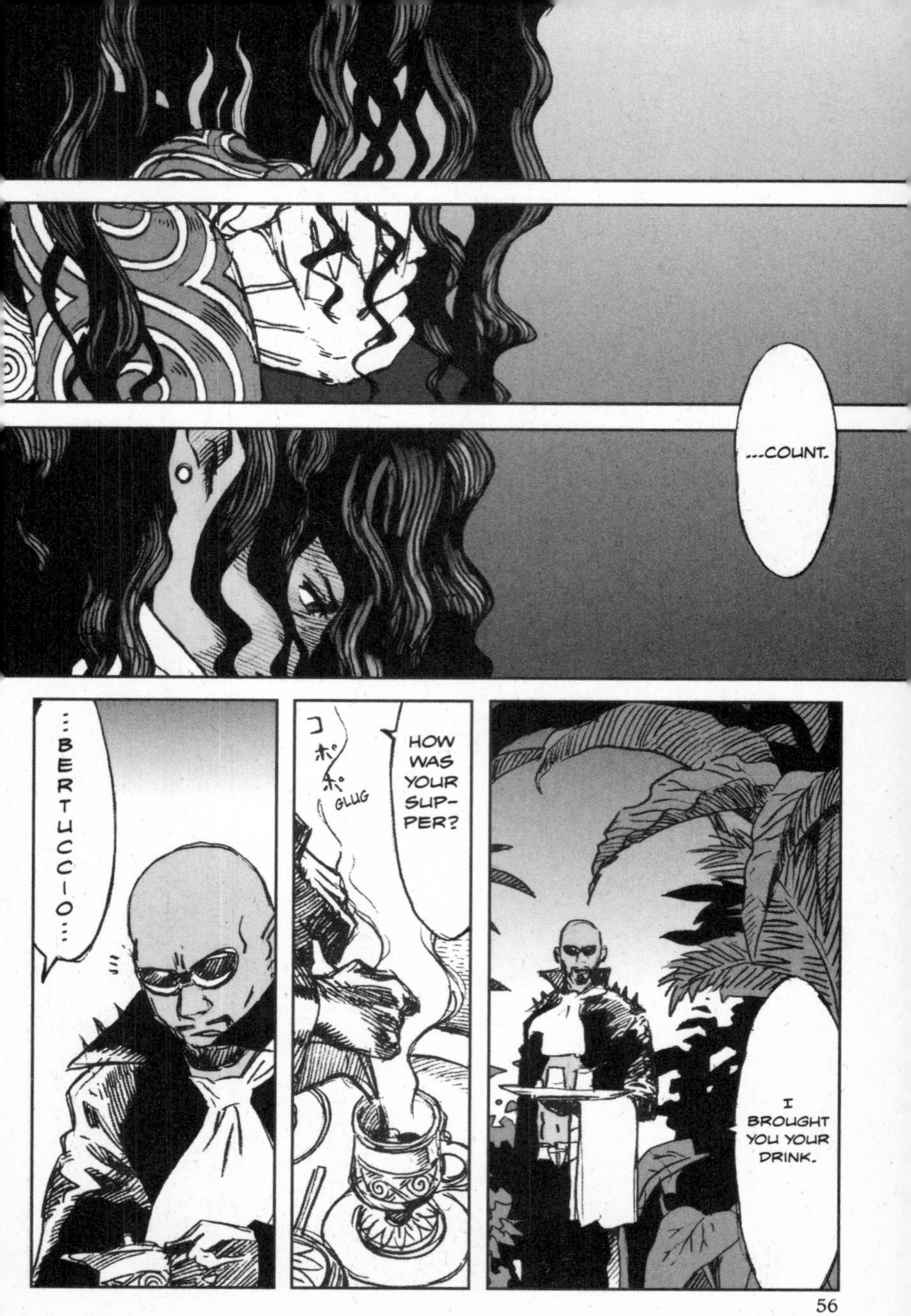
...COUNT.
I BROUGHT YOU YOUR DRINK.
HOW WAS YOUR SUP-PER?
コポポ
GLUG
...BERTUCCIO...

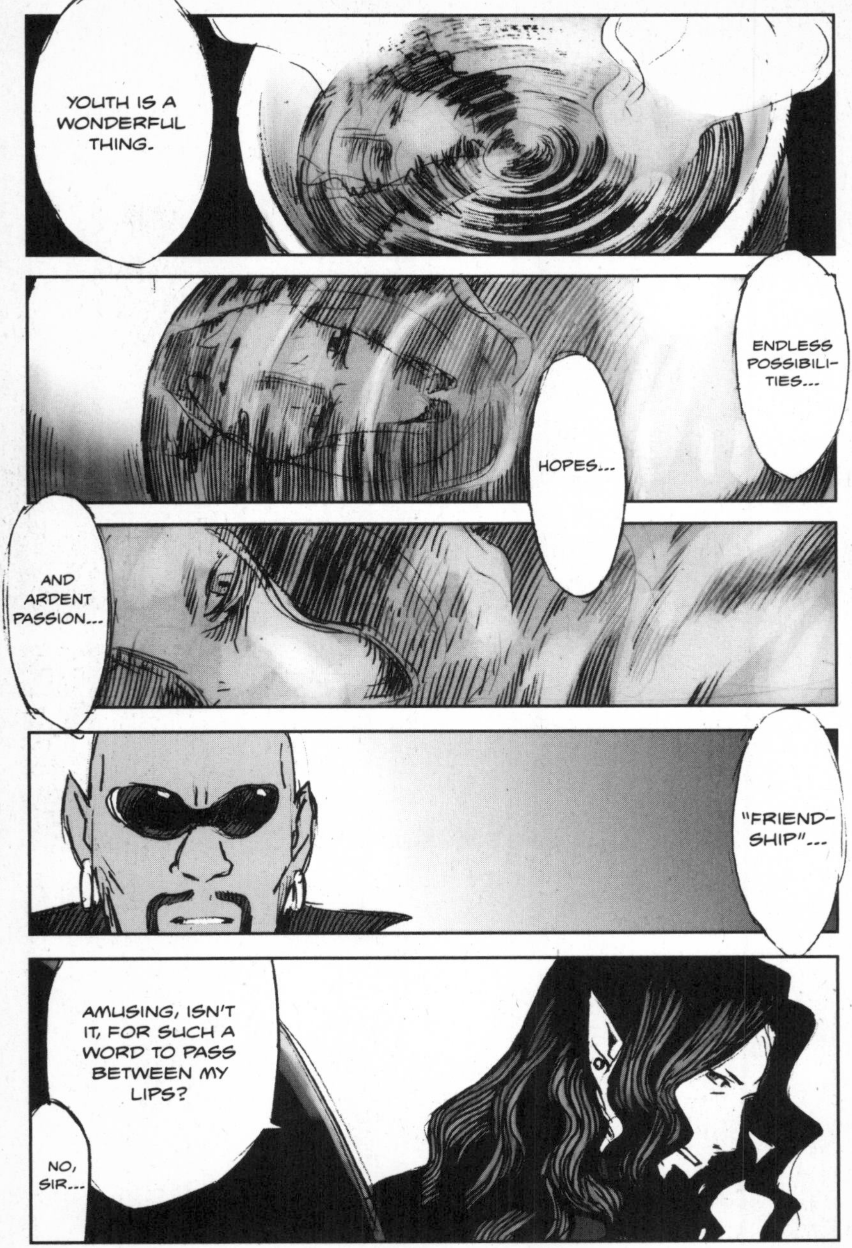
YOUTH IS A WONDERFUL THING.
ENDLESS POSSIBILI-TIES...
HOPES...
AND ARDENT PASSION...
"FRIEND-SHIP"...
AMUSING, ISN'T IT, FOR SUCH A WORD TO PASS BETWEEN MY LIPS?
NO, SIR...

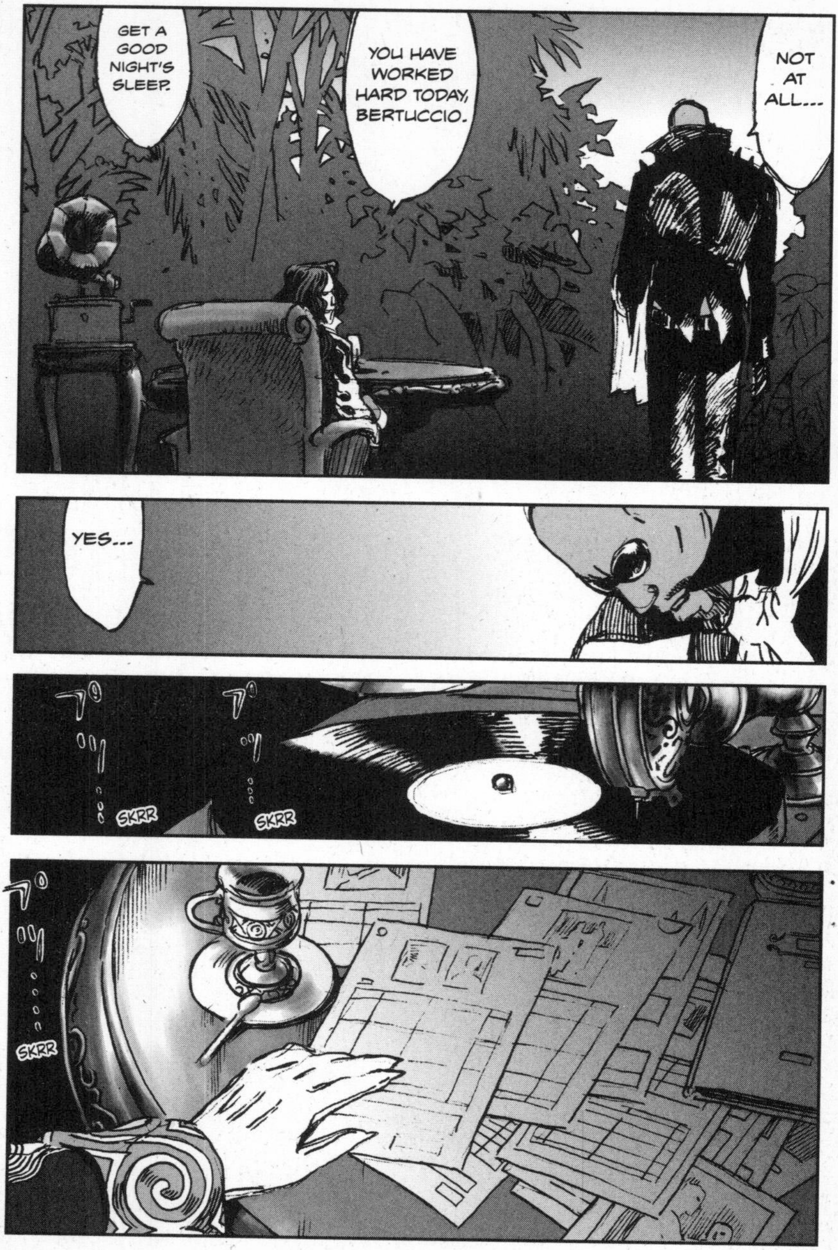
NOT AT ALL...
YOU HAVE WORKED HARD TODAY, BERTUCCIO.
GET A GOOD NIGHT'S SLEEP.
YES...
SKRR
SKRR
SKRR

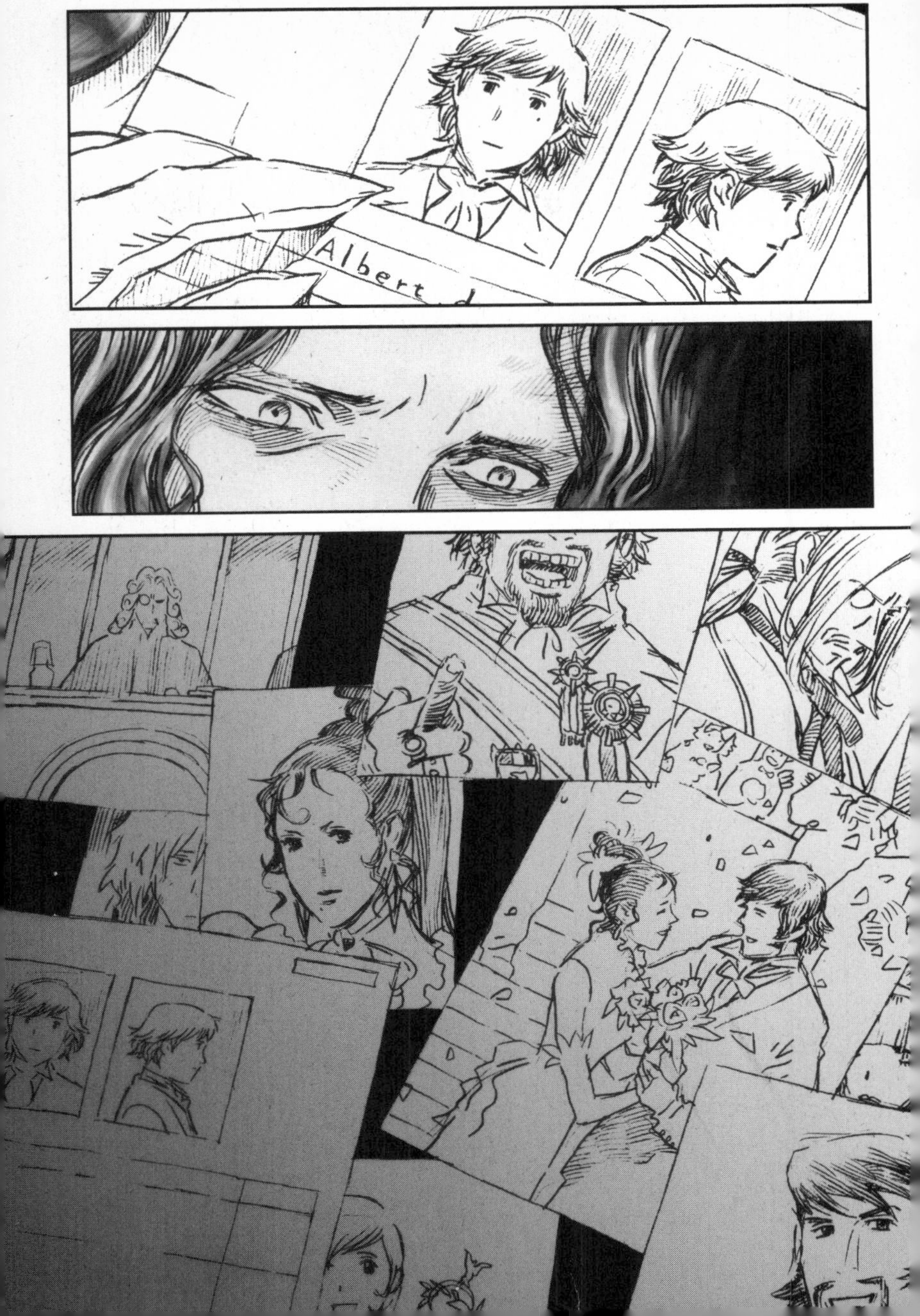
Albert

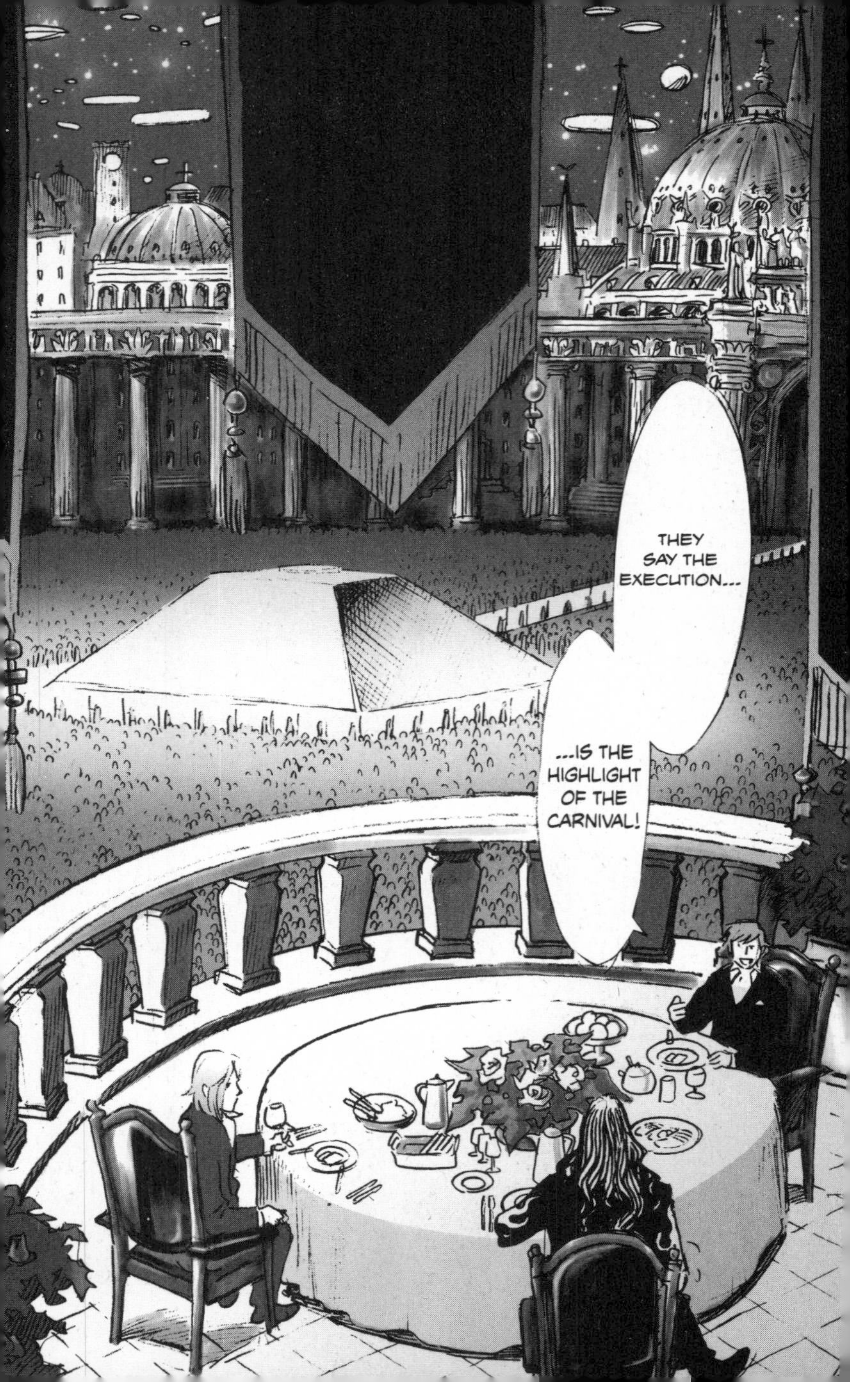
THEY SAY THE EXECUTION...
...IS THE HIGHLIGHT OF THE CARNIVAL!

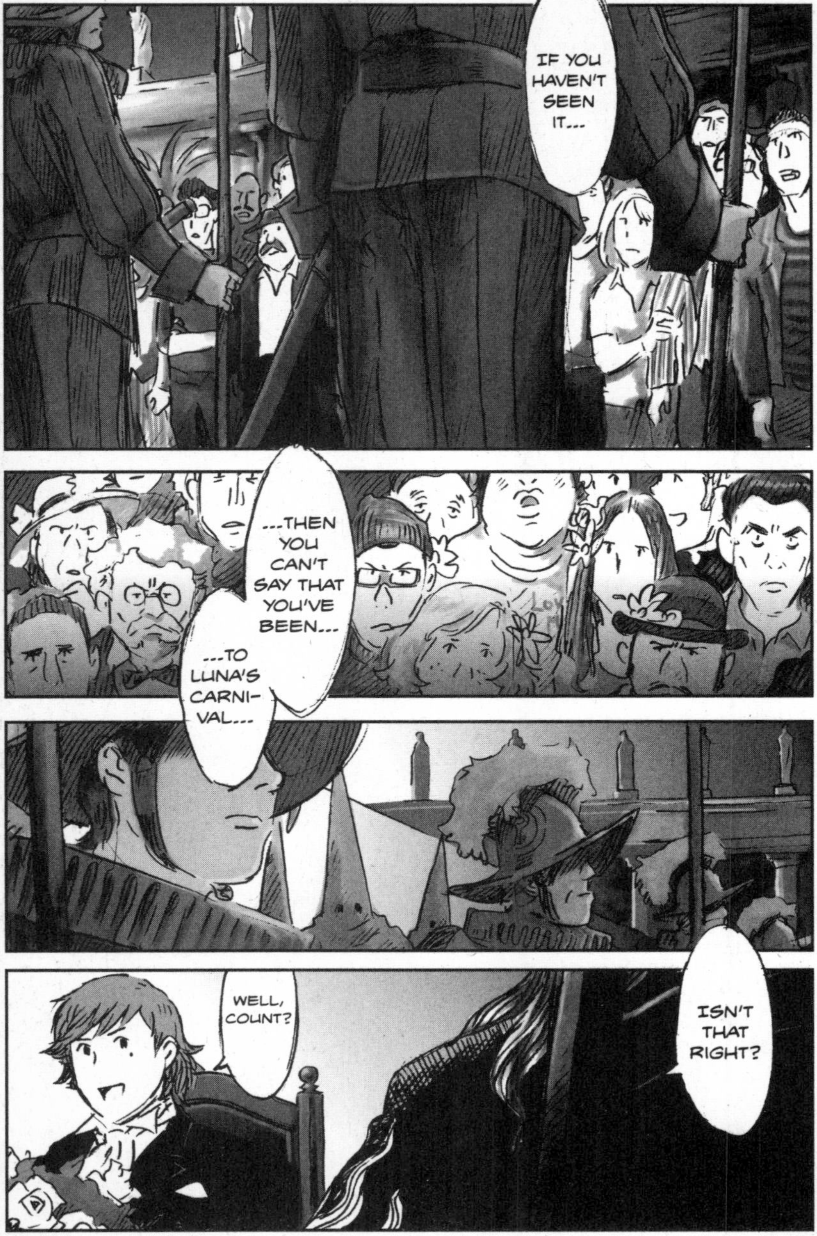
IF YOU HAVEN'T SEEN IT...
...THEN YOU CAN'T SAY THAT YOU'VE BEEN...
...TO LUNA'S CARNI-VAL...
ISN'T THAT RIGHT?
WELL, COUNT?

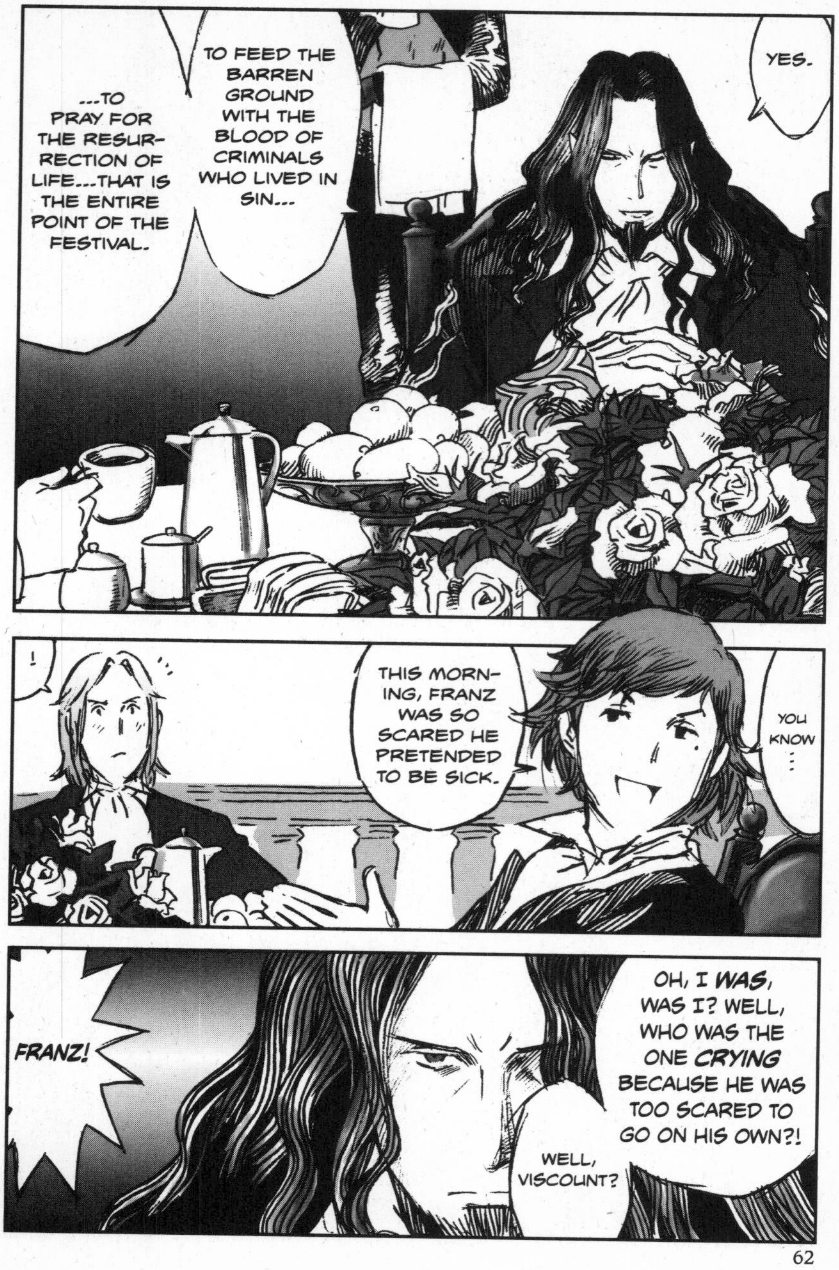
YES.
TO FEED THE BARREN GROUND WITH THE BLOOD OF CRIMINALS WHO LIVED IN SIN...
...TO PRAY FOR THE RESUR-RECTION OF LIFE...THAT IS THE ENTIRE POINT OF THE FESTIVAL.
YOU KNOW...
THIS MORN-ING, FRANZ WAS SO SCARED HE PRETENDED TO BE SICK.
!
OH, I *WAS*, WAS I? WELL, WHO WAS THE ONE *CRYING* BECAUSE HE WAS TOO SCARED TO GO ON HIS OWN?!
WELL, VISCOUNT?
FRANZ!

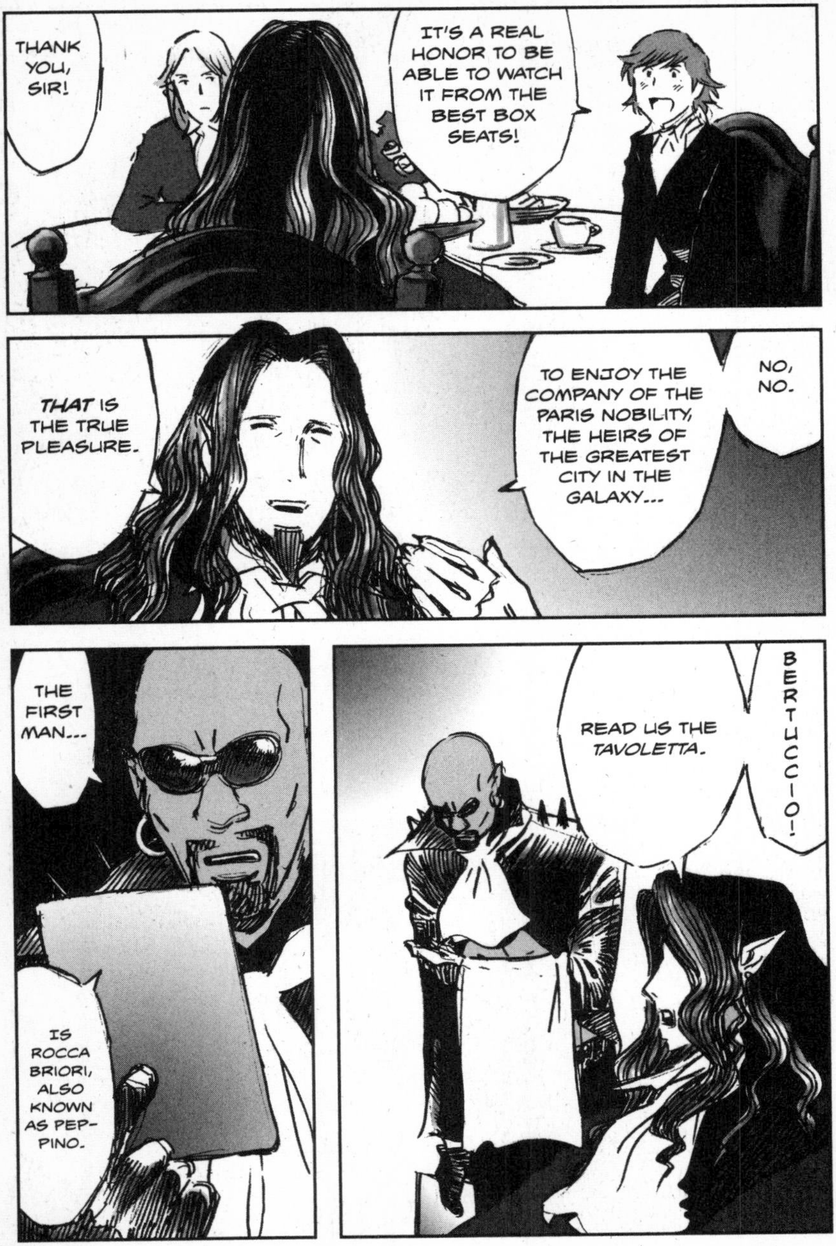
IT'S A REAL HONOR TO BE ABLE TO WATCH IT FROM THE BEST BOX SEATS!
THANK YOU, SIR!
NO, NO.
TO ENJOY THE COMPANY OF THE PARIS NOBILITY, THE HEIRS OF THE GREATEST CITY IN THE GALAXY...
THAT IS THE TRUE PLEASURE.
BERTUCCIO!
READ US THE *TAVOLETTA*.
THE FIRST MAN...
IS ROCCA BRIORI, ALSO KNOWN AS PEP-PINO.

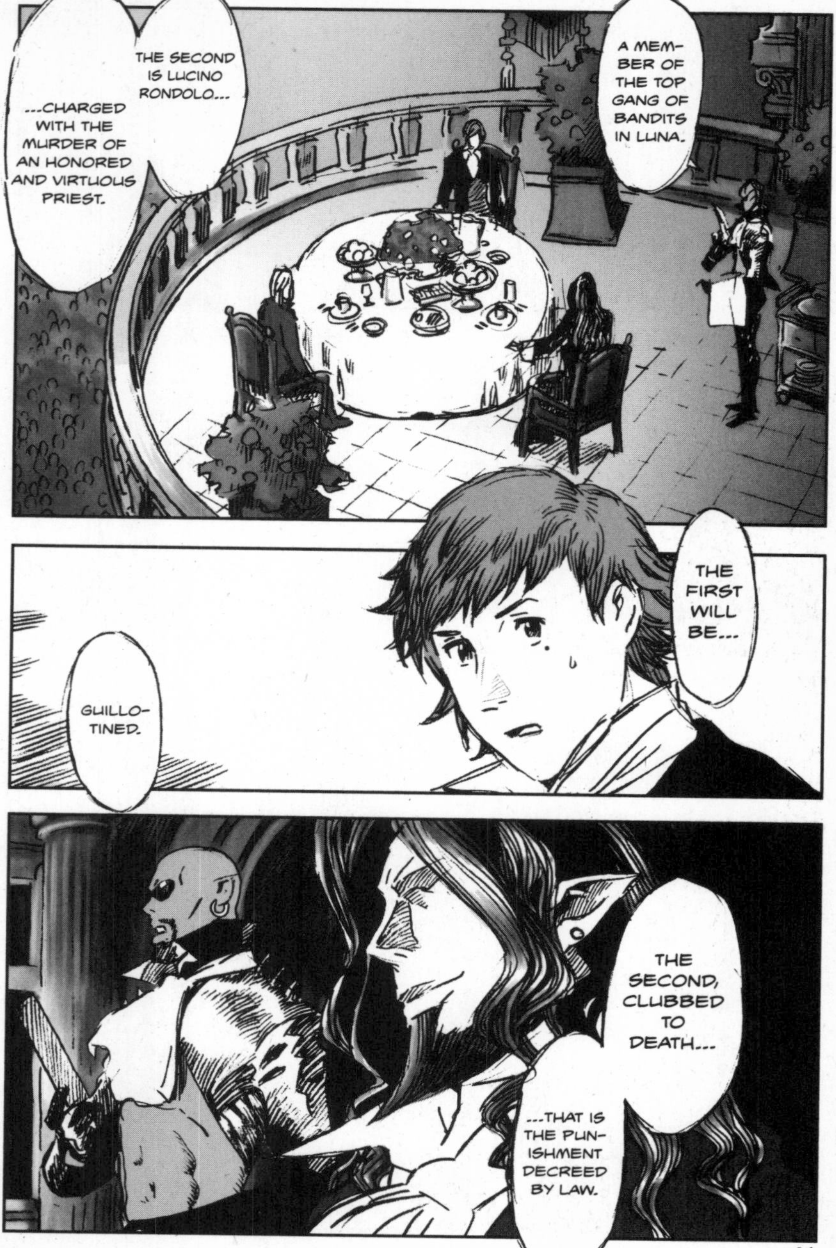
A MEM-BER OF THE TOP GANG OF BANDITS IN LUNA.
THE SECOND IS LUCINO RONDOLO...
...CHARGED WITH THE MURDER OF AN HONORED AND VIRTUOUS PRIEST.
THE FIRST WILL BE...
GUILLO-TINED.
THE SECOND, CLUBBED TO DEATH...
...THAT IS THE PUN-ISHMENT DECREED BY LAW.

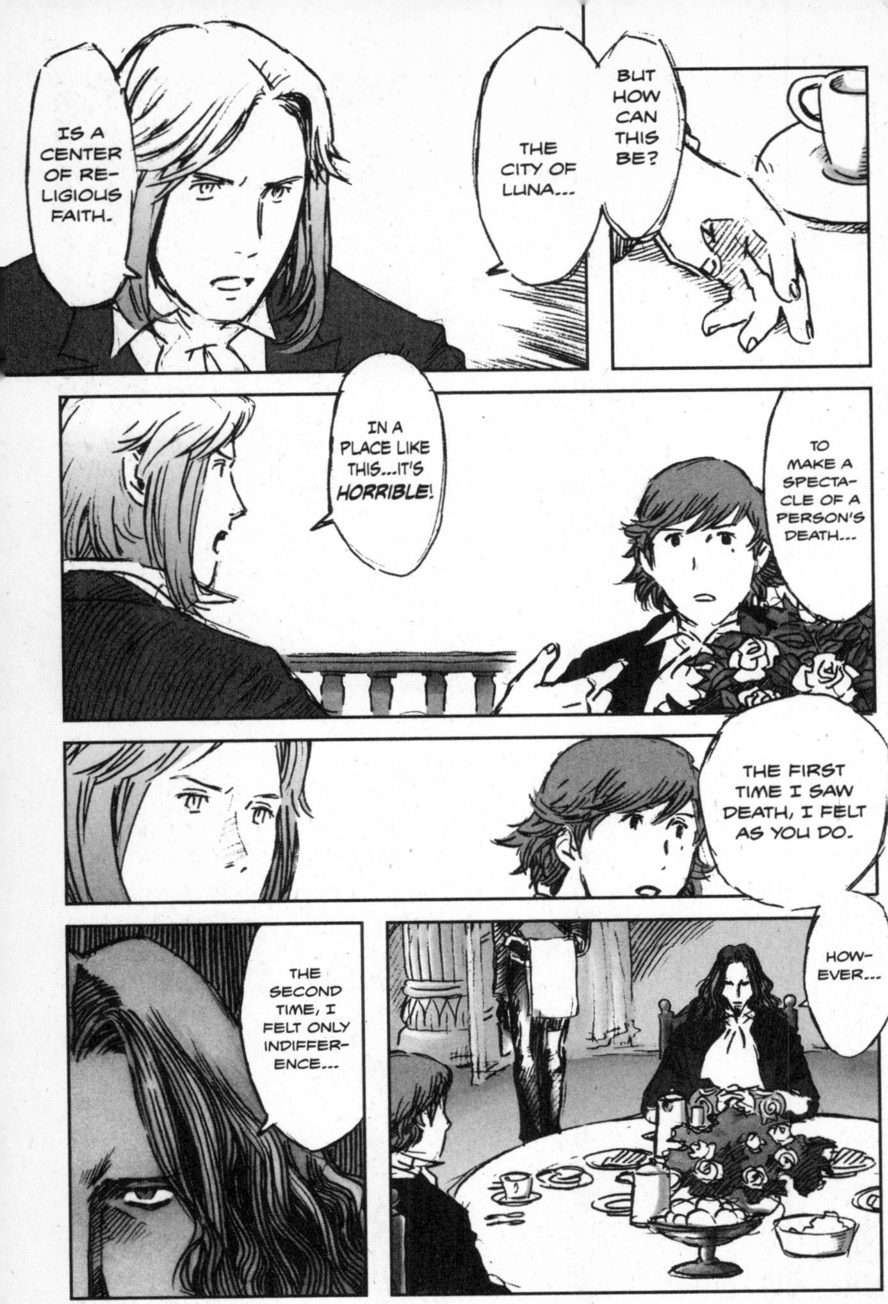
BUT HOW CAN THIS BE?
THE CITY OF LUNA...
IS A CENTER OF RE-LIGIOUS FAITH.
TO MAKE A SPECTA-CLE OF A PERSON'S DEATH...
IN A PLACE LIKE THIS...IT'S *HORRIBLE*!
THE FIRST TIME I SAW DEATH, I FELT AS YOU DO.
HOW-EVER...
THE SECOND TIME, I FELT ONLY INDIFFER-ENCE...

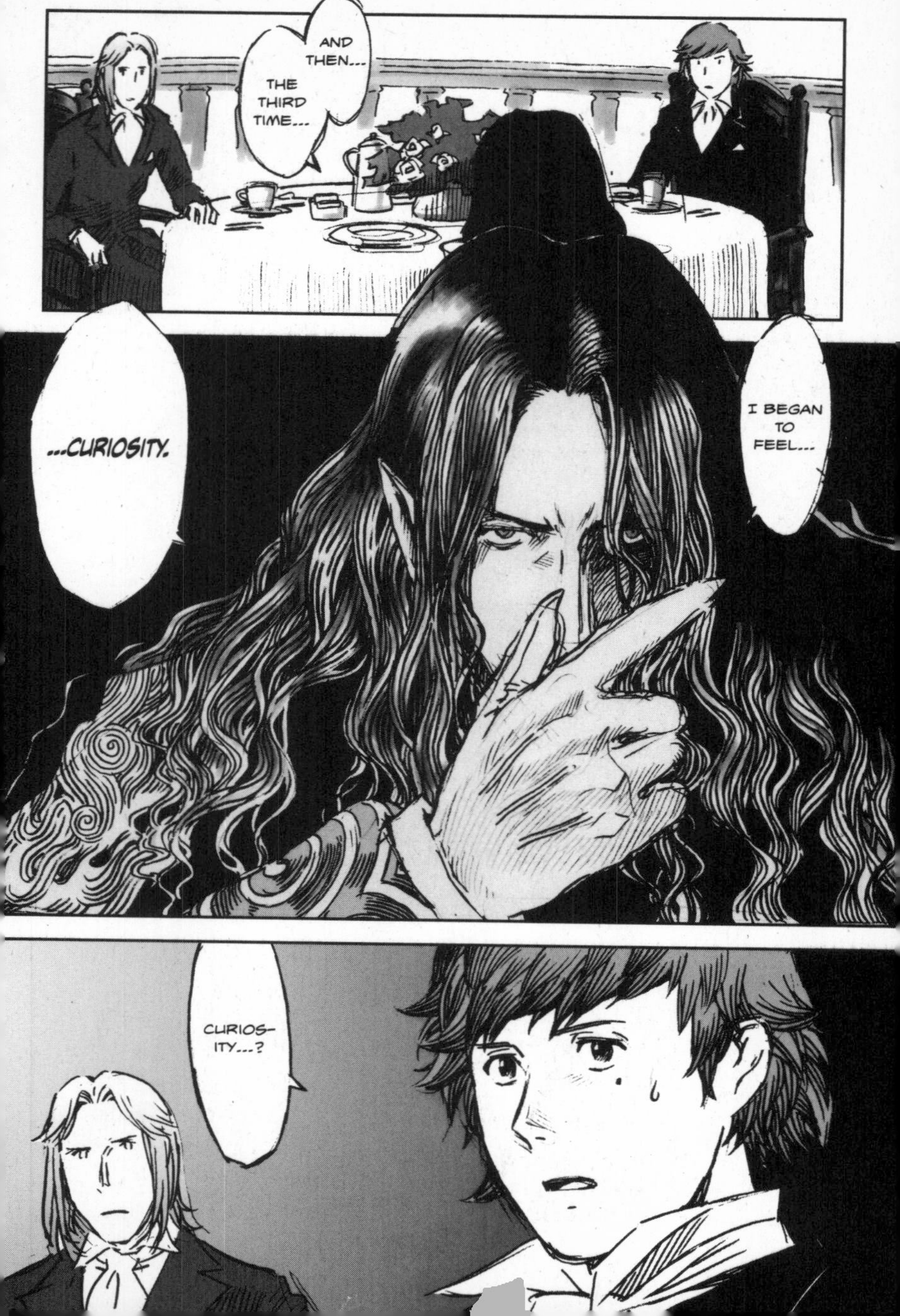
AND THEN...
THE THIRD TIME...
I BEGAN TO FEEL...
...CURIOSITY.
CURIOS-ITY...?

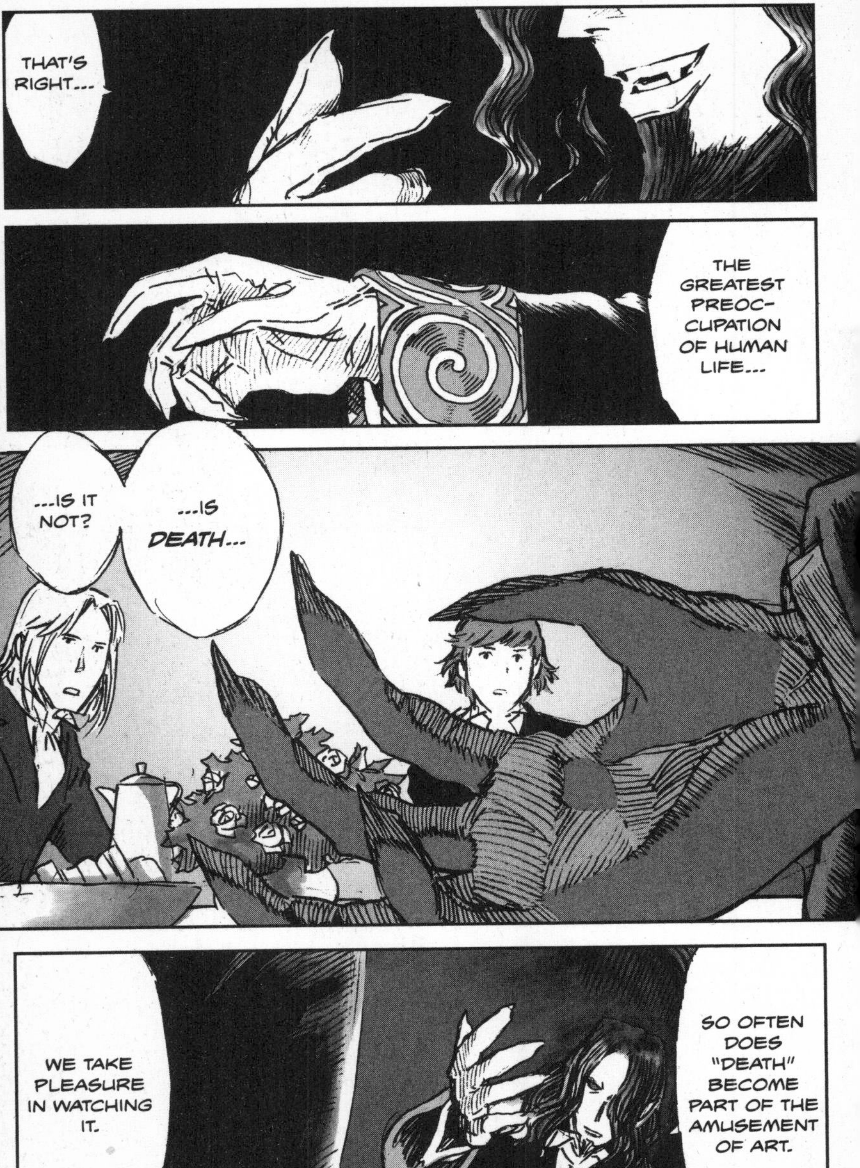
THAT'S RIGHT...
THE GREATEST PREOC-CUPATION OF HUMAN LIFE...
...IS DEATH...
...IS IT NOT?
SO OFTEN DOES "DEATH" BECOME PART OF THE AMUSEMENT OF ART.
WE TAKE PLEASURE IN WATCHING IT.

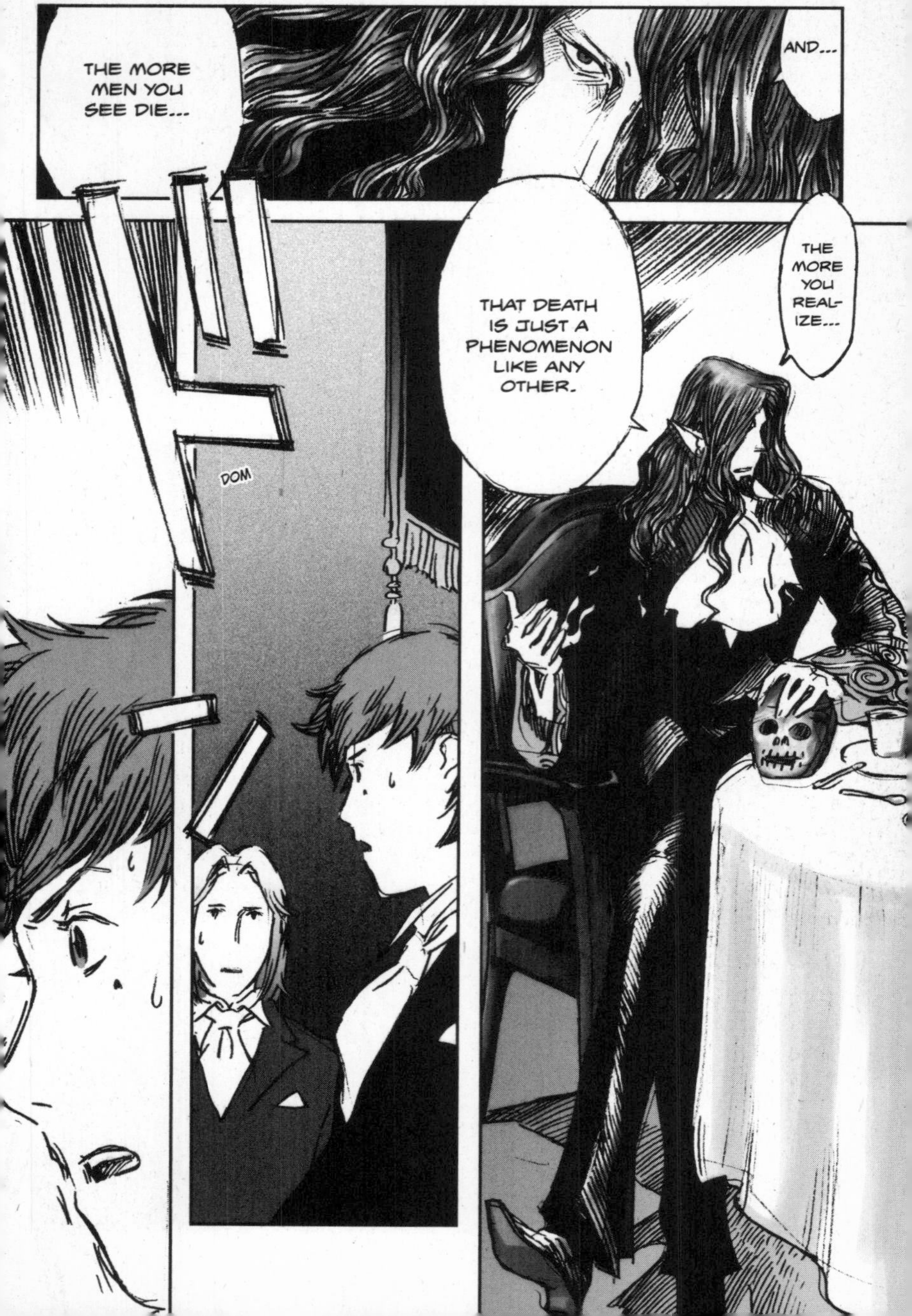
THE MORE MEN YOU SEE DIE...
AND...
DOM
THE MORE YOU REAL-IZE...
THAT DEATH IS JUST A PHENOMENON LIKE ANY OTHER.

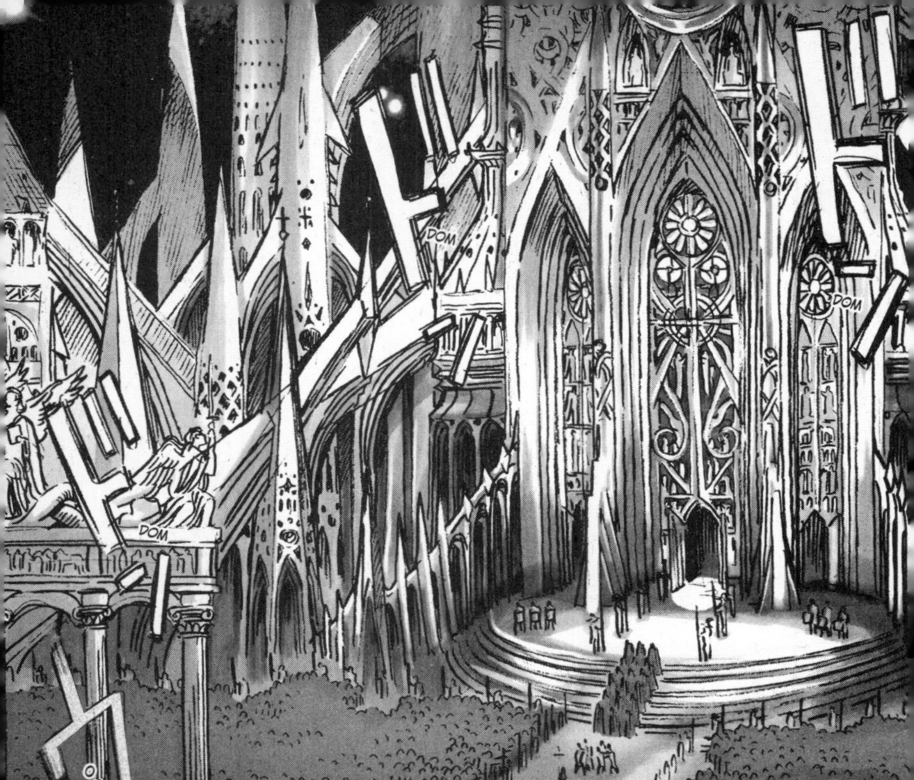
DOM
DOM
DOM
OOOOHHHH

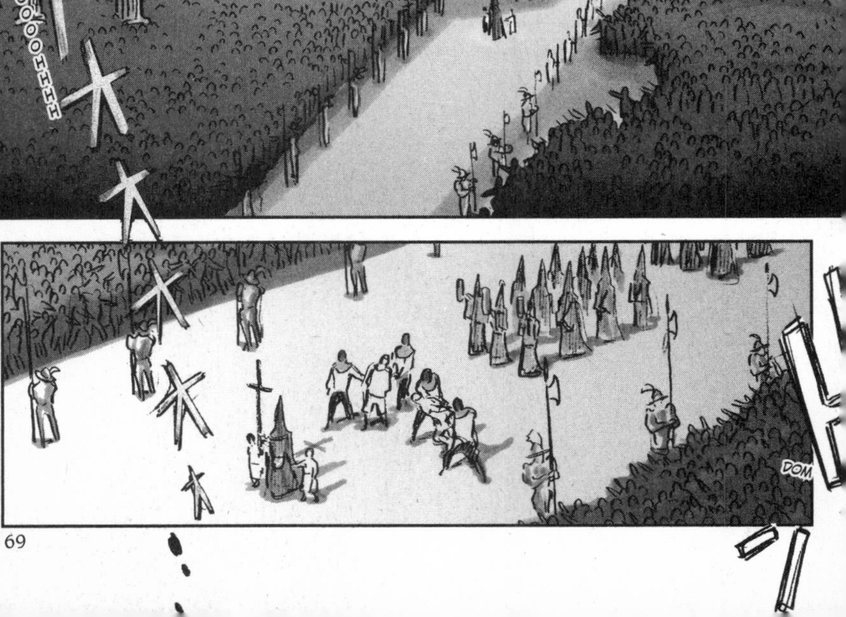
DOM

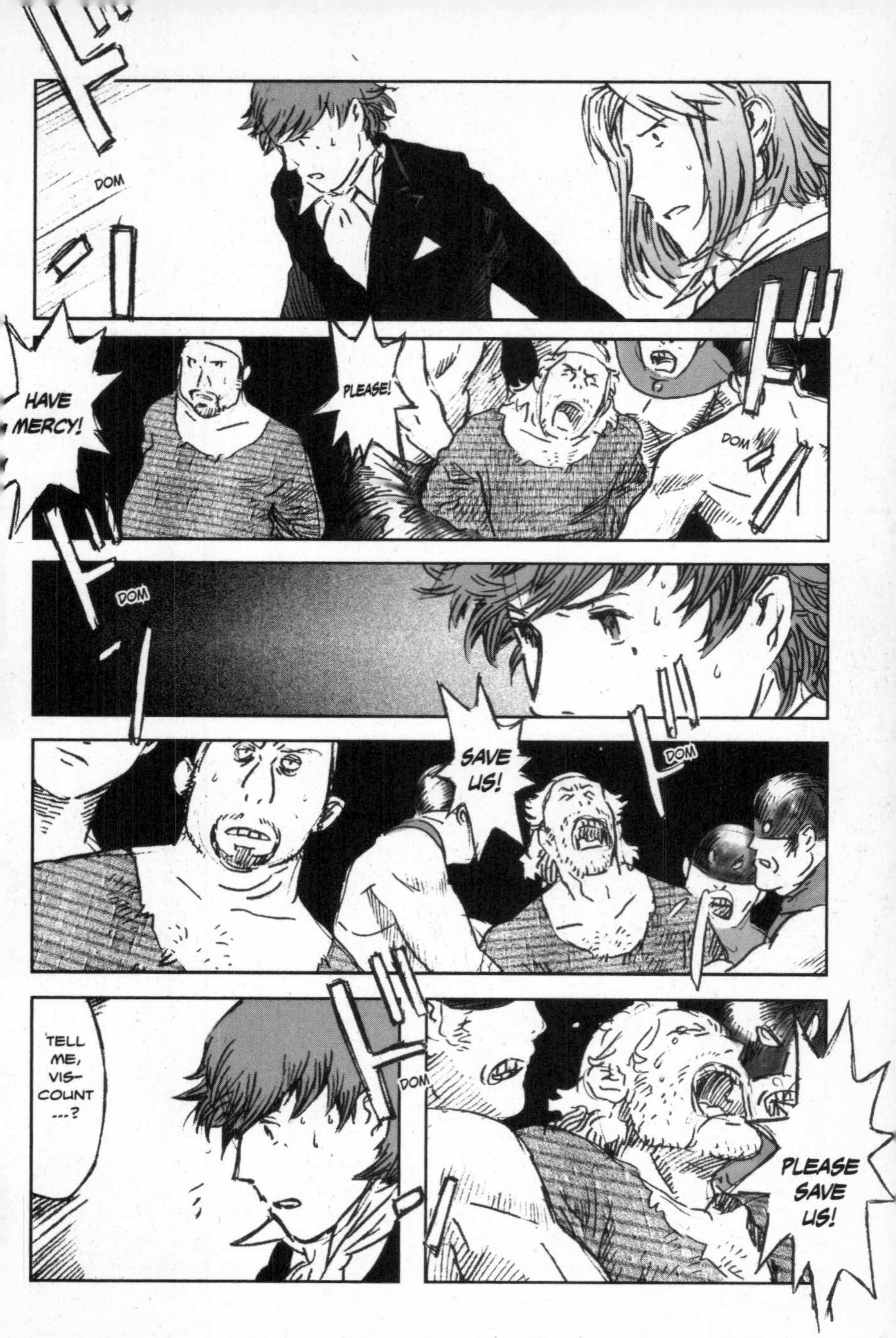
DOM
DOM
PLEASE!
HAVE MERCY!
DOM
DOM
SAVE US!
PLEASE SAVE US!
DOM
TELL ME, VIS-COUNT ...?

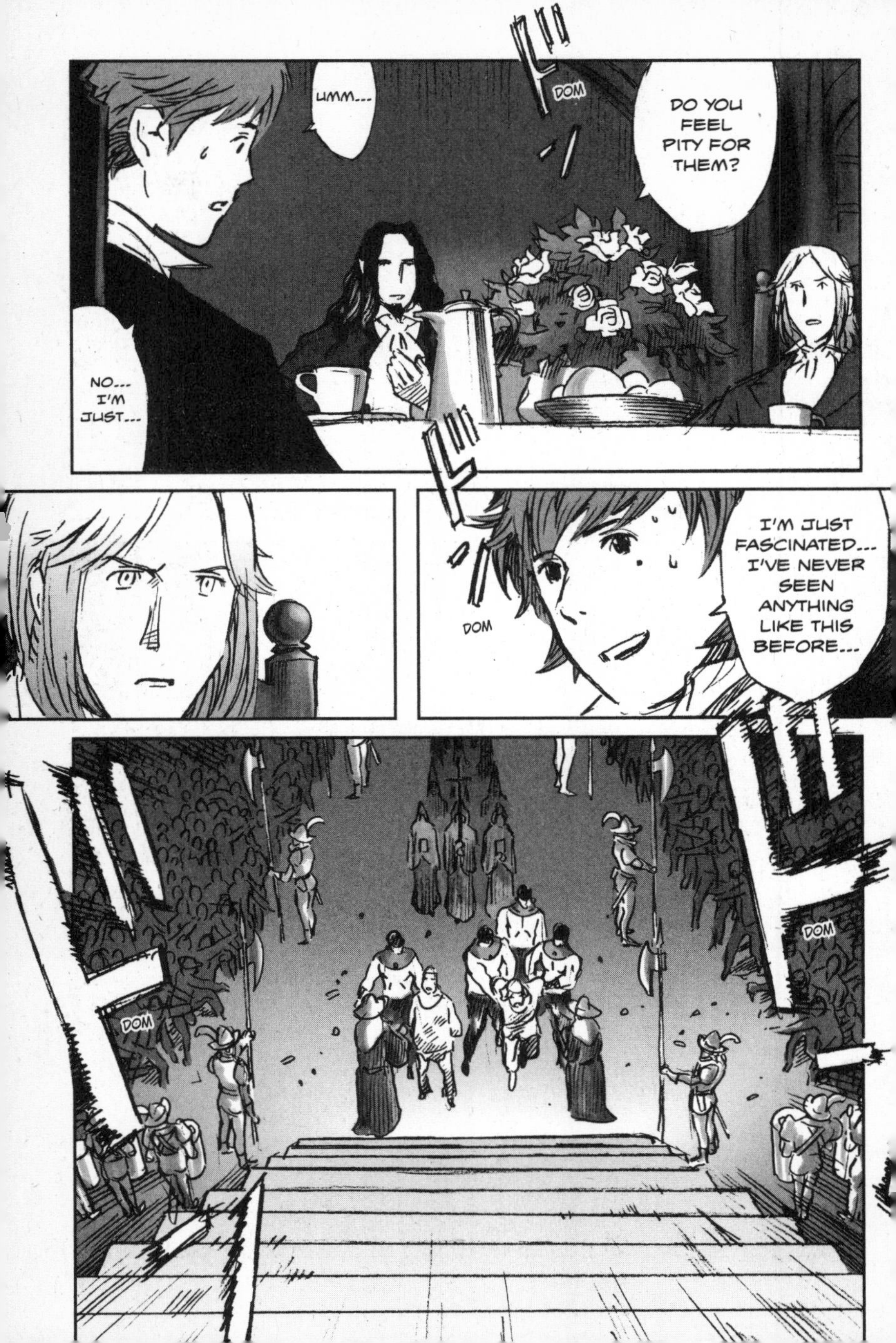
DO YOU FEEL PITY FOR THEM?
DOM
UMM...
NO... I'M JUST...
I'M JUST FASCINATED... I'VE NEVER SEEN ANYTHING LIKE THIS BEFORE...
DOM
DOM
DOM

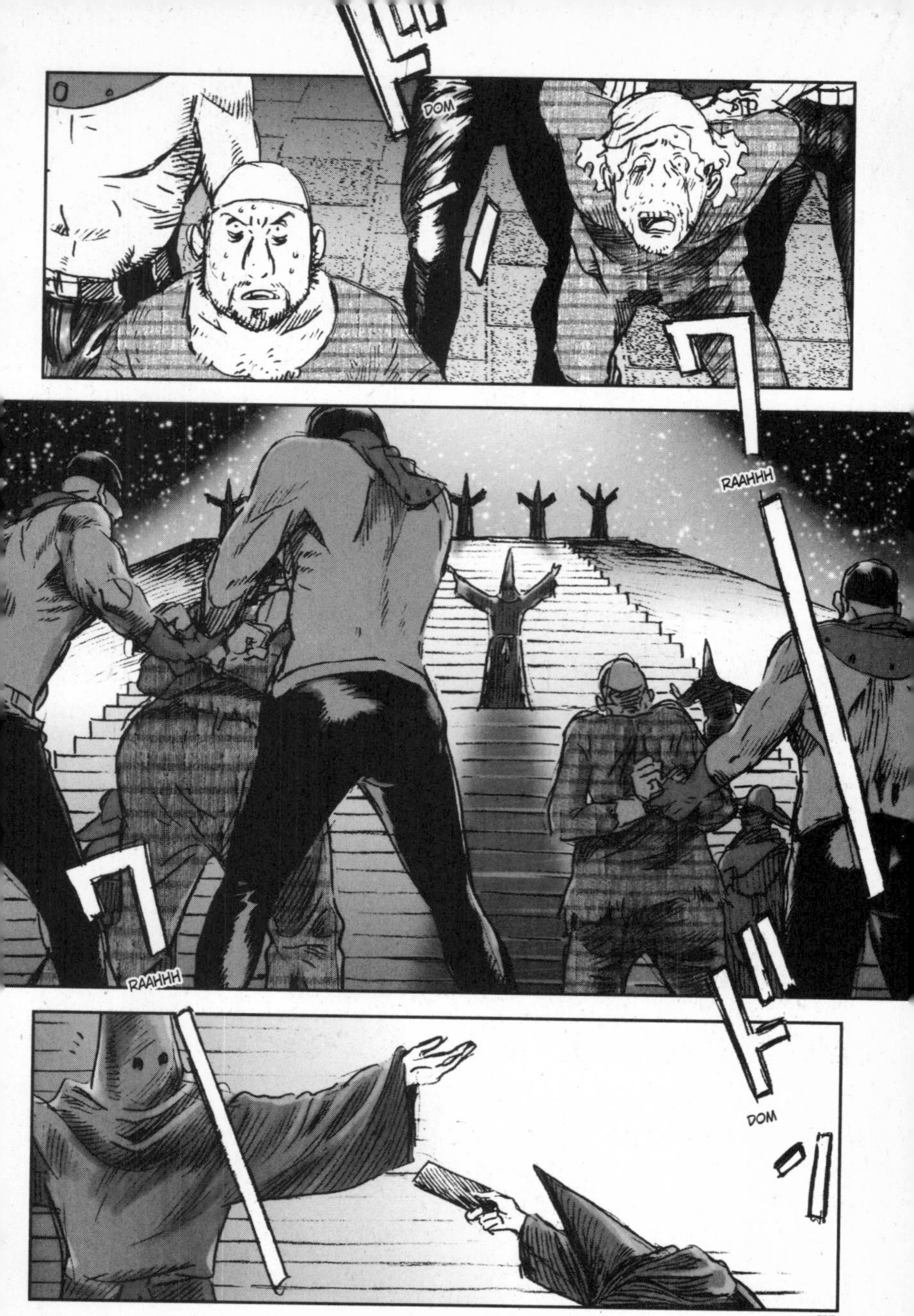
DOM
RAAHHH
RAAHHH
DOM

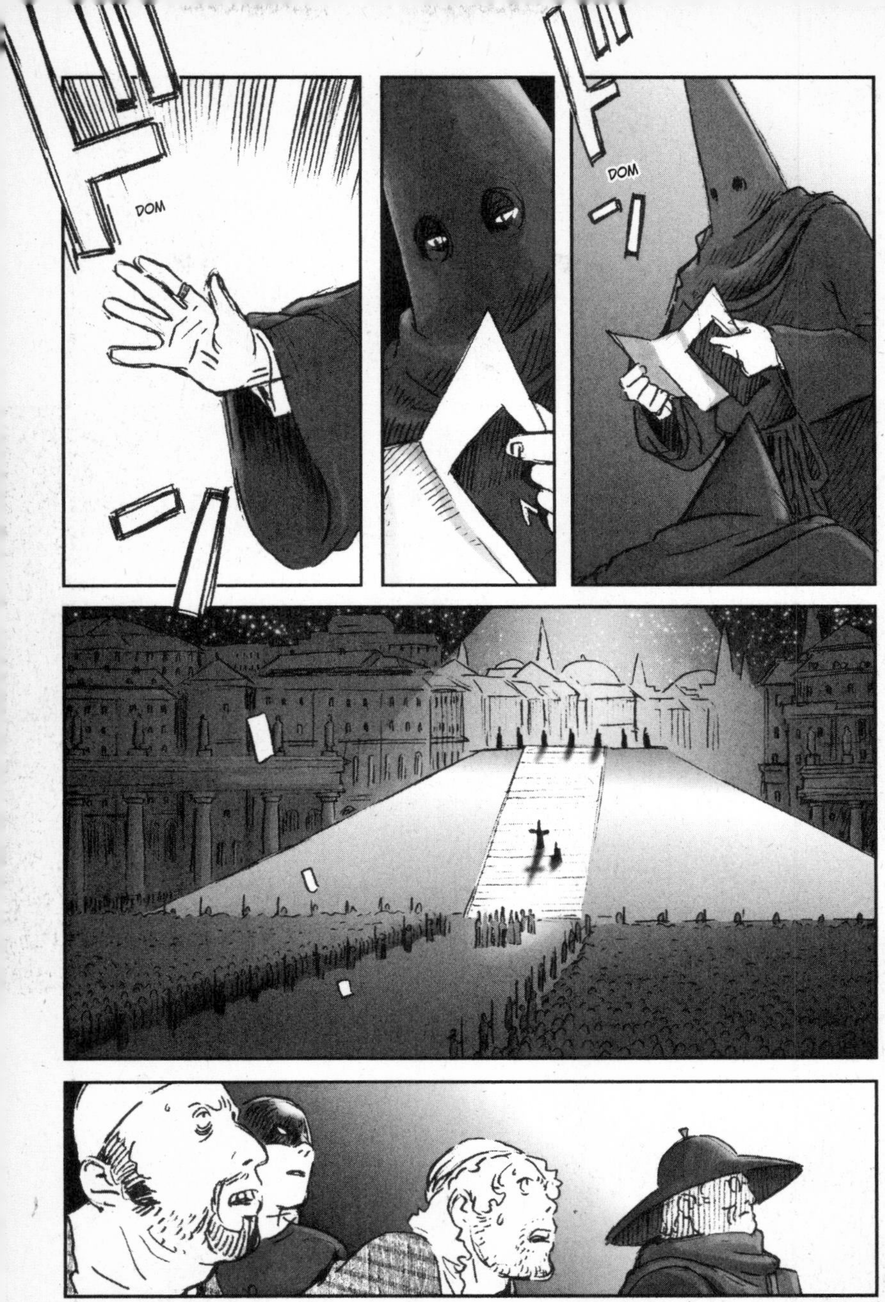
DOM
DOM

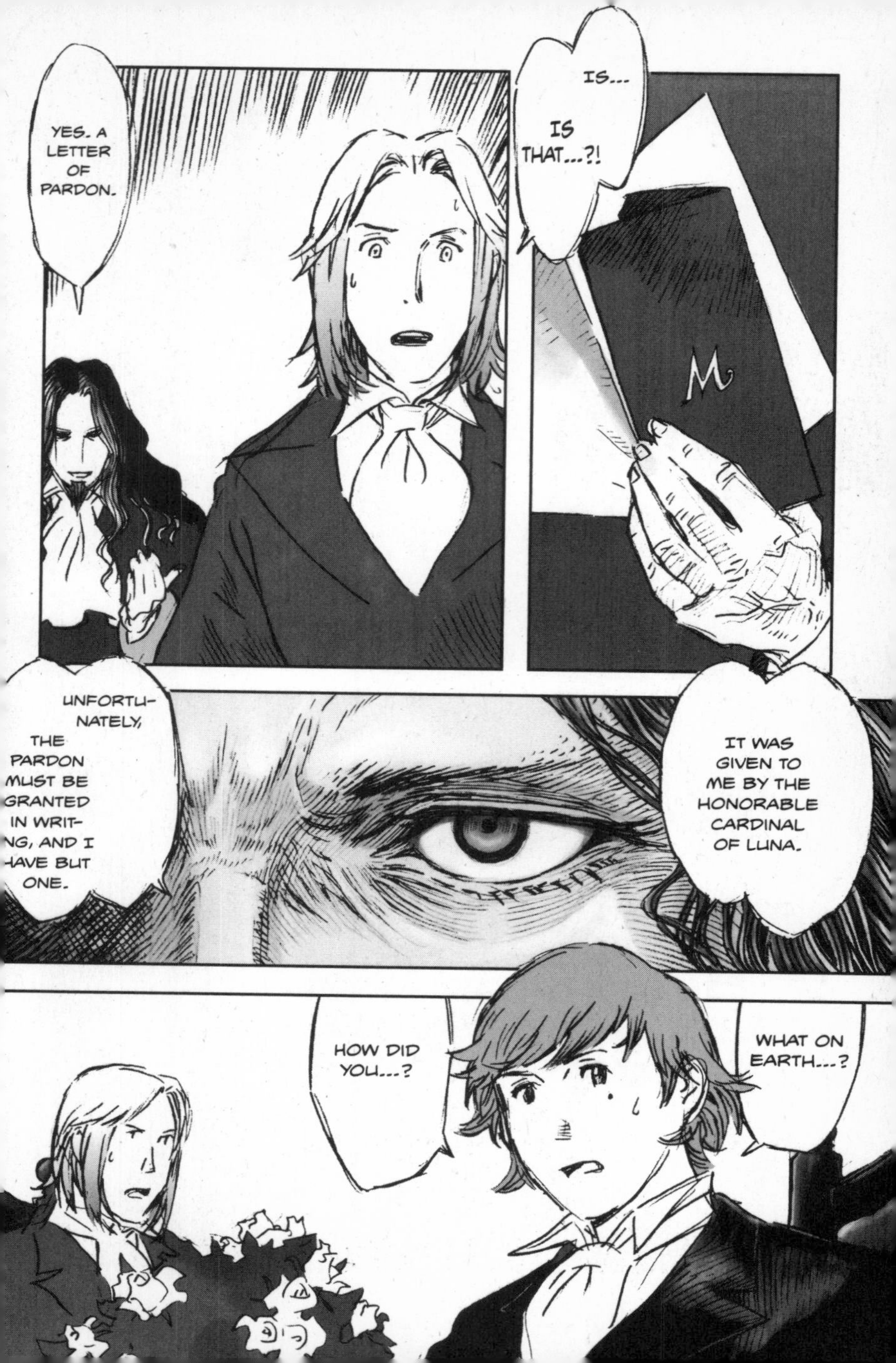
IS... IS THAT...?!
YES. A LETTER OF PARDON.
IT WAS GIVEN TO ME BY THE HONORABLE CARDINAL OF LUNA.
UNFORTU- NATELY, THE PARDON MUST BE GRANTED IN WRIT- NG, AND I HAVE BUT ONE.
WHAT ON EARTH...?
HOW DID YOU...?

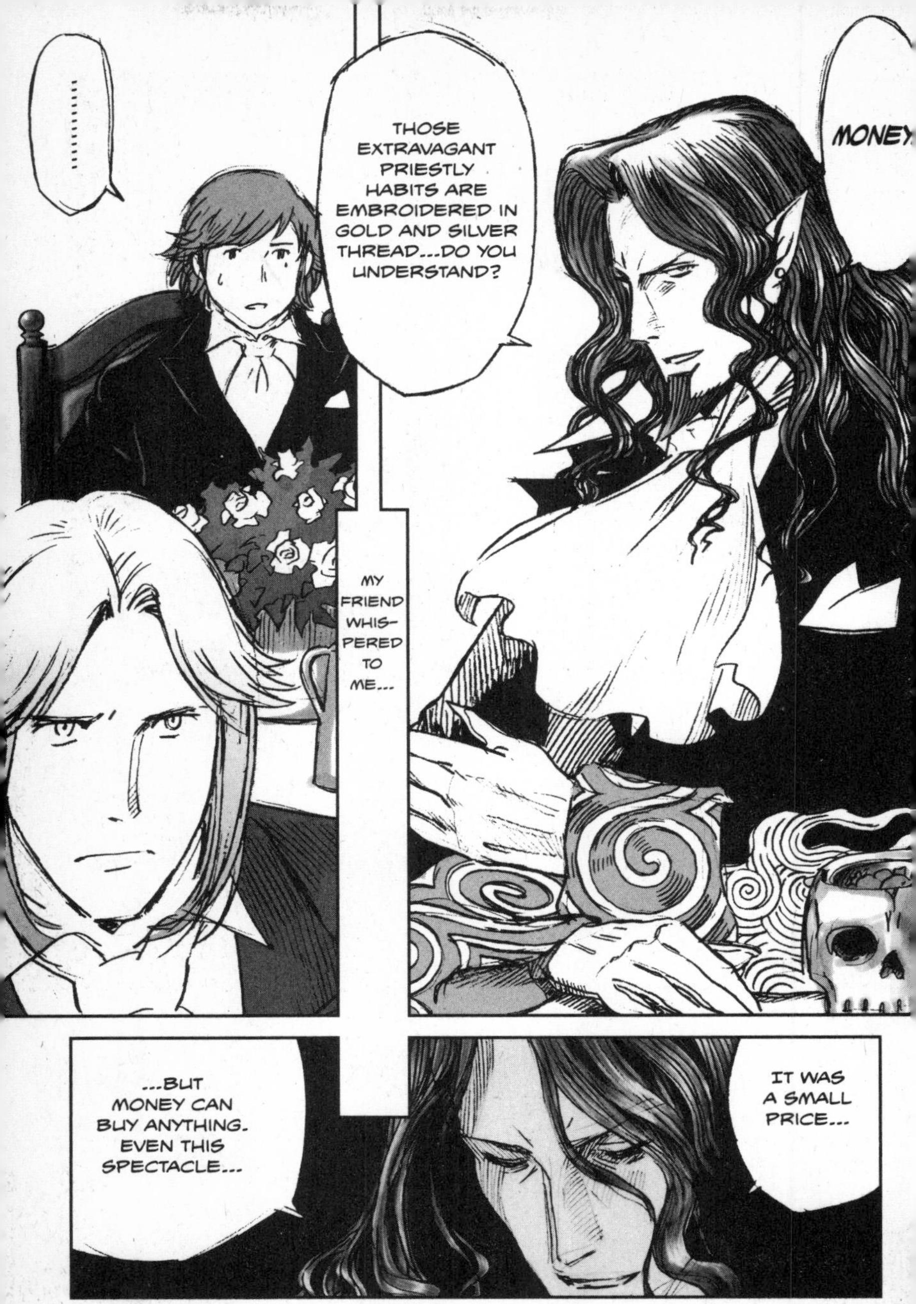
MONEY
THOSE EXTRAVAGANT PRIESTLY HABITS ARE EMBROIDERED IN GOLD AND SILVER THREAD...DO YOU UNDERSTAND?
MY FRIEND WHISPERED TO ME...
......
IT WAS A SMALL PRICE...
...BUT MONEY CAN BUY ANYTHING. EVEN THIS SPECTACLE...

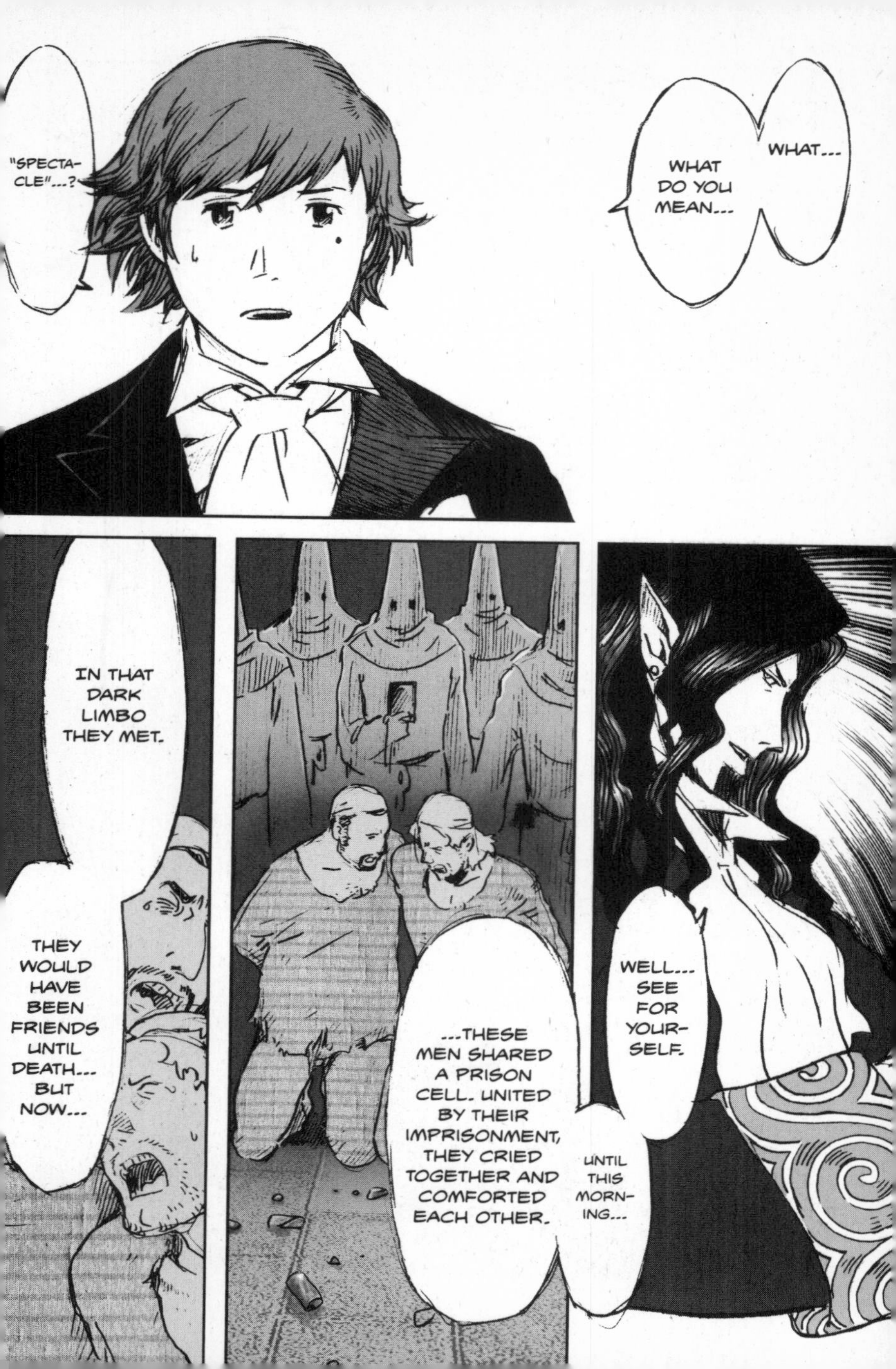
WHAT...
WHAT DO YOU MEAN...
"SPECTACLE"...?
WELL... SEE FOR YOURSELF.
UNTIL THIS MORNING...
...THESE MEN SHARED A PRISON CELL. UNITED BY THEIR IMPRISONMENT, THEY CRIED TOGETHER AND COMFORTED EACH OTHER.
IN THAT DARK LIMBO THEY MET.
THEY WOULD HAVE BEEN FRIENDS UNTIL DEATH... BUT NOW...

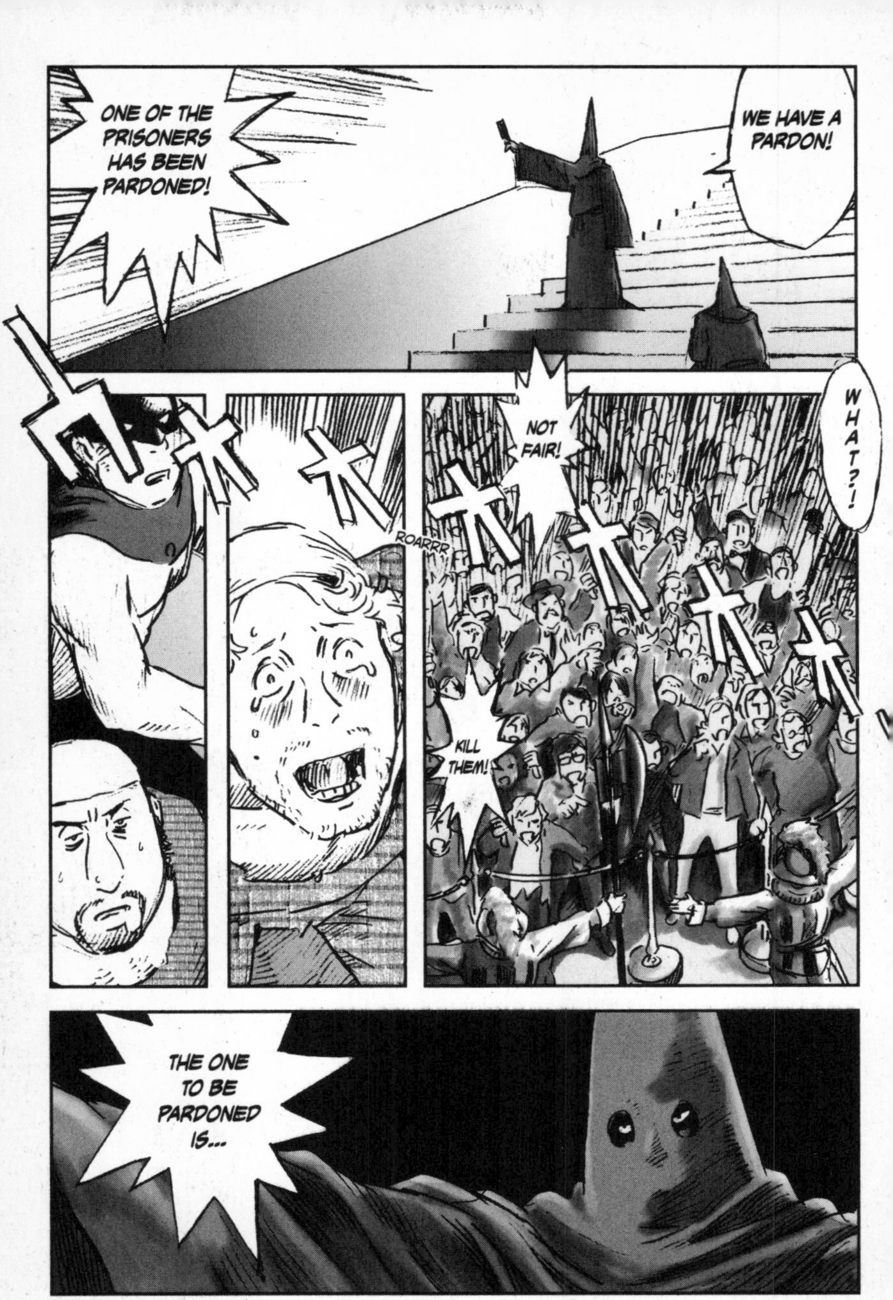
WE HAVE A PARDON!
ONE OF THE PRISONERS HAS BEEN PARDONED!
WHAT?!
NOT FAIR!
ROARRR
KILL THEM!
THE ONE TO BE PARDONED IS...

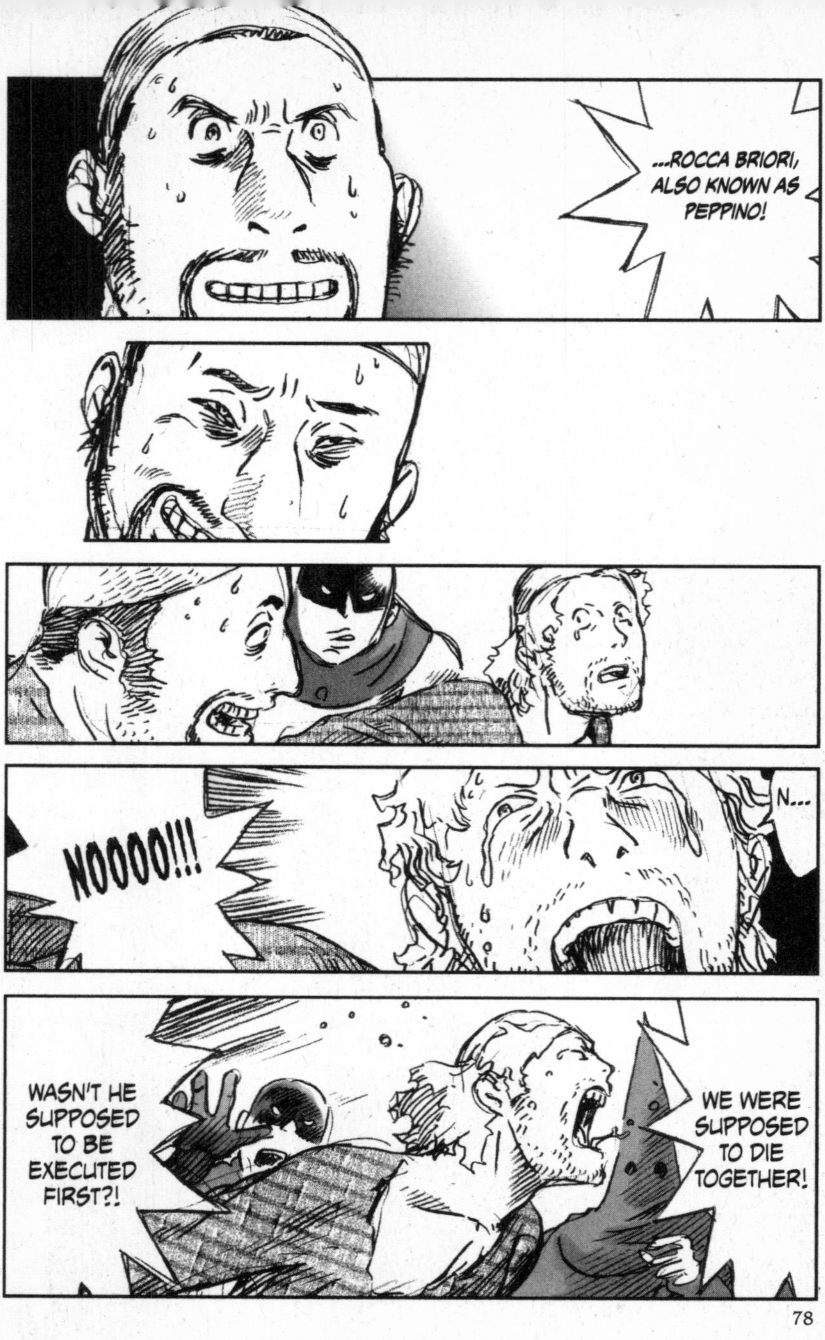
...ROCCA BRIORI, ALSO KNOWN AS PEPPINO!
N...
NOOOO!!!
WE WERE SUPPOSED TO DIE TOGETHER!
WASN'T HE SUPPOSED TO BE EXECUTED FIRST?!

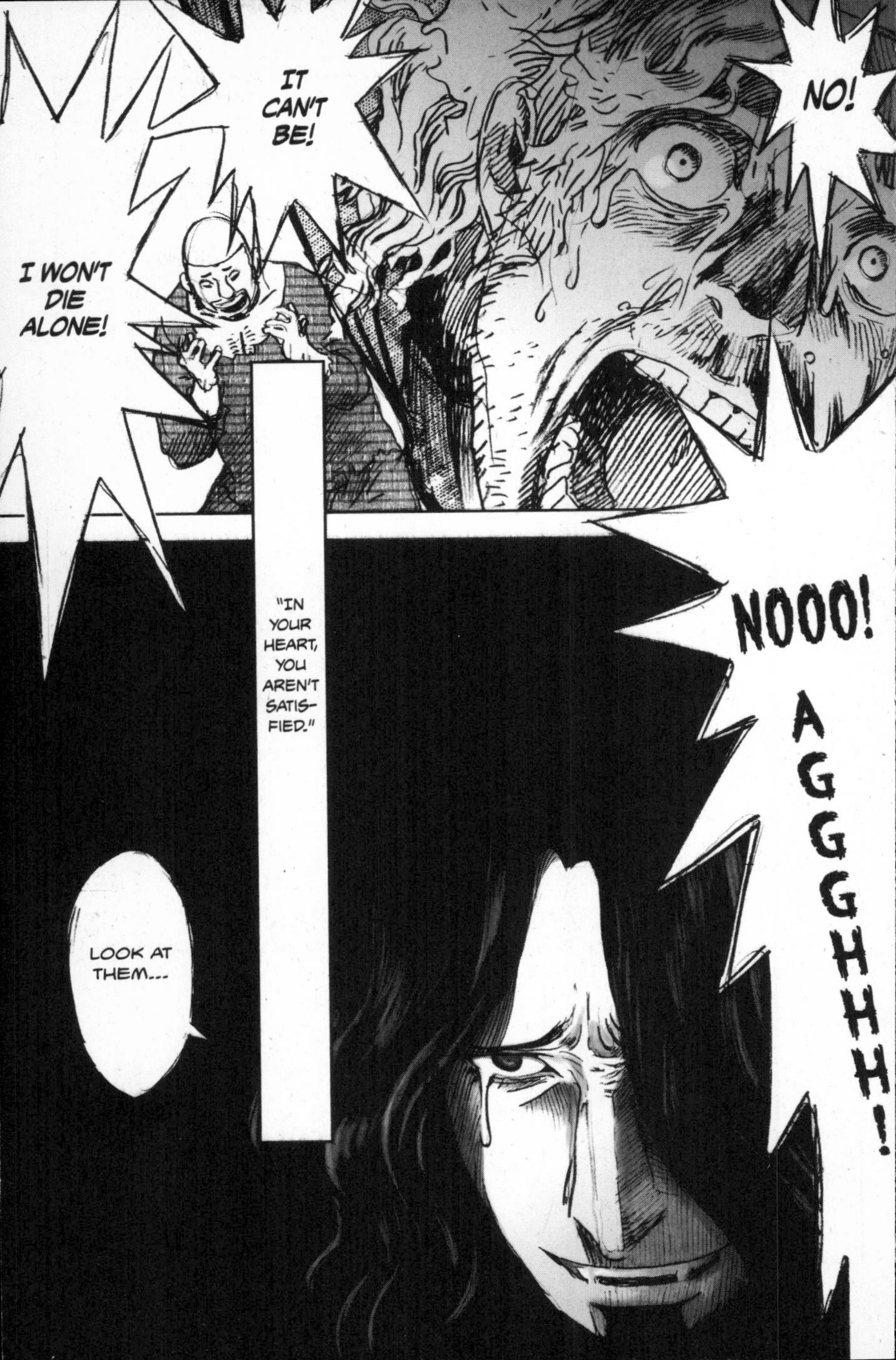
NO!
IT CAN'T BE!
I WON'T DIE ALONE!
NOOO! AGGGHHH!
"IN YOUR HEART, YOU AREN'T SATIS-FIED."
LOOK AT THEM...

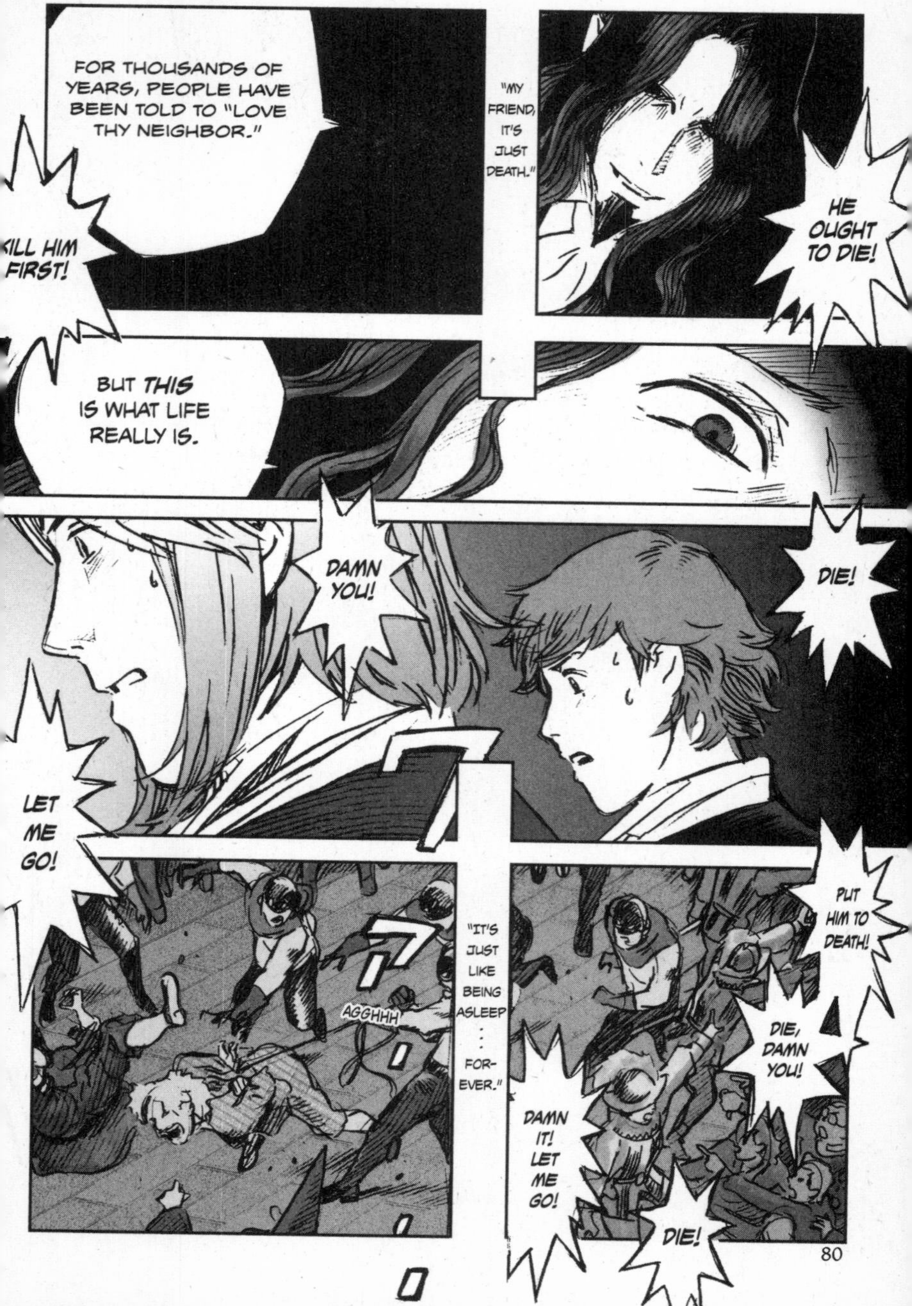
"MY FRIEND, IT'S JUST DEATH."
HE OUGHT TO DIE!
FOR THOUSANDS OF YEARS, PEOPLE HAVE BEEN TOLD TO "LOVE THY NEIGHBOR."
ILL HIM FIRST!
BUT THIS IS WHAT LIFE REALLY IS.
DIE!
DAMN YOU!
LET ME GO!
PUT HIM TO DEATH!
DIE, DAMN YOU!
DAMN IT! LET ME GO!
DIE!
"IT'S JUST LIKE BEING ASLEEP . . . FOR-EVER."
AGGHHH

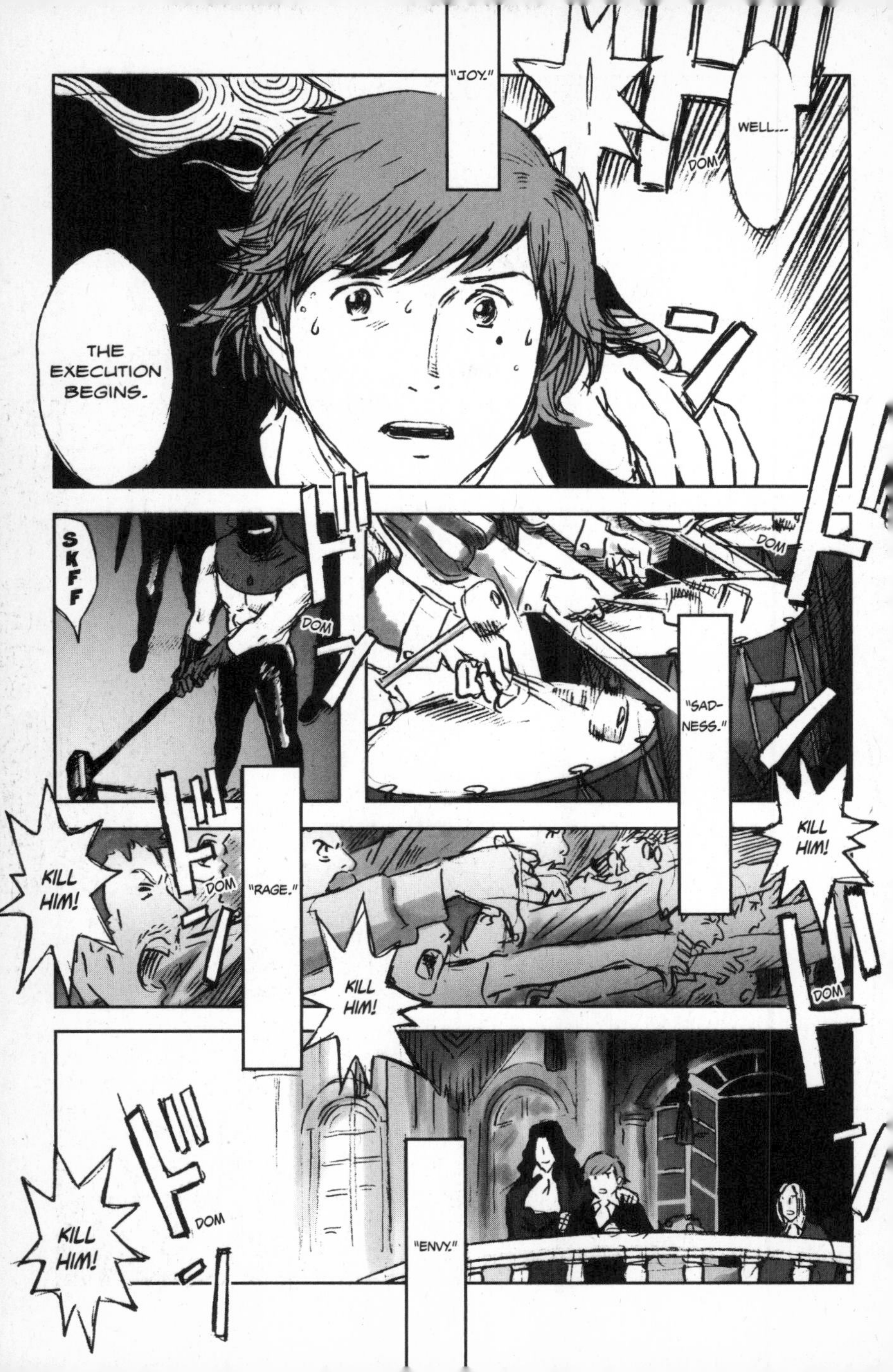
WELL...
DOM
"JOY."
THE EXECUTION BEGINS.
DOM
"SAD-NESS."
DOM
SKFF
KILL HIM!
DOM
"RAGE."
KILL HIM!
DOM
KILL HIM!
"ENVY."
DOM
KILL HIM!

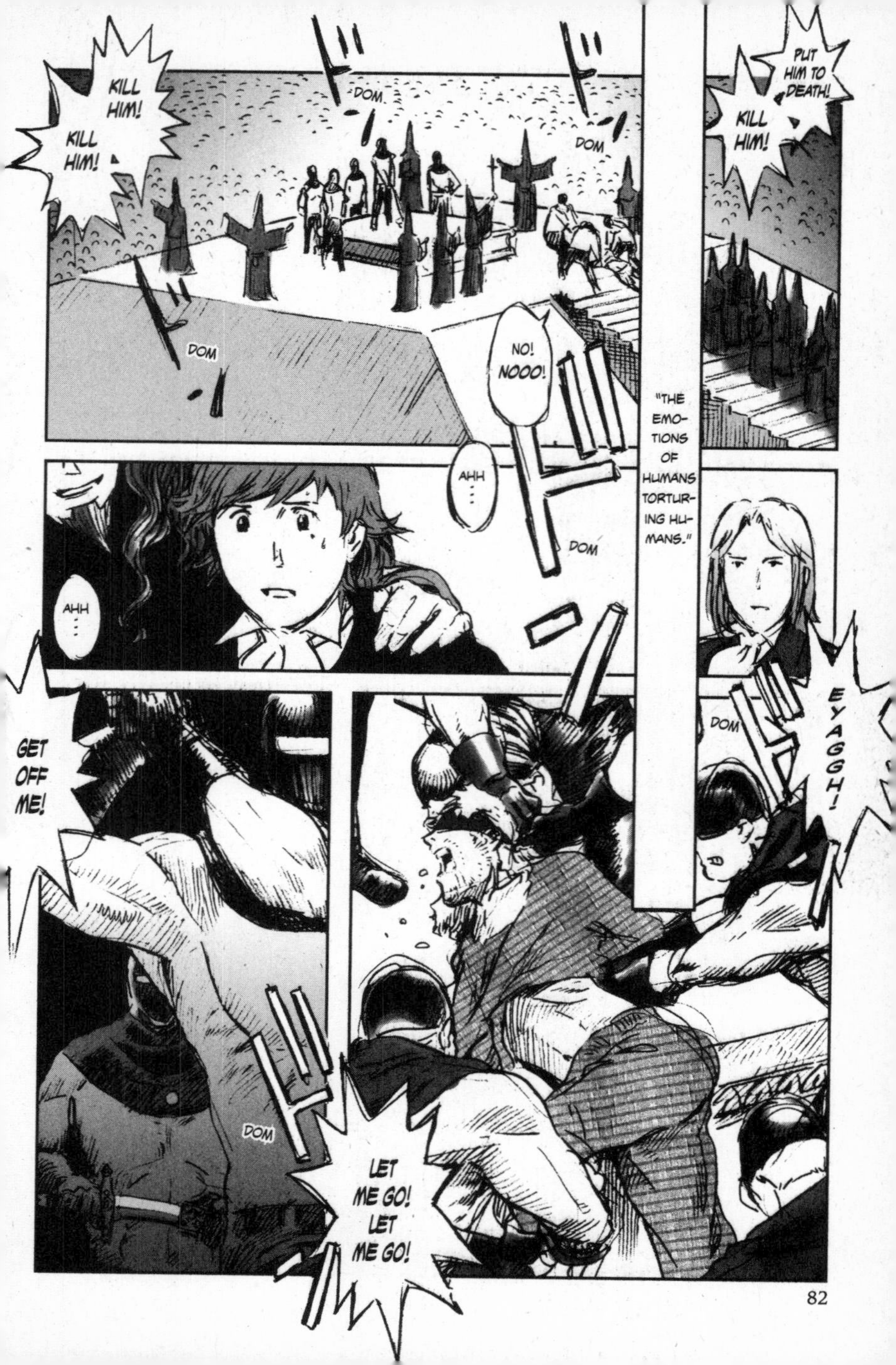
PUT HIM TO DEATH!
KILL HIM!
"THE EMO- TIONS OF HUMANS TORTUR- ING HU- MANS."
DOM
DOM
KILL HIM!
KILL HIM!
DOM
NO! NOOO!
AHH...
DOM
AHH...
EYAGGH!
DOM
LET ME GO! LET ME GO!
GET OFF ME!
DOM

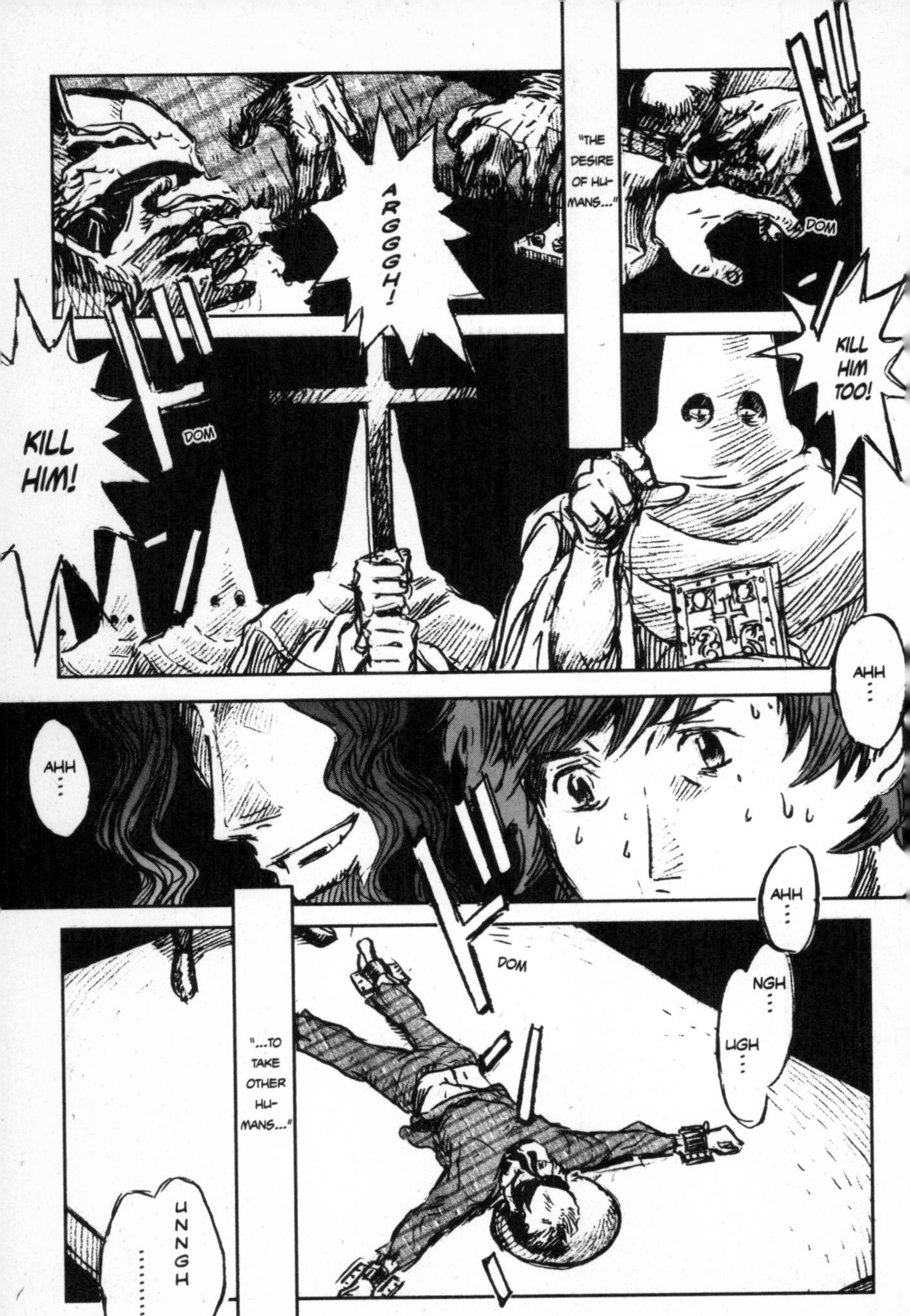
"THE DESIRE OF HU-MANS..."
DOM
ARGGGH!
KILL HIM TOO!
DOM
KILL HIM!
AHH...
AHH...
AHH...
NGH...
UGH...
DOM
"...TO TAKE OTHER HU-MANS..."
UNNGH......

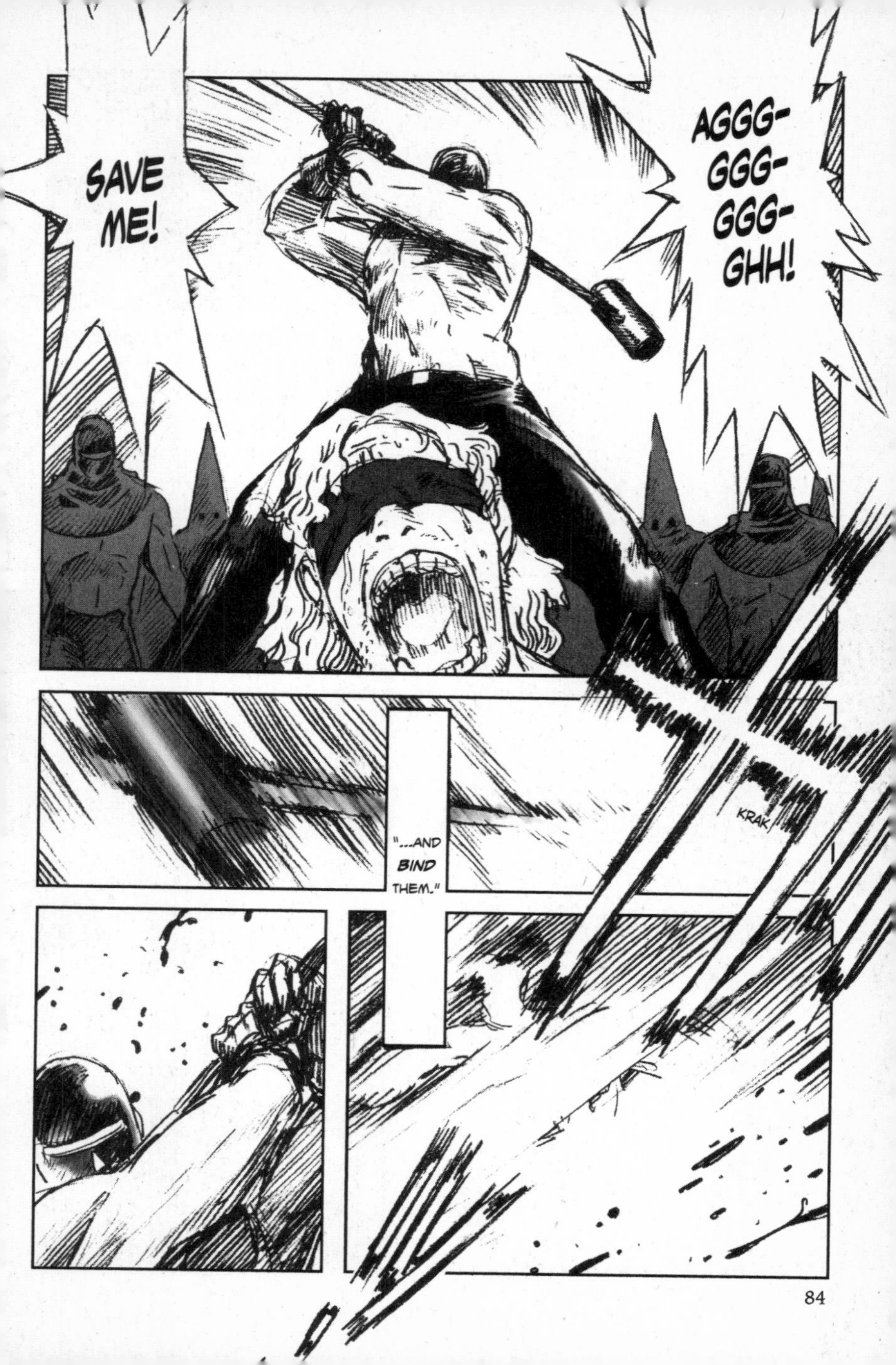
AGGG-GGG-GGG-GHH!
SAVE ME!
KRAK
"...AND BIND THEM."

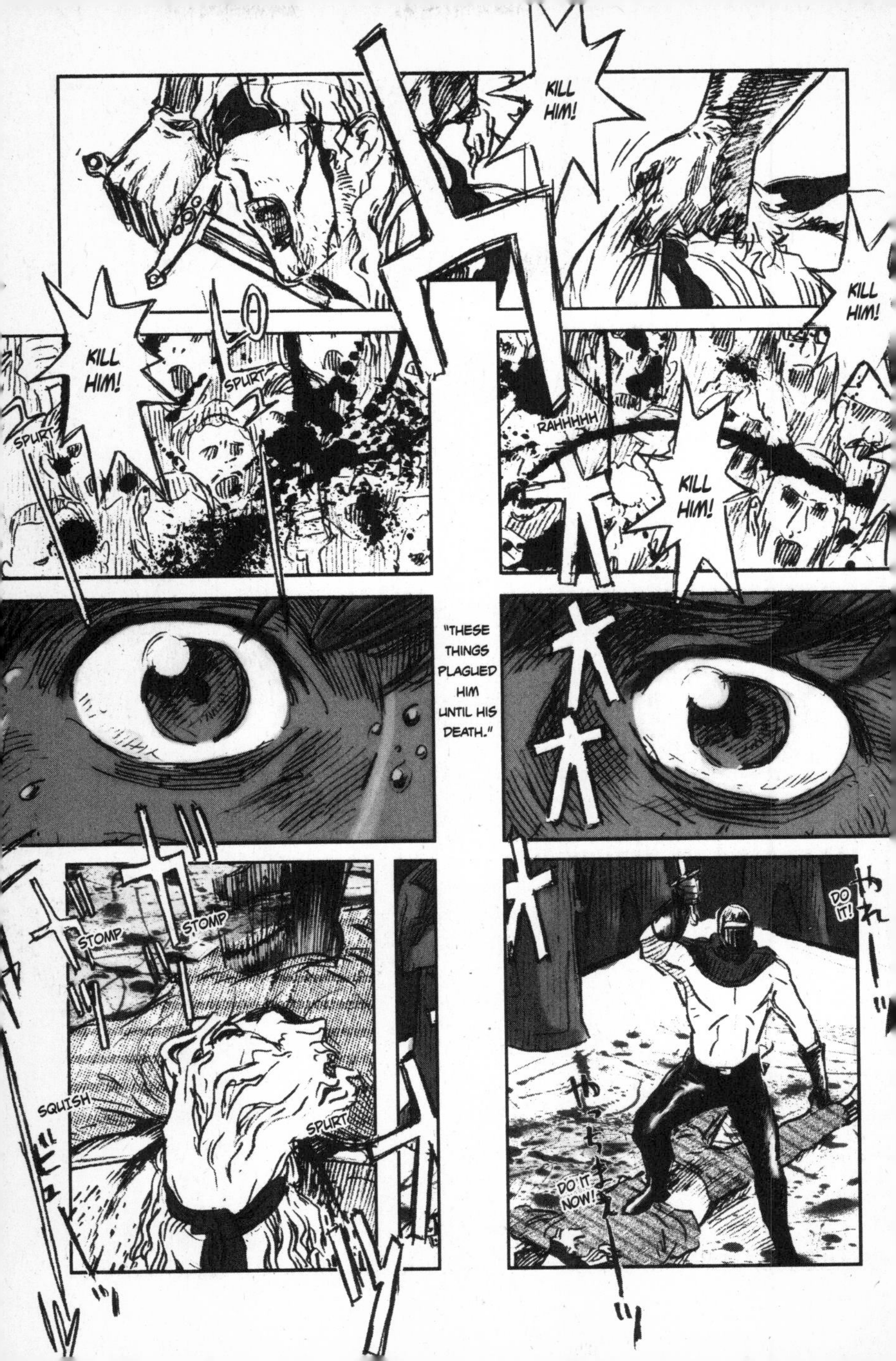

KILL HIM!
KILL HIM!
RAHHHHH
KILL HIM!
KILL HIM!
SPURT
SPURT
"THESE THINGS PLAGUED HIM UNTIL HIS DEATH."
DO IT!
DO IT NOW!
STOMP
STOMP
SQUISH
SPURT

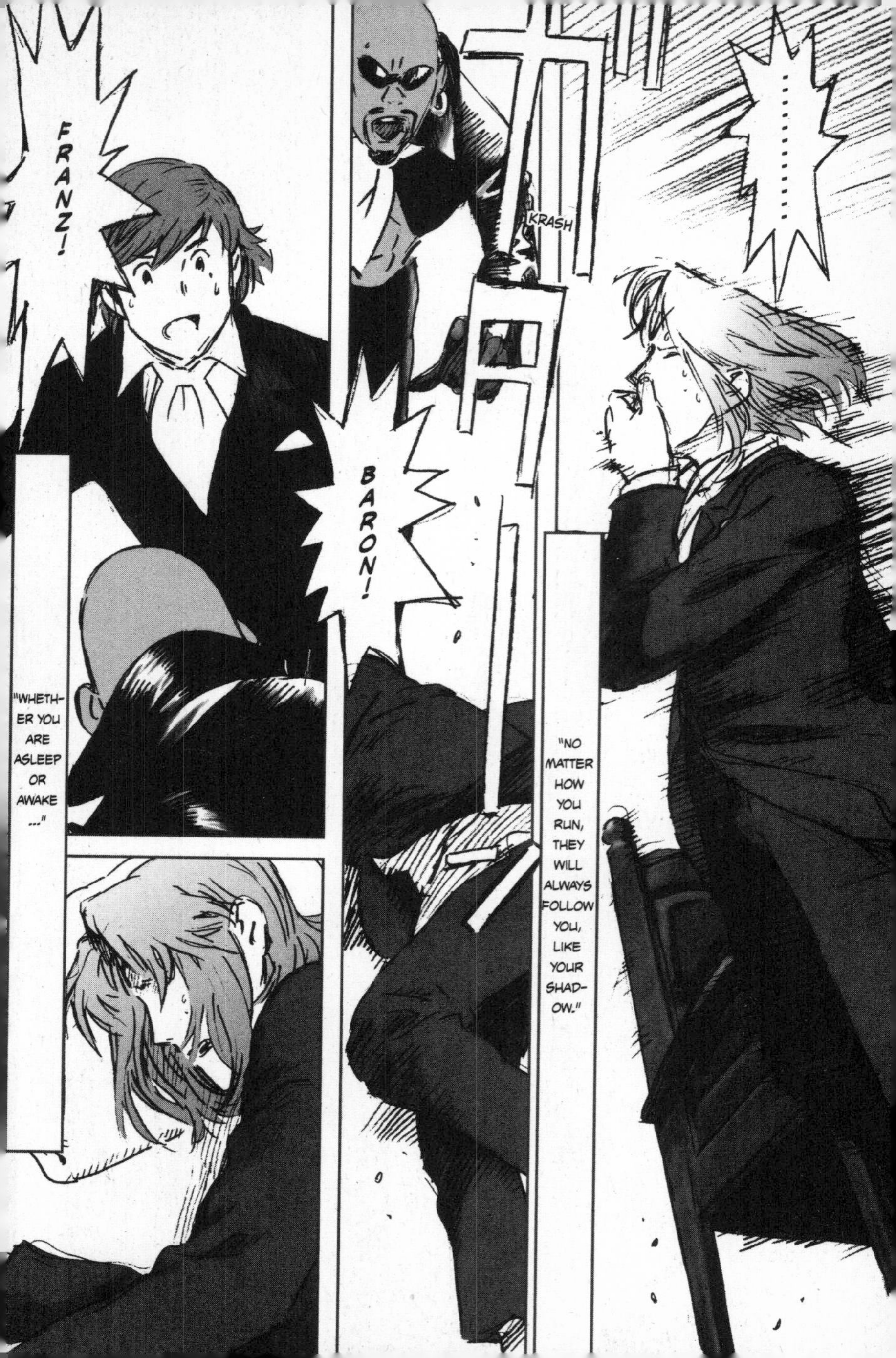
......
"NO MATTER HOW YOU RUN, THEY WILL ALWAYS FOLLOW YOU, LIKE YOUR SHADOW."
KRASH
BARON!
FRANZ!
"WHETHER YOU ARE ASLEEP OR AWAKE..."

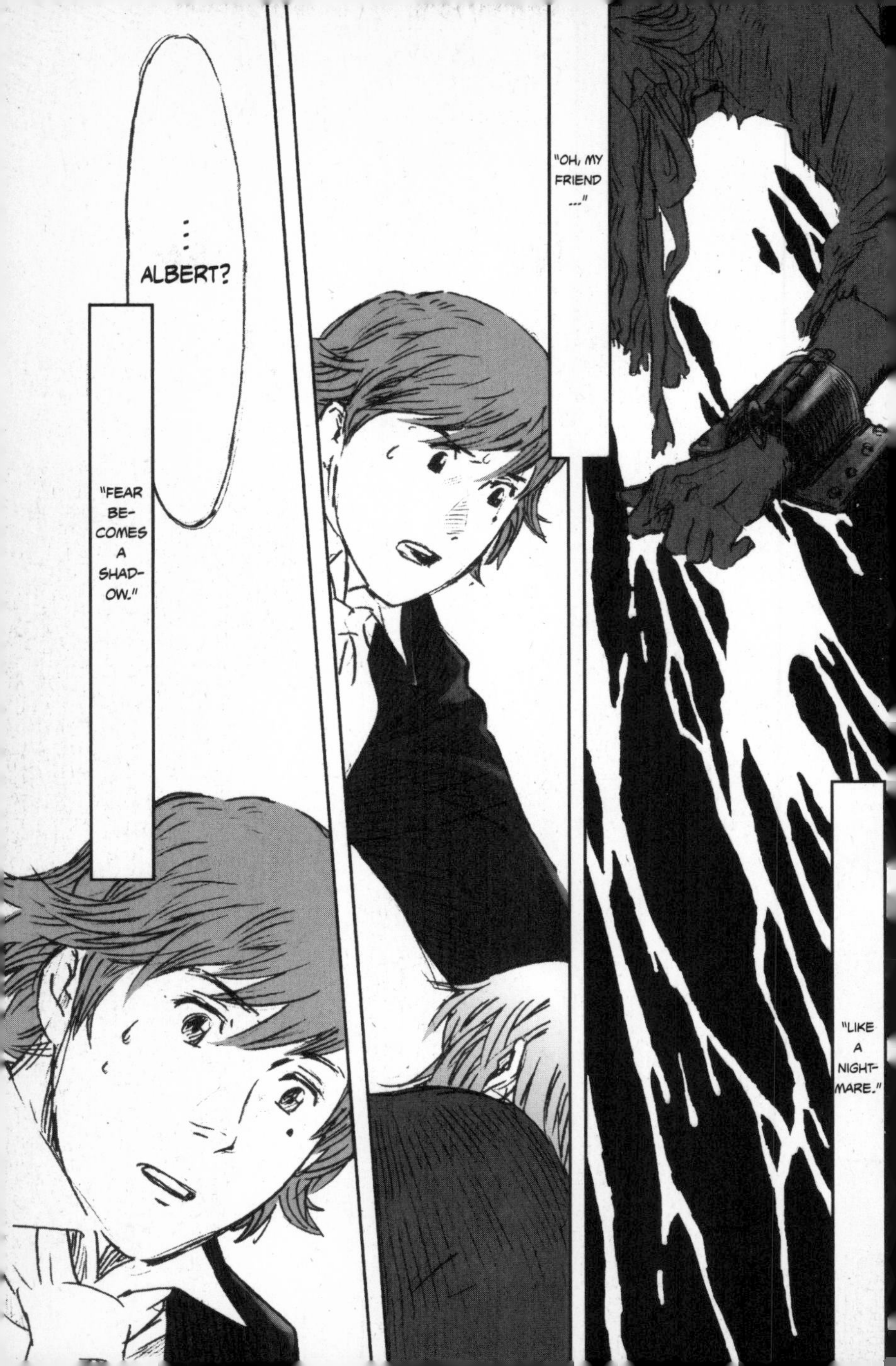
"OH, MY FRIEND ..."
"LIKE A NIGHTMARE."
... ALBERT?
"FEAR BECOMES A SHADOW."

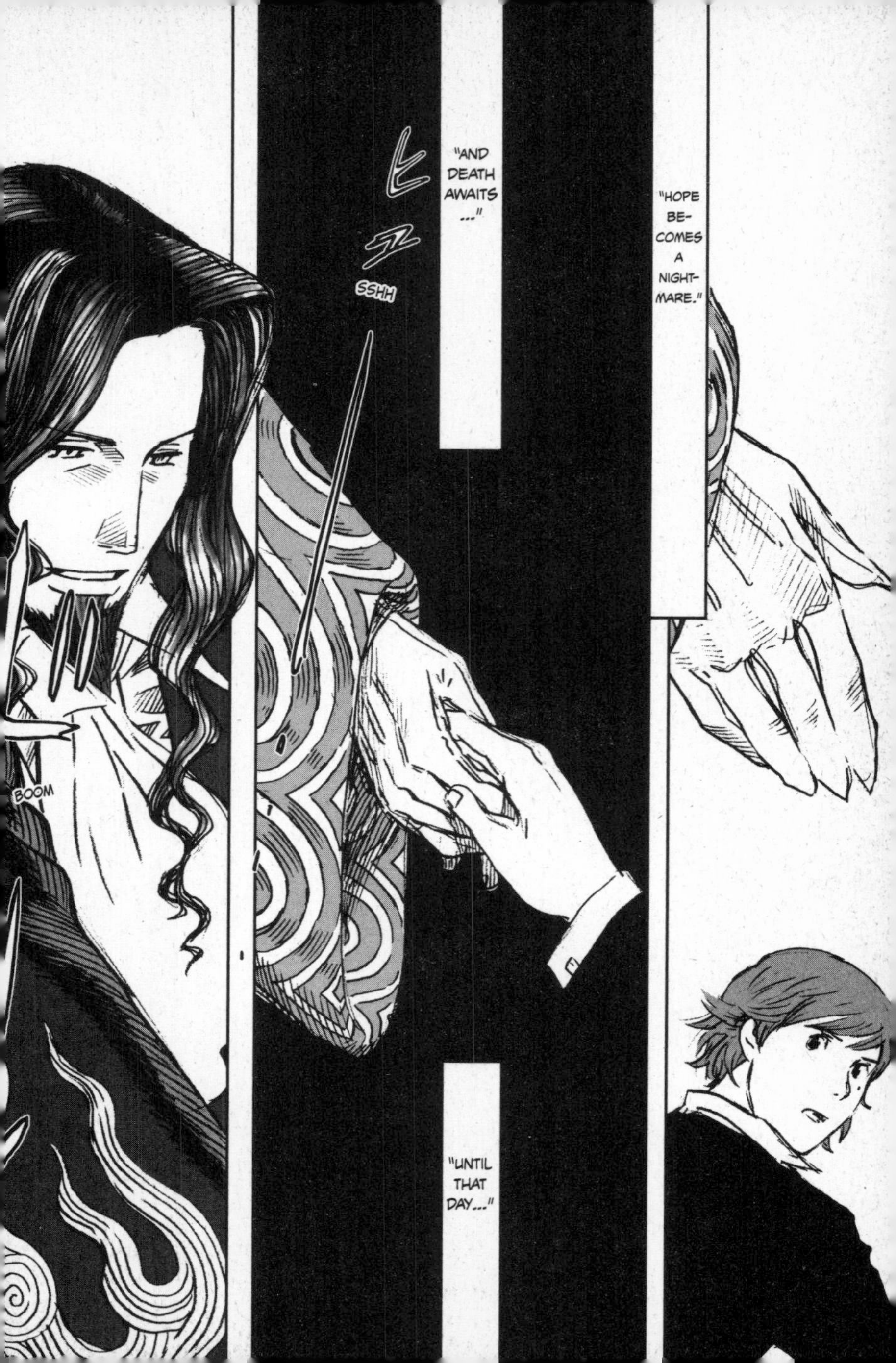
"HOPE BE-COMES A NIGHT-MARE."
"AND DEATH AWAITS..."
"UNTIL THAT DAY..."
SSHH
BOOM

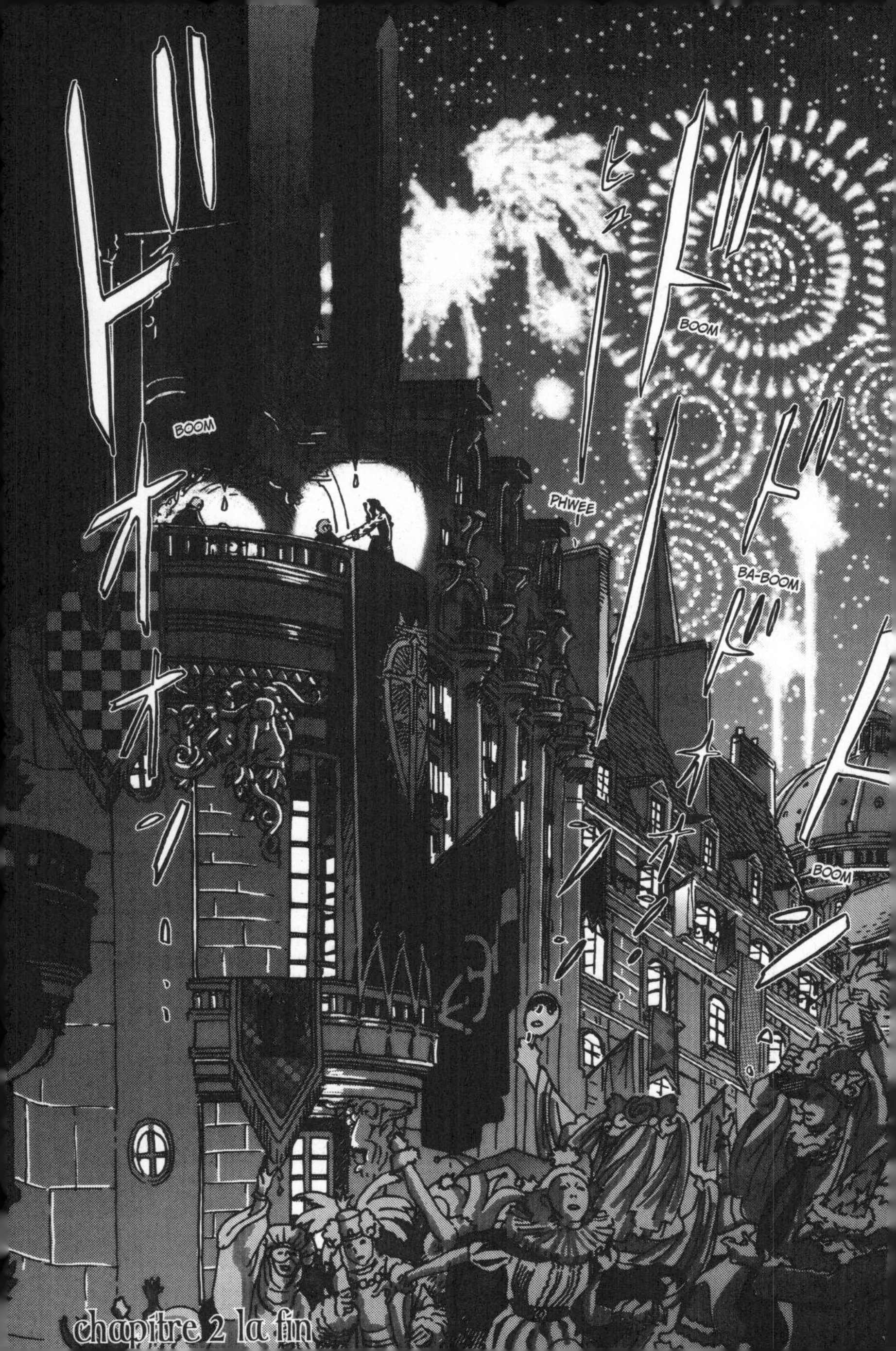
BOOM
PHWEE
BA-BOOM
BOOM
BOOM
chapitre 2 la fin

Gankutsuou

The Count of Monte Cristo

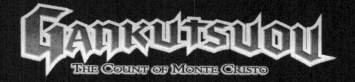

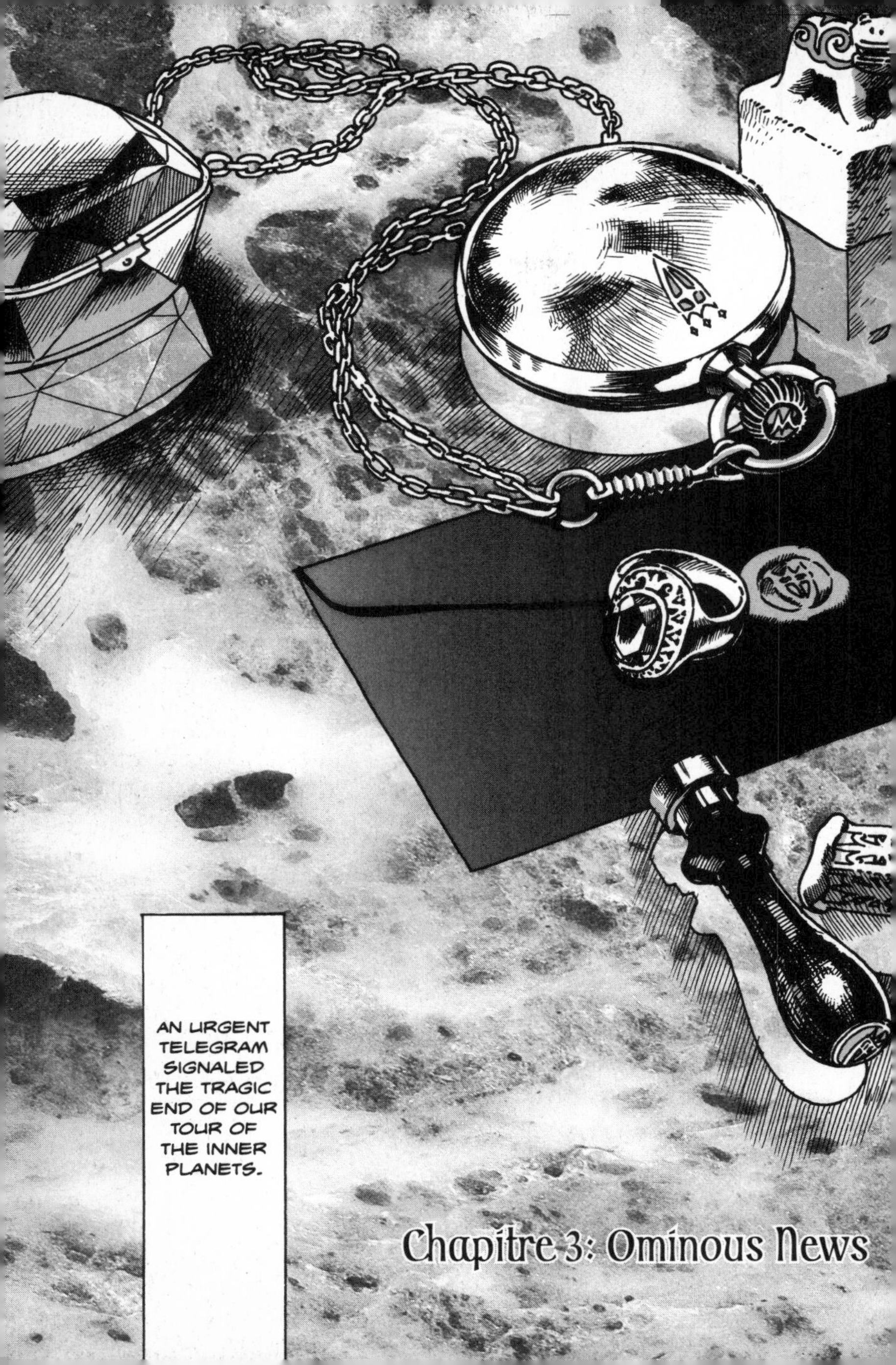
AN URGENT TELEGRAM SIGNALED THE TRAGIC END OF OUR TOUR OF THE INNER PLANETS.
Chapitre 3: Ominous News

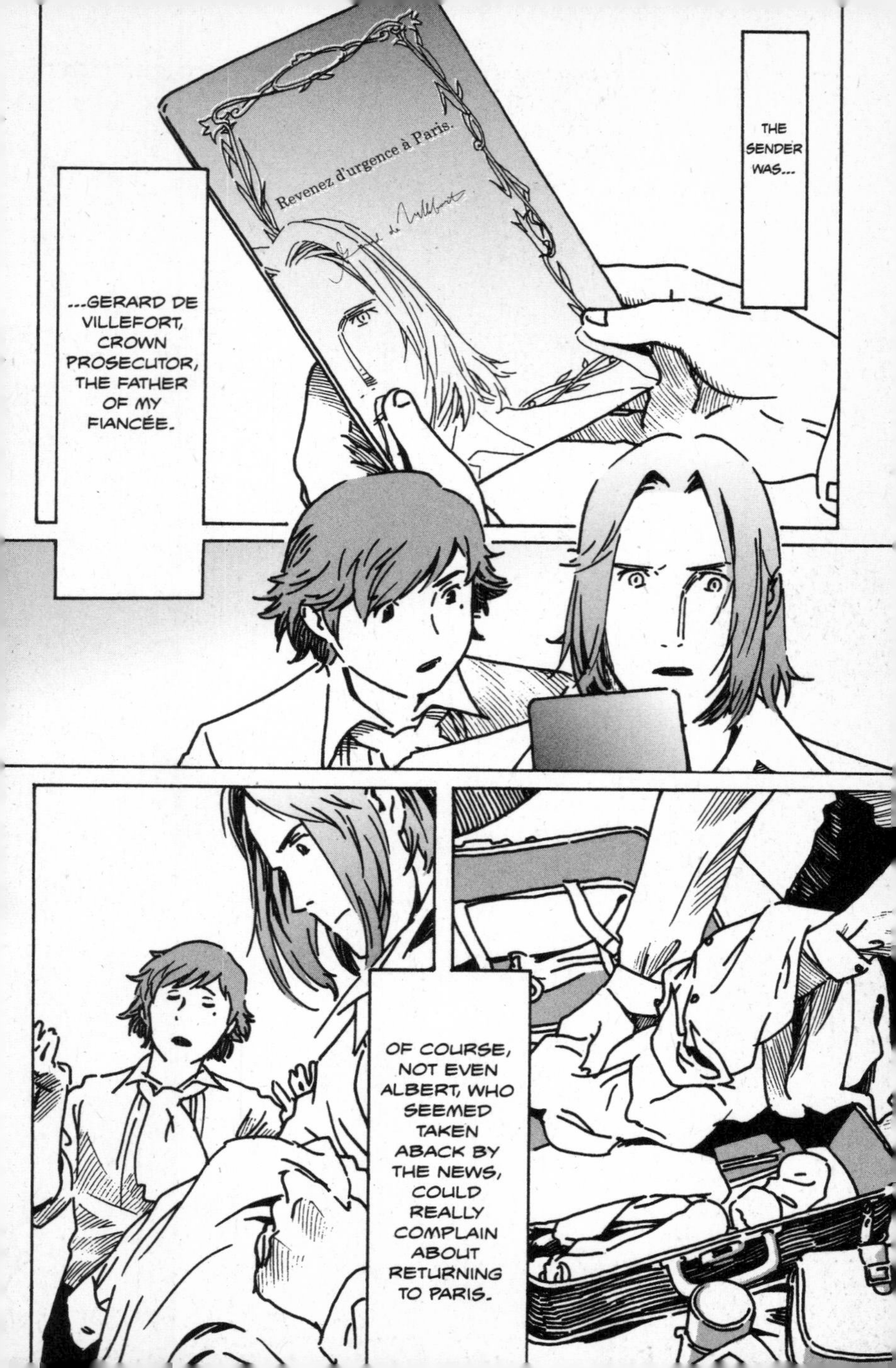
THE SENDER WAS...
Revenez d'urgence à Paris.
...GERARD DE VILLEFORT, CROWN PROSECUTOR, THE FATHER OF MY FIANCÉE.
OF COURSE, NOT EVEN ALBERT, WHO SEEMED TAKEN ABACK BY THE NEWS, COULD REALLY COMPLAIN ABOUT RETURNING TO PARIS.

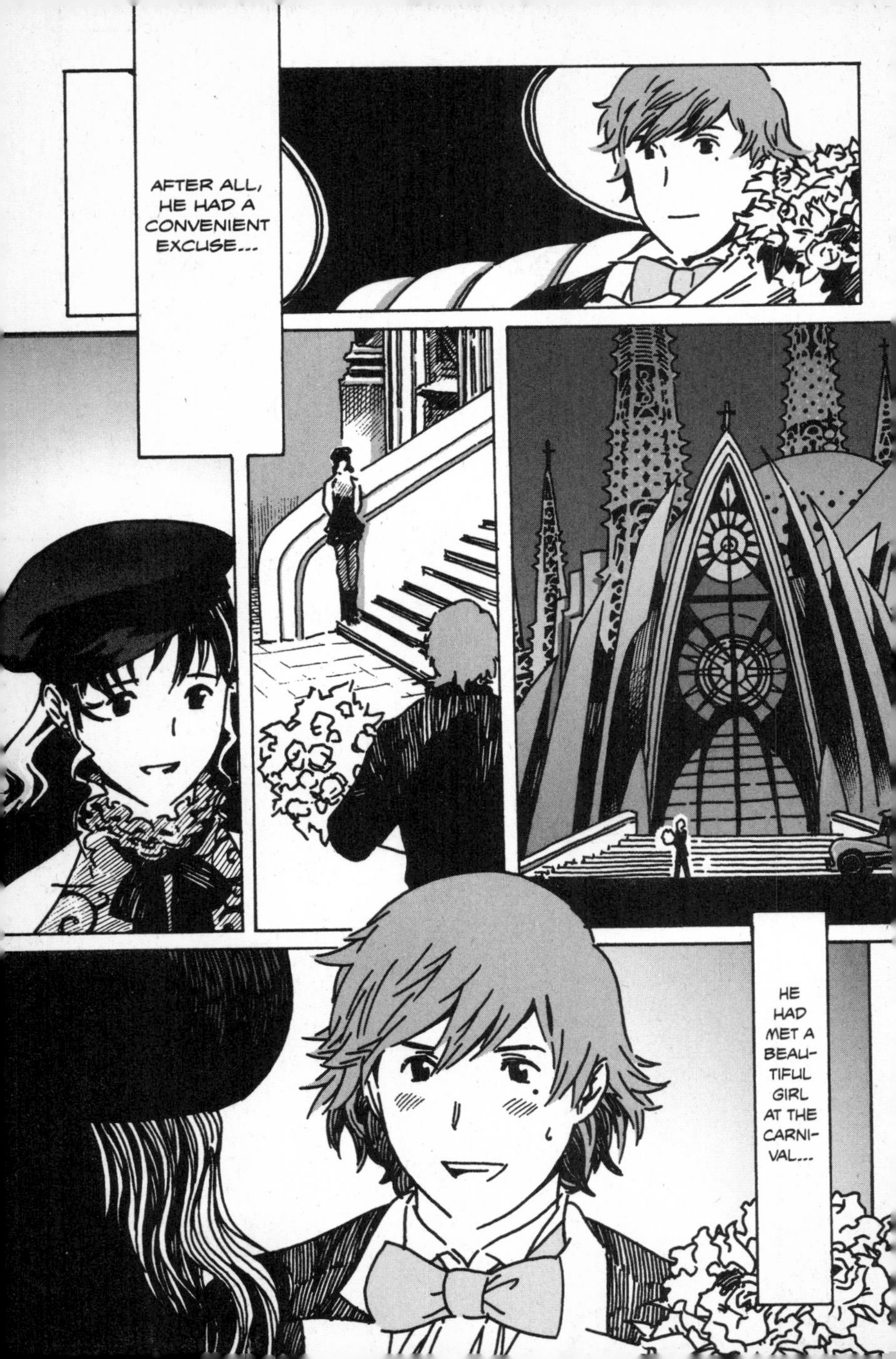
AFTER ALL, HE HAD A CONVENIENT EXCUSE...
HE HAD MET A BEAU-TIFUL GIRL AT THE CARNI-VAL...

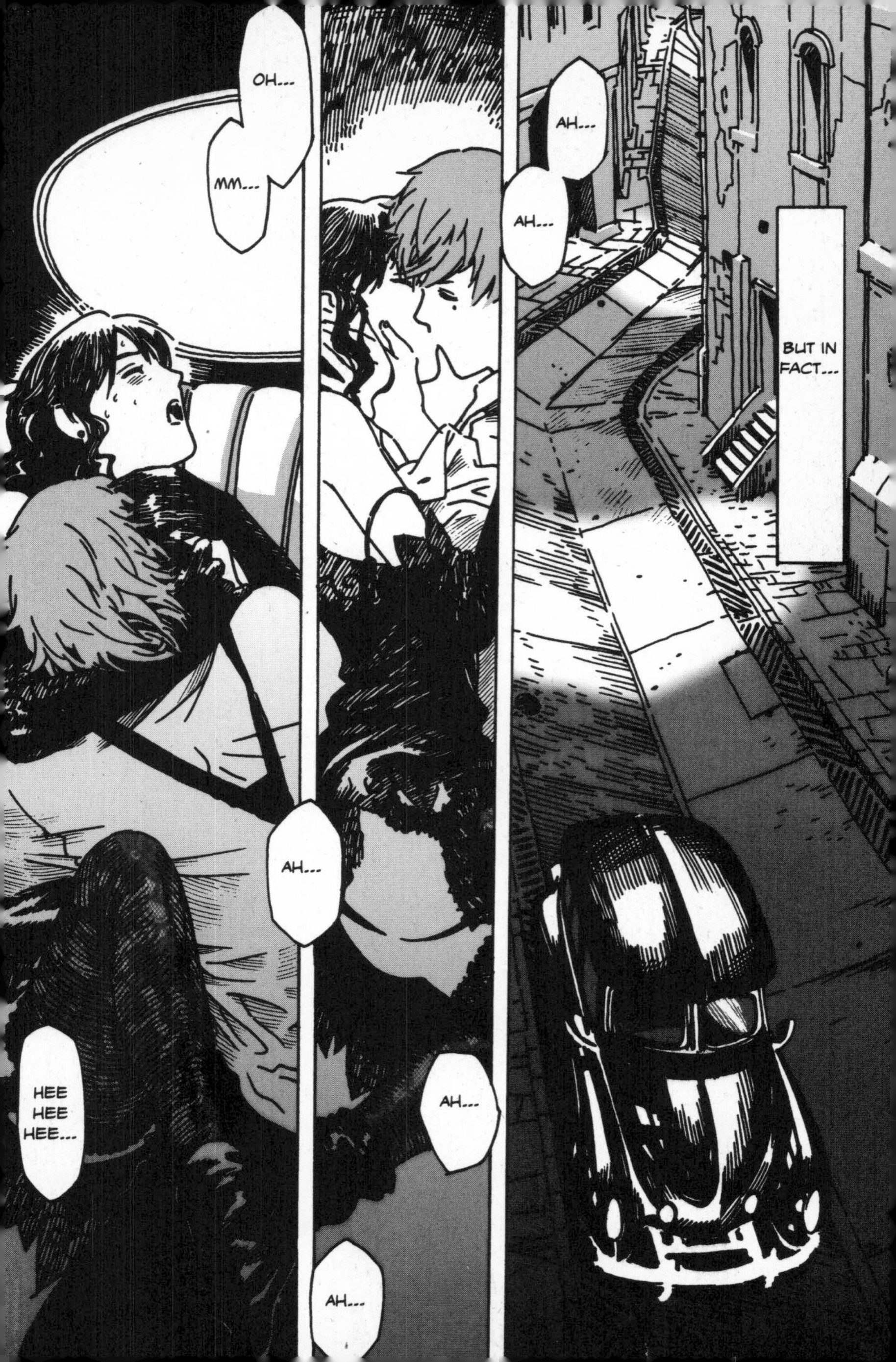
BUT IN FACT...
AH...
AH...
AH...
AH...
AH...
OH...
MM...
HEE HEE HEE...

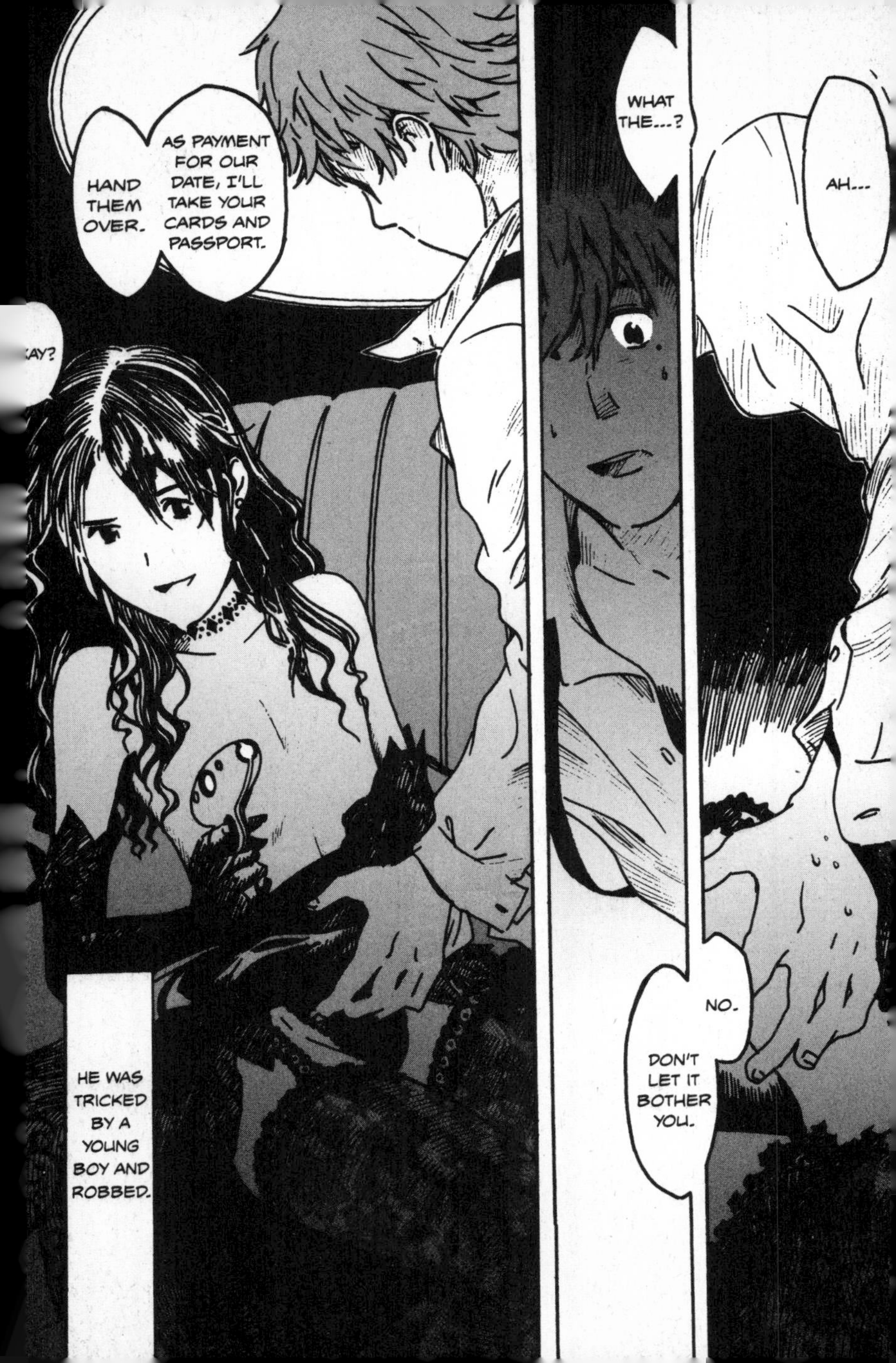
AH...
NO.
DON'T LET IT BOTHER YOU.
WHAT THE...?
AS PAYMENT FOR OUR DATE, I'LL TAKE YOUR CARDS AND PASSPORT.
HAND THEM OVER.
HE WAS TRICKED BY A YOUNG BOY AND ROBBED.

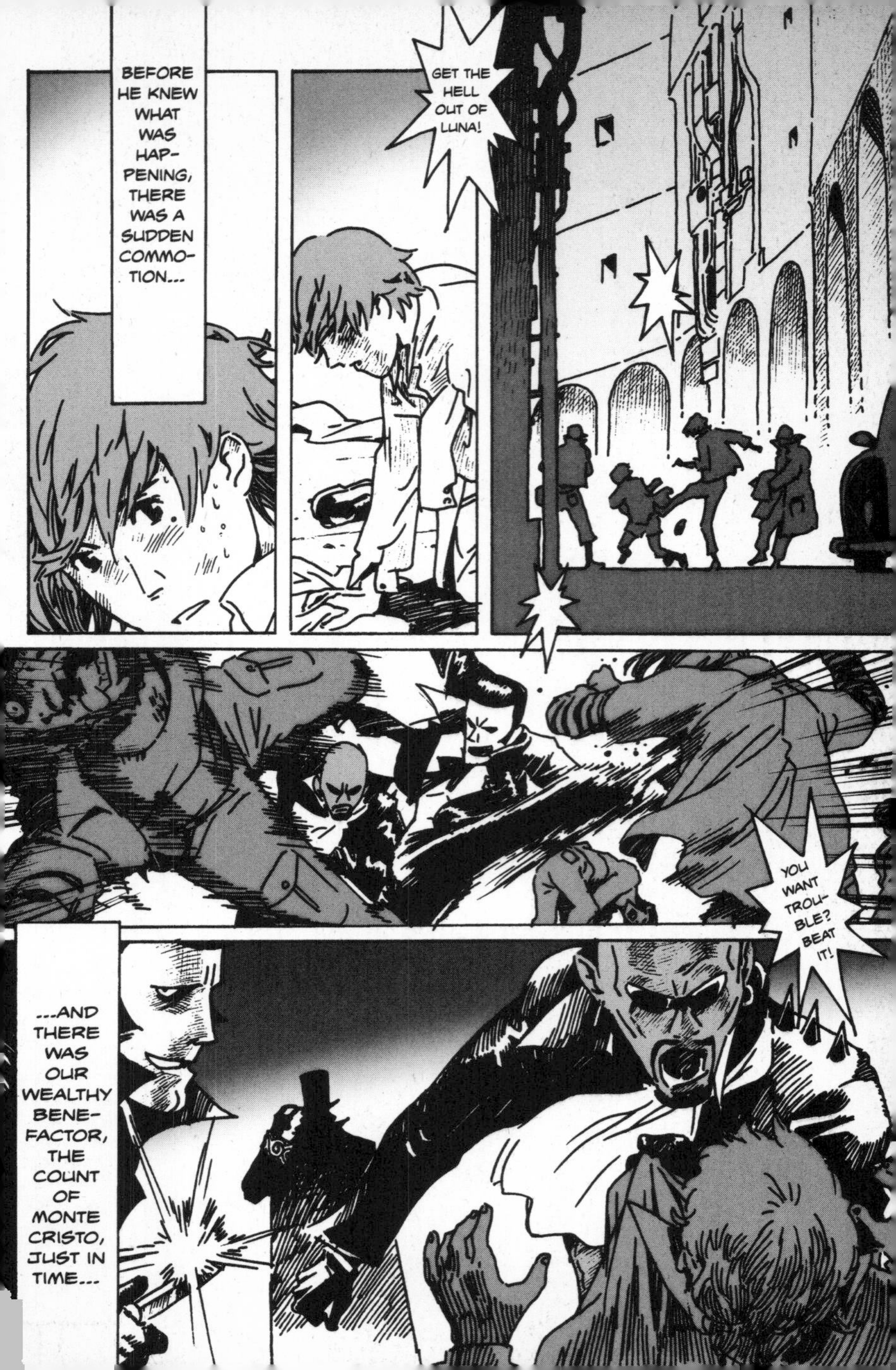
GET THE HELL OUT OF LUNA!
BEFORE HE KNEW WHAT WAS HAPPENING, THERE WAS A SUDDEN COMMOTION...
YOU WANT TROUBLE? BEAT IT!
...AND THERE WAS OUR WEALTHY BENEFACTOR, THE COUNT OF MONTE CRISTO, JUST IN TIME...

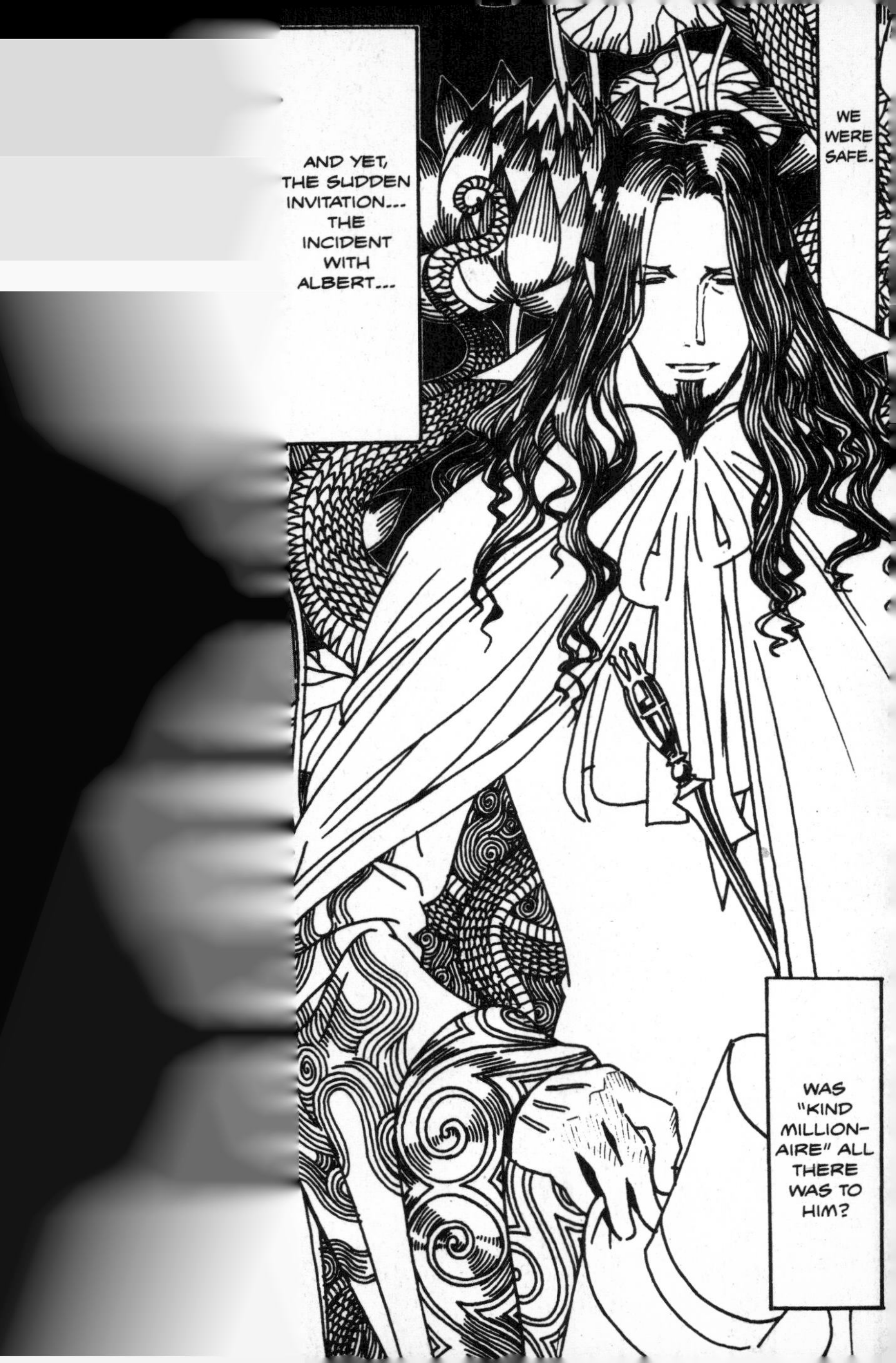
WE WERE SAFE.
AND YET, THE SUDDEN INVITATION... THE INCIDENT WITH ALBERT...
WAS "KIND MILLION-AIRE" ALL THERE WAS TO HIM?

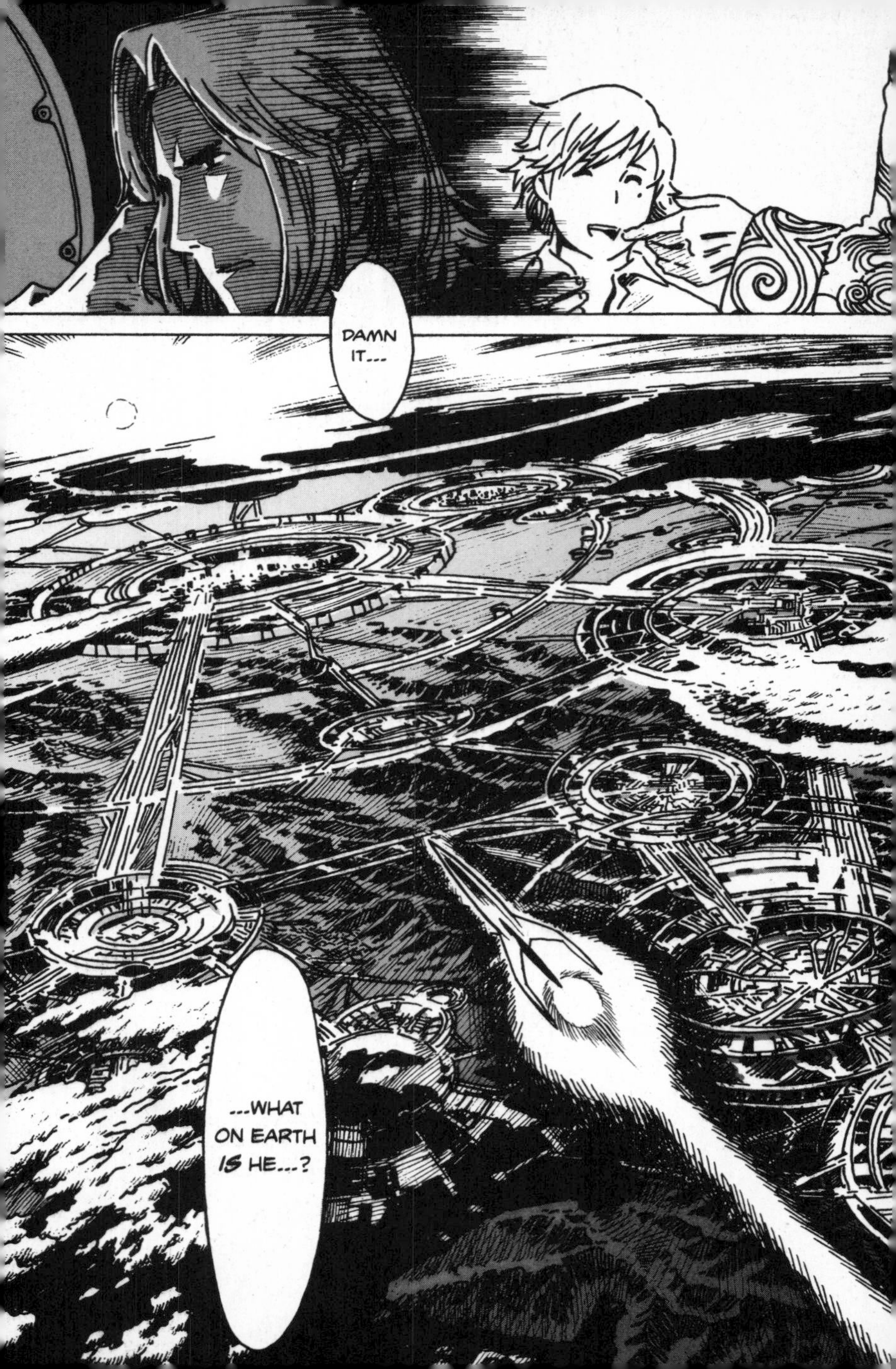
DAMN IT...
...WHAT ON EARTH IS HE...?

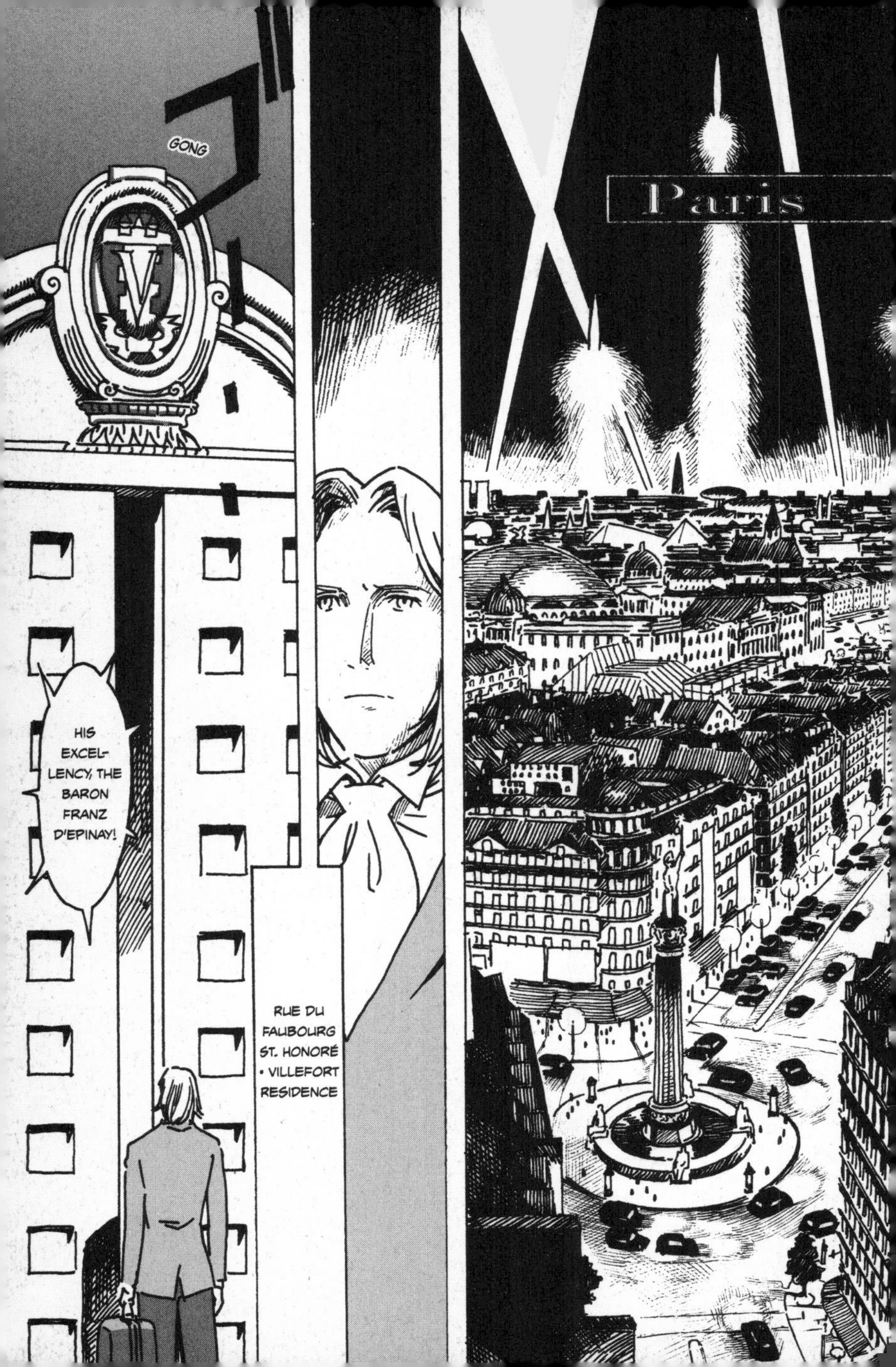
Paris
RUE DU FAUBOURG ST. HONORÉ • VILLEFORT RESIDENCE
GONG
HIS EXCELLENCY, THE BARON FRANZ D'EPINAY!

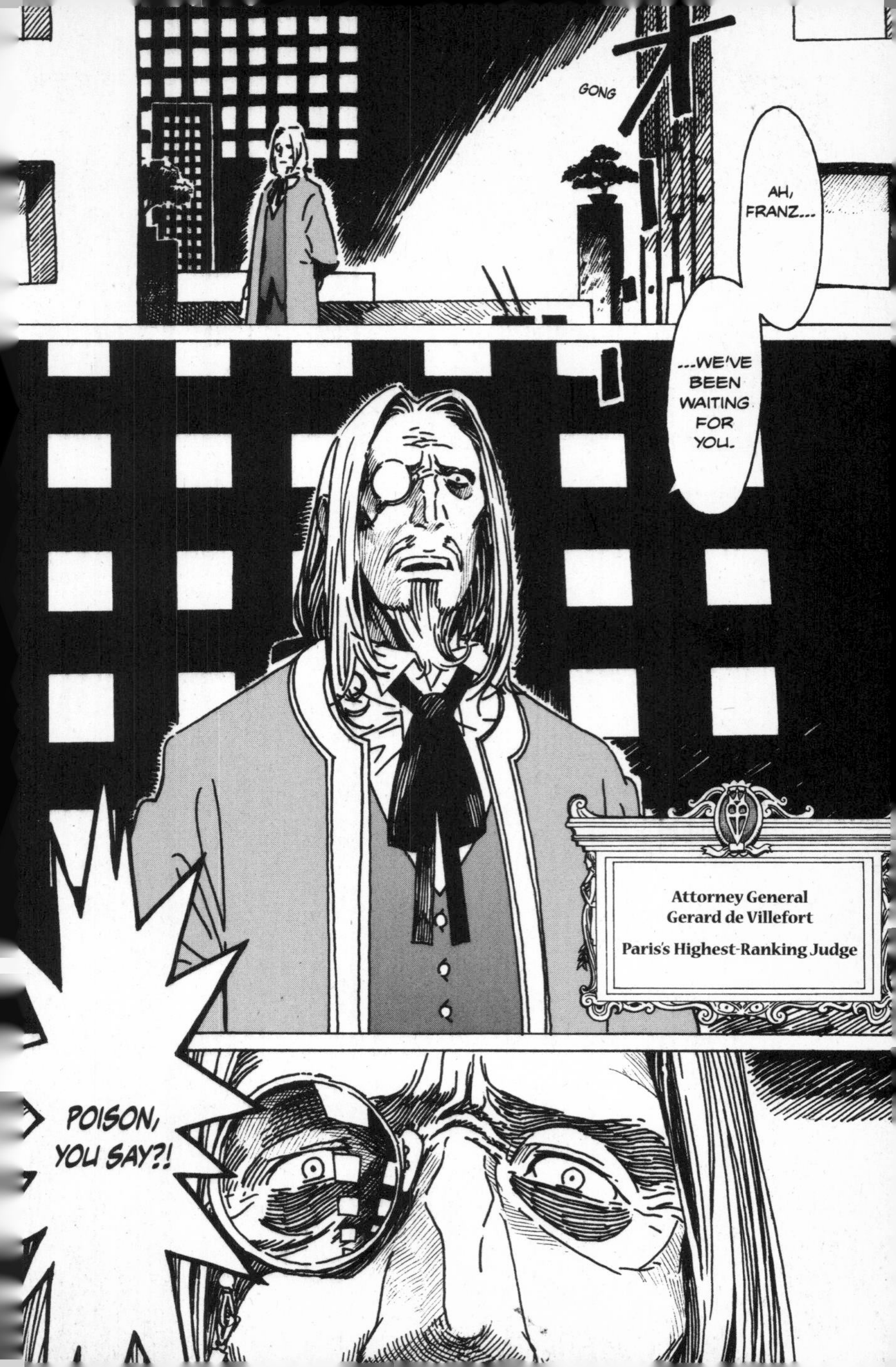
GONG
AH, FRANZ...
...WE'VE BEEN WAITING FOR YOU.
Attorney General Gerard de Villefort
Paris's Highest-Ranking Judge
POISON, YOU SAY?!

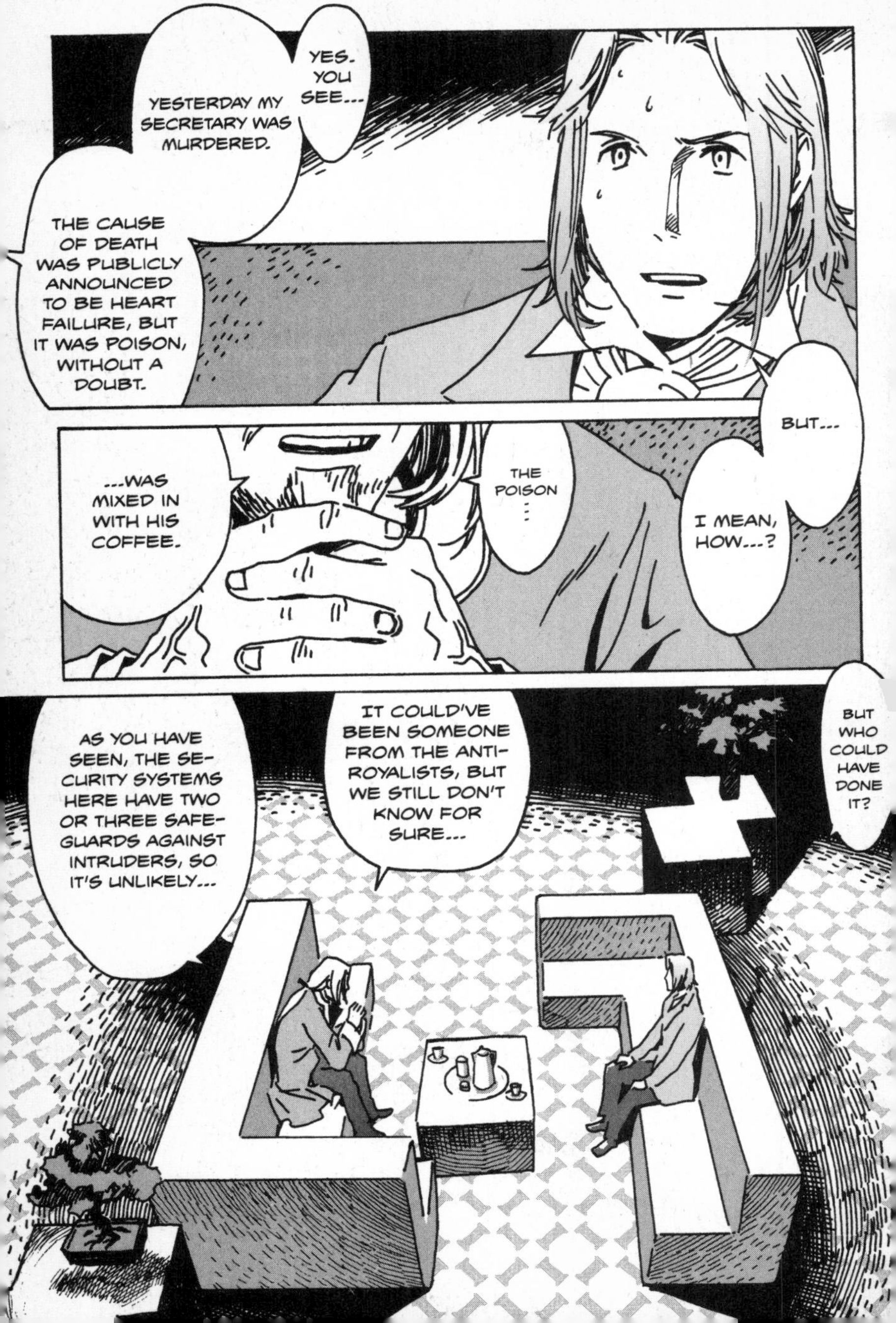

YES. YOU SEE...
YESTERDAY MY SECRETARY WAS MURDERED.
THE CAUSE OF DEATH WAS PUBLICLY ANNOUNCED TO BE HEART FAILURE, BUT IT WAS POISON, WITHOUT A DOUBT.
BUT...
I MEAN, HOW...?
THE POISON ...
...WAS MIXED IN WITH HIS COFFEE.
BUT WHO COULD HAVE DONE IT?
IT COULD'VE BEEN SOMEONE FROM THE ANTI-ROYALISTS, BUT WE STILL DON'T KNOW FOR SURE...
AS YOU HAVE SEEN, THE SE-CURITY SYSTEMS HERE HAVE TWO OR THREE SAFE-GUARDS AGAINST INTRUDERS, SO IT'S UNLIKELY...

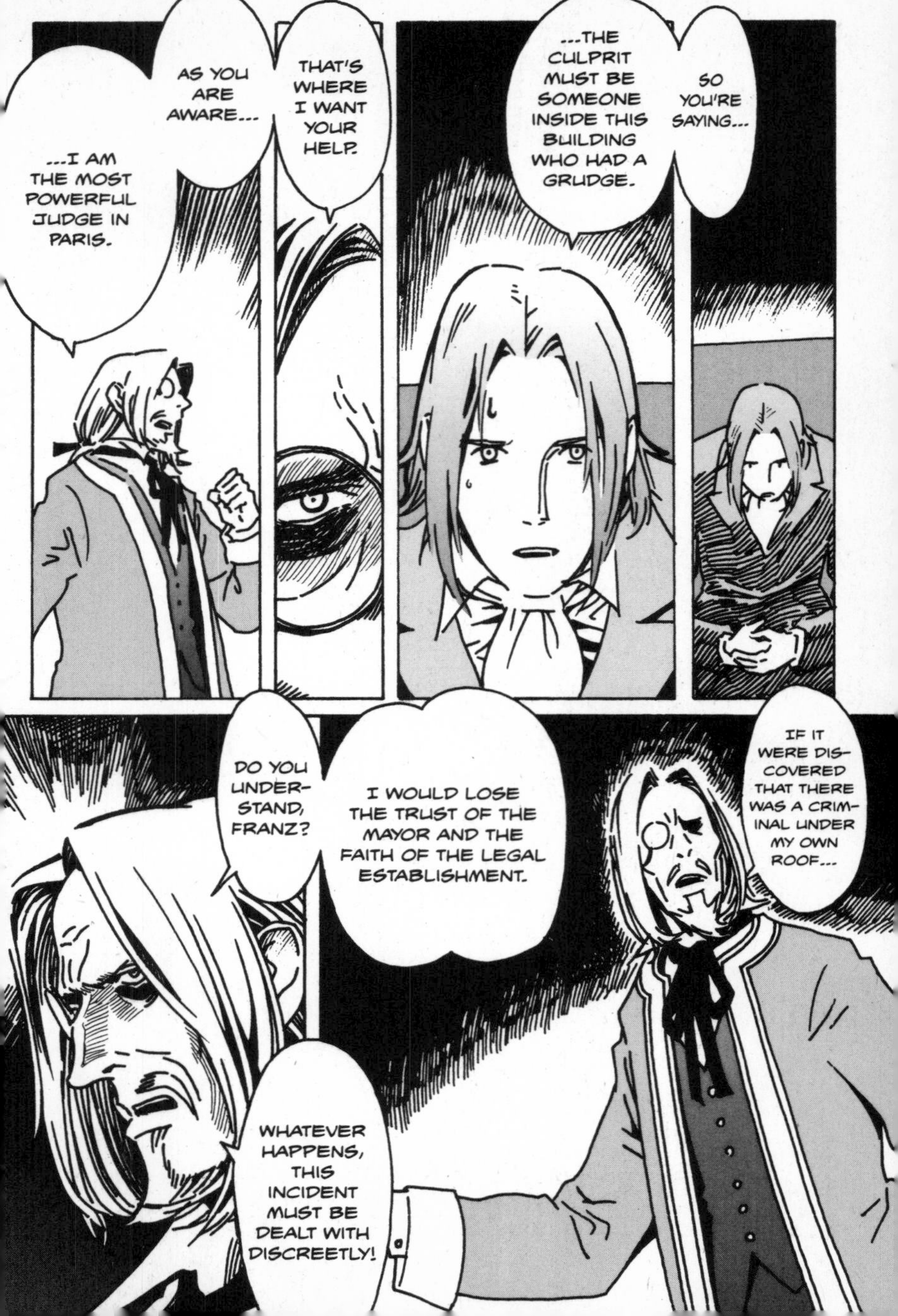
SO YOU'RE SAYING...
...THE CULPRIT MUST BE SOMEONE INSIDE THIS BUILDING WHO HAD A GRUDGE.
THAT'S WHERE I WANT YOUR HELP.
AS YOU ARE AWARE...
...I AM THE MOST POWERFUL JUDGE IN PARIS.
IF IT WERE DIS-COVERED THAT THERE WAS A CRIM-INAL UNDER MY OWN ROOF...
I WOULD LOSE THE TRUST OF THE MAYOR AND THE FAITH OF THE LEGAL ESTABLISHMENT.
DO YOU UNDER-STAND, FRANZ?
WHATEVER HAPPENS, THIS INCIDENT MUST BE DEALT WITH DISCREETLY!

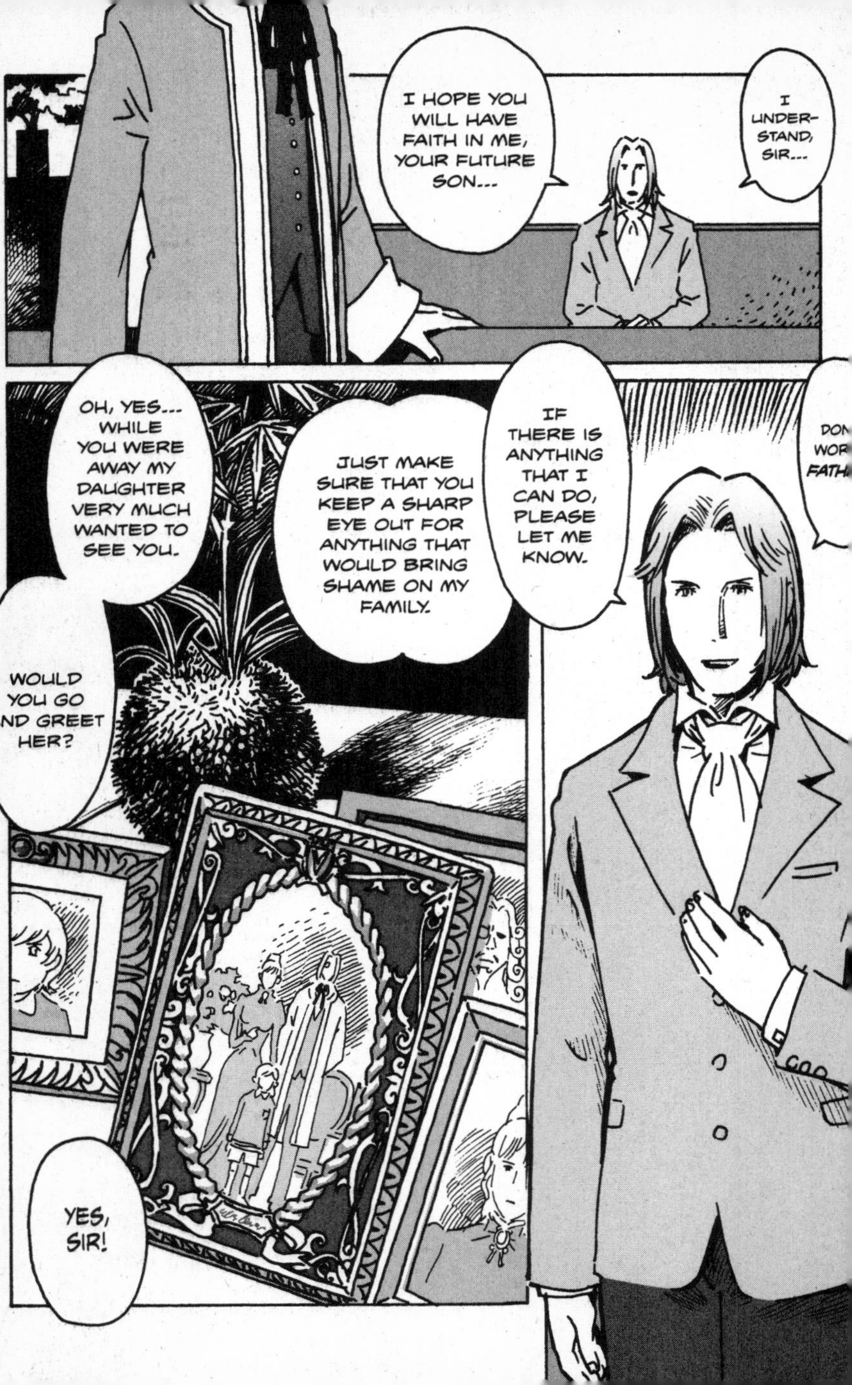
I UNDER-STAND, SIR...
I HOPE YOU WILL HAVE FAITH IN ME, YOUR FUTURE SON...
IF THERE IS ANYTHING THAT I CAN DO, PLEASE LET ME KNOW.
JUST MAKE SURE THAT YOU KEEP A SHARP EYE OUT FOR ANYTHING THAT WOULD BRING SHAME ON MY FAMILY.
OH, YES... WHILE YOU WERE AWAY MY DAUGHTER VERY MUCH WANTED TO SEE YOU.
WOULD YOU GO AND GREET HER?
YES, SIR!

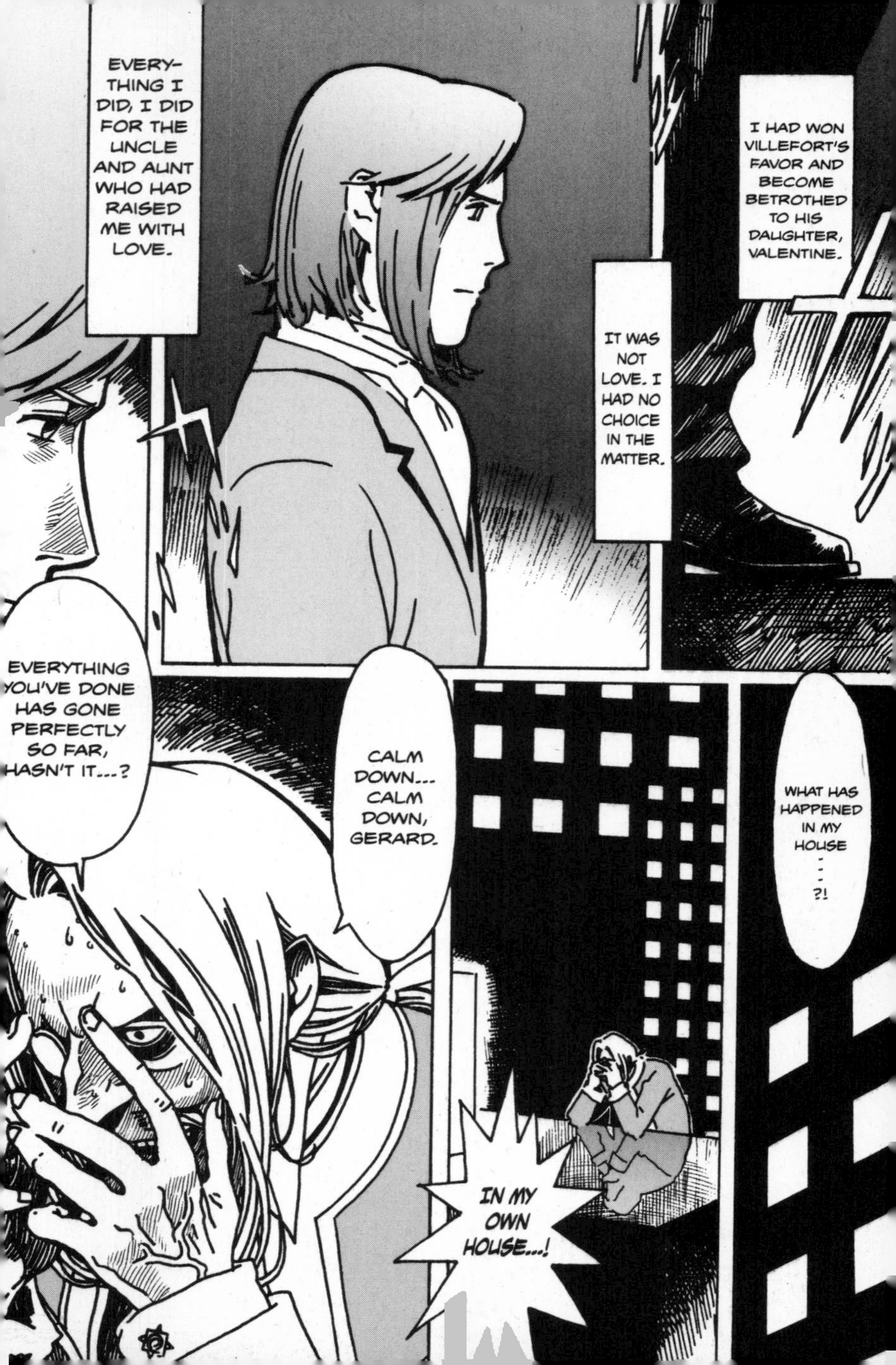
I HAD WON VILLEFORT'S FAVOR AND BECOME BETROTHED TO HIS DAUGHTER, VALENTINE.
IT WAS NOT LOVE. I HAD NO CHOICE IN THE MATTER.
EVERYTHING I DID, I DID FOR THE UNCLE AND AUNT WHO HAD RAISED ME WITH LOVE.
WHAT HAS HAPPENED IN MY HOUSE...?!
IN MY OWN HOUSE...!
CALM DOWN... CALM DOWN, GERARD.
EVERYTHING YOU'VE DONE HAS GONE PERFECTLY SO FAR, HASN'T IT...?

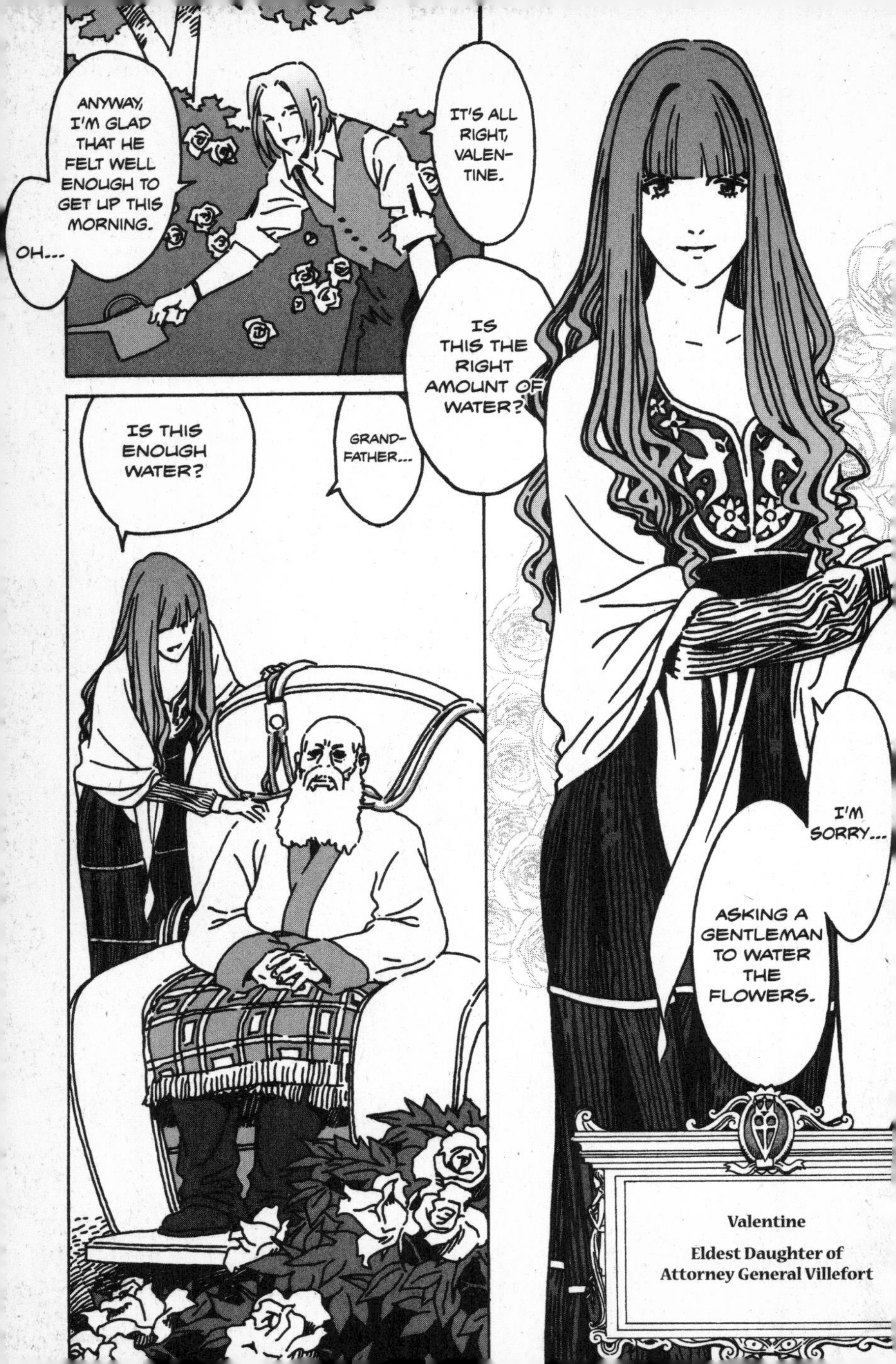
I'M SORRY...
ASKING A GENTLEMAN TO WATER THE FLOWERS.
IS THIS THE RIGHT AMOUNT OF WATER?
Valentine
Eldest Daughter of Attorney General Villefort
IT'S ALL RIGHT, VALENTINE.
ANYWAY, I'M GLAD THAT HE FELT WELL ENOUGH TO GET UP THIS MORNING.
OH...
GRANDFATHER...
IS THIS ENOUGH WATER?

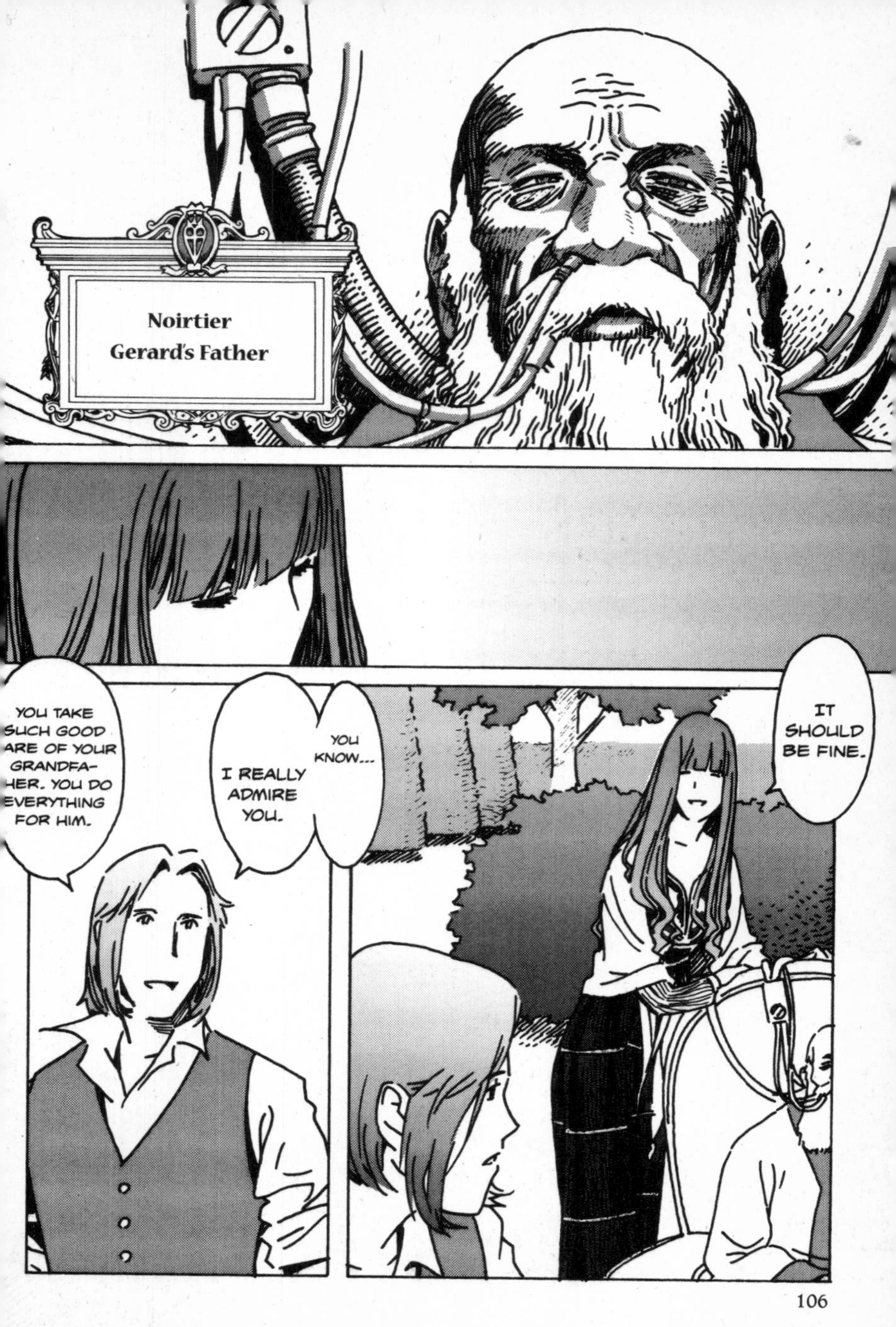
Noirtier
Gerard's Father
IT SHOULD BE FINE.
YOU KNOW...
I REALLY ADMIRE YOU.
YOU TAKE SUCH GOOD ARE OF YOUR GRANDFA-HER. YOU DO EVERYTHING FOR HIM.

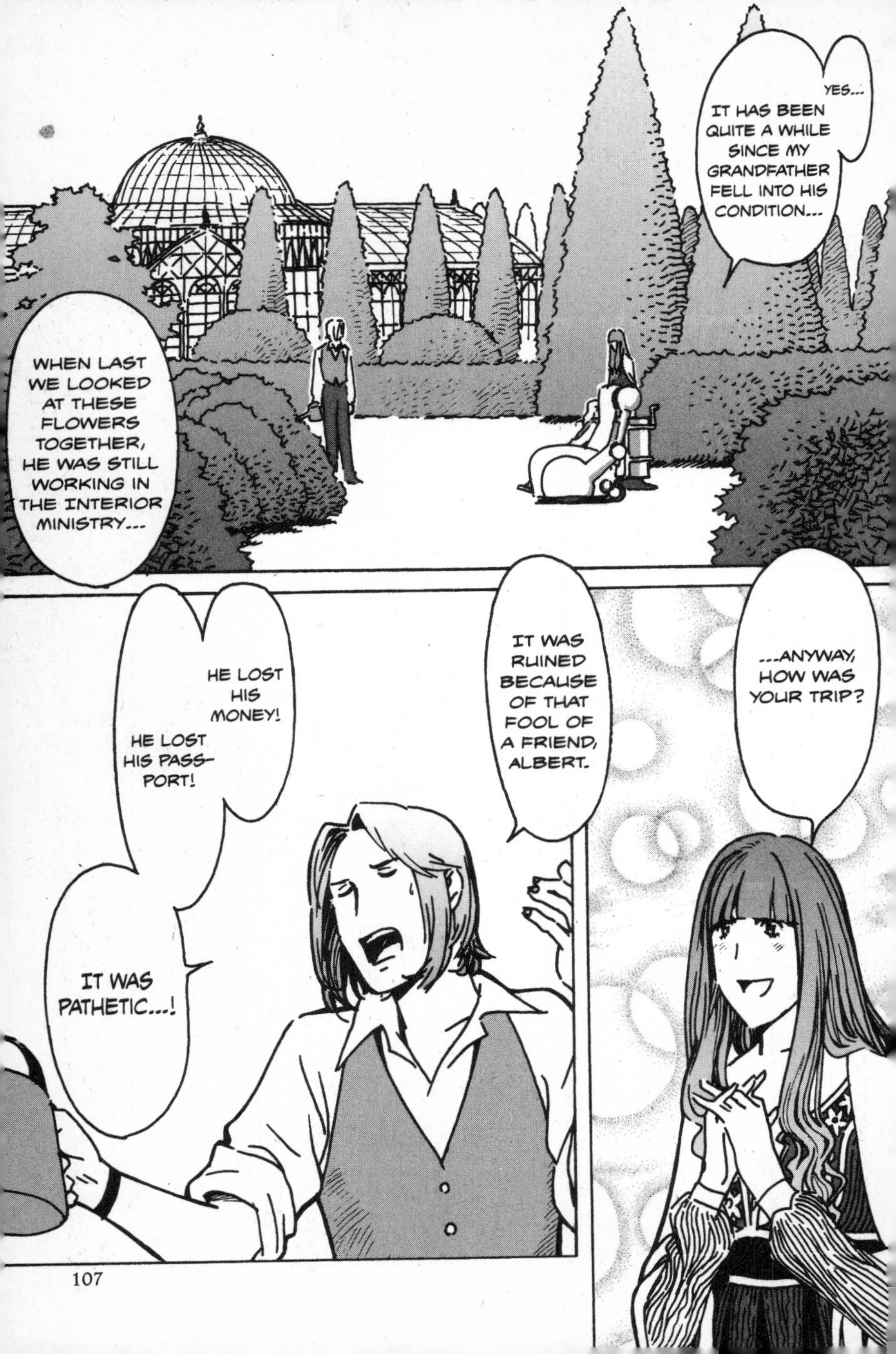
YES... IT HAS BEEN QUITE A WHILE SINCE MY GRANDFATHER FELL INTO HIS CONDITION...
WHEN LAST WE LOOKED AT THESE FLOWERS TOGETHER, HE WAS STILL WORKING IN THE INTERIOR MINISTRY...
...ANYWAY, HOW WAS YOUR TRIP?
IT WAS RUINED BECAUSE OF THAT FOOL OF A FRIEND, ALBERT.
HE LOST HIS MONEY!
HE LOST HIS PASS-PORT!
IT WAS PATHETIC...!

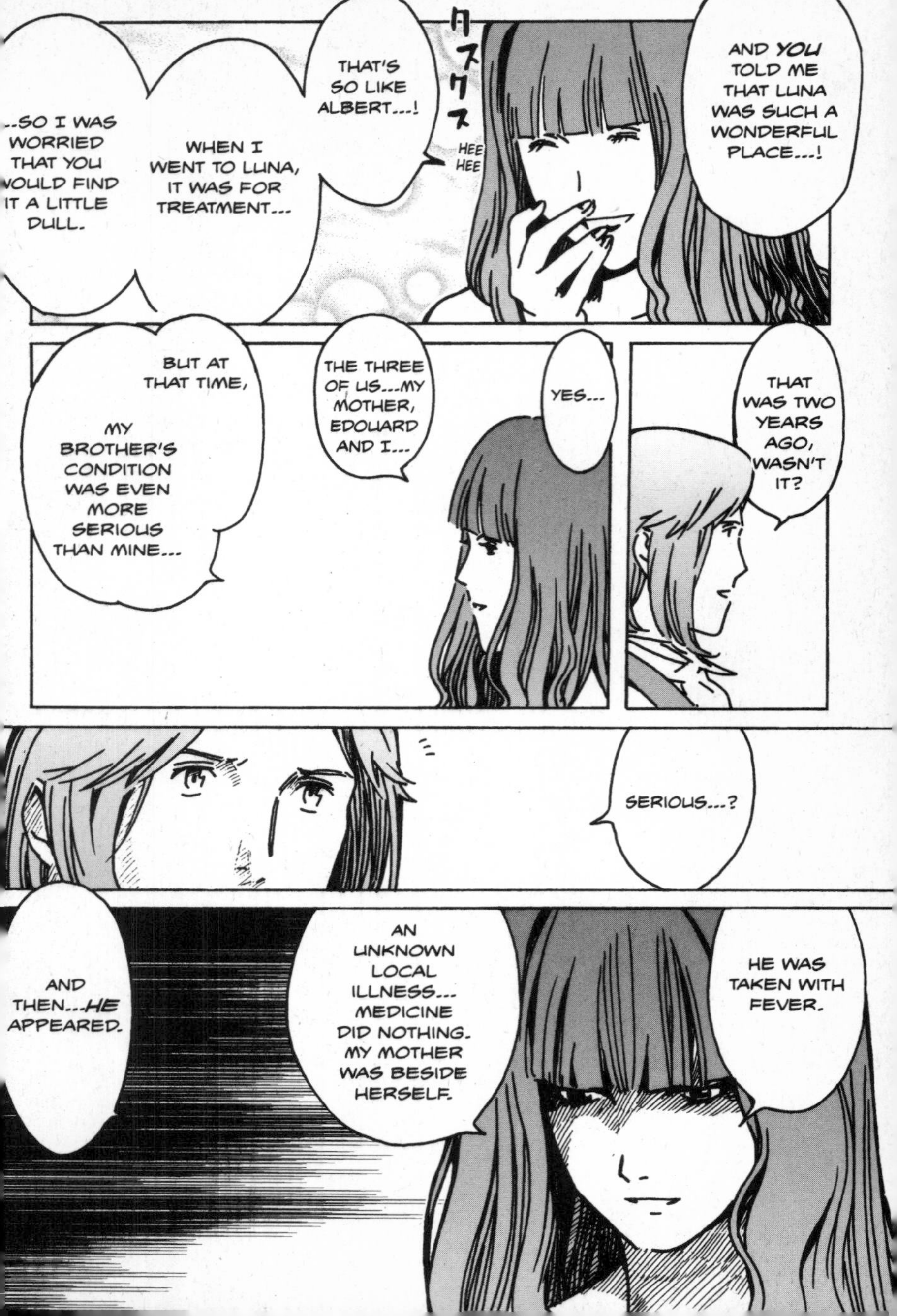
AND *YOU* TOLD ME THAT LUNA WAS SUCH A WONDERFUL PLACE...!
クスクス
HEE HEE
THAT'S SO LIKE ALBERT...!
WHEN I WENT TO LUNA, IT WAS FOR TREATMENT...
...SO I WAS WORRIED THAT YOU WOULD FIND IT A LITTLE DULL.
THAT WAS TWO YEARS AGO, WASN'T IT?
YES...
THE THREE OF US...MY MOTHER, EDOUARD AND I...
BUT AT THAT TIME,
MY BROTHER'S CONDITION WAS EVEN MORE SERIOUS THAN MINE...
SERIOUS...?
HE WAS TAKEN WITH FEVER.
AN UNKNOWN LOCAL ILLNESS... MEDICINE DID NOTHING. MY MOTHER WAS BESIDE HERSELF.
AND THEN...*HE* APPEARED.

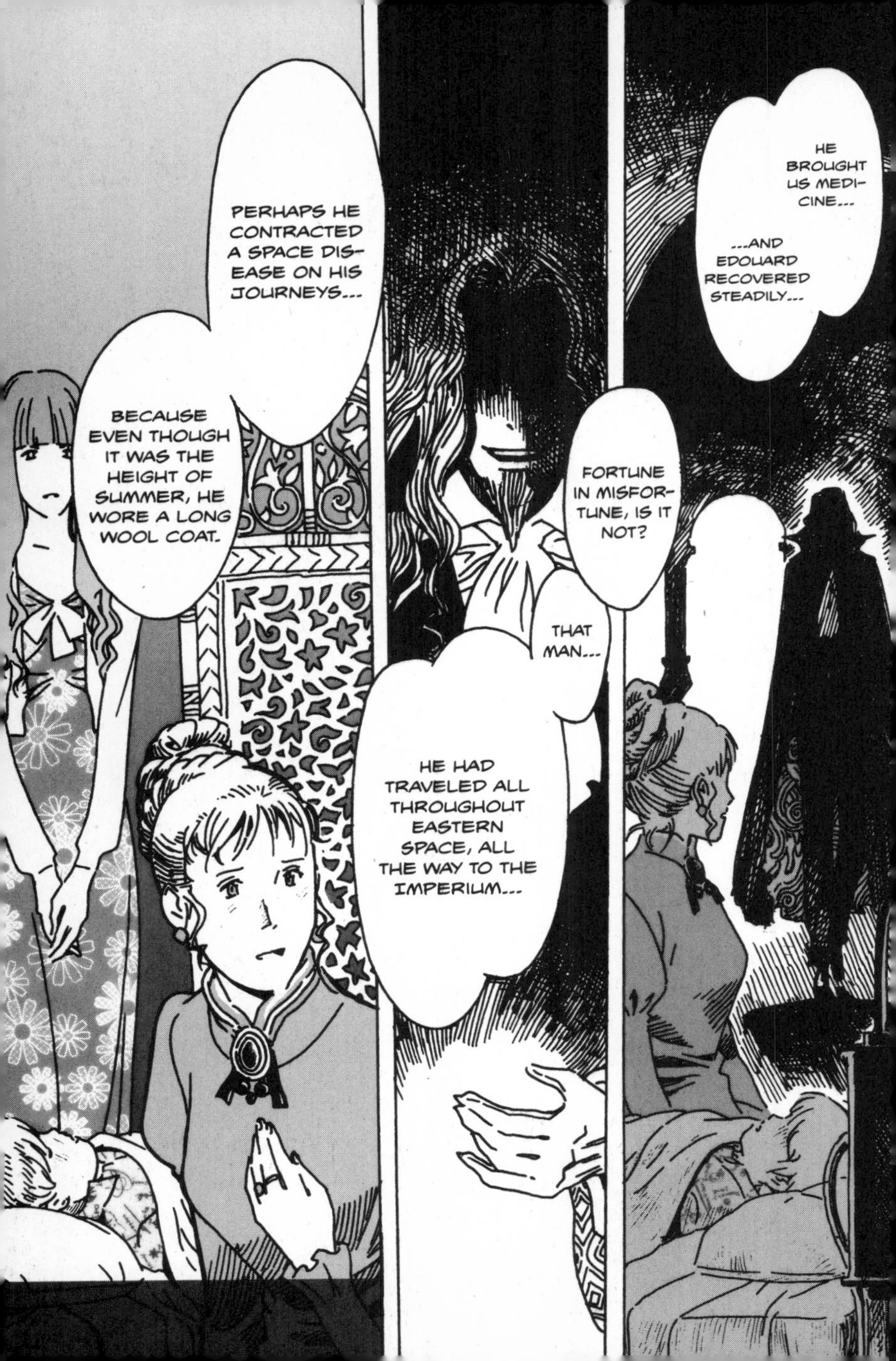
HE BROUGHT US MEDICINE...
...AND EDOUARD RECOVERED STEADILY...
FORTUNE IN MISFORTUNE, IS IT NOT?
THAT MAN...
HE HAD TRAVELED ALL THROUGHOUT EASTERN SPACE, ALL THE WAY TO THE IMPERIUM...
PERHAPS HE CONTRACTED A SPACE DISEASE ON HIS JOURNEYS...
BECAUSE EVEN THOUGH IT WAS THE HEIGHT OF SUMMER, HE WORE A LONG WOOL COAT.

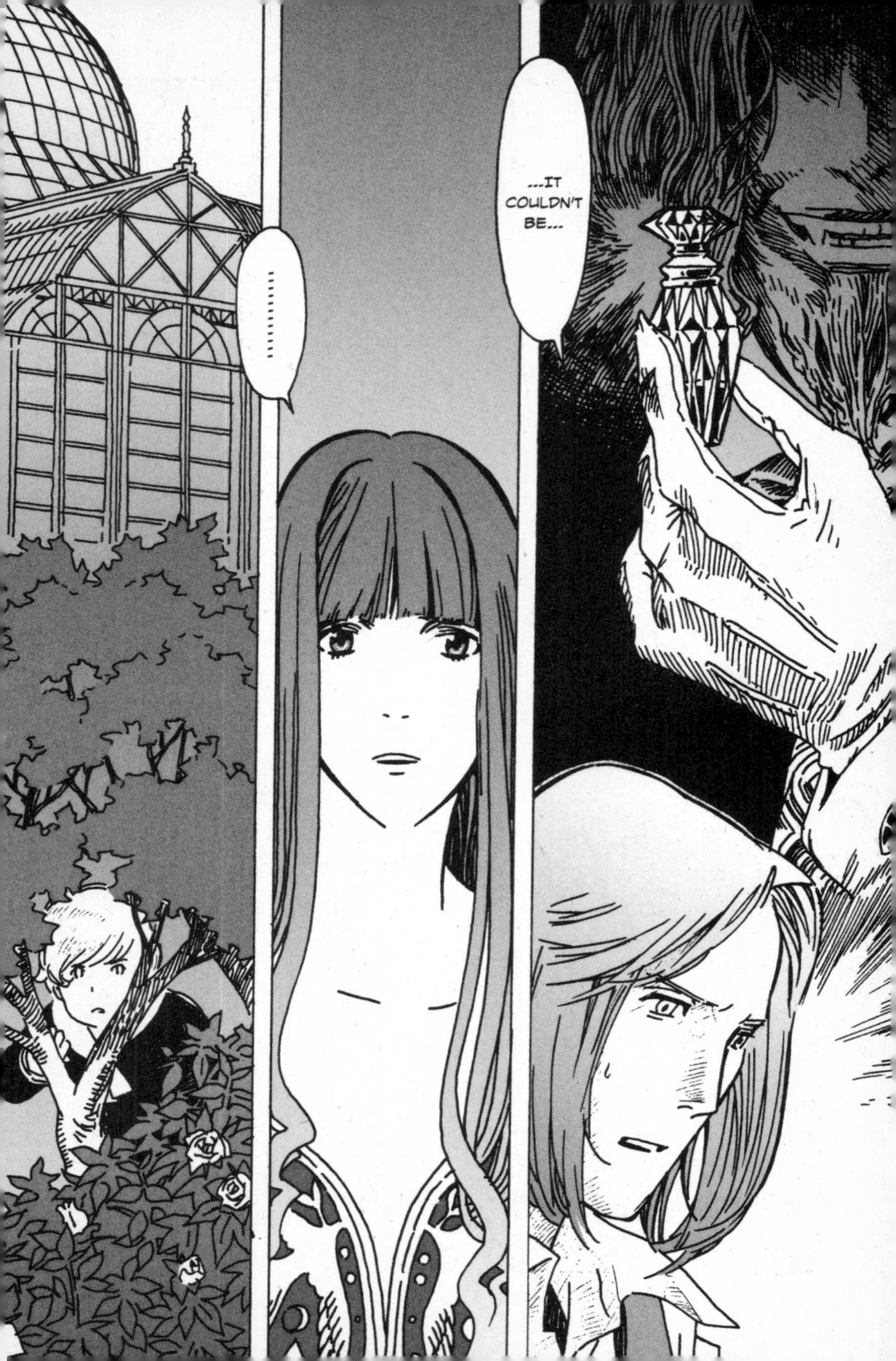
...IT COULDN'T BE...
......

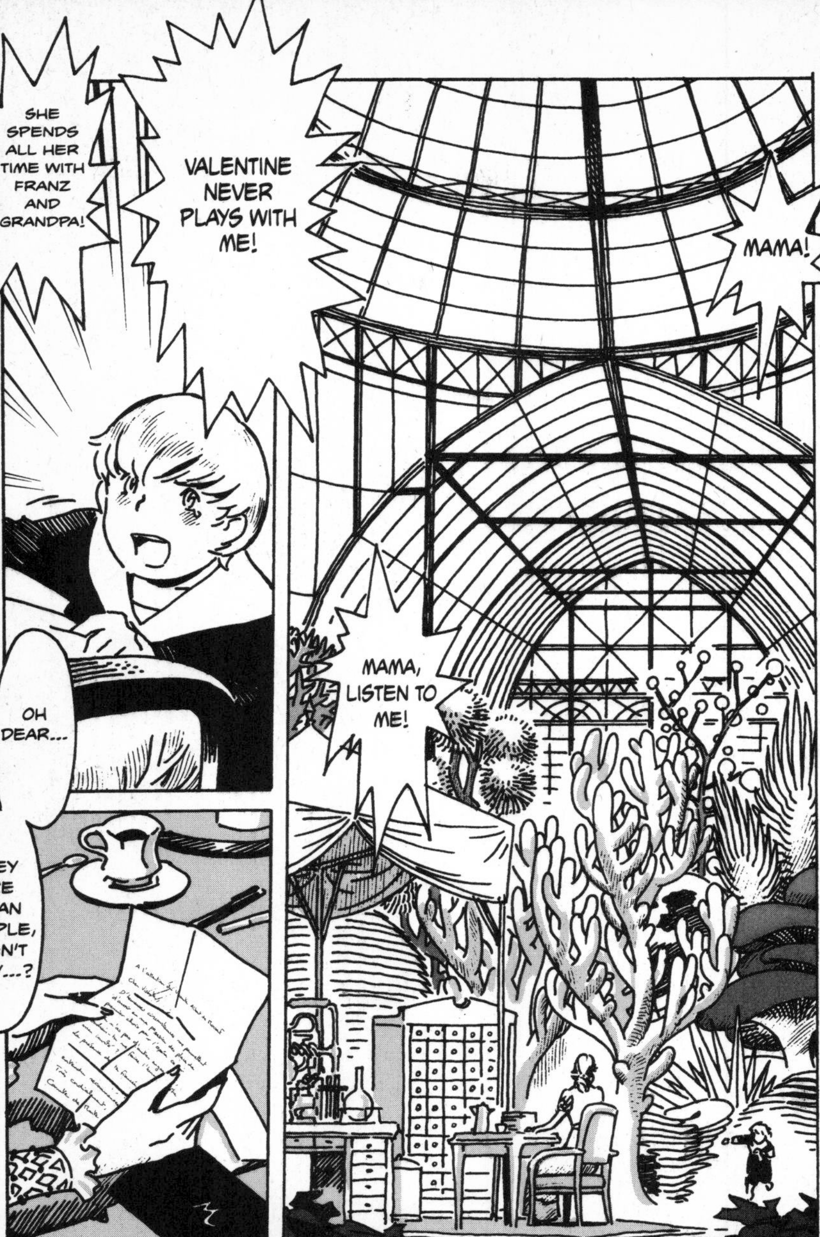
MAMA!
MAMA, LISTEN TO ME!
VALENTINE NEVER PLAYS WITH ME!
SHE SPENDS ALL HER TIME WITH FRANZ AND GRANDPA!
OH DEAR...
THEY ARE MEAN PEOPLE, AREN'T THEY...?

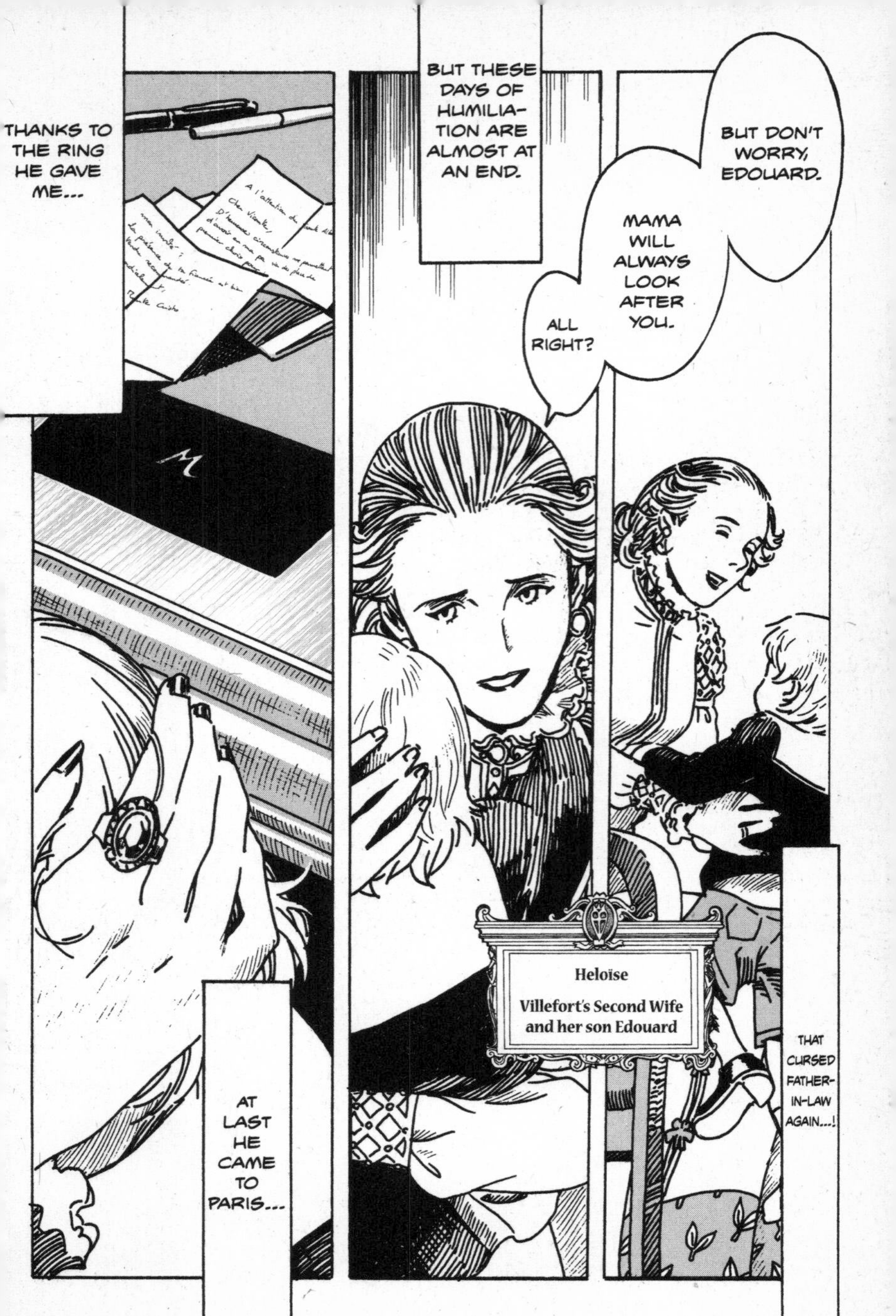
BUT DON'T WORRY, EDOUARD.
MAMA WILL ALWAYS LOOK AFTER YOU.
ALL RIGHT?
THAT CURSED FATHER-IN-LAW AGAIN...!
BUT THESE DAYS OF HUMILIATION ARE ALMOST AT AN END.
Heloïse
Villefort's Second Wife and her son Edouard
THANKS TO THE RING HE GAVE ME...
AT LAST HE CAME TO PARIS...

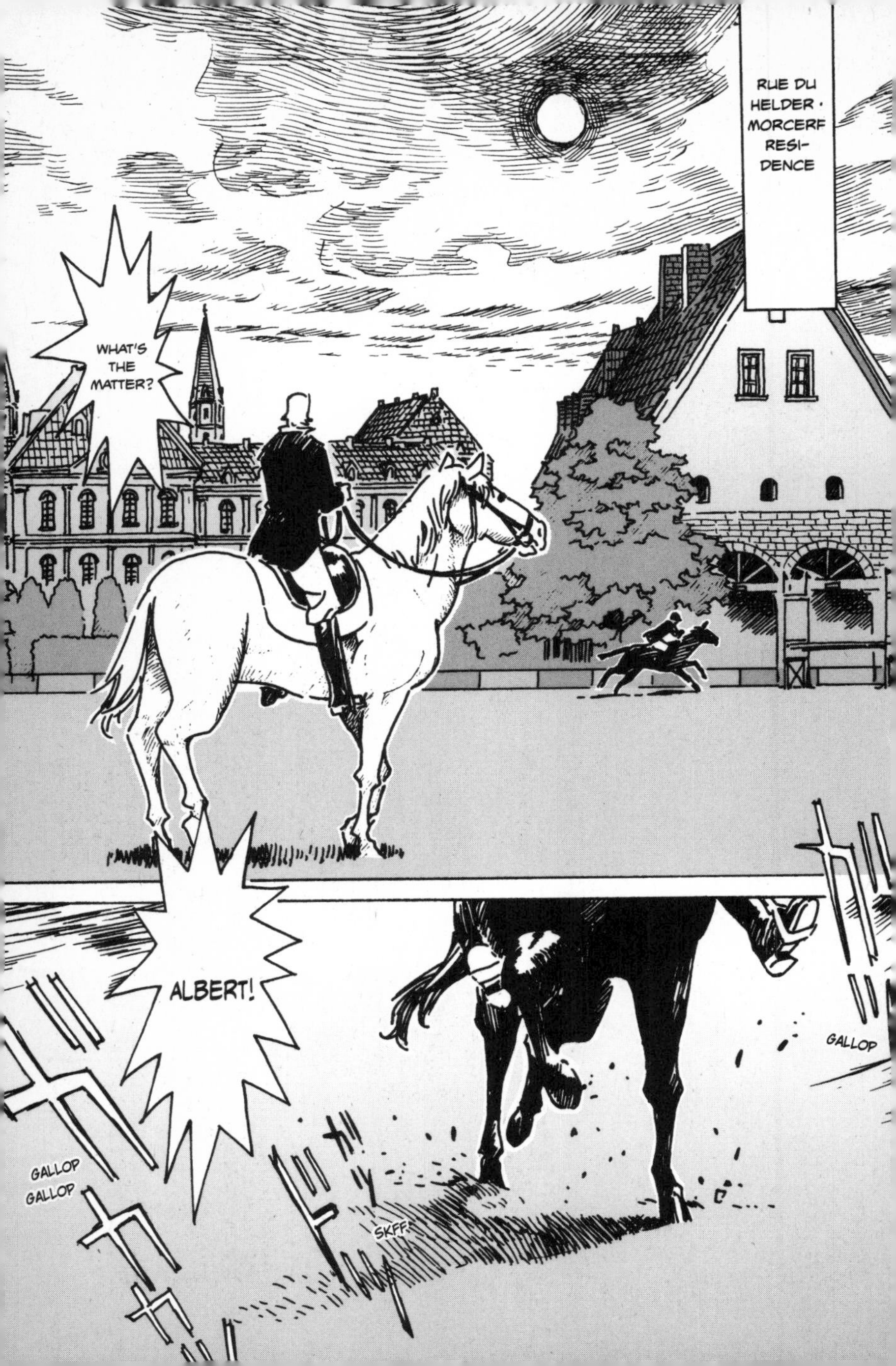
RUE DU HELDER · MORCERF RESI-DENCE
WHAT'S THE MATTER?
GALLOP
ALBERT!
SKFF
GALLOP GALLOP

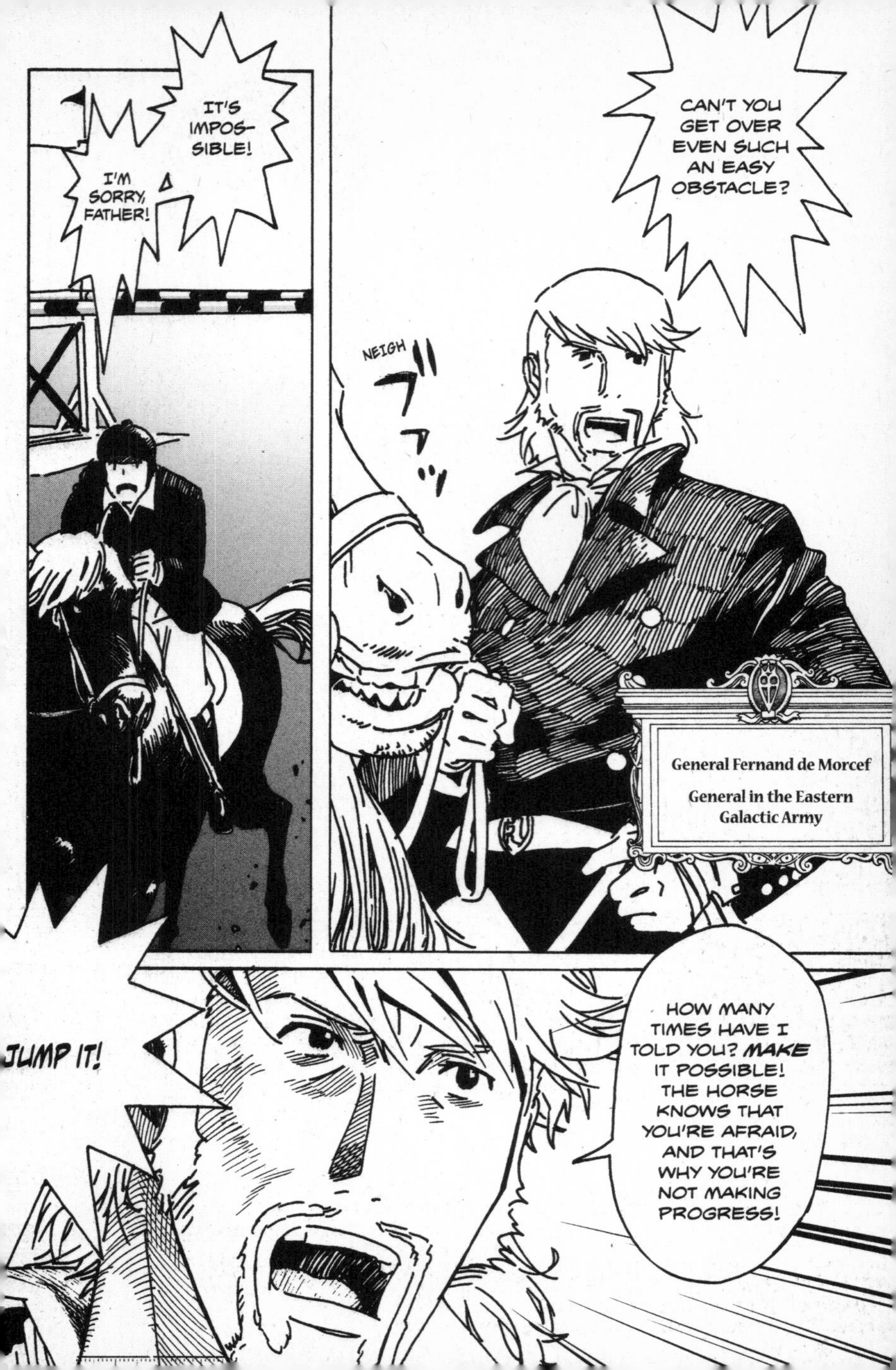
CAN'T YOU GET OVER EVEN SUCH AN EASY OBSTACLE?
NEIGH
General Fernand de Morcef
General in the Eastern Galactic Army
IT'S IMPOS-SIBLE!
I'M SORRY, FATHER!
HOW MANY TIMES HAVE I TOLD YOU? MAKE IT POSSIBLE! THE HORSE KNOWS THAT YOU'RE AFRAID, AND THAT'S WHY YOU'RE NOT MAKING PROGRESS!
JUMP IT!

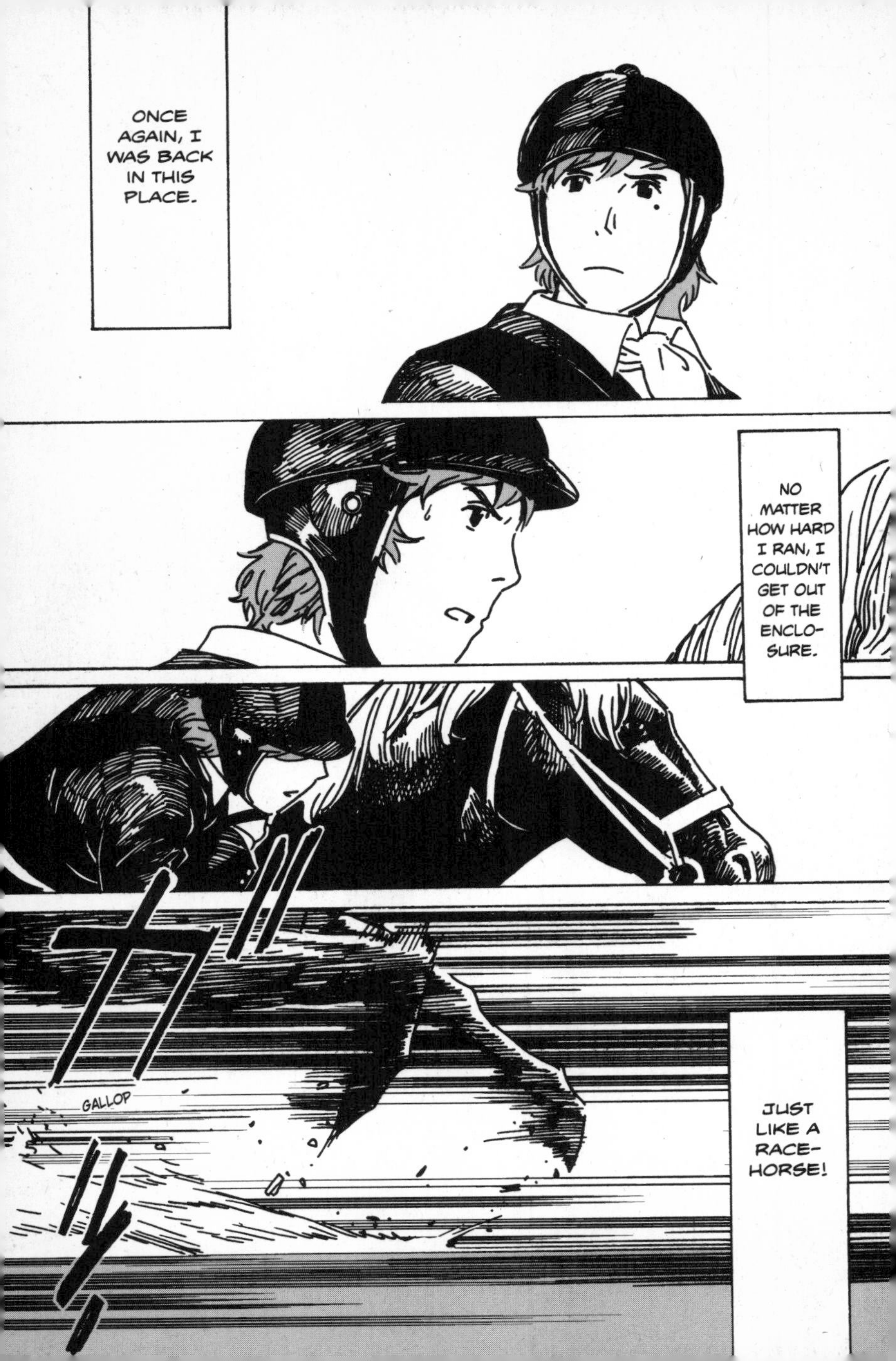
ONCE AGAIN, I WAS BACK IN THIS PLACE.
NO MATTER HOW HARD I RAN, I COULDN'T GET OUT OF THE ENCLO-SURE.
JUST LIKE A RACE-HORSE!
GALLOP

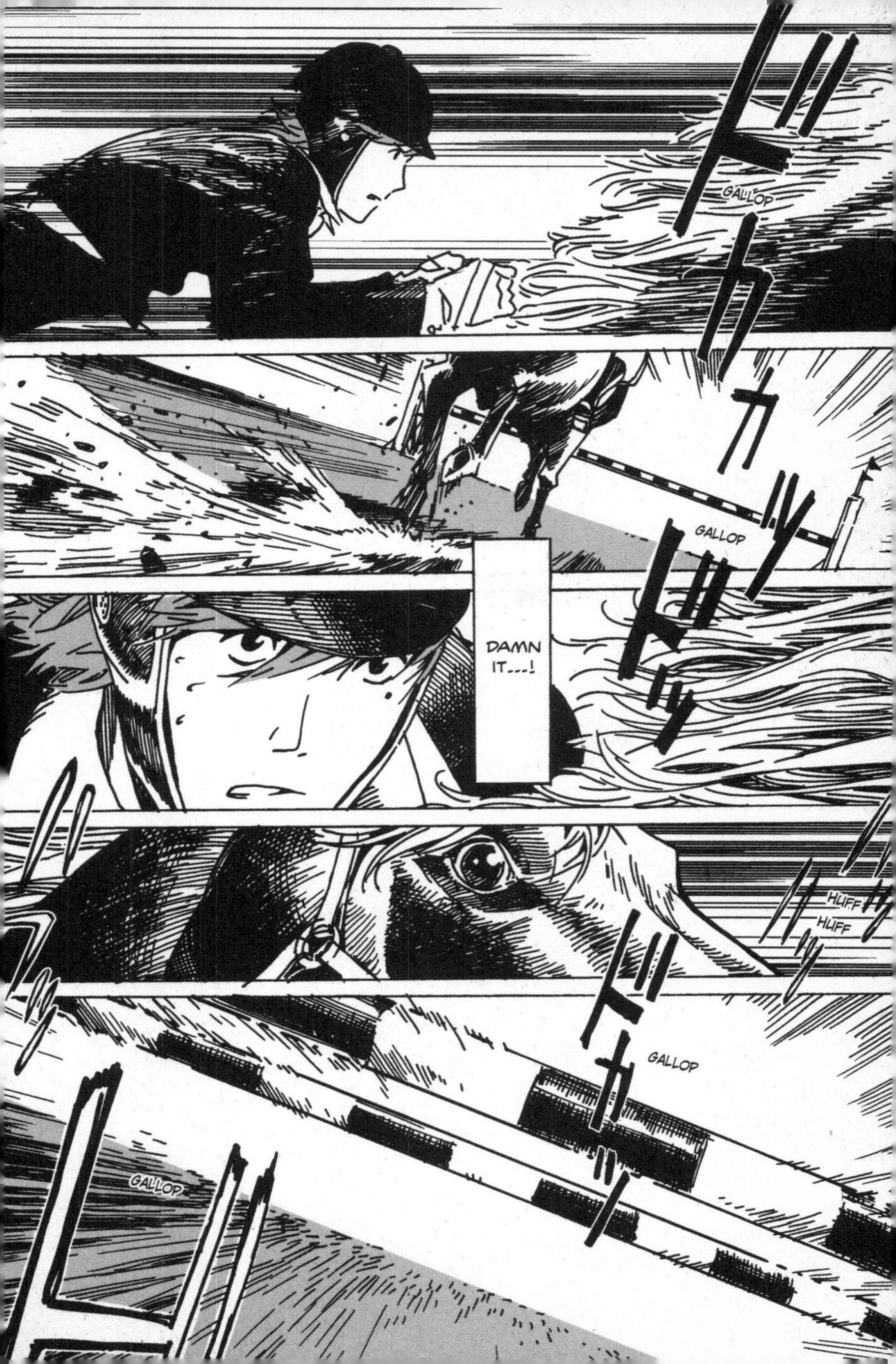
GALLOP
GALLOP
DAMN IT...!
HUFF
HUFF
GALLOP
GALLOP

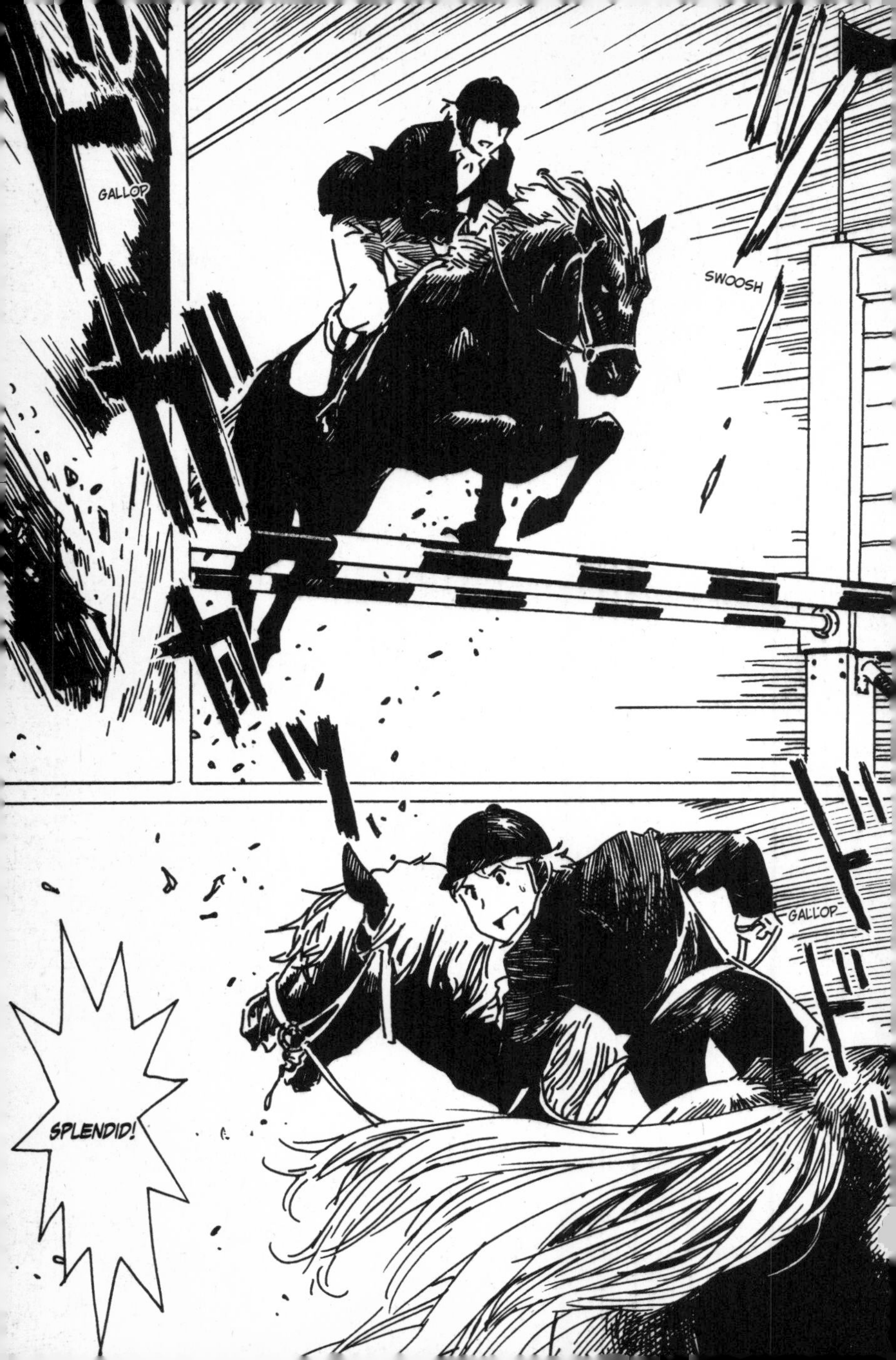
SWOOSH
GALLOP
GALLOP
SPLENDID!

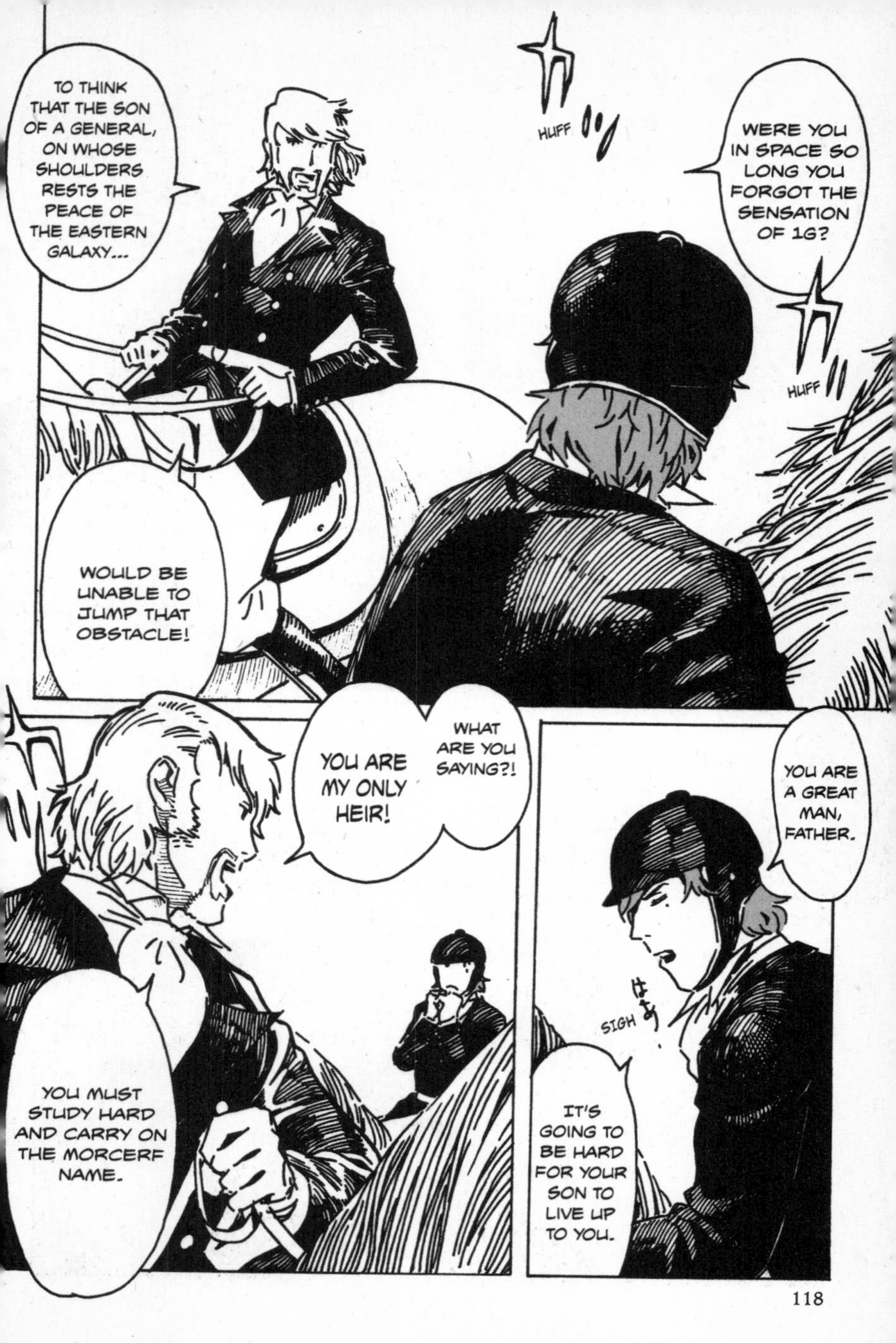
WERE YOU IN SPACE SO LONG YOU FORGOT THE SENSATION OF 1G?
HUFF
HUFF
TO THINK THAT THE SON OF A GENERAL, ON WHOSE SHOULDERS RESTS THE PEACE OF THE EASTERN GALAXY...
WOULD BE UNABLE TO JUMP THAT OBSTACLE!
YOU ARE A GREAT MAN, FATHER.
はぁ
SIGH
IT'S GOING TO BE HARD FOR YOUR SON TO LIVE UP TO YOU.
WHAT ARE YOU SAYING?!
YOU ARE MY ONLY HEIR!
YOU MUST STUDY HARD AND CARRY ON THE MORCERF NAME.

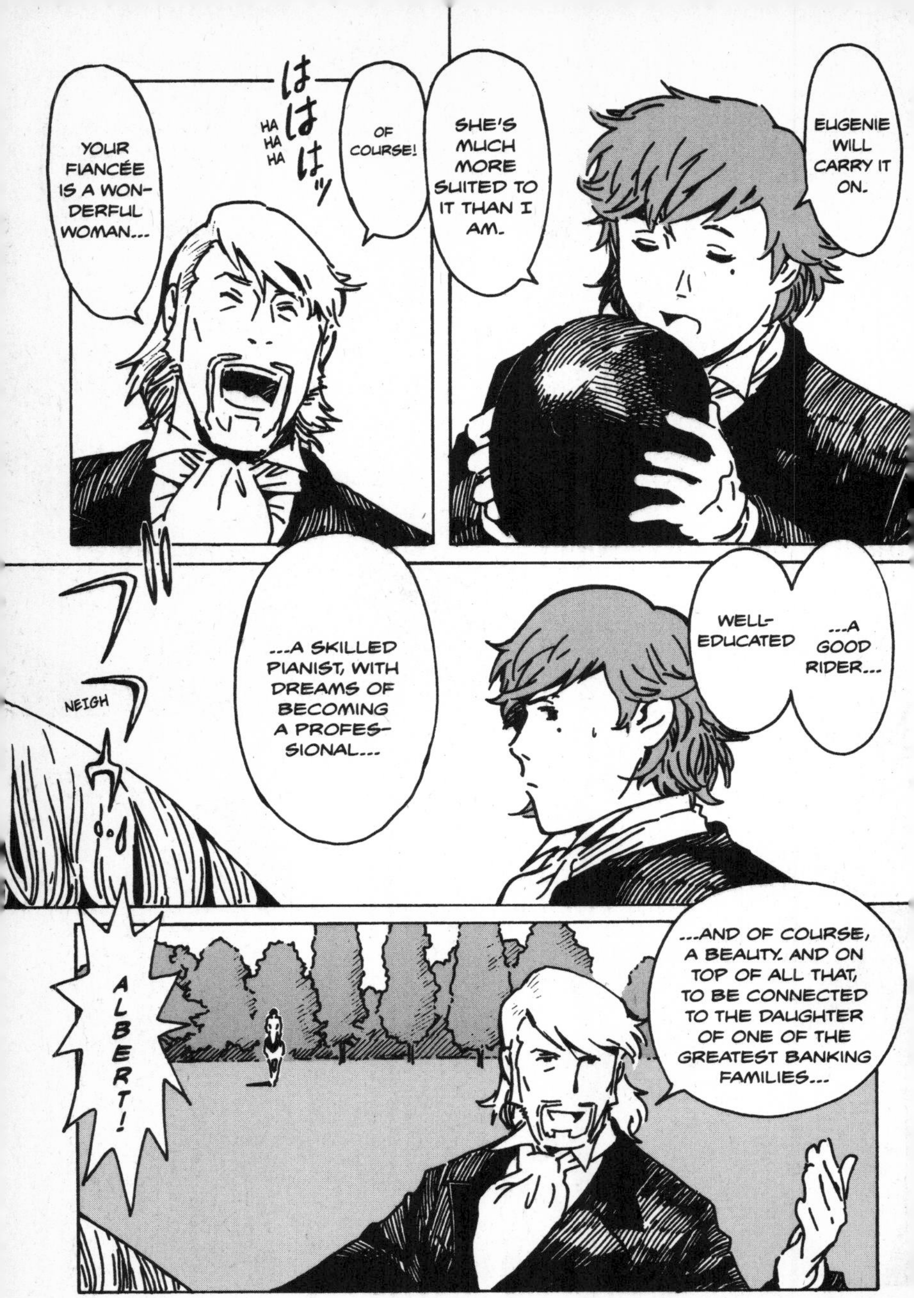
EUGENIE WILL CARRY IT ON.
SHE'S MUCH MORE SUITED TO IT THAN I AM.
OF COURSE!
ははは ッ
HA HA HA
YOUR FIANCÉE IS A WON-DERFUL WOMAN...
WELL-EDUCATED
...A GOOD RIDER...
...A SKILLED PIANIST, WITH DREAMS OF BECOMING A PROFES-SIONAL...
NEIGH
...AND OF COURSE, A BEAUTY. AND ON TOP OF ALL THAT, TO BE CONNECTED TO THE DAUGHTER OF ONE OF THE GREATEST BANKING FAMILIES...
ALBERT!

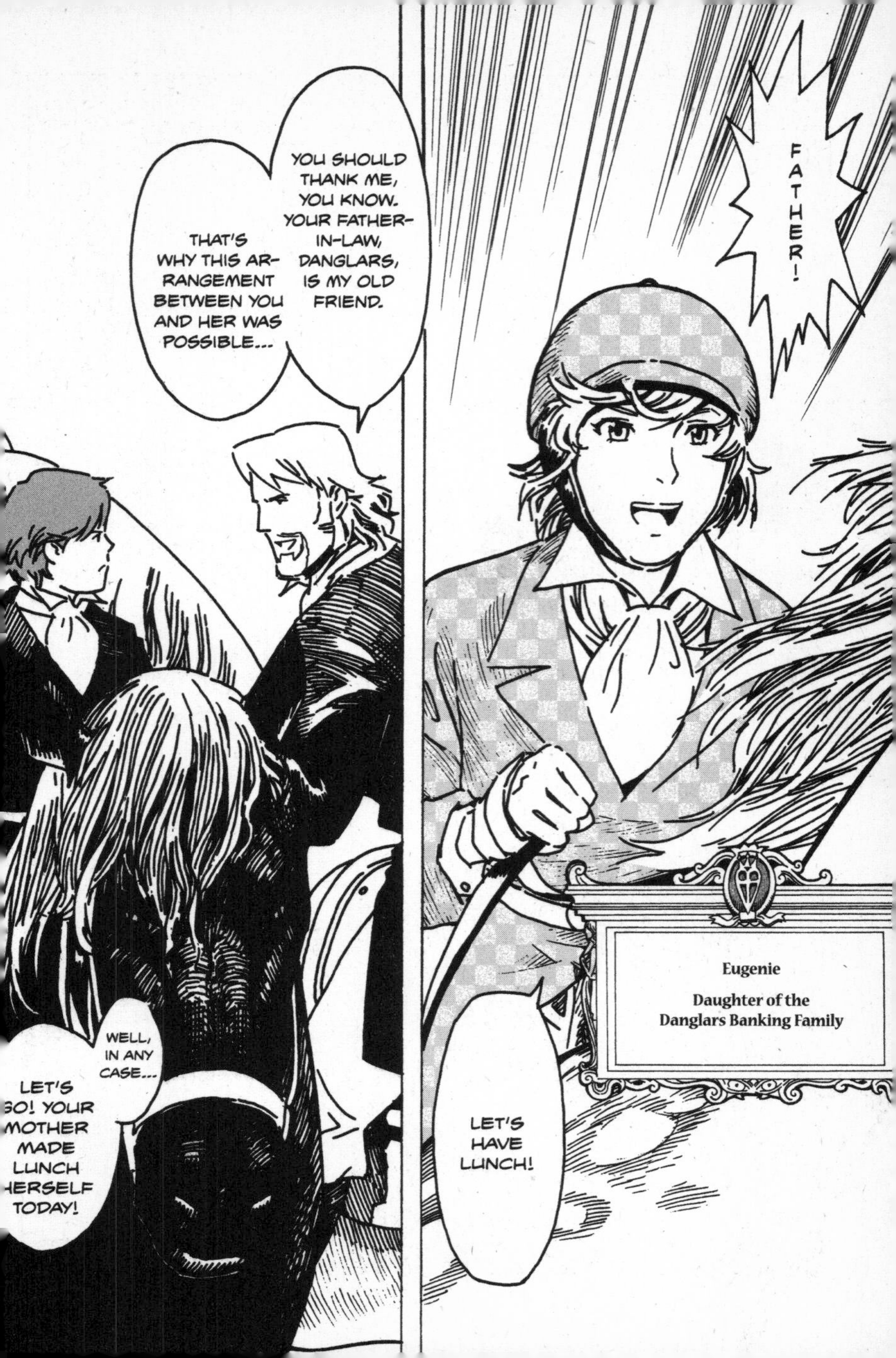
FATHER!
Eugenie
Daughter of the Danglars Banking Family
LET'S HAVE LUNCH!
YOU SHOULD THANK ME, YOU KNOW. YOUR FATHER-IN-LAW, DANGLARS, IS MY OLD FRIEND.
THAT'S WHY THIS ARRANGEMENT BETWEEN YOU AND HER WAS POSSIBLE...
WELL, IN ANY CASE...
LET'S GO! YOUR MOTHER MADE LUNCH HERSELF TODAY!

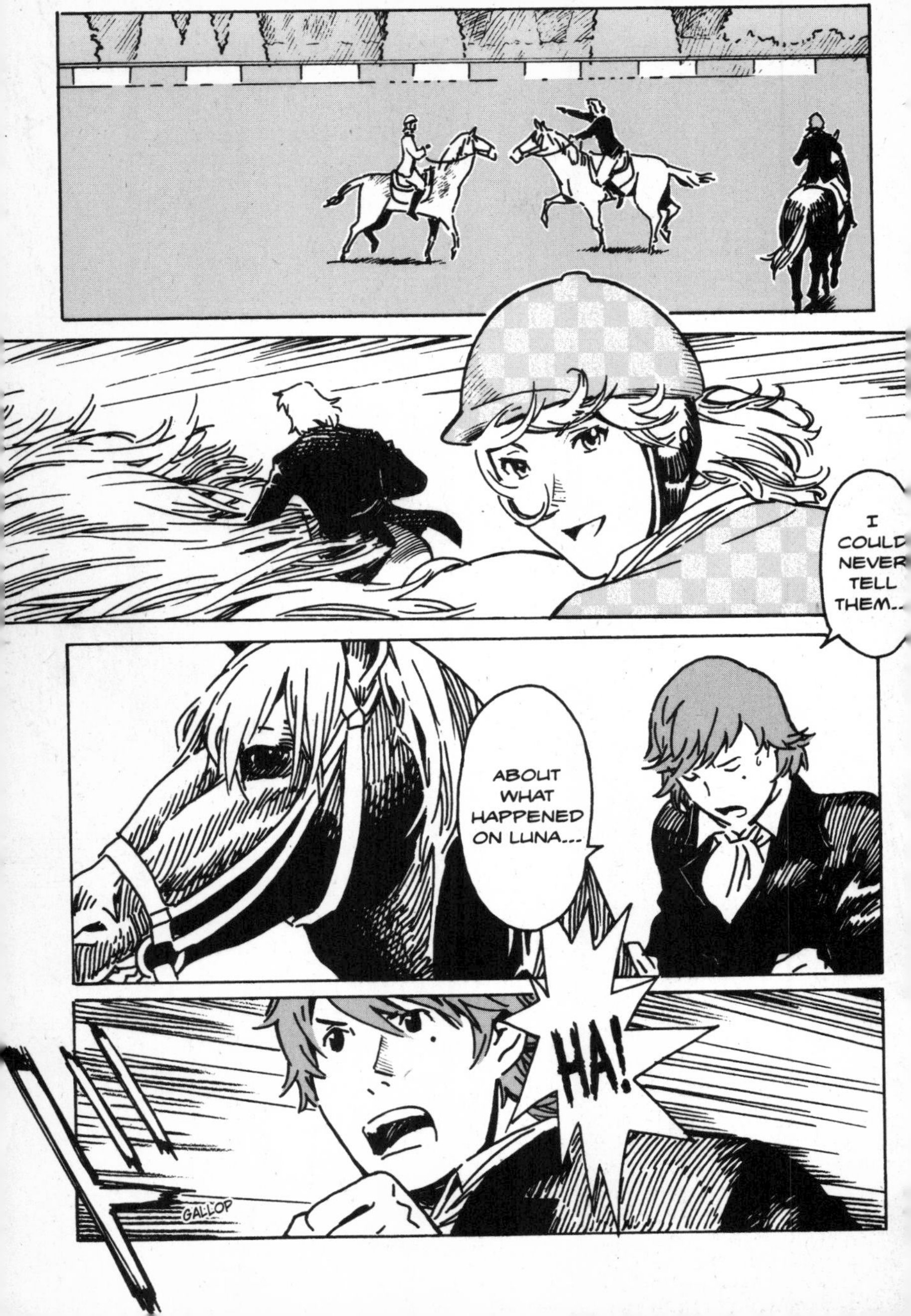
I COULD NEVER TELL THEM...
ABOUT WHAT HAPPENED ON LUNA...
HA!
GALLOP

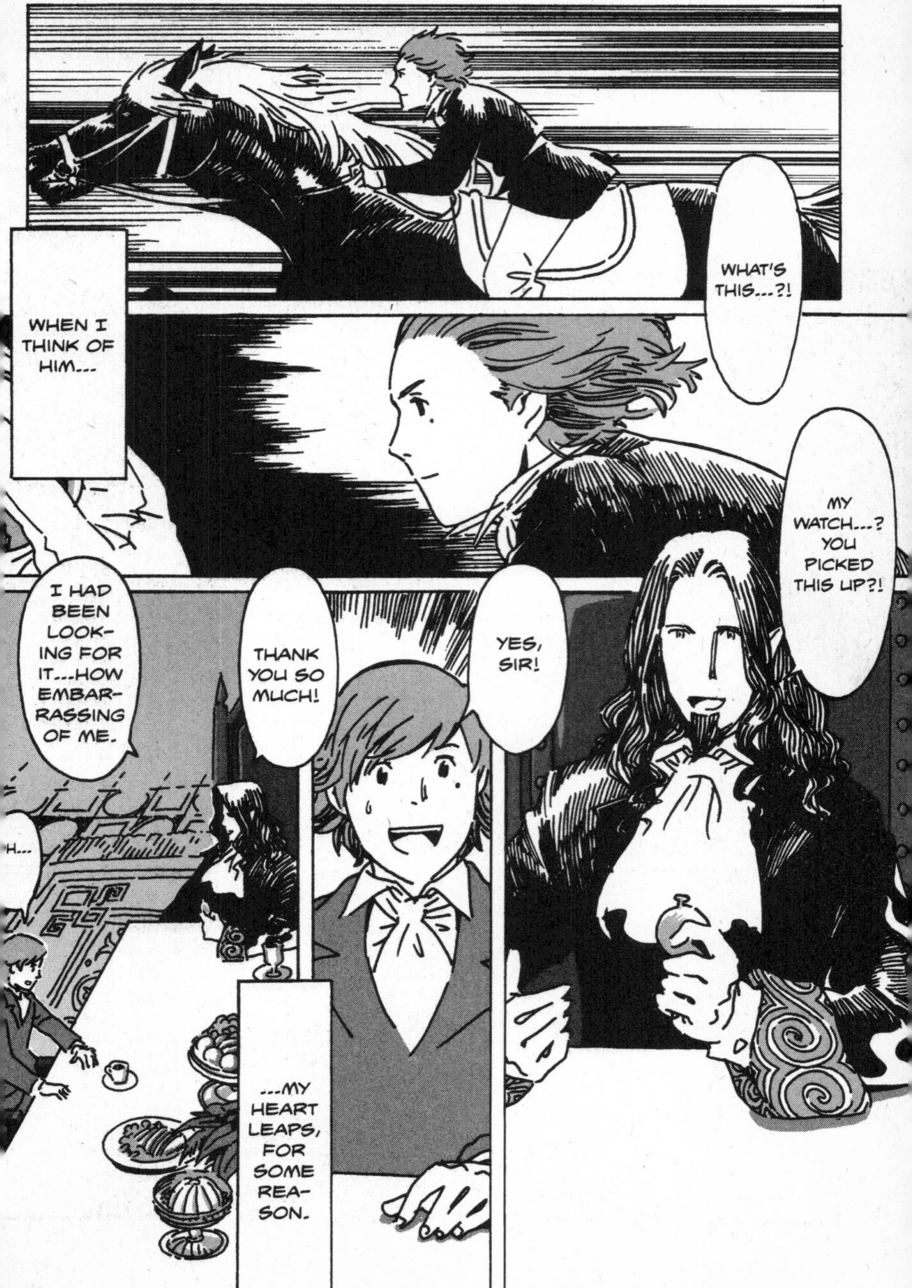
WHAT'S THIS...?!
WHEN I THINK OF HIM...
MY WATCH...? YOU PICKED THIS UP?!
YES, SIR!
THANK YOU SO MUCH!
I HAD BEEN LOOKING FOR IT...HOW EMBARRASSING OF ME.
...MY HEART LEAPS, FOR SOME REASON.

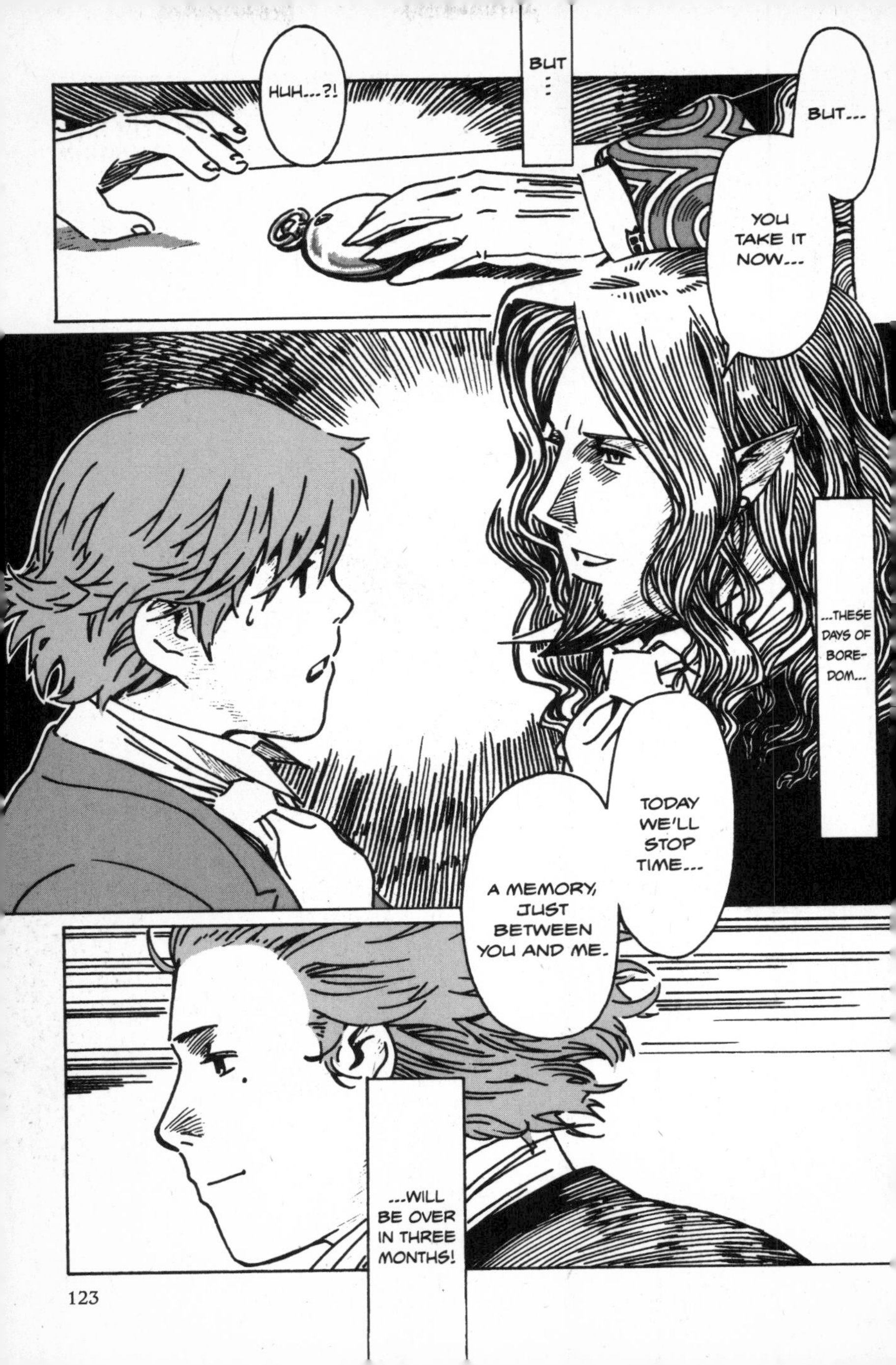
BUT...
YOU TAKE IT NOW...
BUT...
HUH...?!
...THESE DAYS OF BOREDOM...
TODAY WE'LL STOP TIME...
A MEMORY, JUST BETWEEN YOU AND ME.
...WILL BE OVER IN THREE MONTHS!

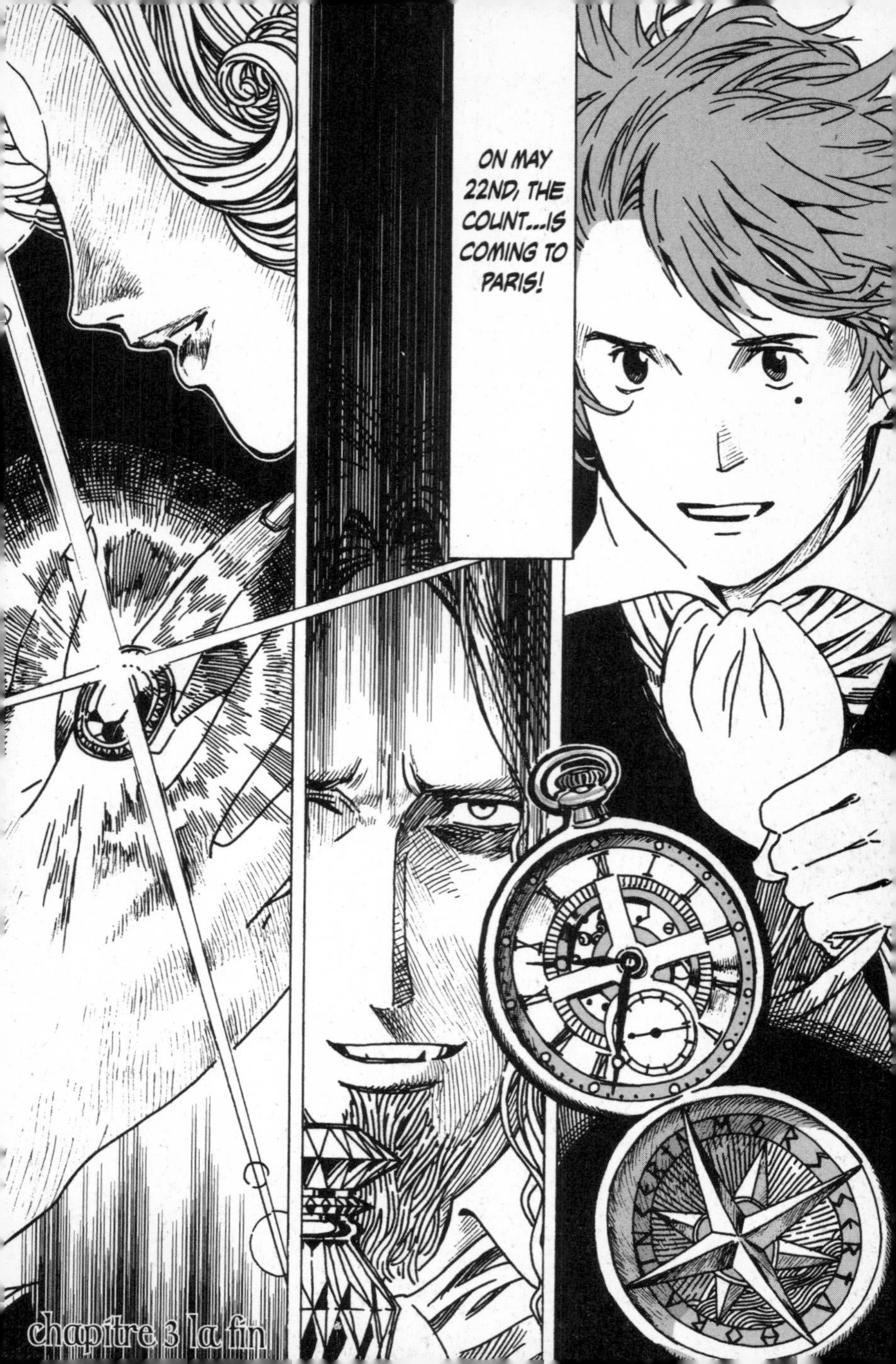
ON MAY 22ND, THE COUNT...IS COMING TO PARIS!
chapitre 3 la fin

Chapitre 4: Château d'If

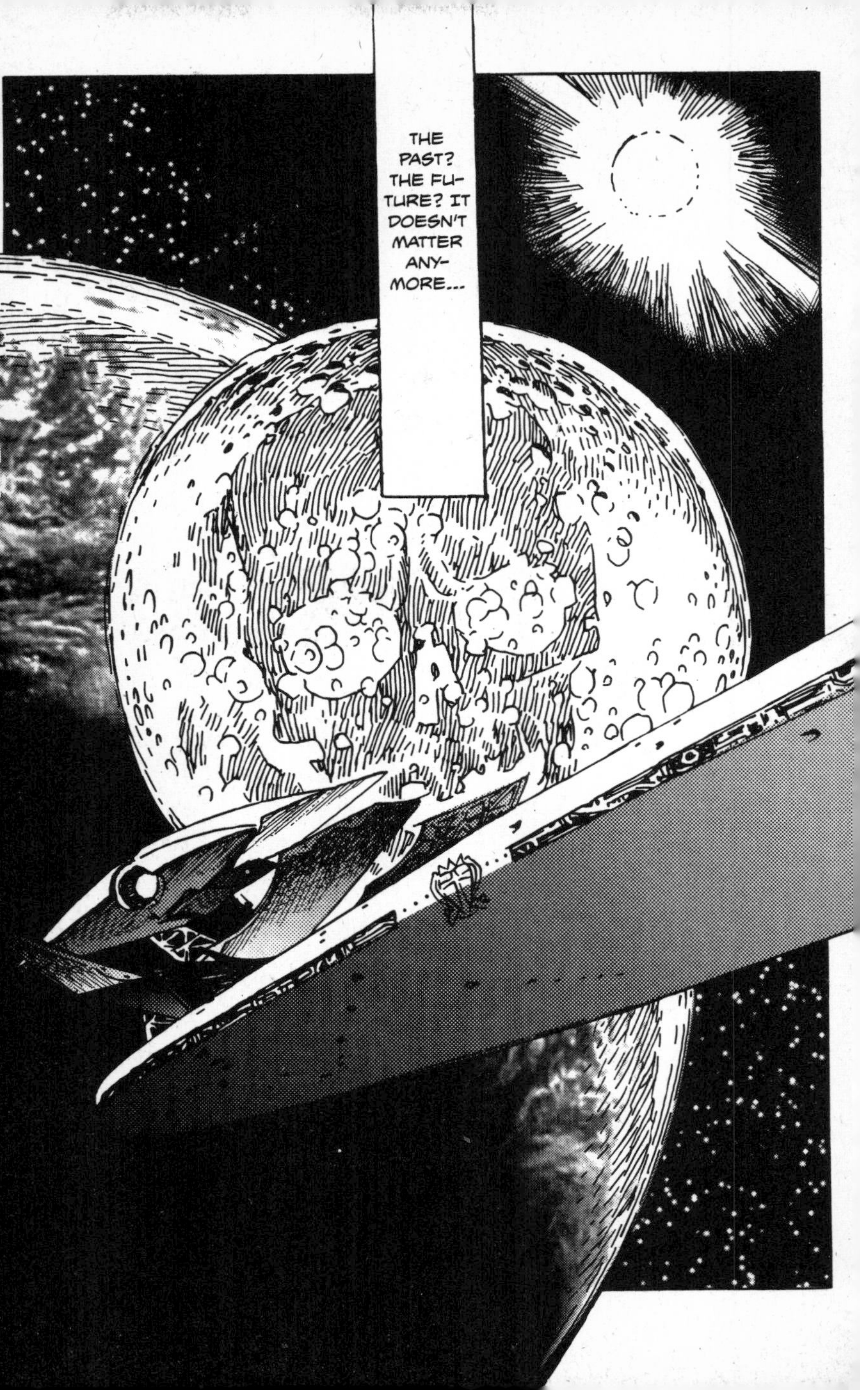
THE PAST? THE FU-TURE? IT DOESN'T MATTER ANY-MORE...

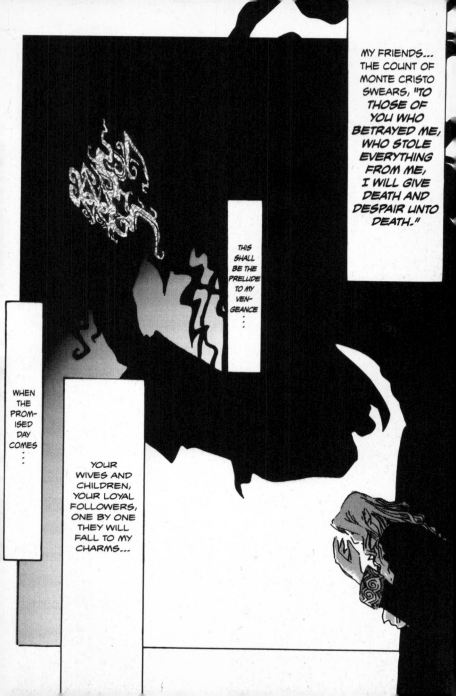

MY FRIENDS... THE COUNT OF MONTE CRISTO SWEARS, *"TO THOSE OF YOU WHO BETRAYED ME, WHO STOLE EVERYTHING FROM ME, I WILL GIVE DEATH AND DESPAIR UNTO DEATH."*

THIS SHALL BE THE PRELUDE TO MY VENGEANCE :

WHEN THE PROMISED DAY COMES :

YOUR WIVES AND CHILDREN, YOUR LOYAL FOLLOWERS, ONE BY ONE THEY WILL FALL TO MY CHARMS...

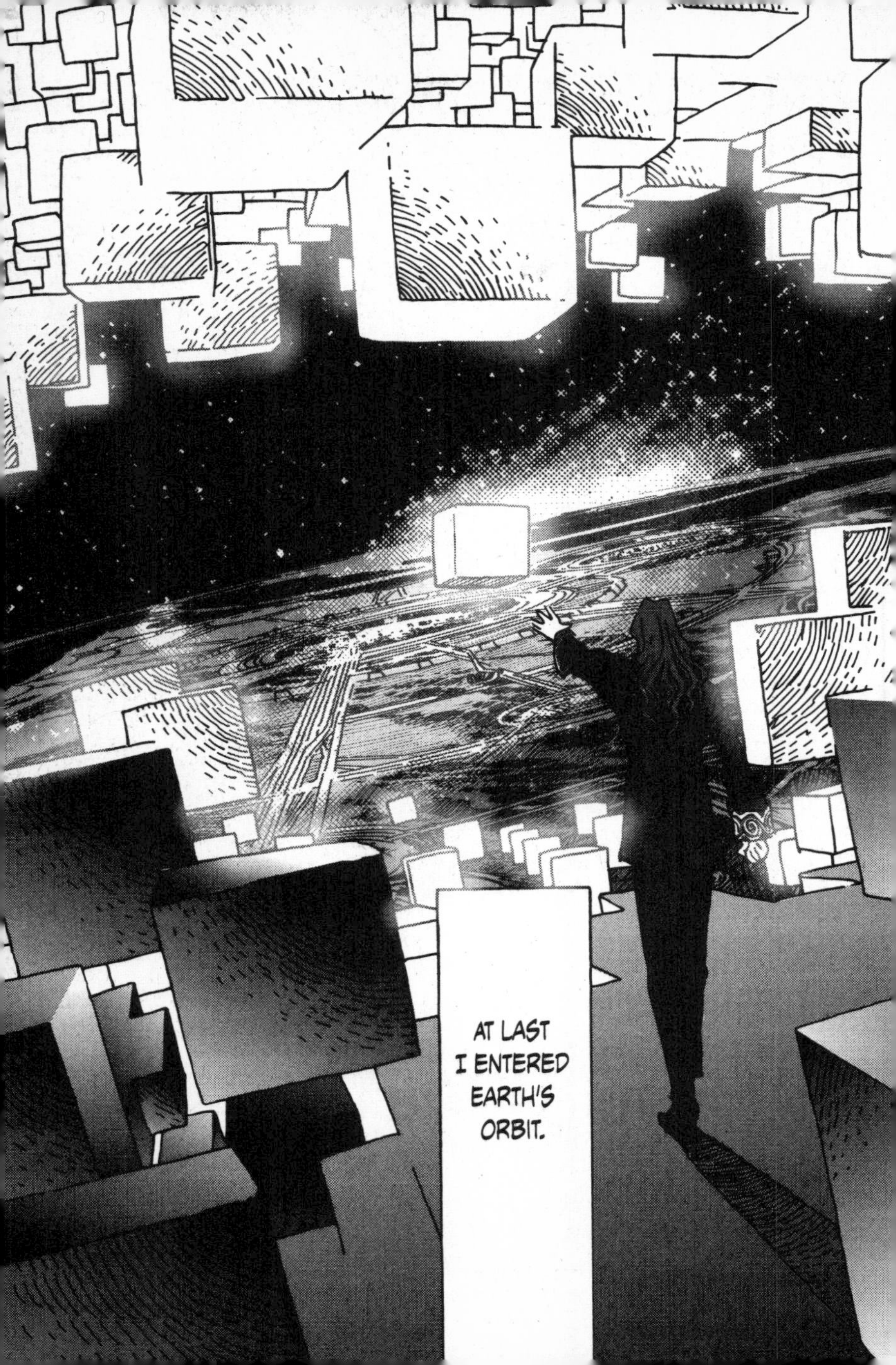
AT LAST
I ENTERED
EARTH'S
ORBIT.

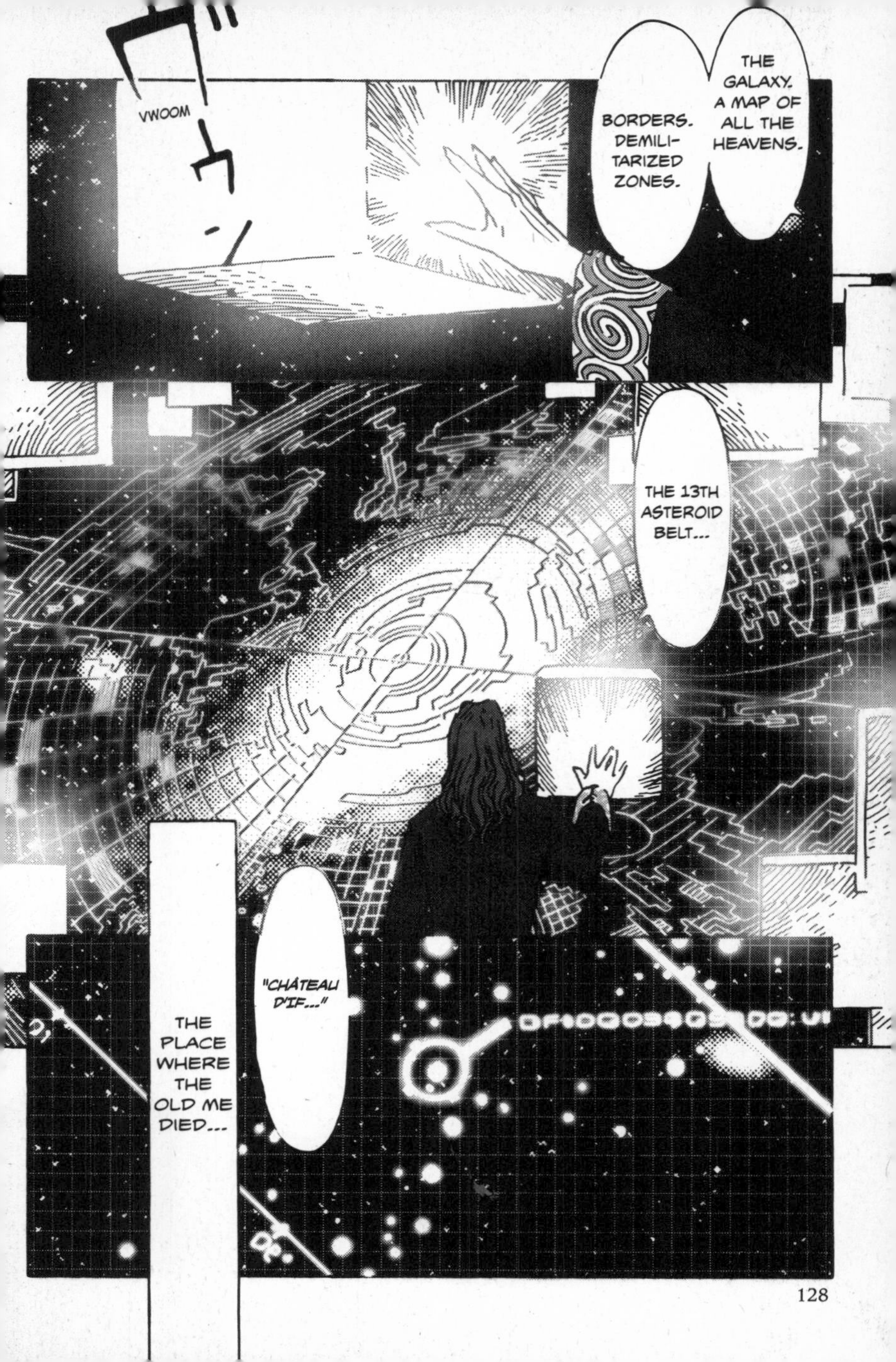
THE GALAXY. A MAP OF ALL THE HEAVENS.
BORDERS. DEMILI-TARIZED ZONES.
VWOOM
THE 13TH ASTEROID BELT...
"CHÂTEAU D'IF..."
THE PLACE WHERE THE OLD ME DIED...

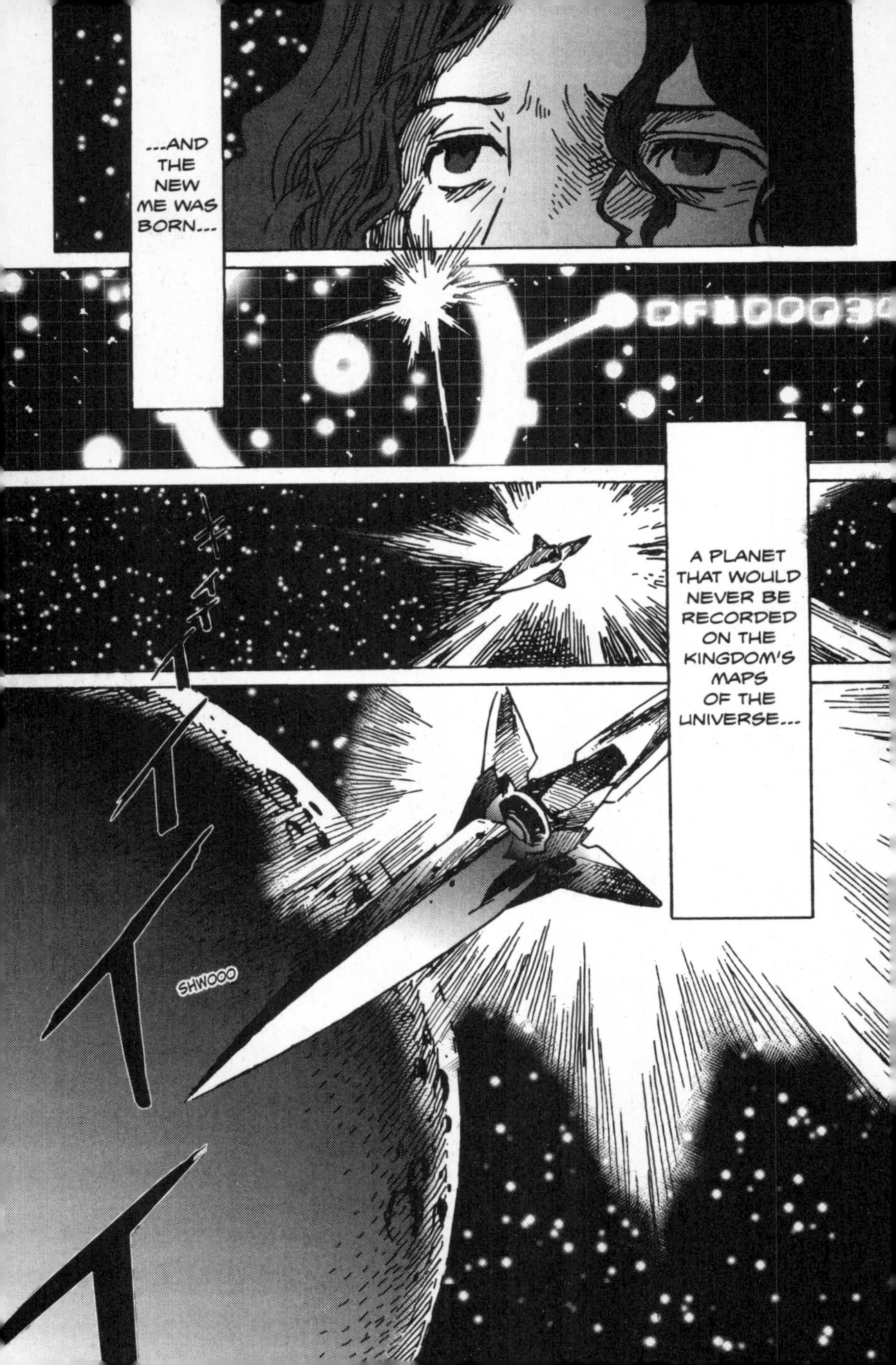
...AND THE NEW ME WAS BORN...
A PLANET THAT WOULD NEVER BE RECORDED ON THE KINGDOM'S MAPS OF THE UNIVERSE...
SHWOOO

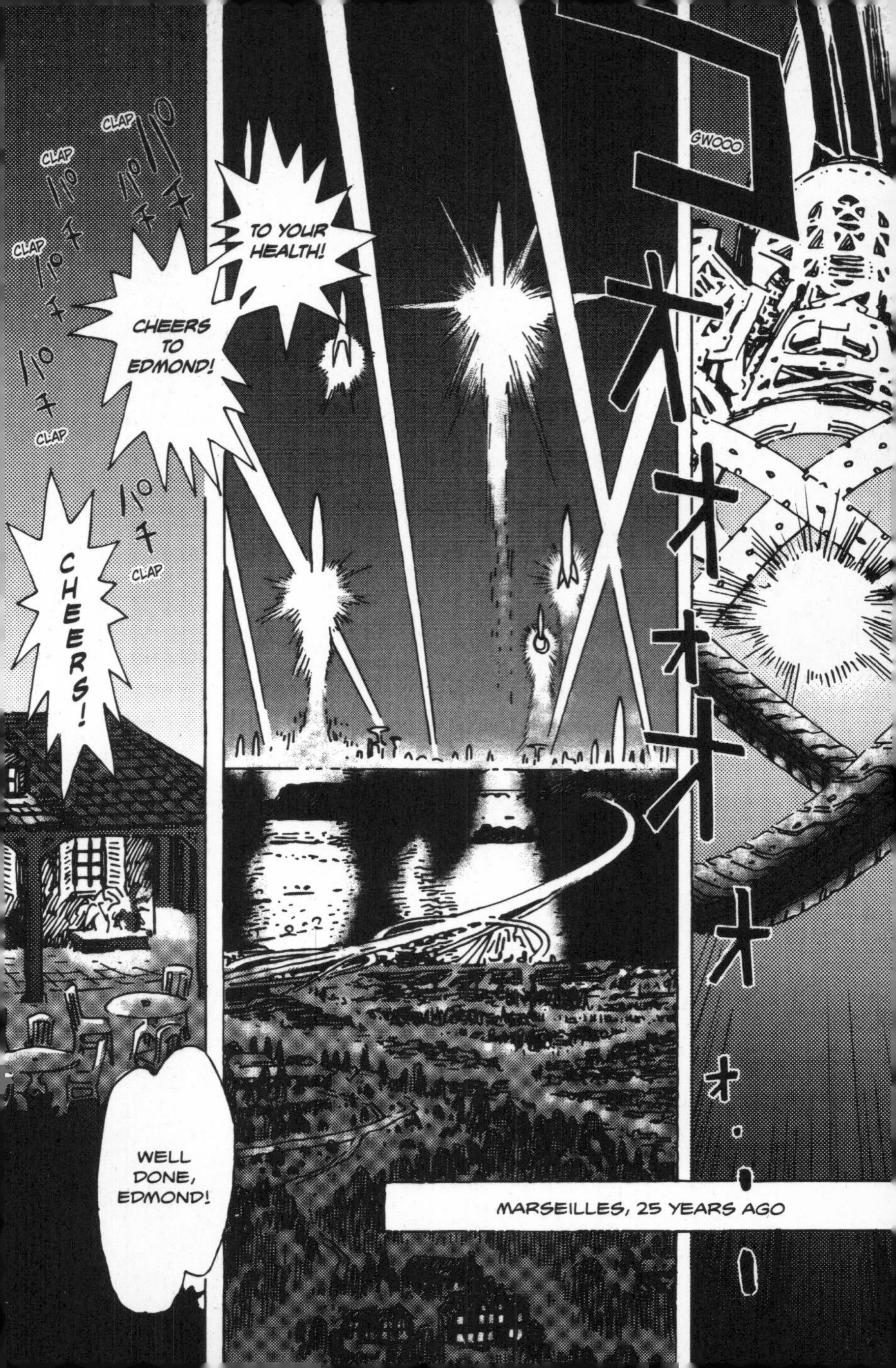
GWOOO
TO YOUR HEALTH!
MARSEILLES, 25 YEARS AGO
CLAP
CLAP
CLAP
CHEERS TO EDMOND!
CLAP
CLAP
CHEERS!
WELL DONE, EDMOND!

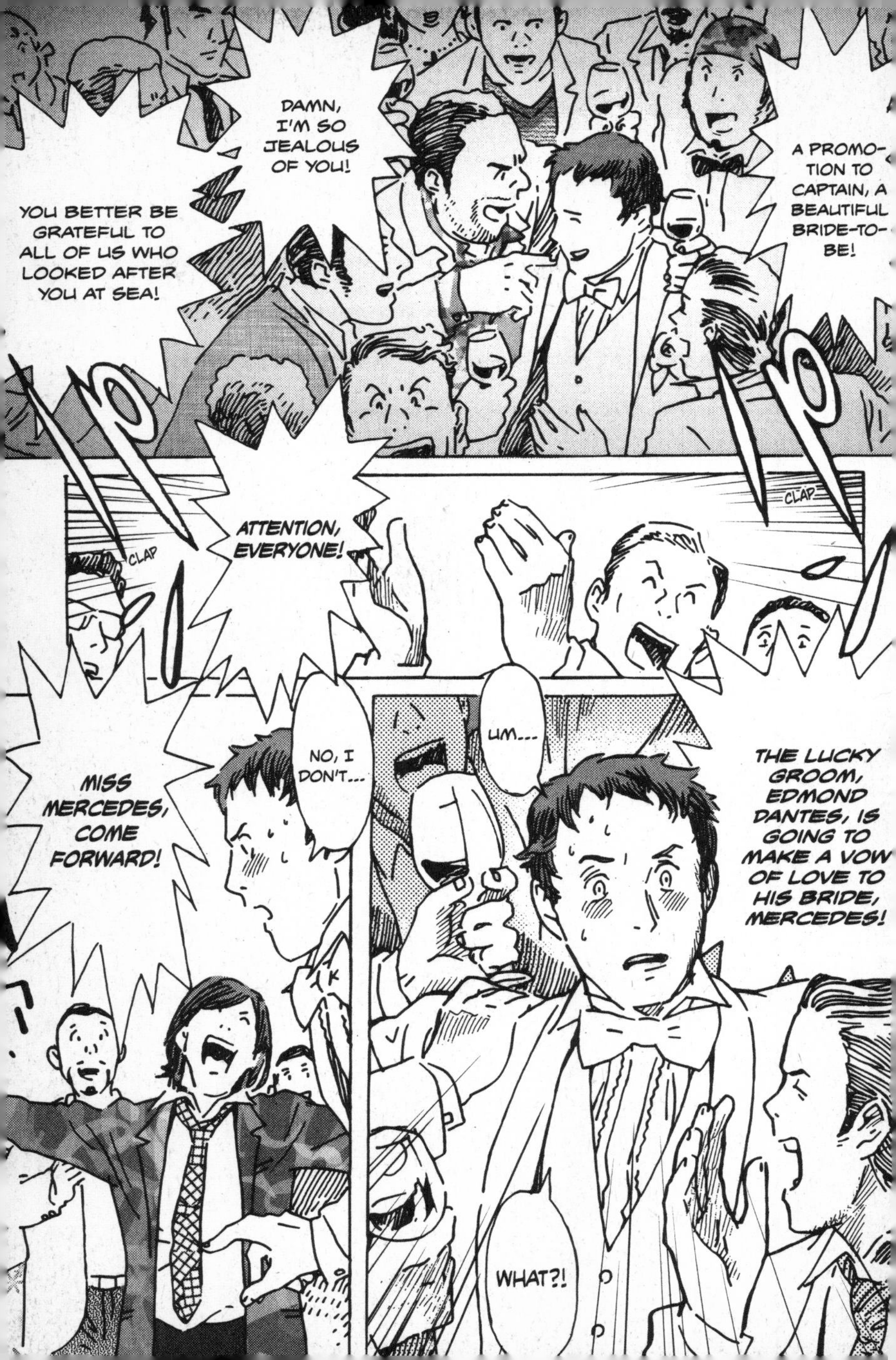
A PROMOTION TO CAPTAIN, A BEAUTIFUL BRIDE-TO-BE!
DAMN, I'M SO JEALOUS OF YOU!
YOU BETTER BE GRATEFUL TO ALL OF US WHO LOOKED AFTER YOU AT SEA!
CLAP
ATTENTION, EVERYONE!
CLAP
THE LUCKY GROOM, EDMOND DANTES, IS GOING TO MAKE A VOW OF LOVE TO HIS BRIDE, MERCEDES!
UM...
WHAT?!
NO, I DON'T...
MISS MERCEDES, COME FORWARD!

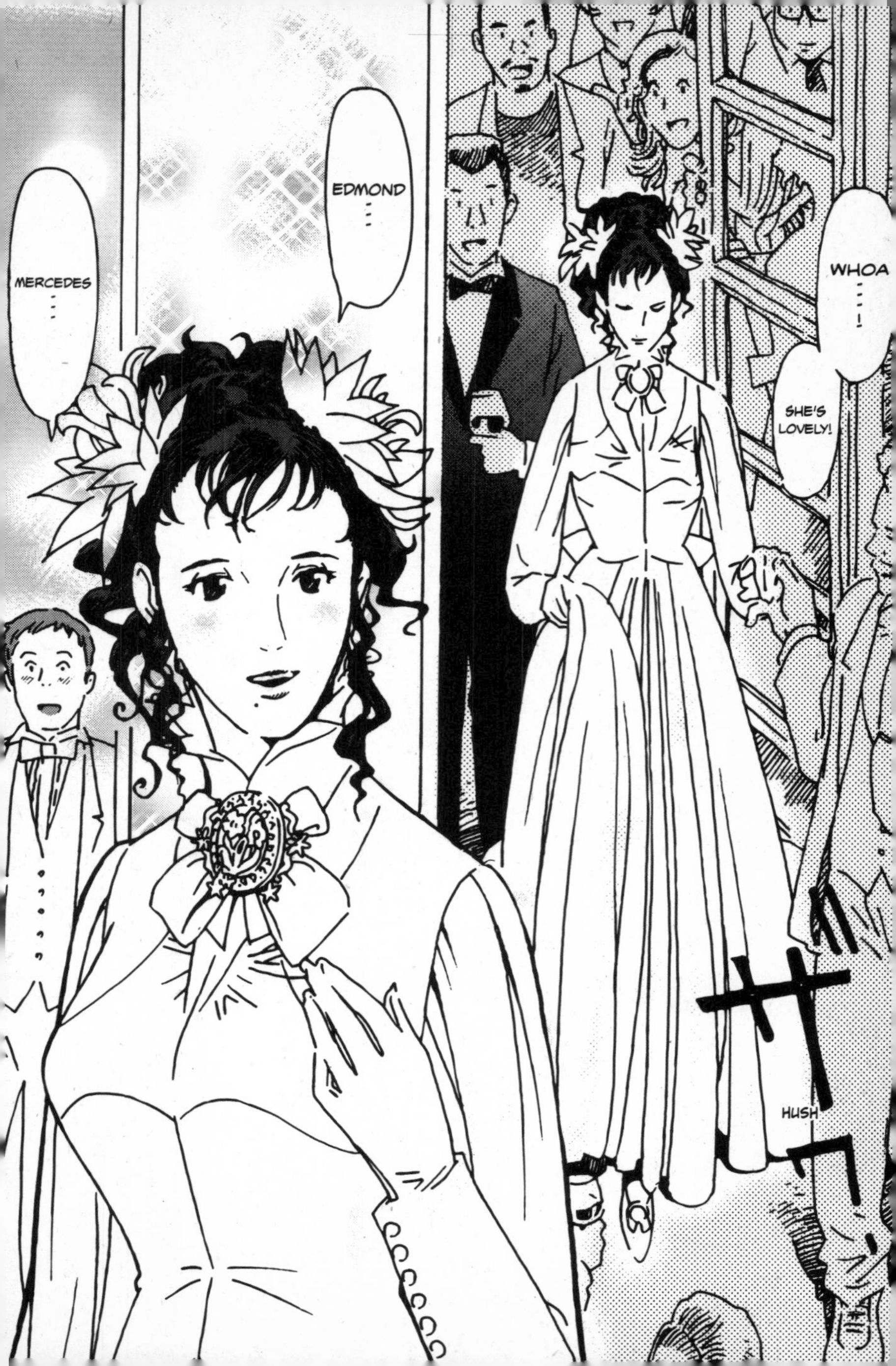
WHOA...!
SHE'S LOVELY!
HUSH
EDMOND...
MERCEDES...

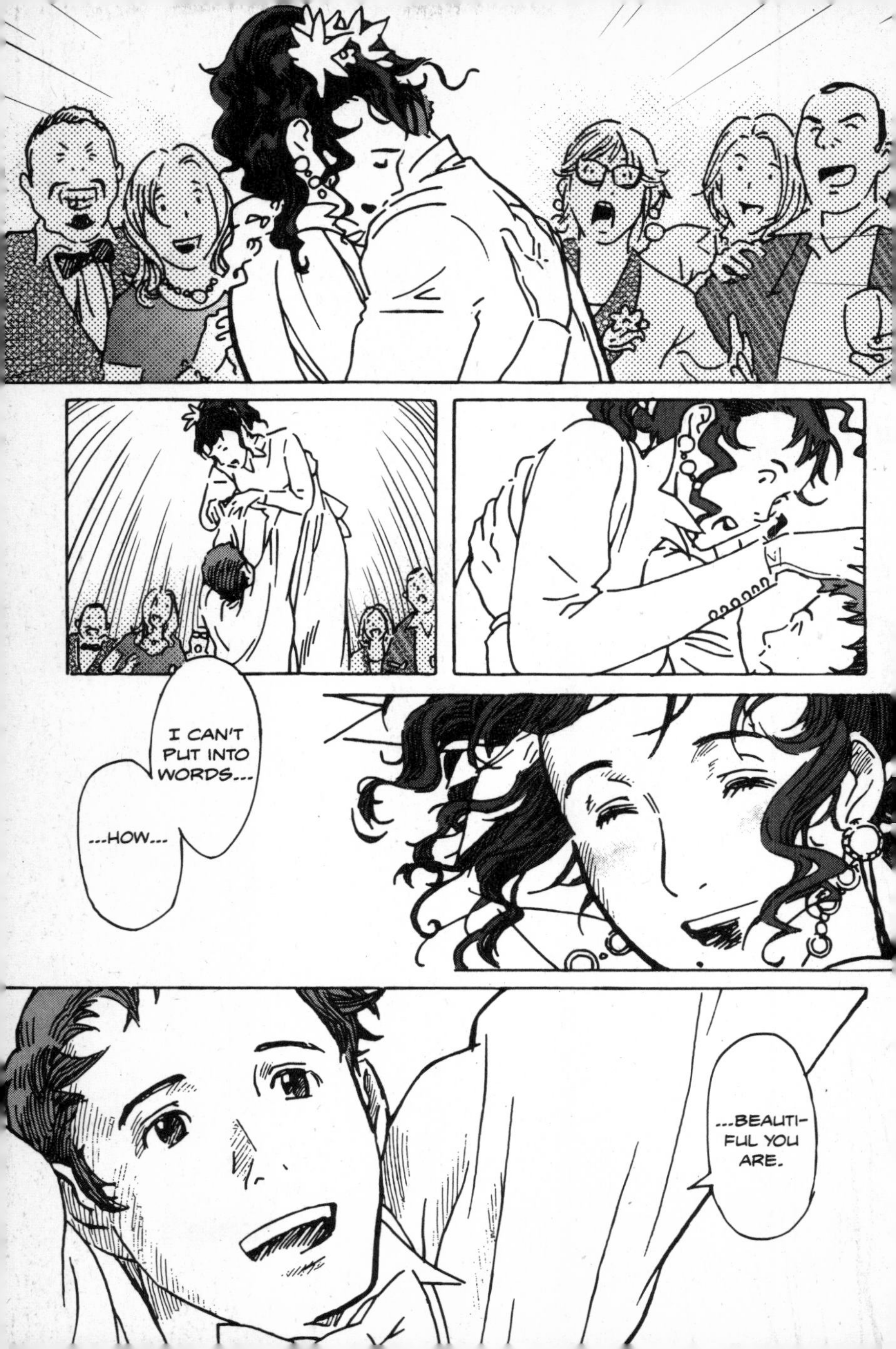
I CAN'T PUT INTO WORDS...
...HOW...
...BEAUTI-FUL YOU ARE.

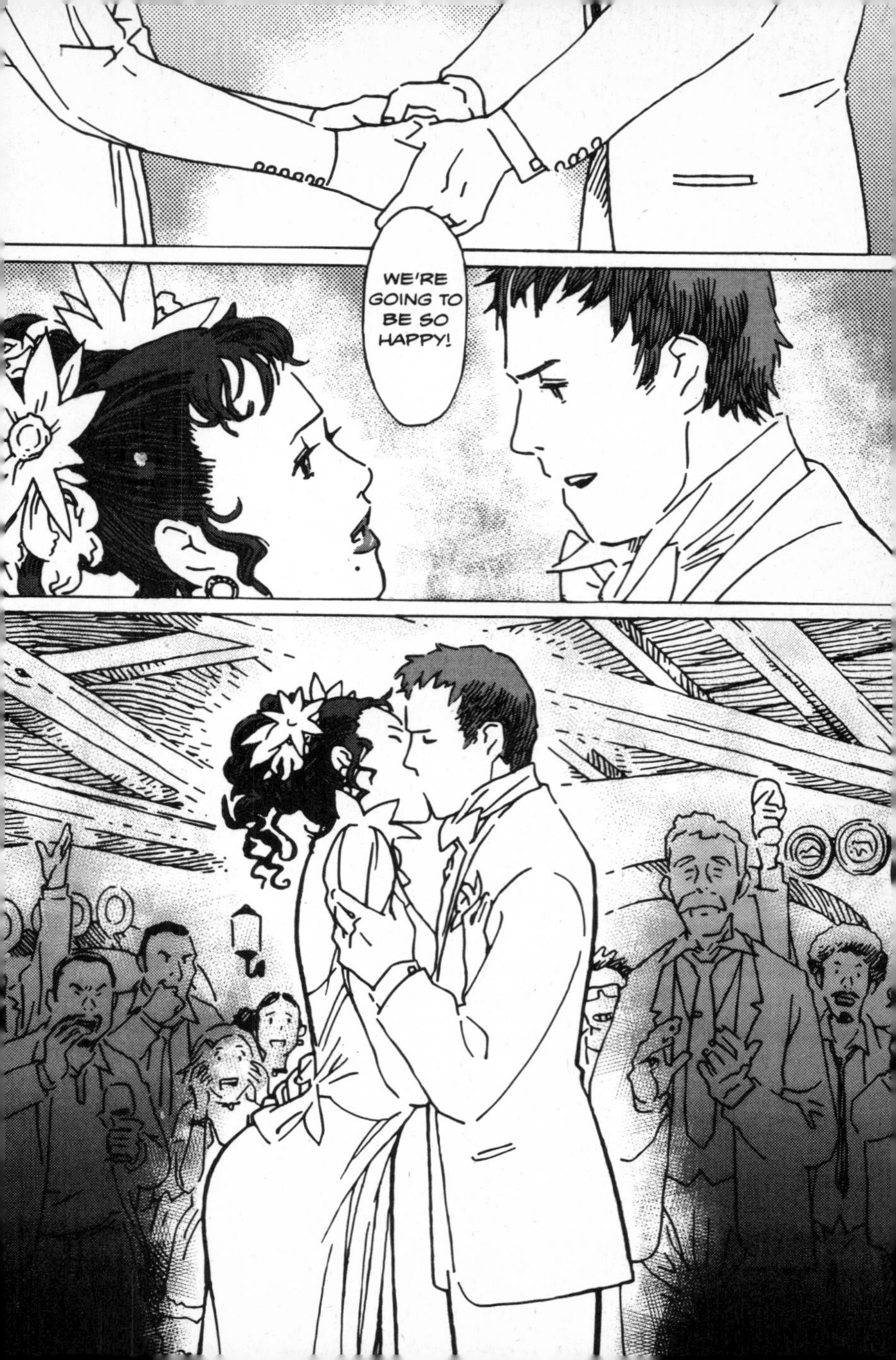
WE'RE GOING TO BE SO HAPPY!

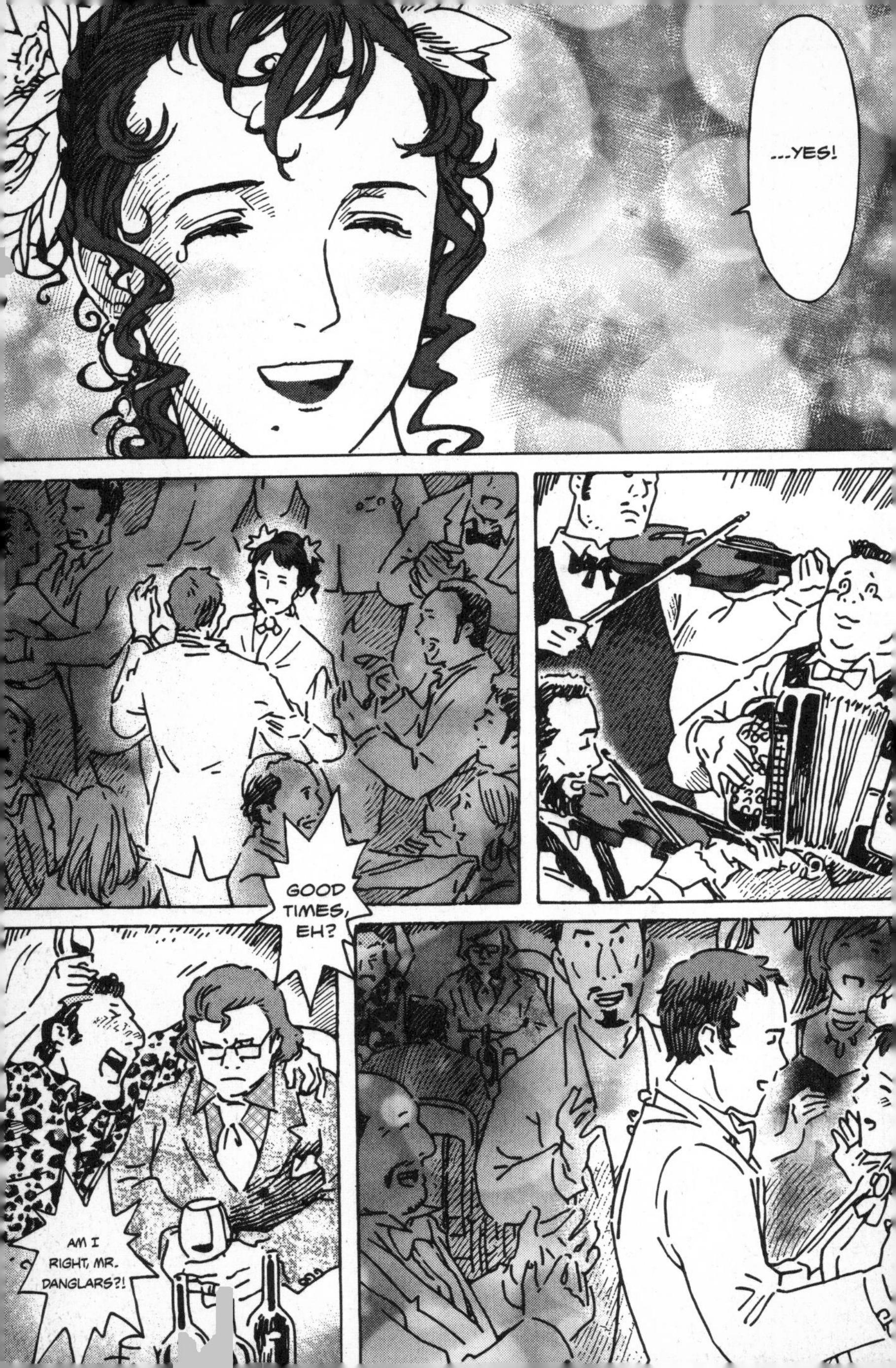
...YES!
GOOD TIMES, EH?
AM I RIGHT, MR. DANGLARS?!

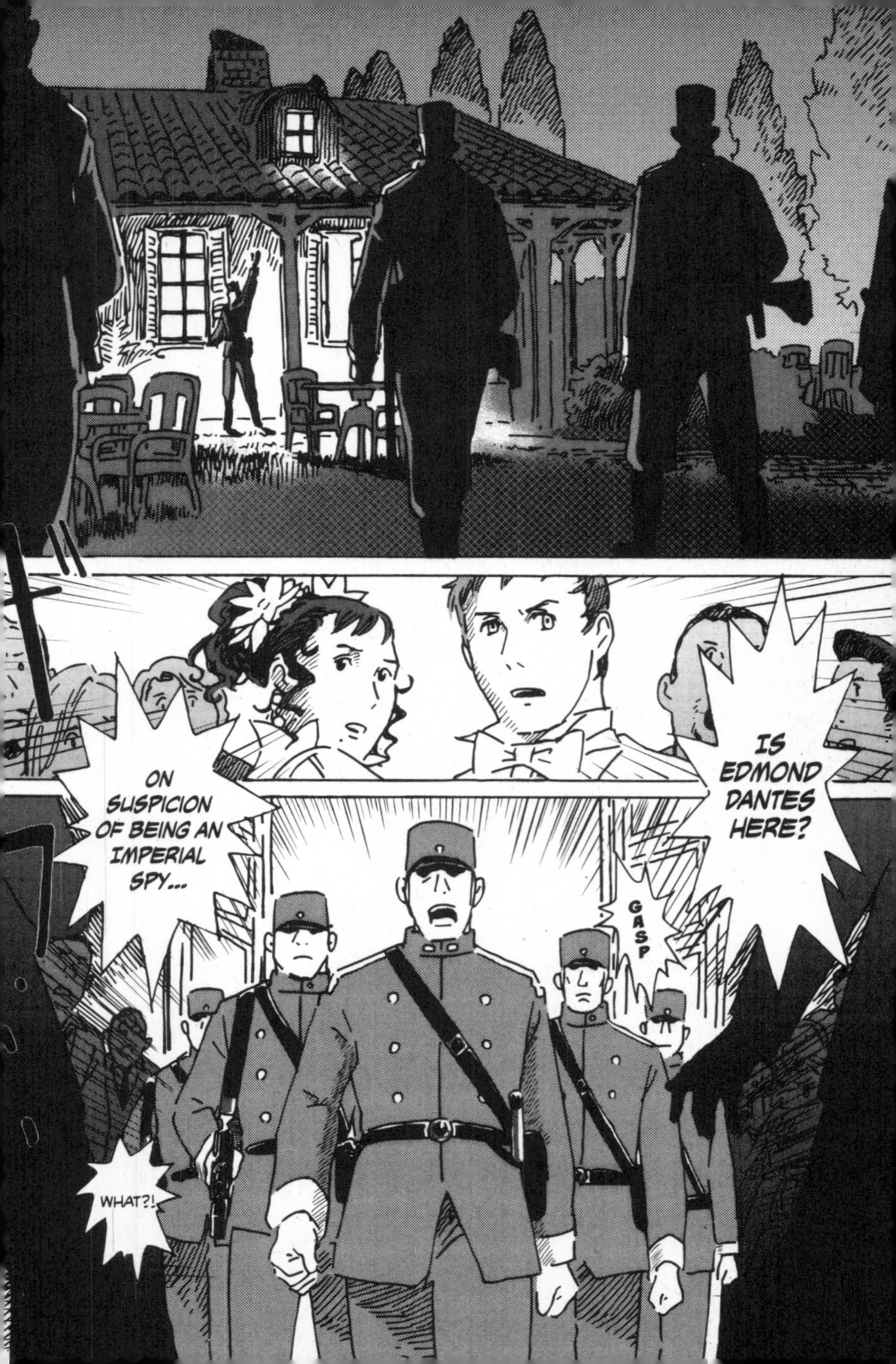
IS EDMOND DANTES HERE?
GASP
ON SUSPICION OF BEING AN IMPERIAL SPY...
WHAT?!

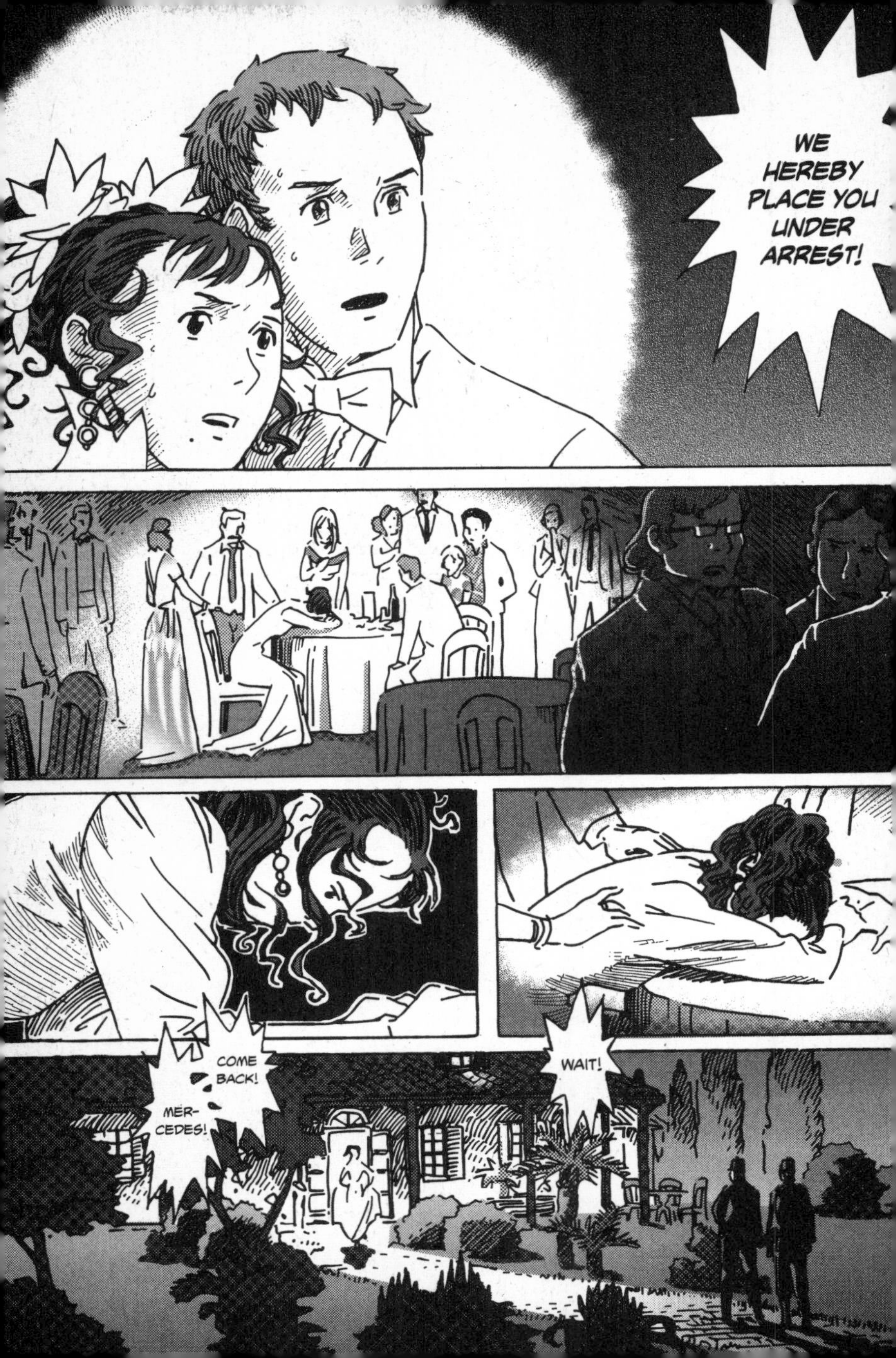
WE HEREBY PLACE YOU UNDER ARREST!
WAIT!
COME BACK!
MER-CEDES!

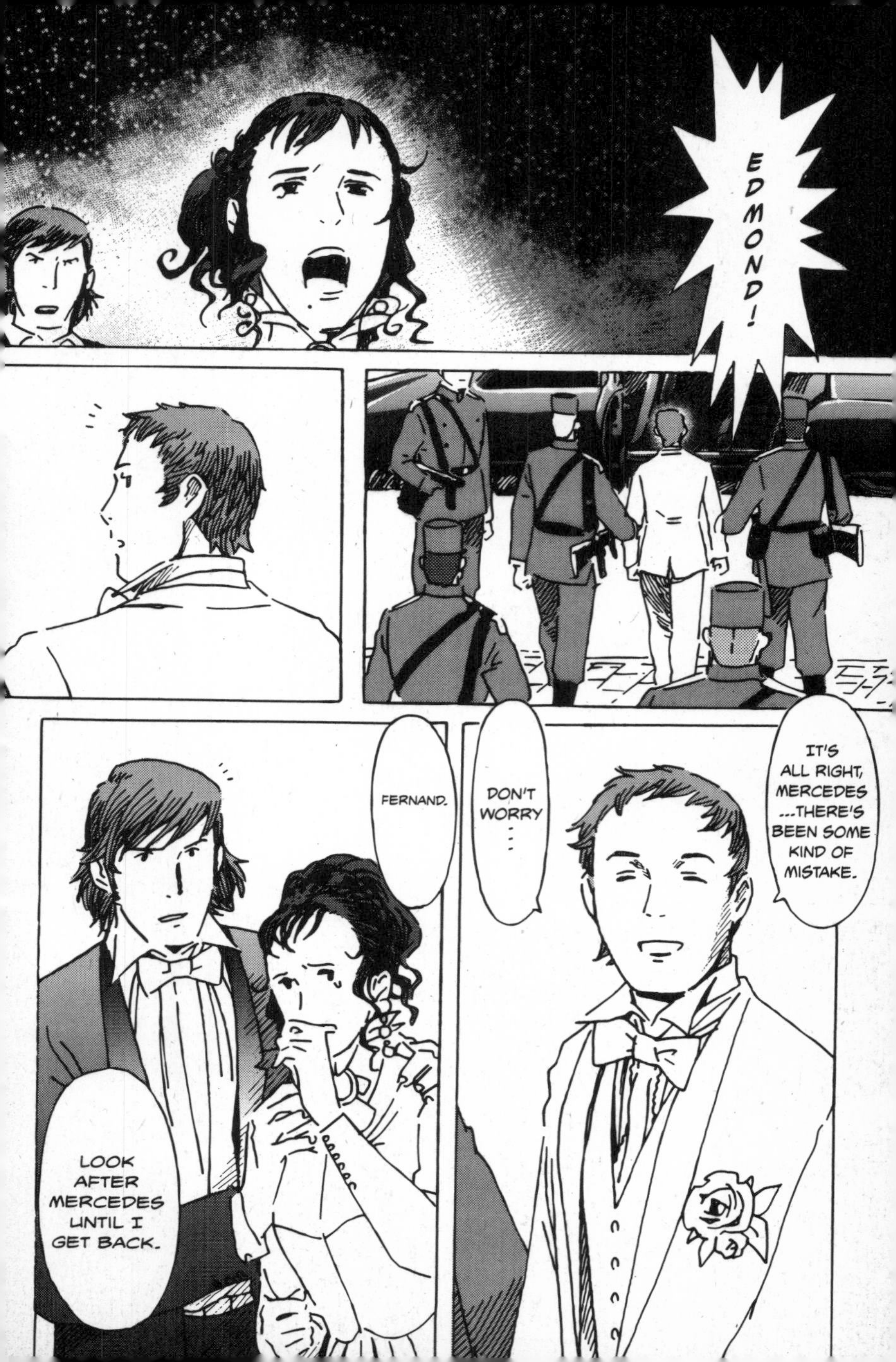
EDMOND!
IT'S ALL RIGHT, MERCEDES ...THERE'S BEEN SOME KIND OF MISTAKE.
DON'T WORRY...
FERNAND.
LOOK AFTER MERCEDES UNTIL I GET BACK.

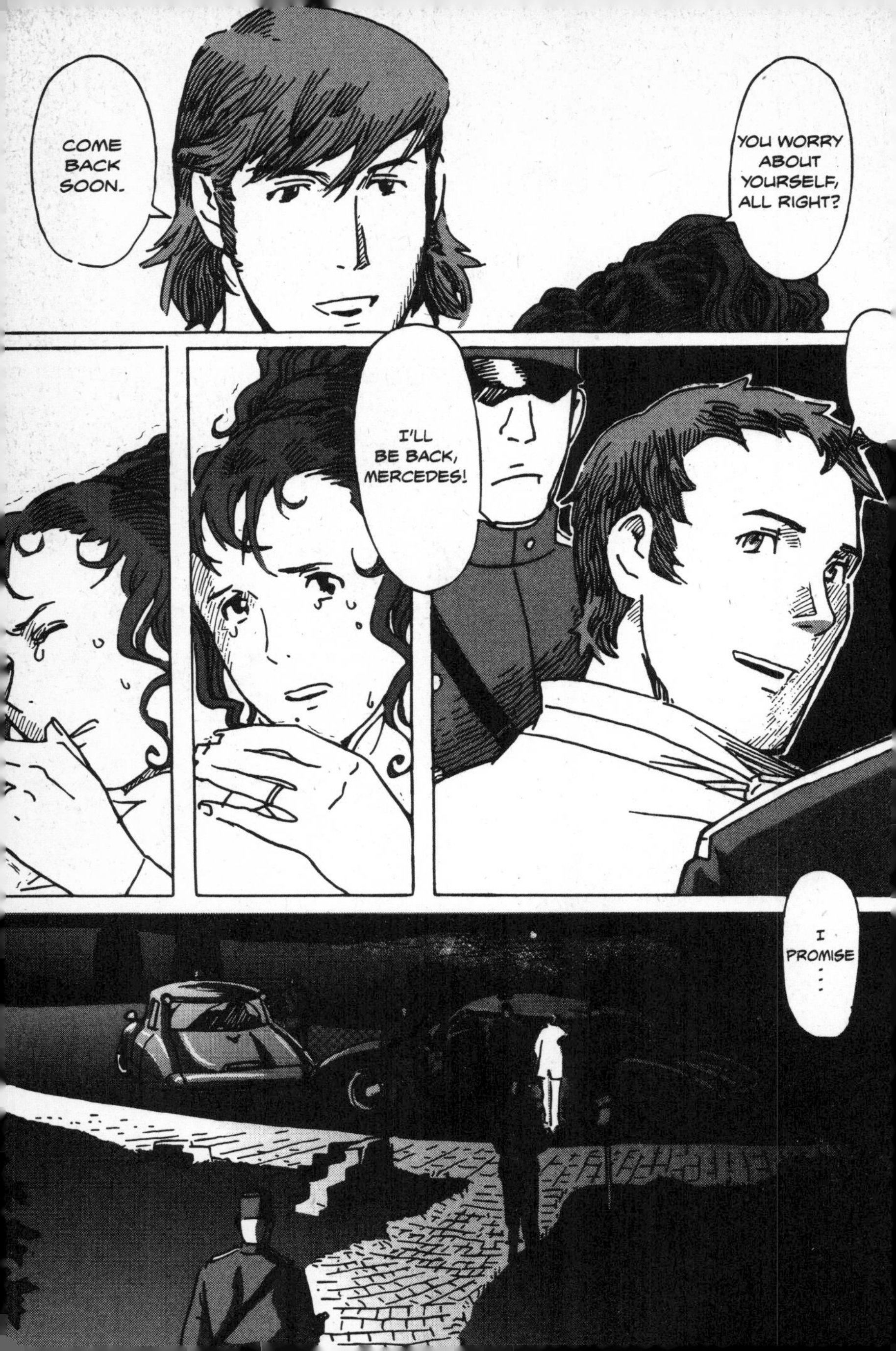
YOU WORRY ABOUT YOURSELF, ALL RIGHT?
COME BACK SOON.
I'LL BE BACK, MERCEDES!
I PROMISE . . .

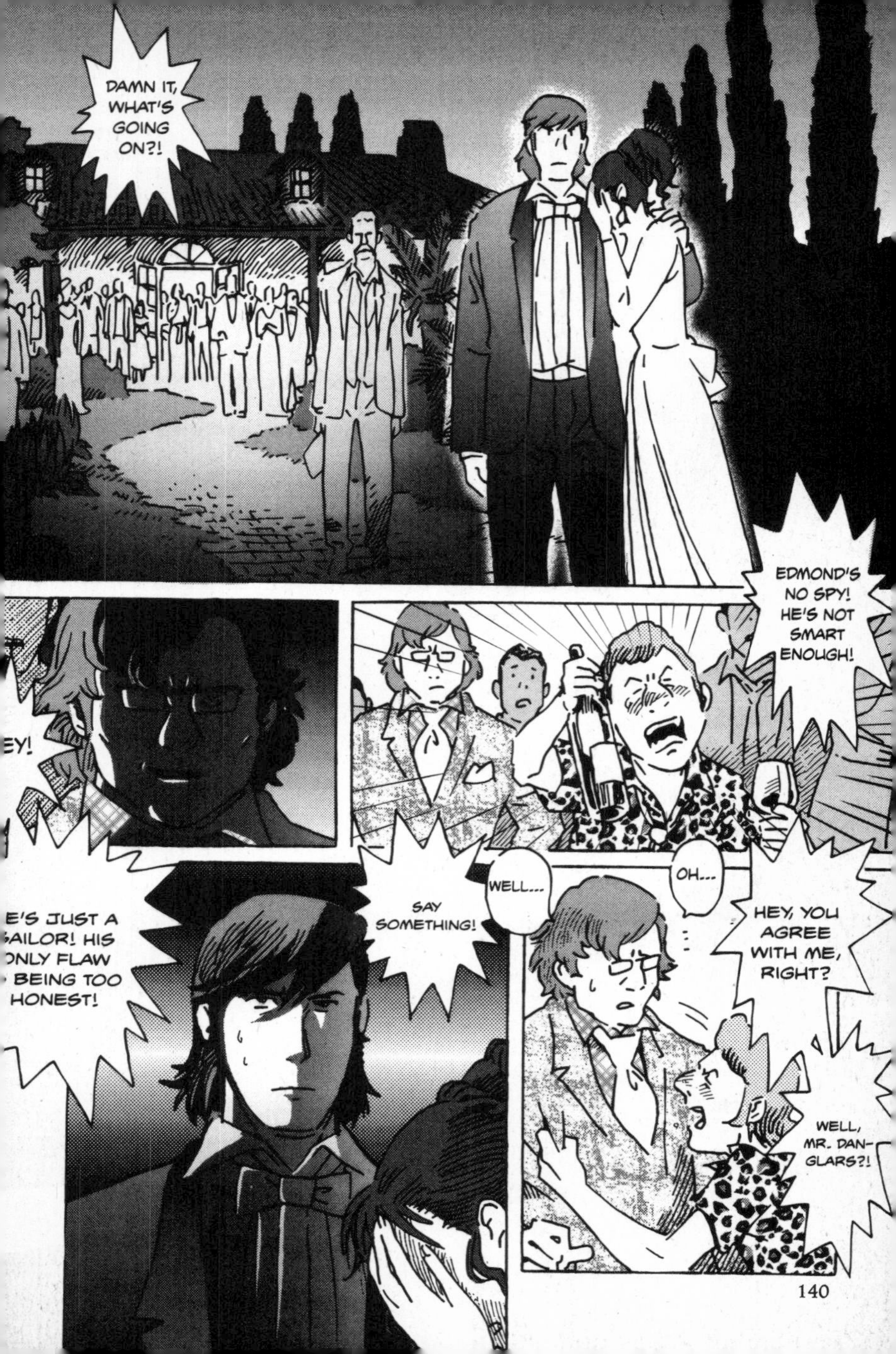
DAMN IT, WHAT'S GOING ON?!
EDMOND'S NO SPY! HE'S NOT SMART ENOUGH!
EY!
HEY, YOU AGREE WITH ME, RIGHT?
OH...
WELL...
WELL, MR. DAN-GLARS?!
SAY SOMETHING!
E'S JUST A AILOR! HIS ONLY FLAW BEING TOO HONEST!

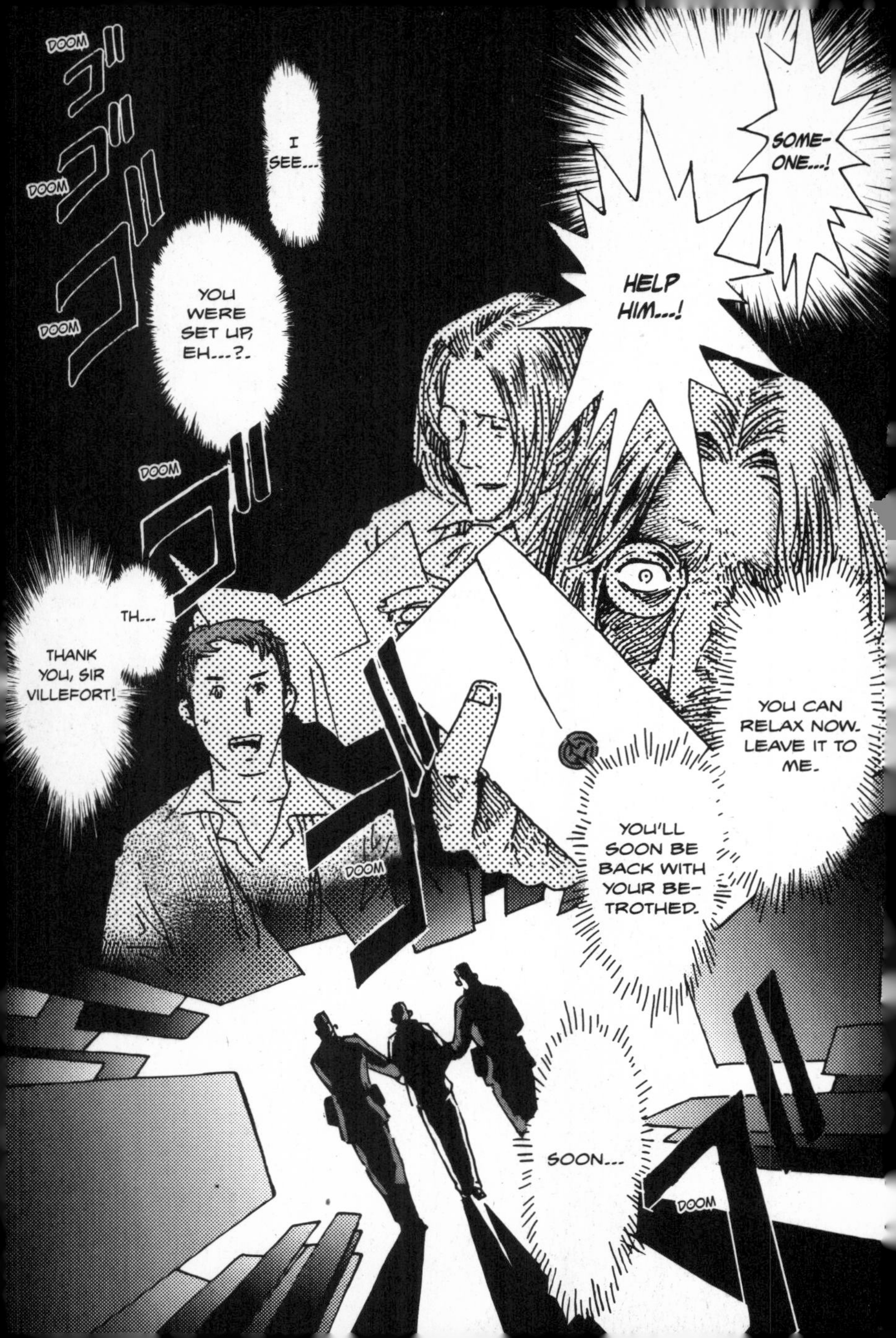
SOME-ONE...!
HELP HIM...!
I SEE...
YOU WERE SET UP, EH...?.
DOOM
DOOM
DOOM
DOOM
YOU CAN RELAX NOW. LEAVE IT TO ME.
YOU'LL SOON BE BACK WITH YOUR BE-TROTHED.
TH...
THANK YOU, SIR VILLEFORT!
DOOM
SOON...
DOOM

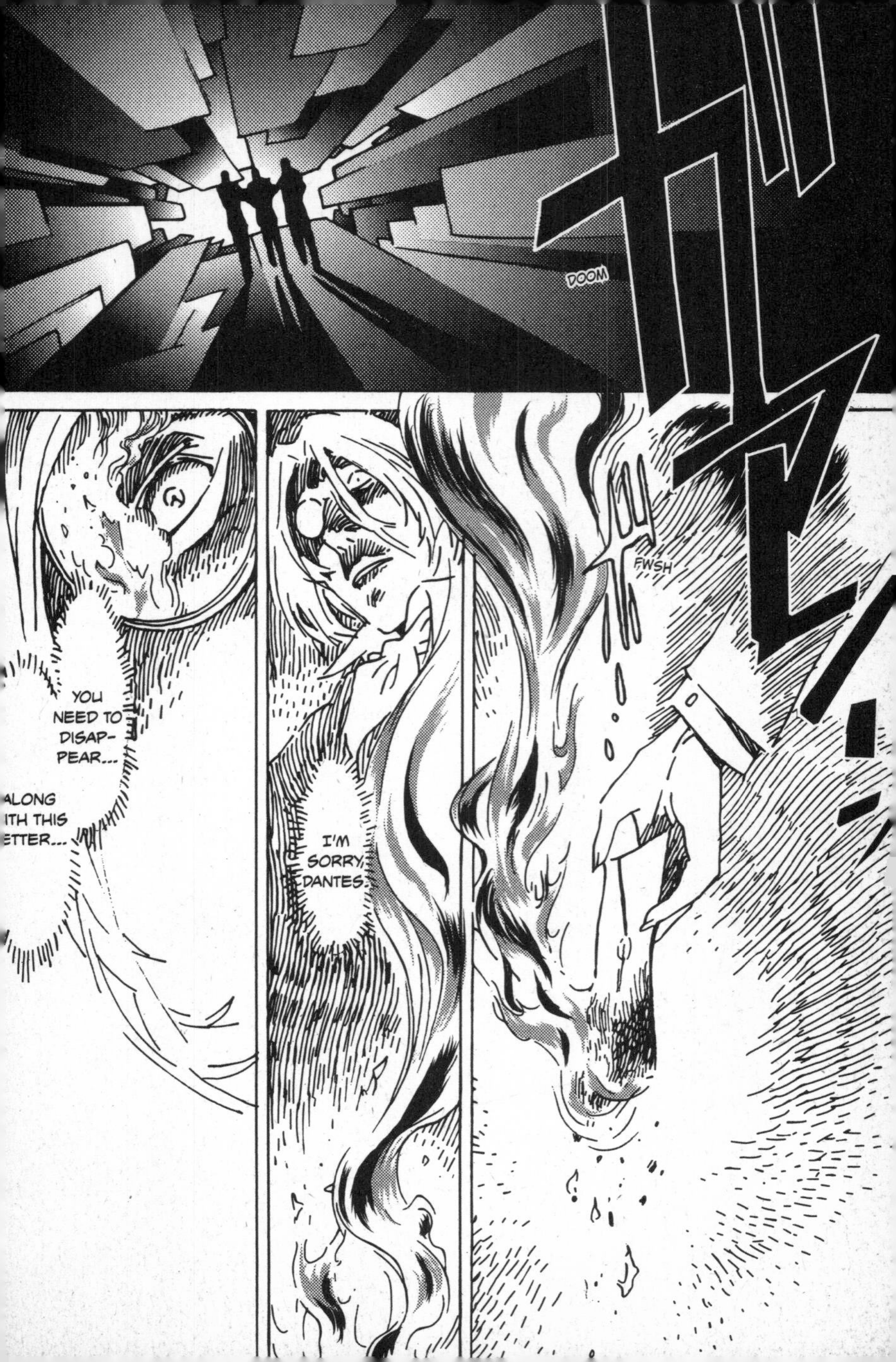
DOOM
FWSH
I'M SORRY, DANTES.
YOU NEED TO DISAP-PEAR...
ALONG ITH THIS ETTER...

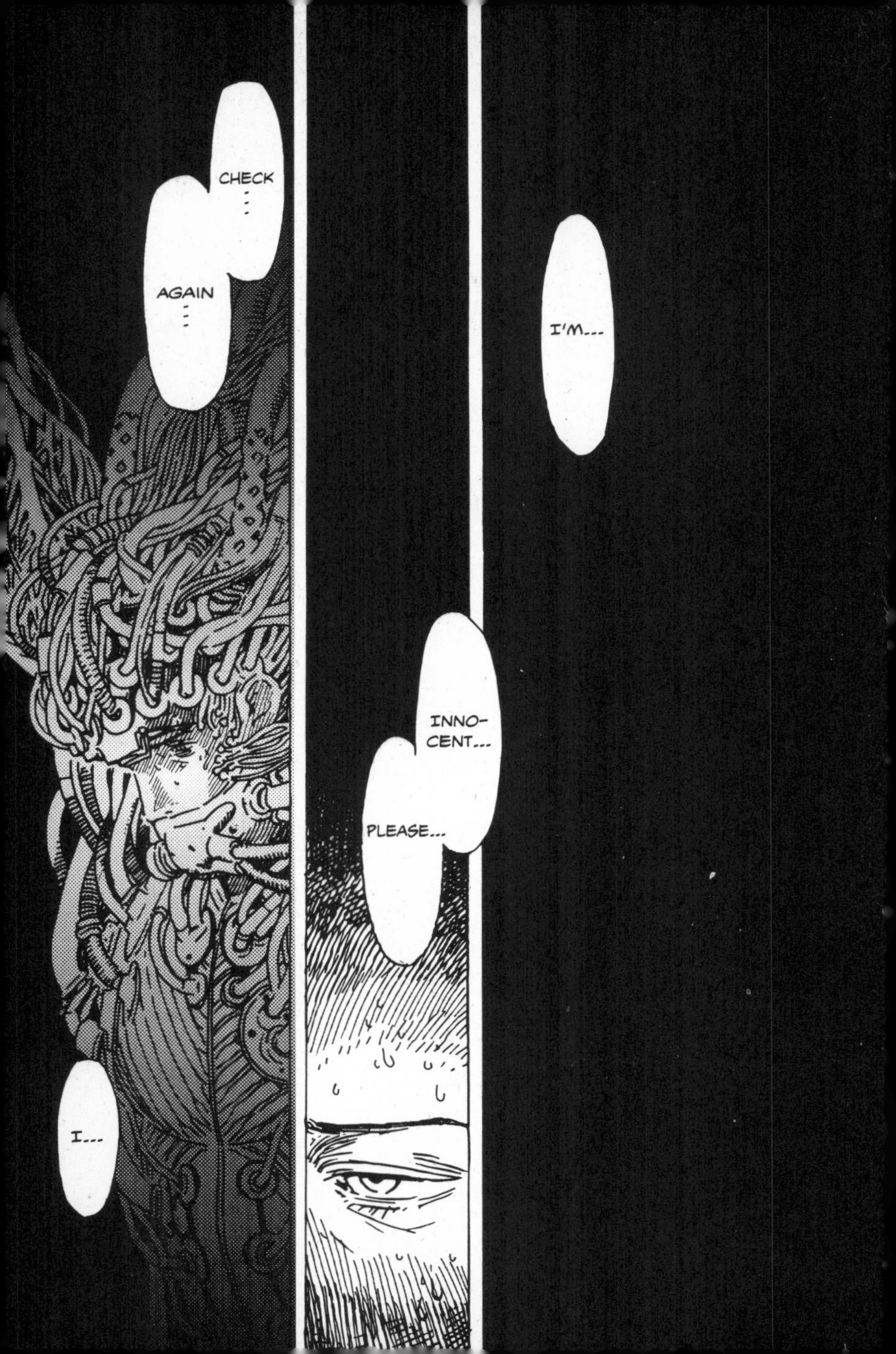
I'M...
INNO-CENT...
PLEASE...
CHECK...
AGAIN...
I...

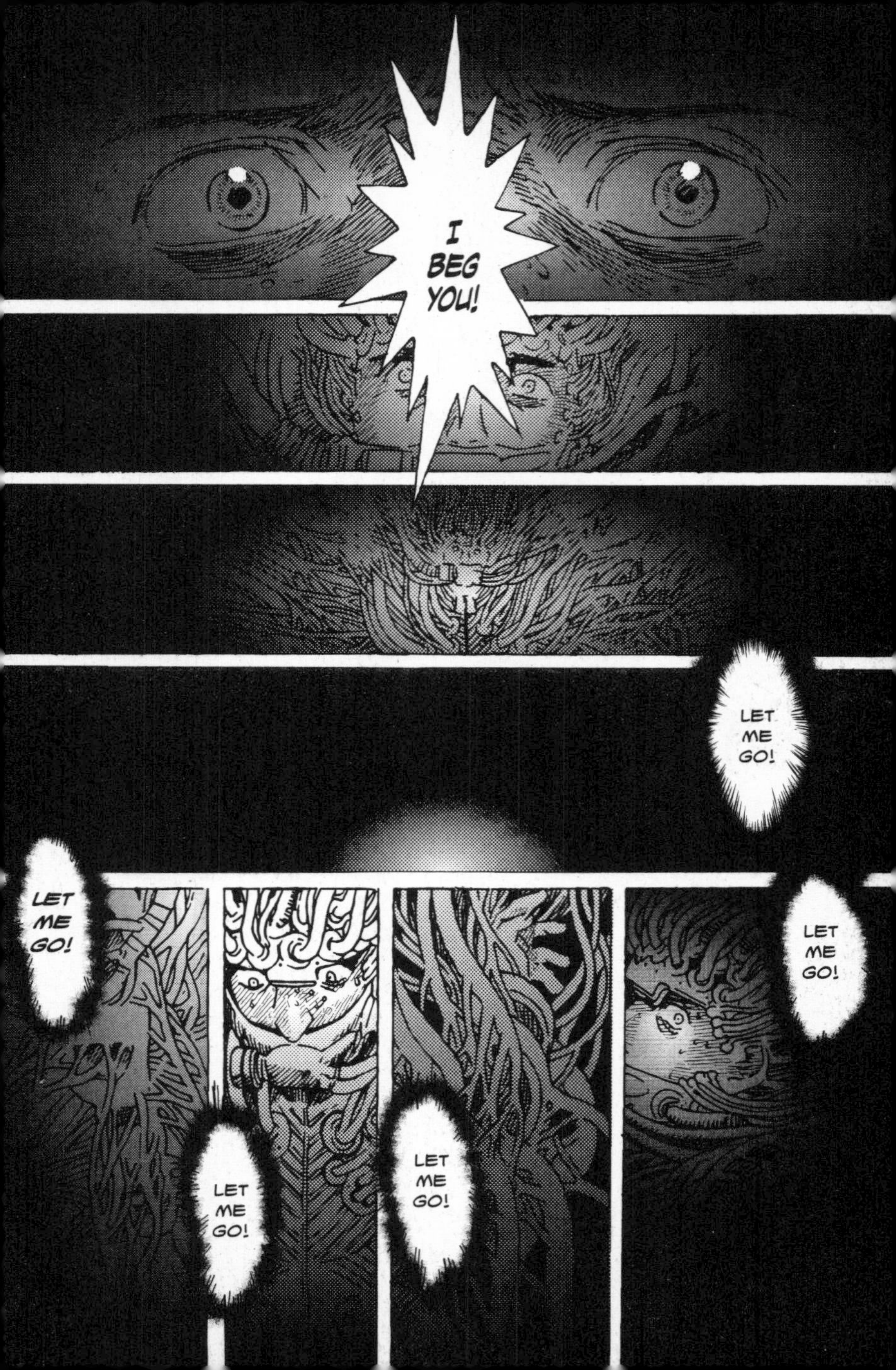
I BEG YOU!
LET ME GO!
LET ME GO!
LET ME GO!
LET ME GO!
LET ME GO!

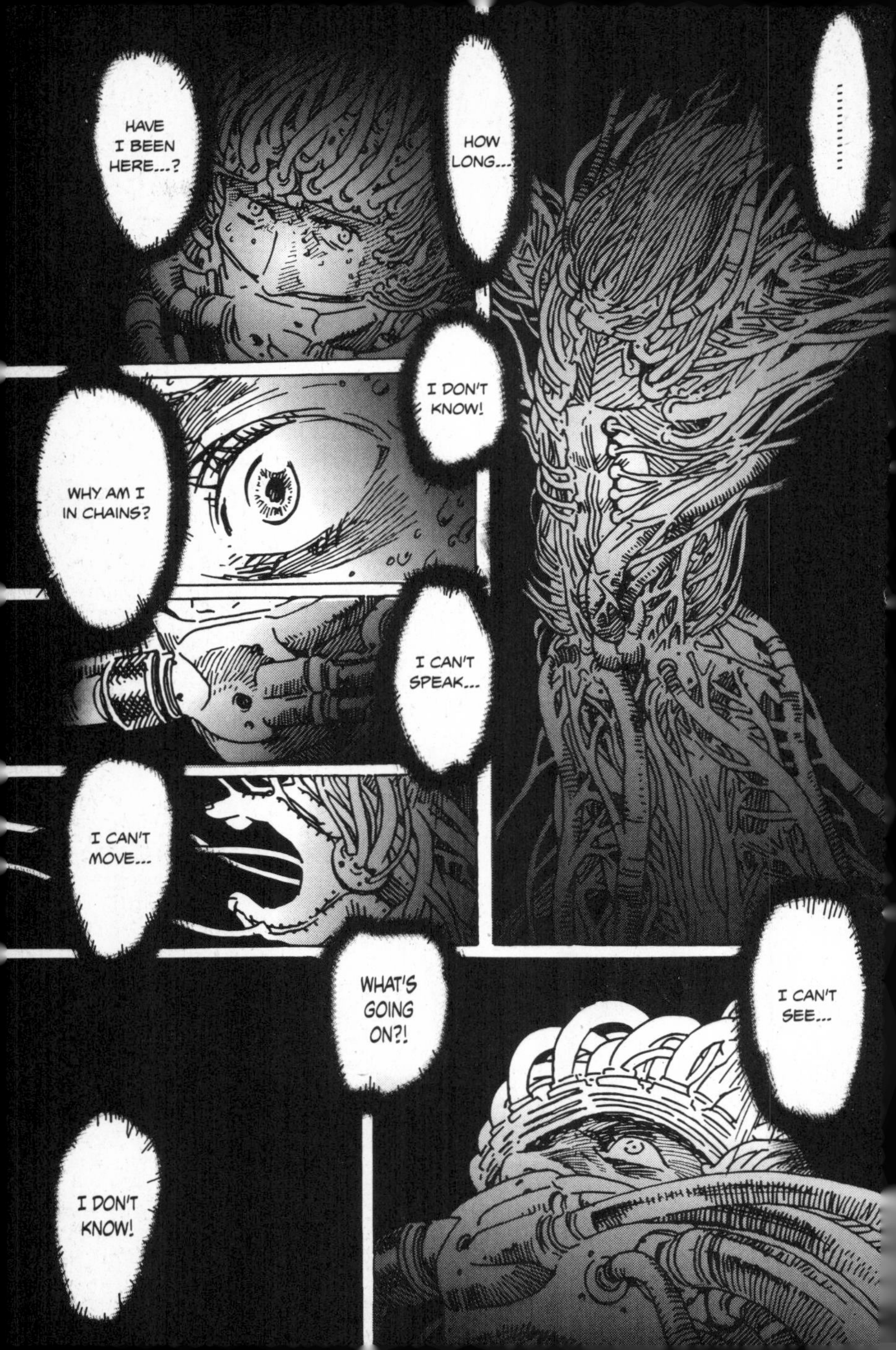
......
HOW LONG...
HAVE I BEEN HERE...?
I DON'T KNOW!
WHY AM I IN CHAINS?
I CAN'T SPEAK...
I CAN'T MOVE...
I CAN'T SEE...
WHAT'S GOING ON?!
I DON'T KNOW!

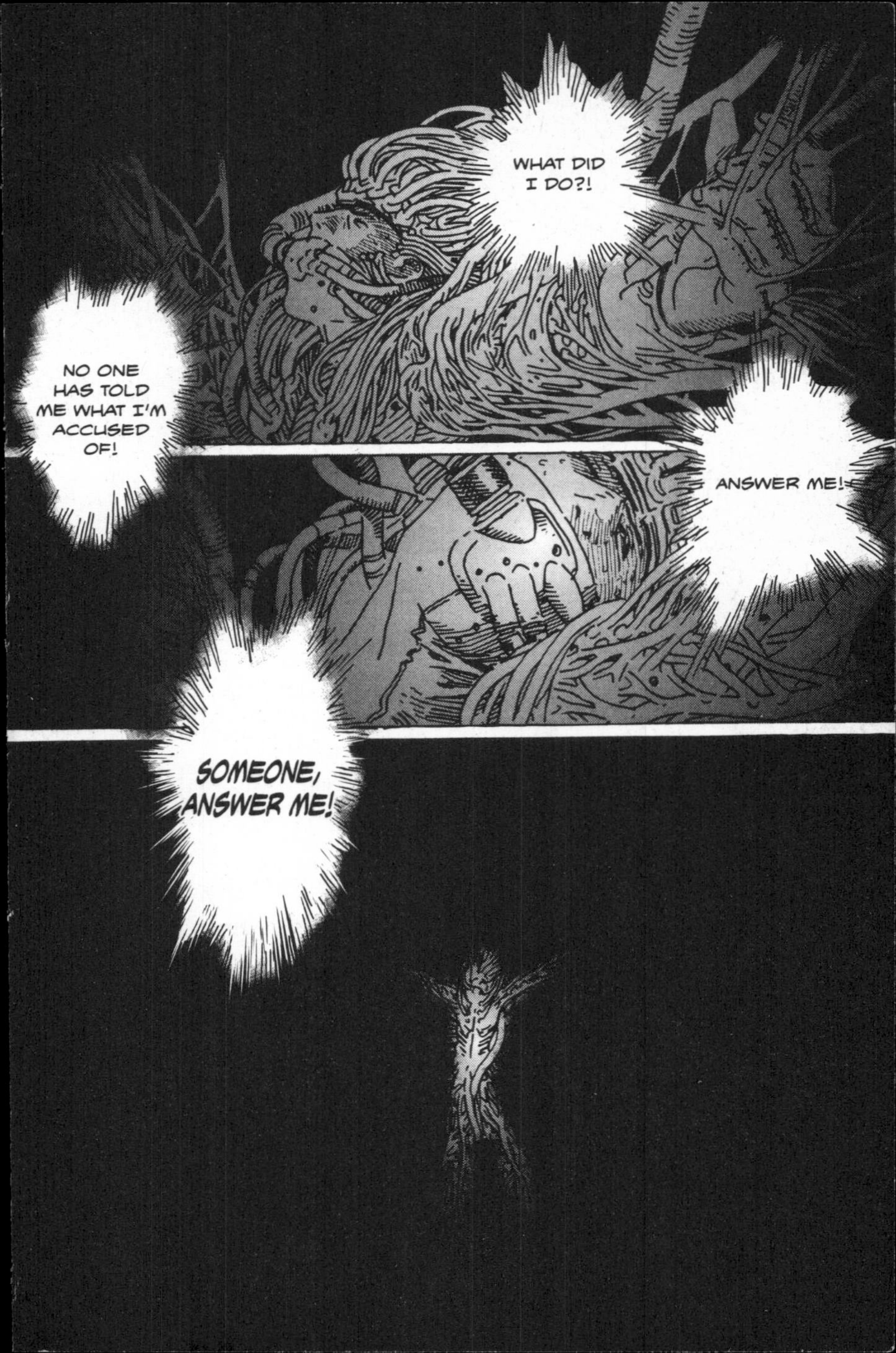
WHAT DID I DO?!
NO ONE HAS TOLD ME WHAT I'M ACCUSED OF!
ANSWER ME!
SOMEONE, ANSWER ME!

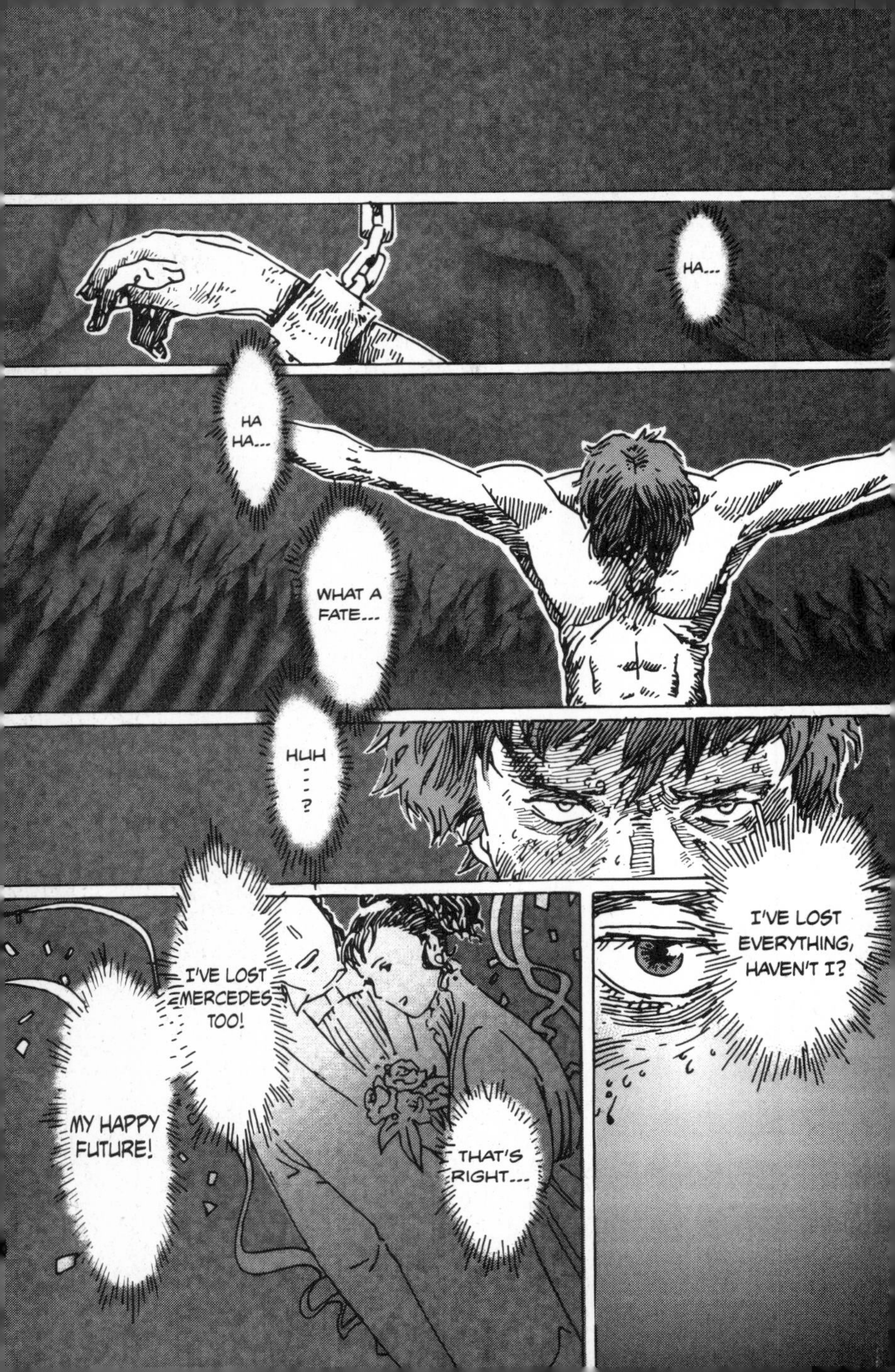
HA...
HA HA...
WHAT A FATE...
HUH...?
I'VE LOST EVERYTHING, HAVEN'T I?
THAT'S RIGHT...
I'VE LOST MERCEDES TOO!
MY HAPPY FUTURE!

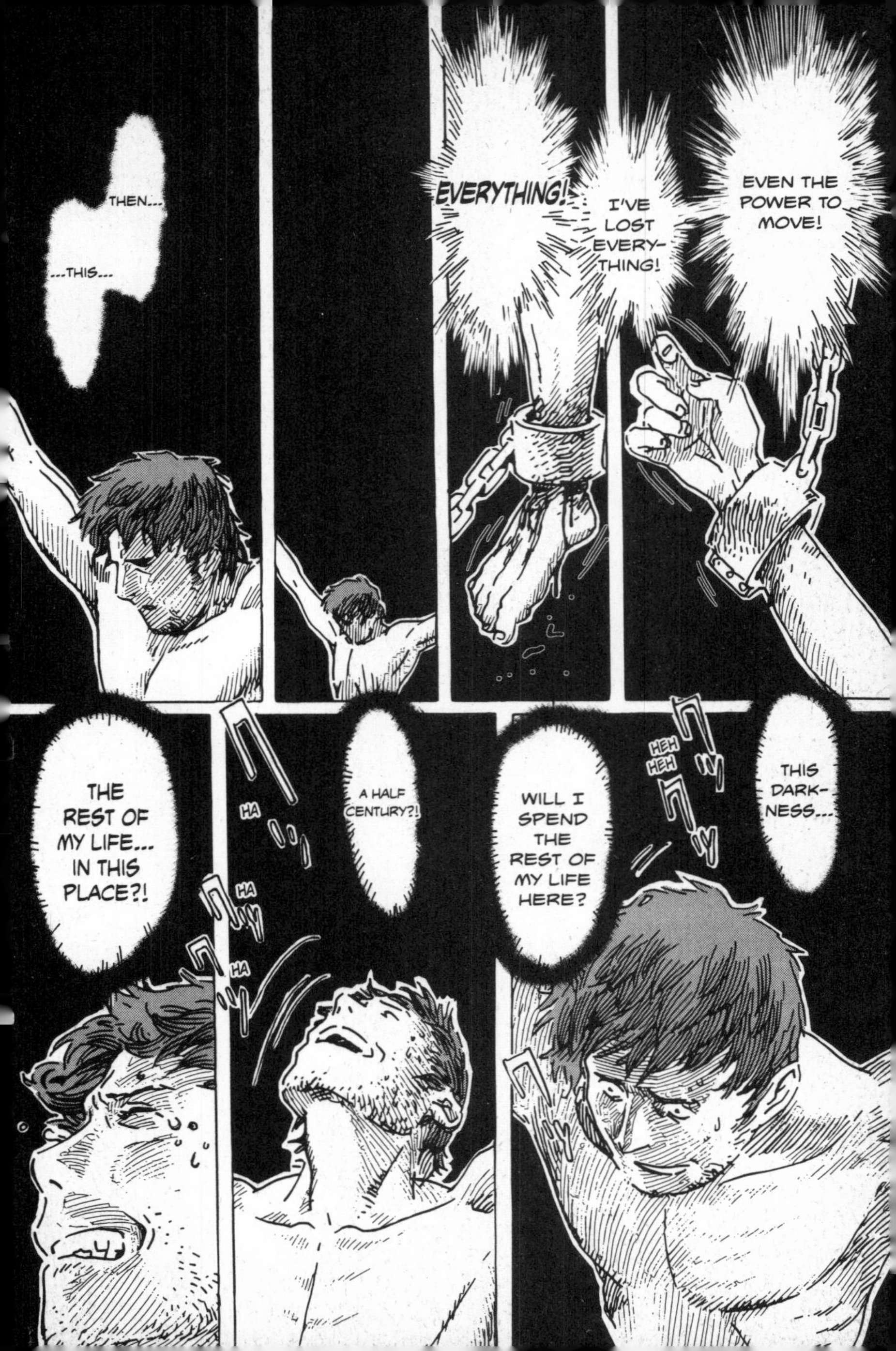

EVEN THE POWER TO MOVE!
I'VE LOST EVERY-THING!
EVERYTHING!
THEN...
...THIS...
THIS DARK-NESS...
HEH HEH
WILL I SPEND THE REST OF MY LIFE HERE?
A HALF CENTURY?!
HA
HA
HA
THE REST OF MY LIFE... IN THIS PLACE?!

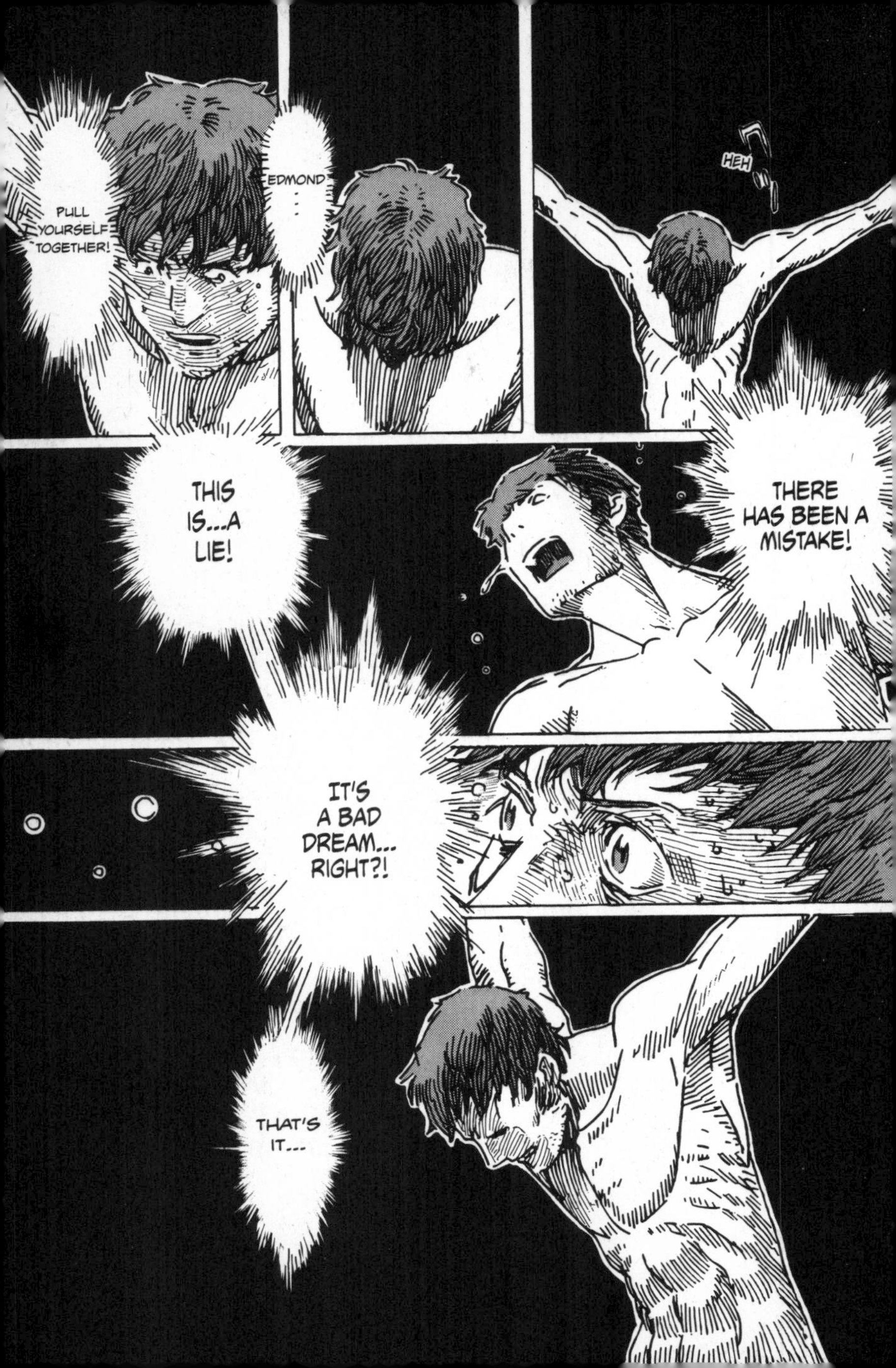
HEH
EDMOND...
PULL YOURSELF TOGETHER!
THERE HAS BEEN A MISTAKE!
THIS IS...A LIE!
IT'S A BAD DREAM... RIGHT?!
THAT'S IT...

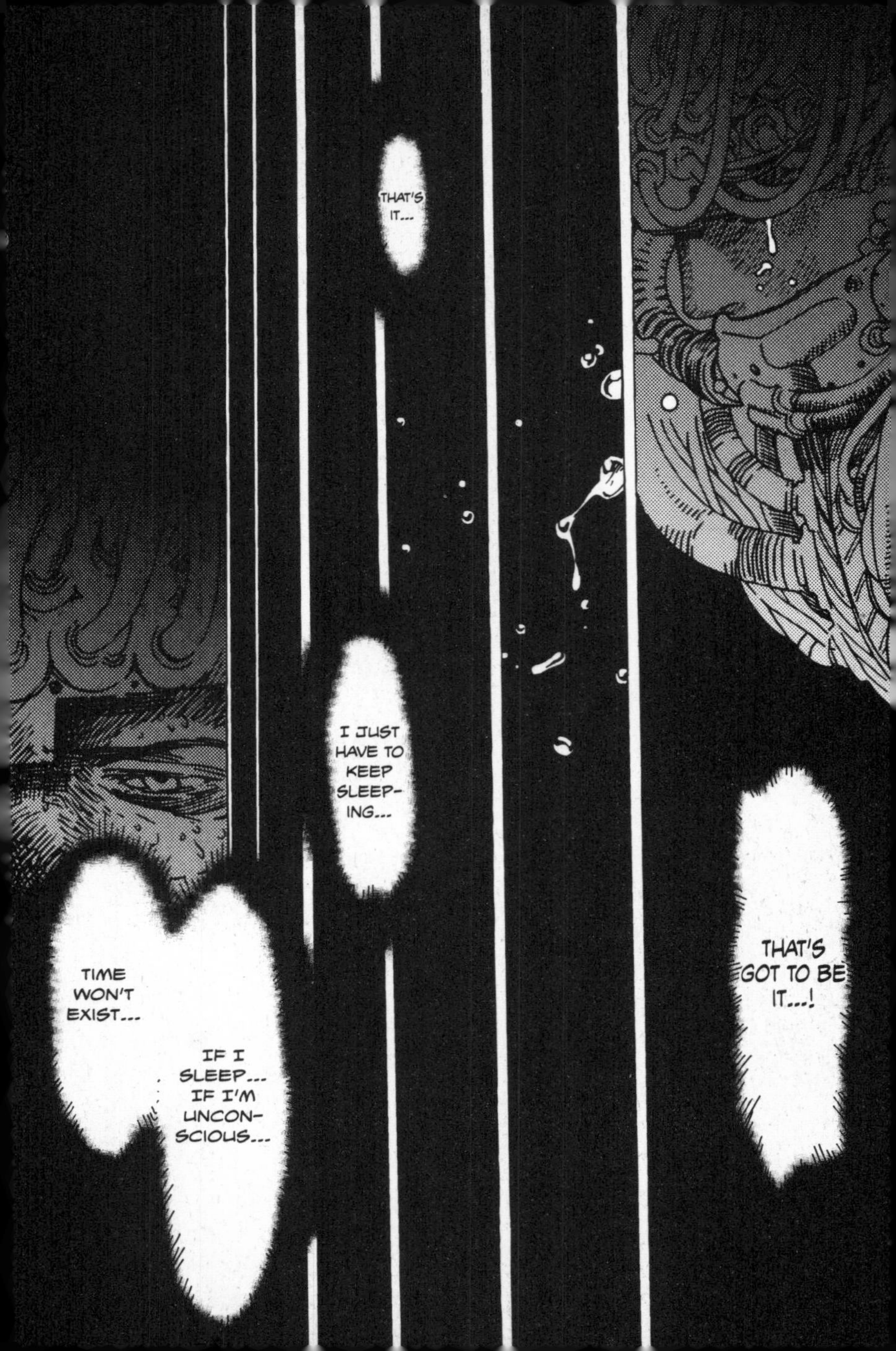
THAT'S GOT TO BE IT...!
THAT'S IT...
I JUST HAVE TO KEEP SLEEPING...
IF I SLEEP... IF I'M UNCONSCIOUS...
TIME WON'T EXIST...

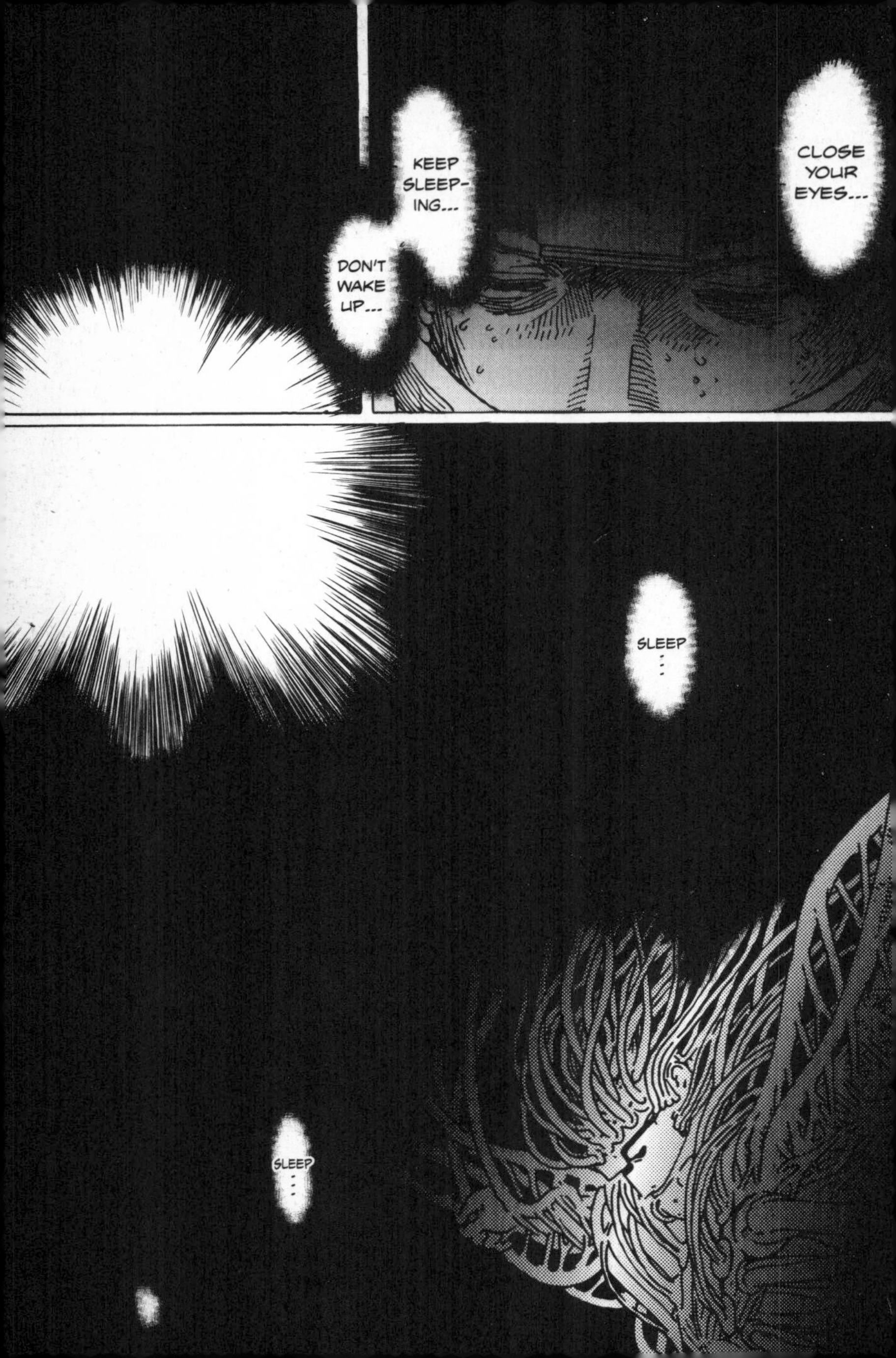
CLOSE YOUR EYES...
KEEP SLEEPING...
DON'T WAKE UP...
SLEEP...
SLEEP...

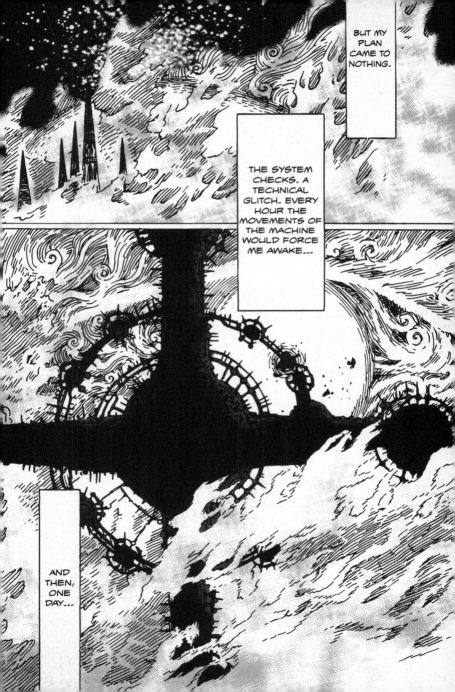

BUT MY PLAN CAME TO NOTHING.

THE SYSTEM CHECKS. A TECHNICAL GLITCH. EVERY HOUR THE MOVEMENTS OF THE MACHINE WOULD FORCE ME AWAKE...

AND THEN, ONE DAY...

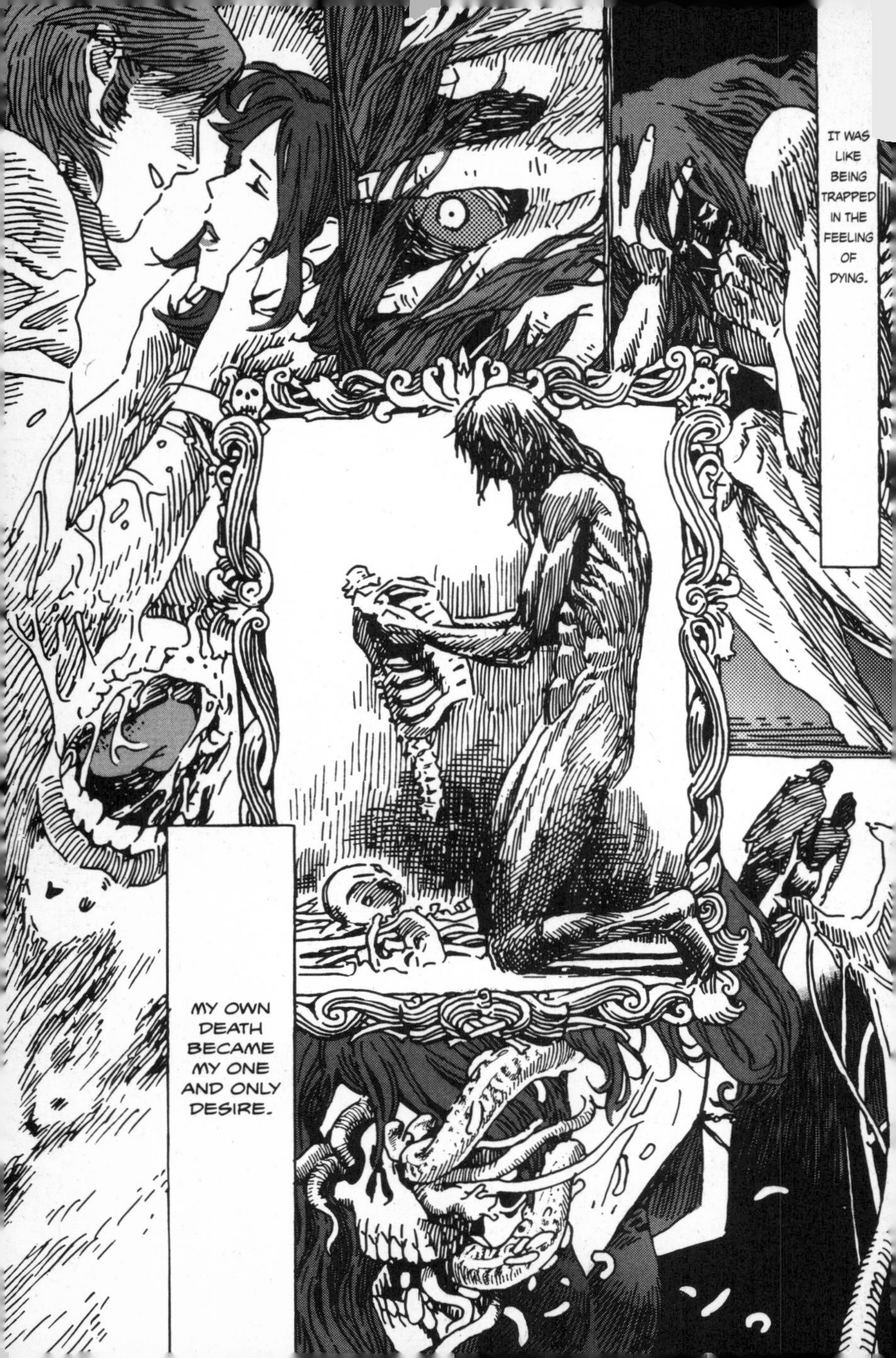
IT WAS LIKE BEING TRAPPED IN THE FEELING OF DYING.
MY OWN DEATH BECAME MY ONE AND ONLY DESIRE.

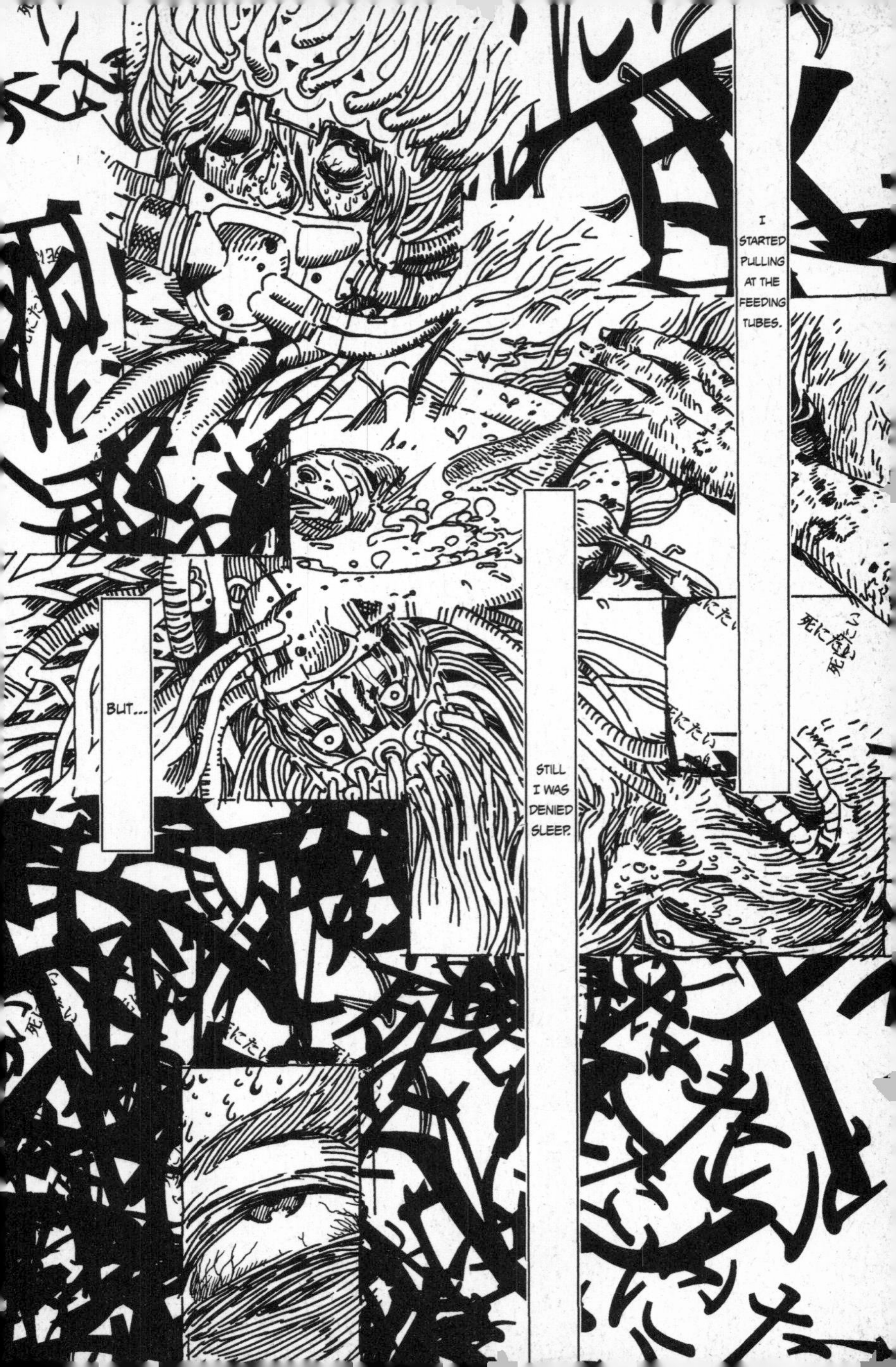
I STARTED PULLING AT THE FEEDING TUBES.
STILL I WAS DENIED SLEEP.
BUT...

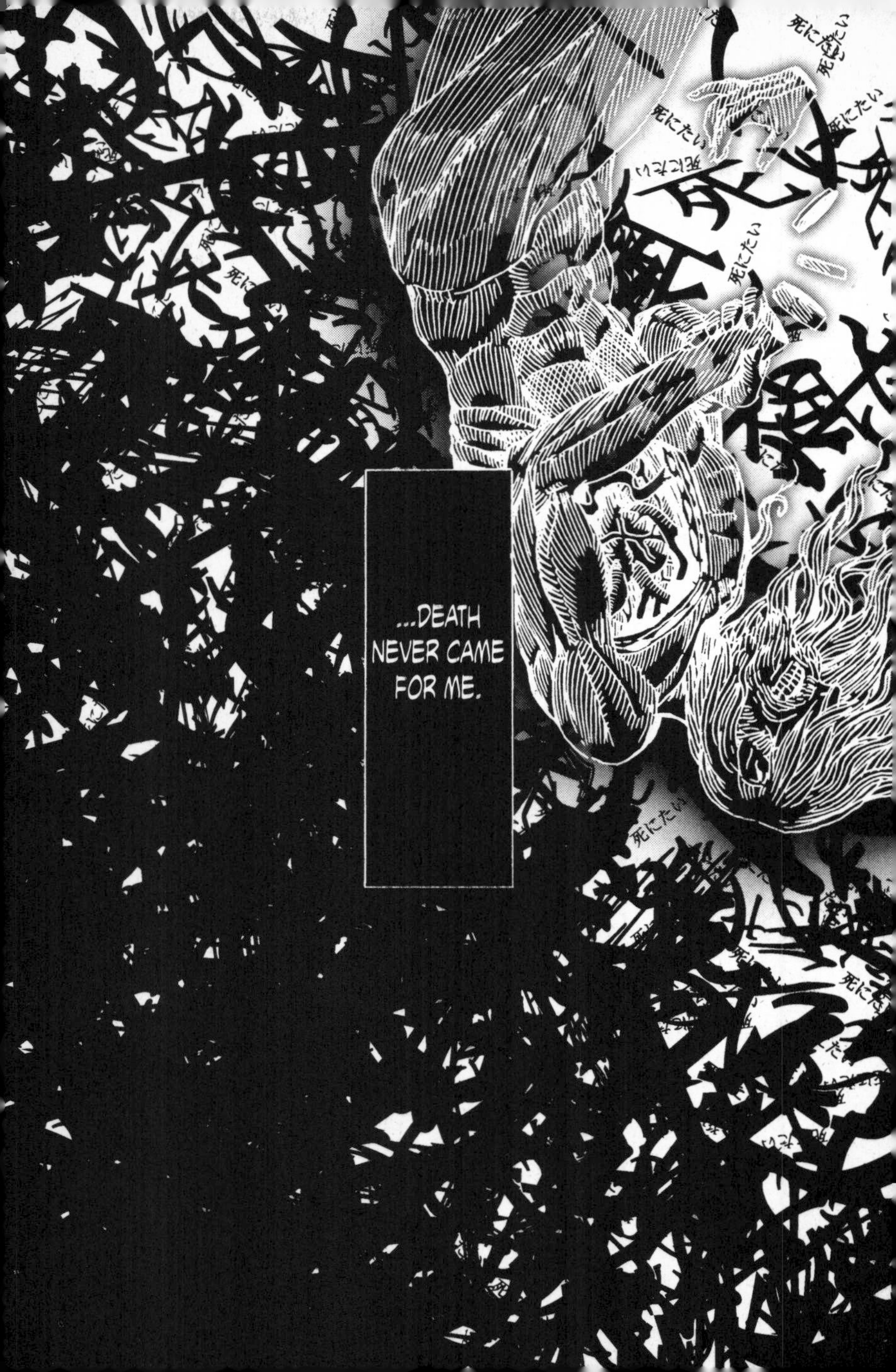
...DEATH NEVER CAME FOR ME.

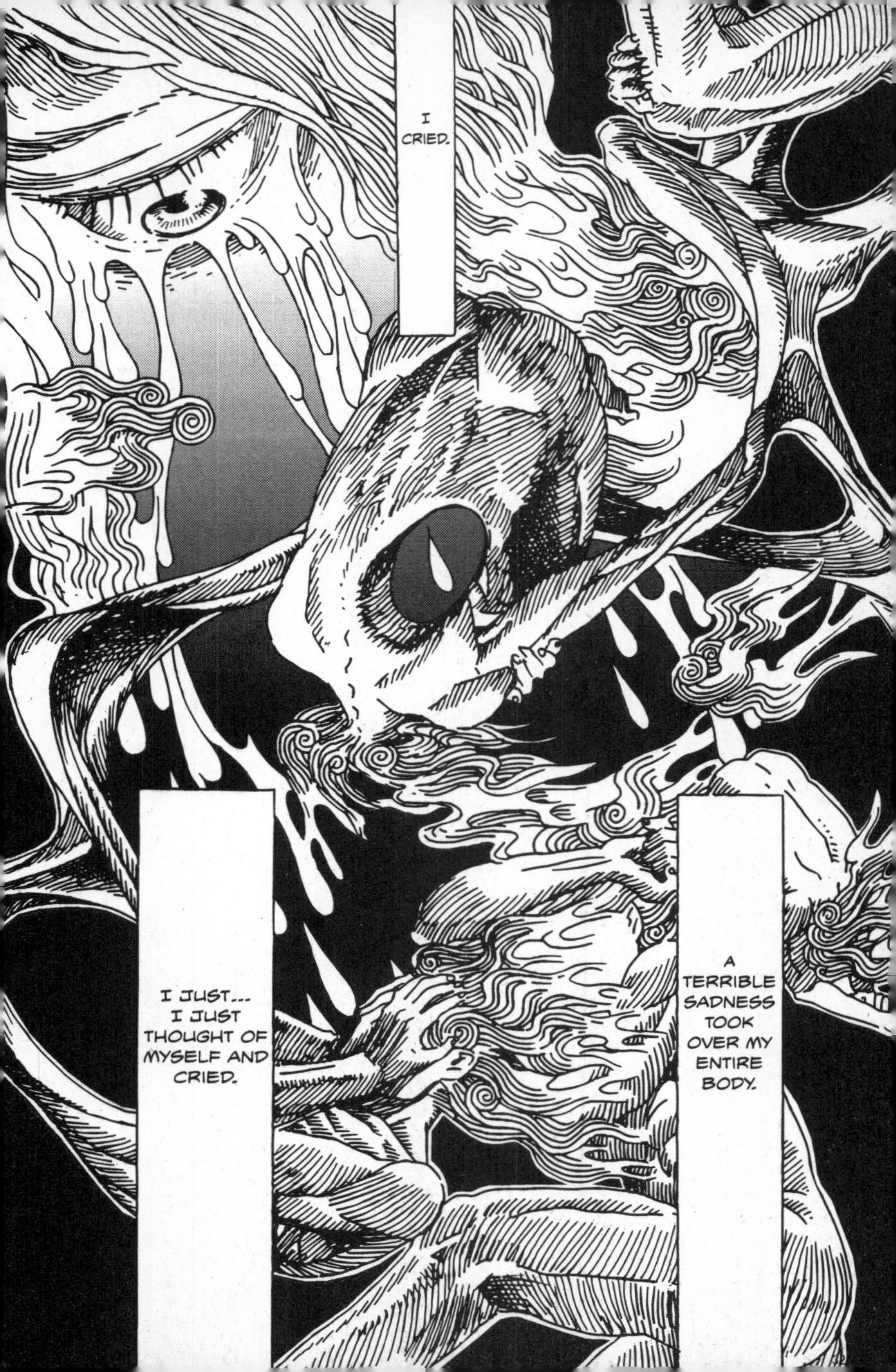
I CRIED.
A TERRIBLE SADNESS TOOK OVER MY ENTIRE BODY.
I JUST... I JUST THOUGHT OF MYSELF AND CRIED.

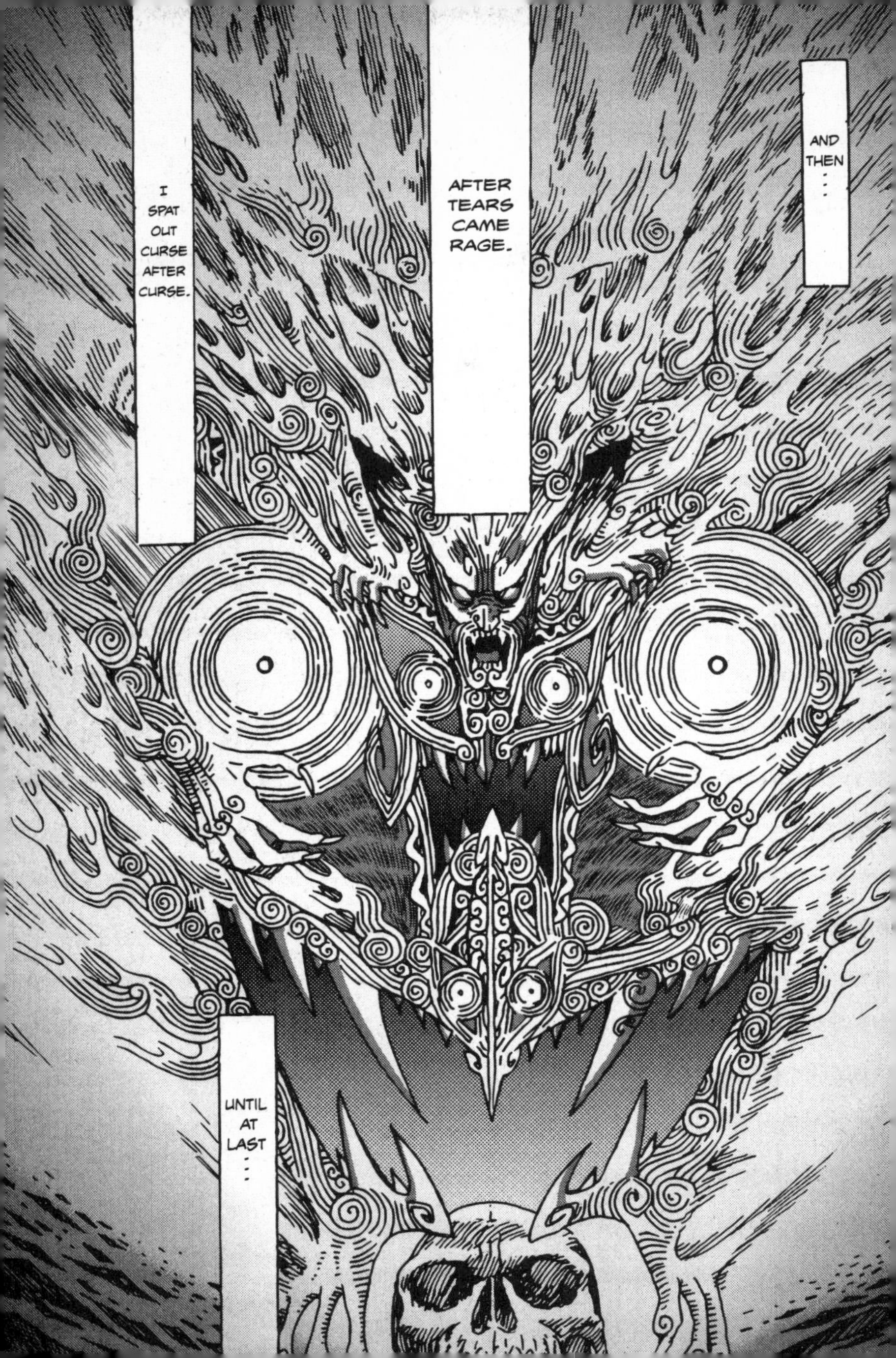
AND THEN . . .
AFTER TEARS CAME RAGE.
I SPAT OUT CURSE AFTER CURSE.
UNTIL AT LAST . . .

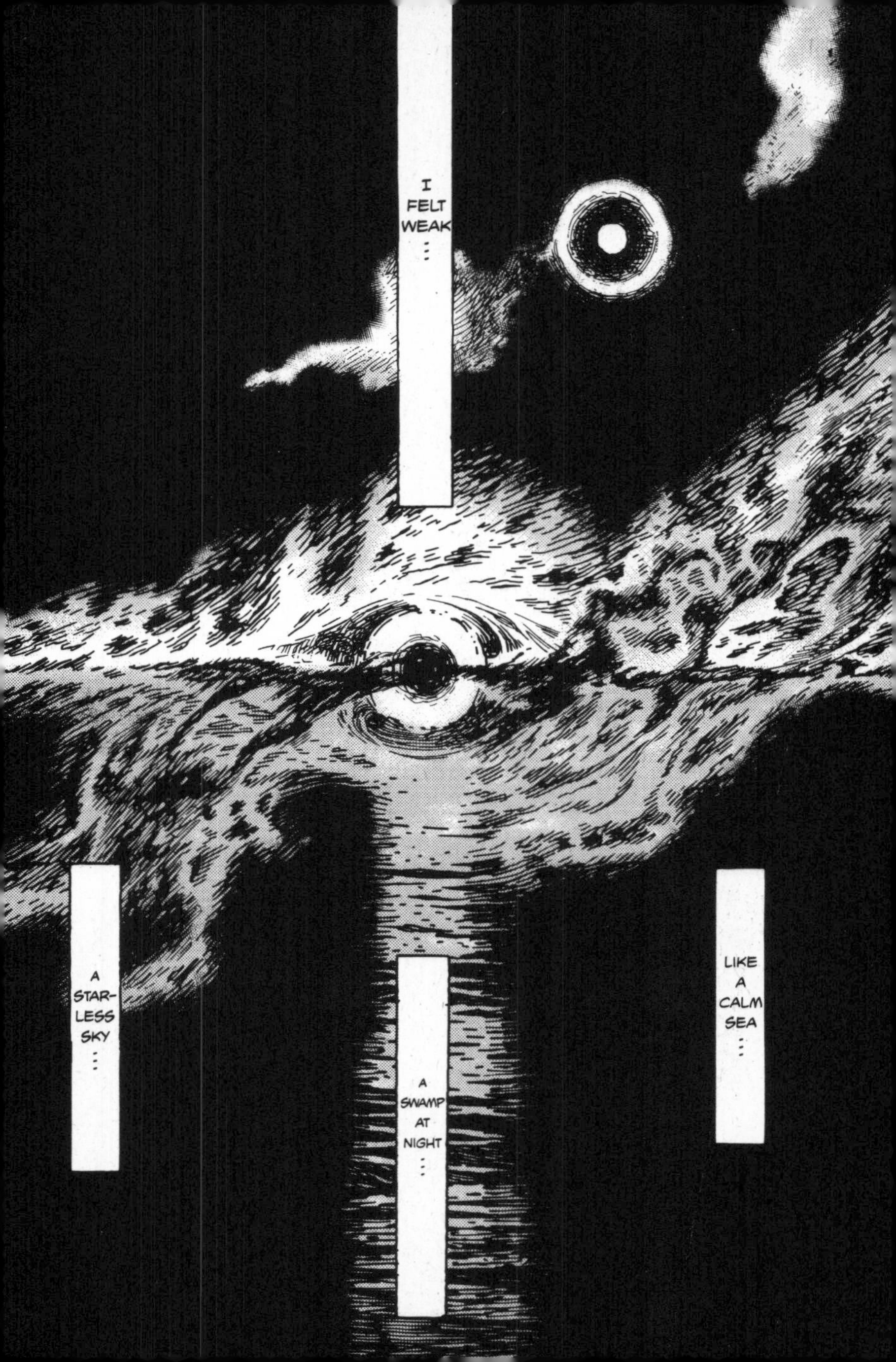
I FELT WEAK...
LIKE A CALM SEA...
A SWAMP AT NIGHT...
A STAR-LESS SKY...

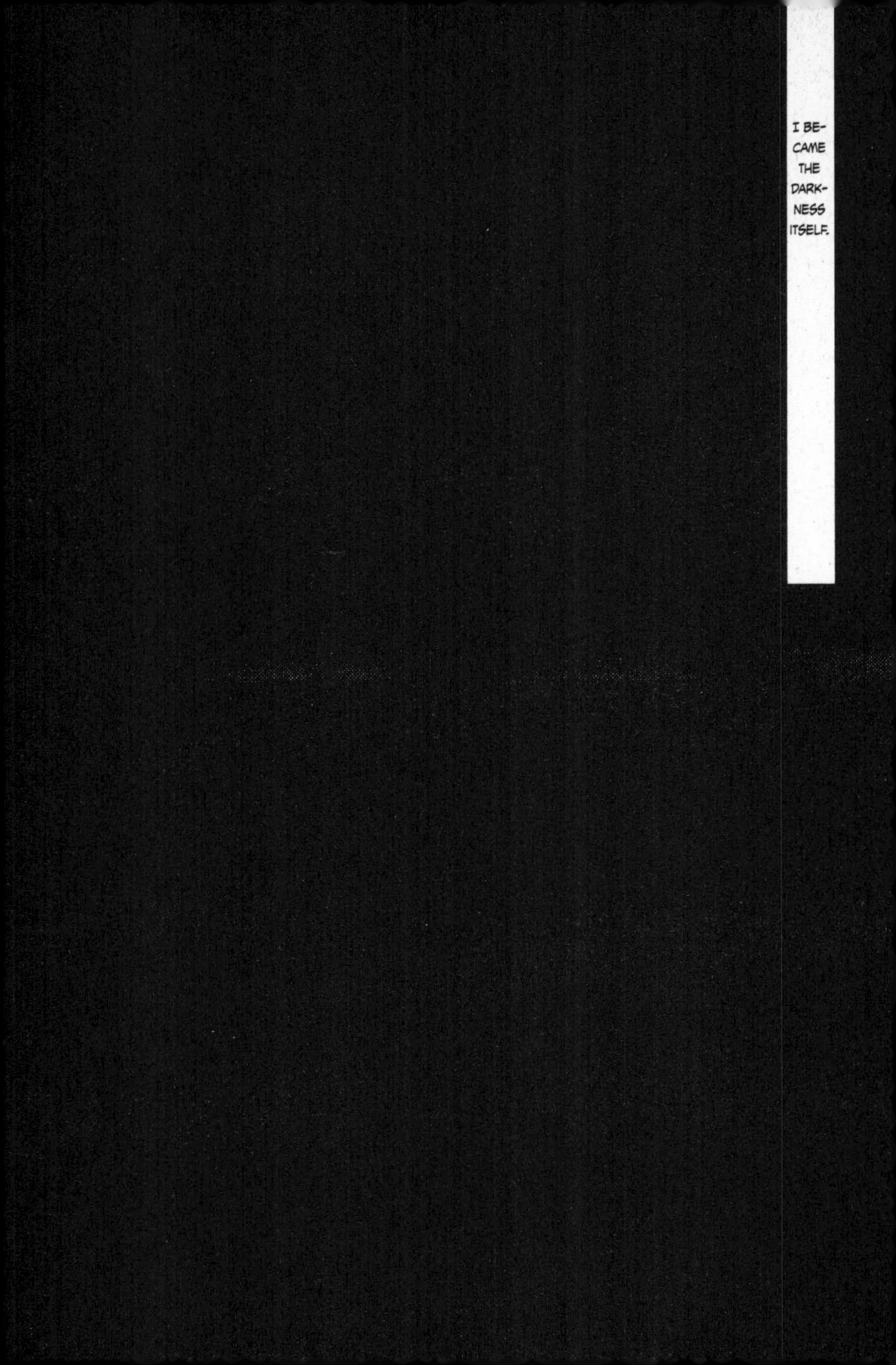
I BECAME THE DARKNESS ITSELF.

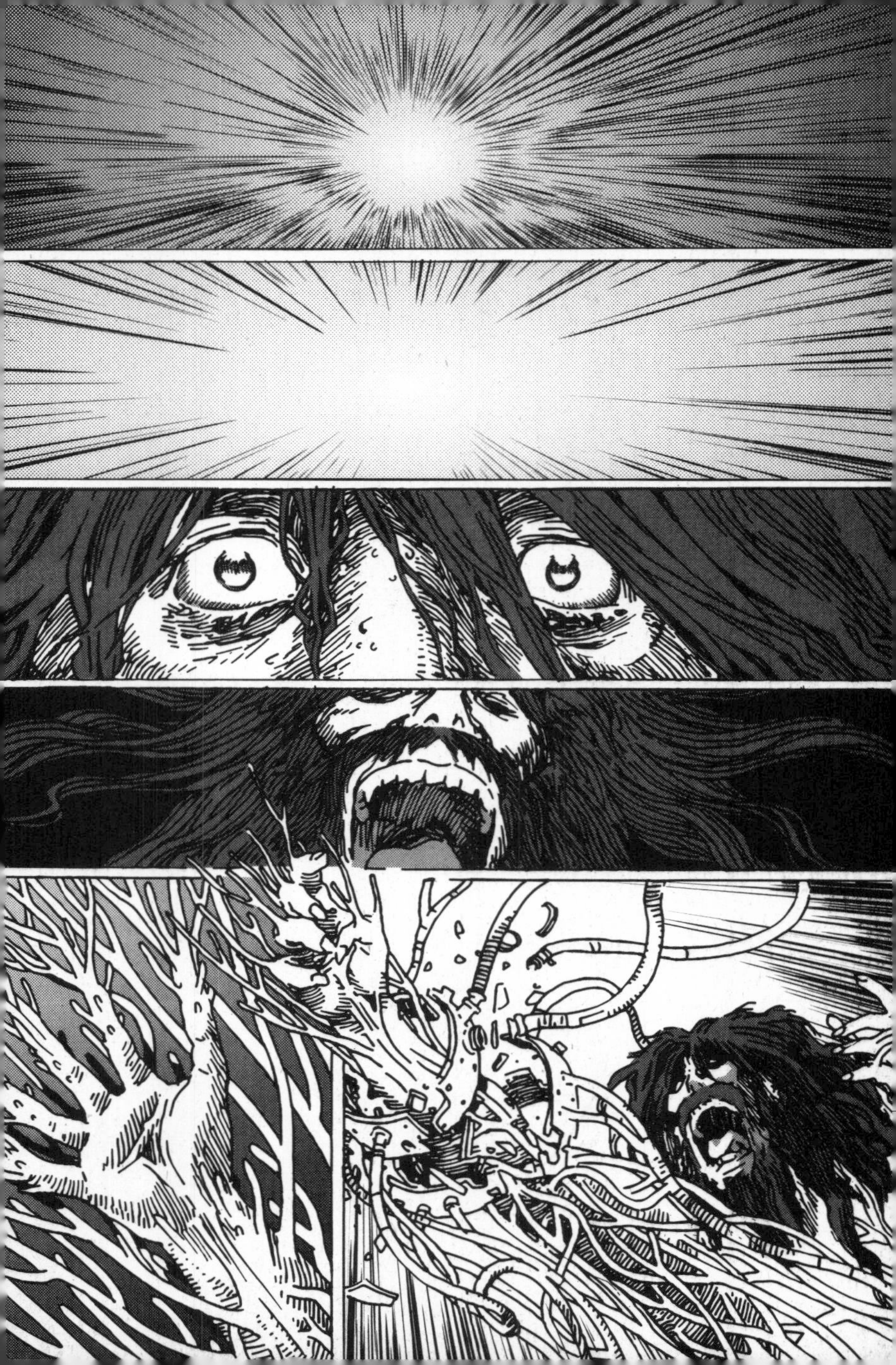

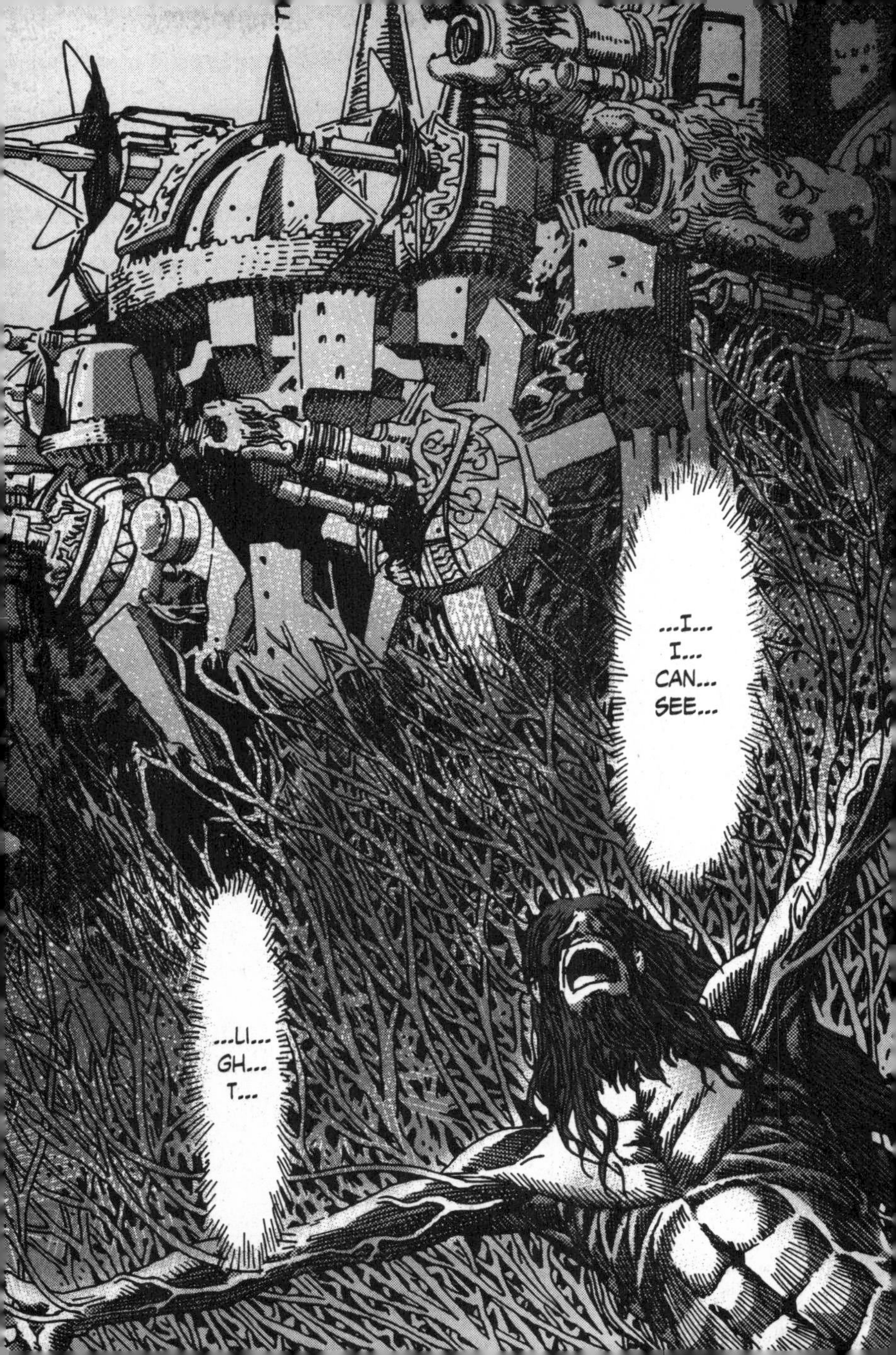
...I... I... CAN... SEE...
...LI... GH... T...

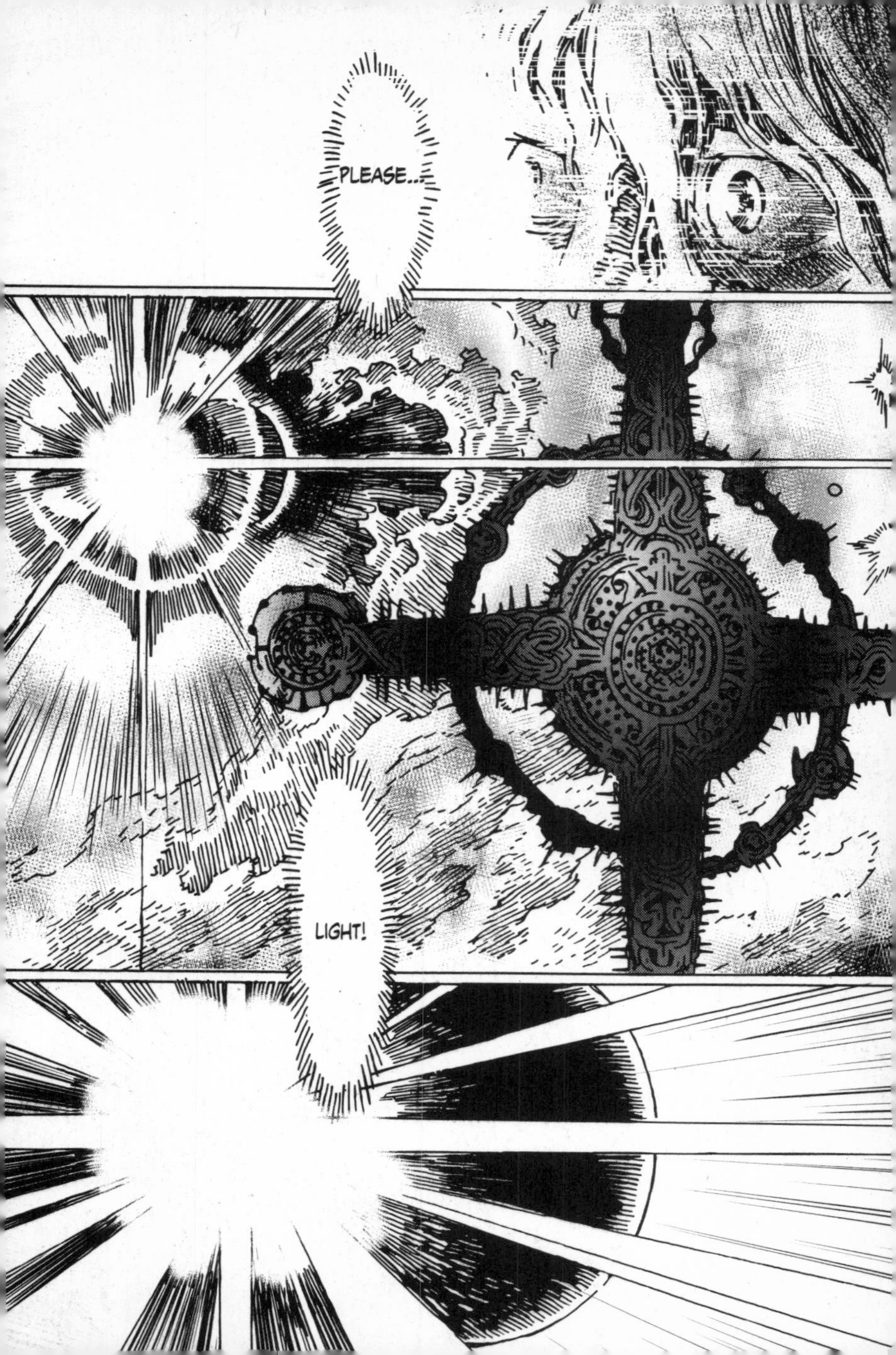
PLEASE...
LIGHT!

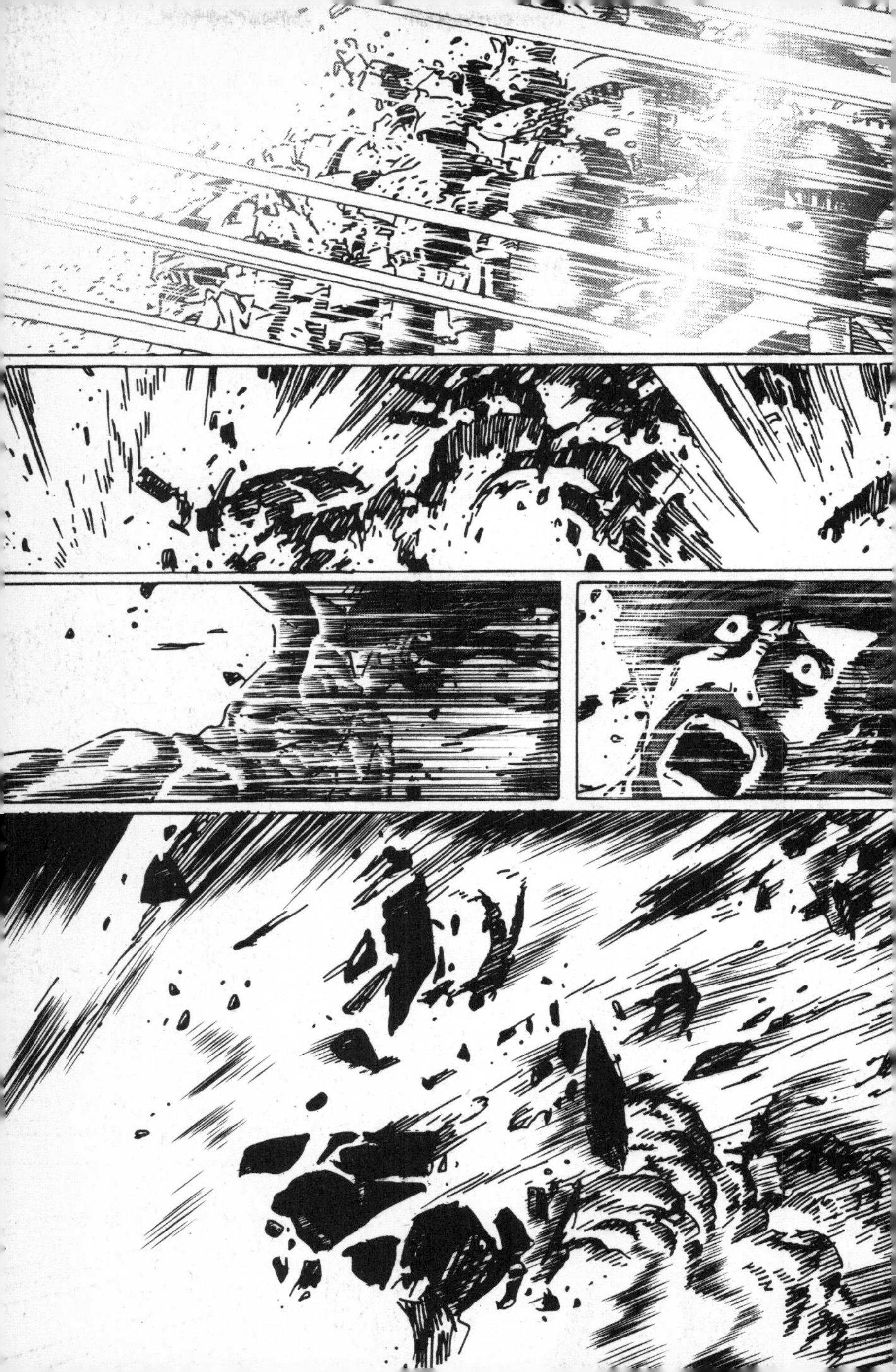

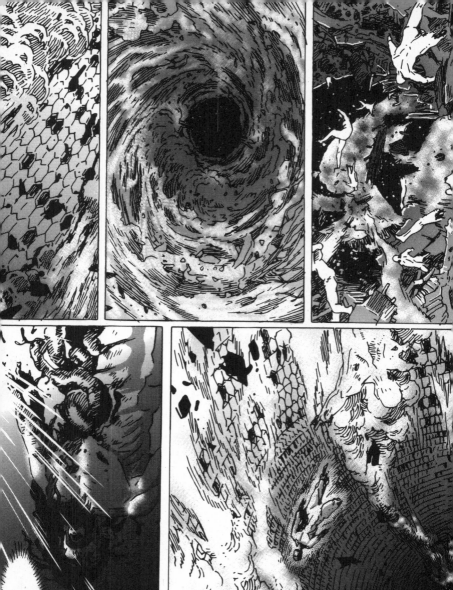

I...

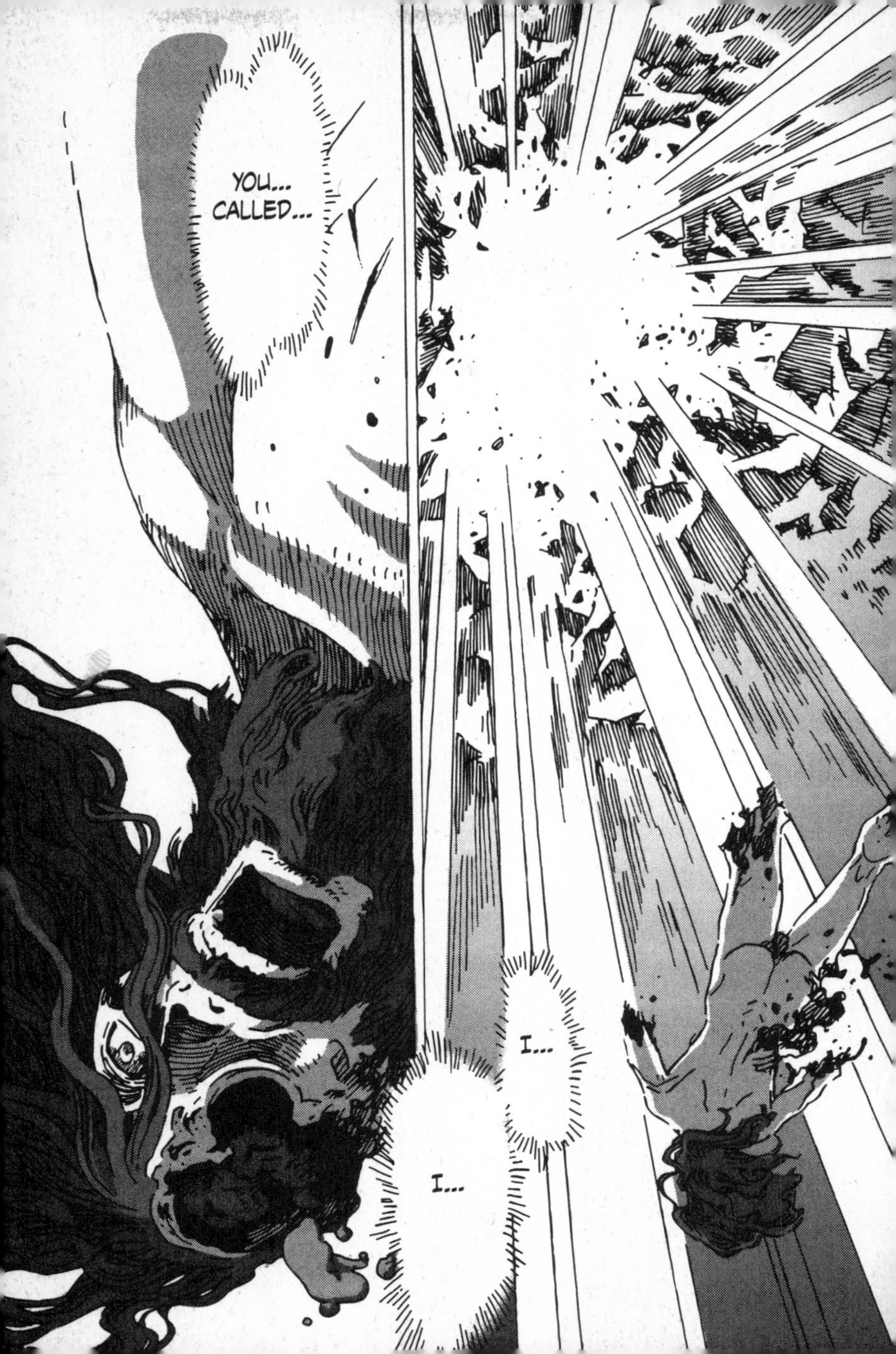
I...
I...
YOU... CALLED...

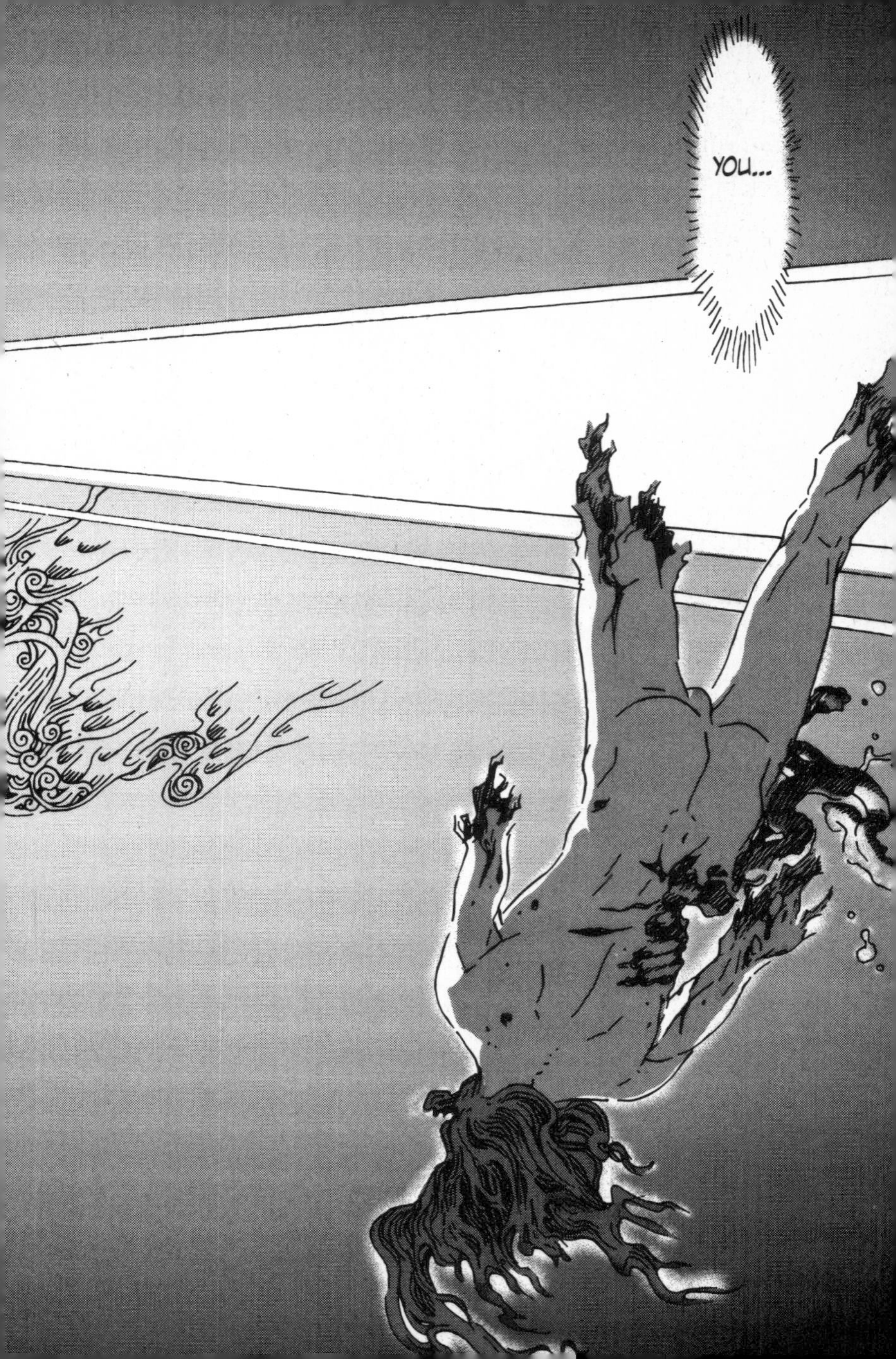
YOU...

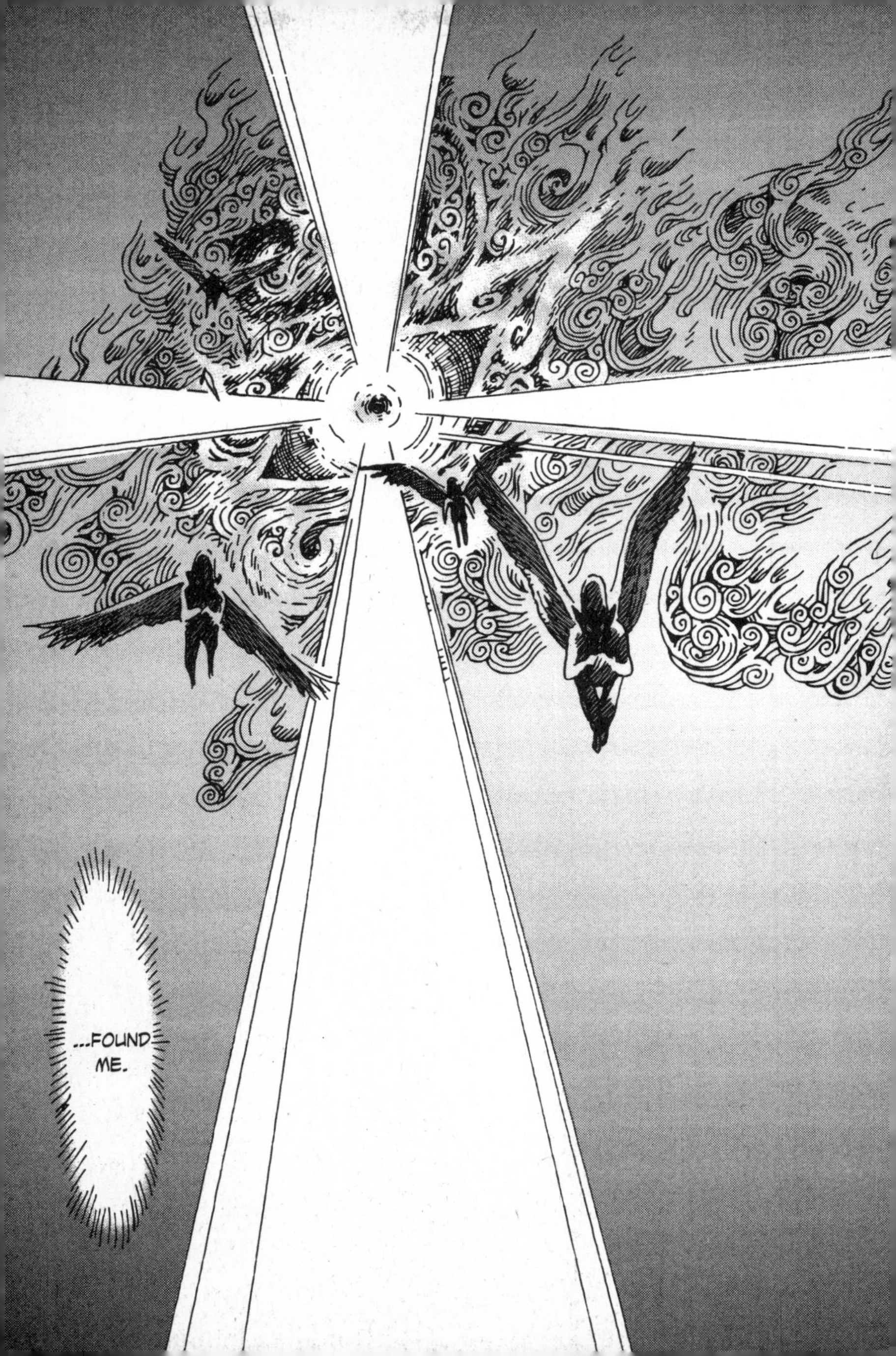
...FOUND ME.

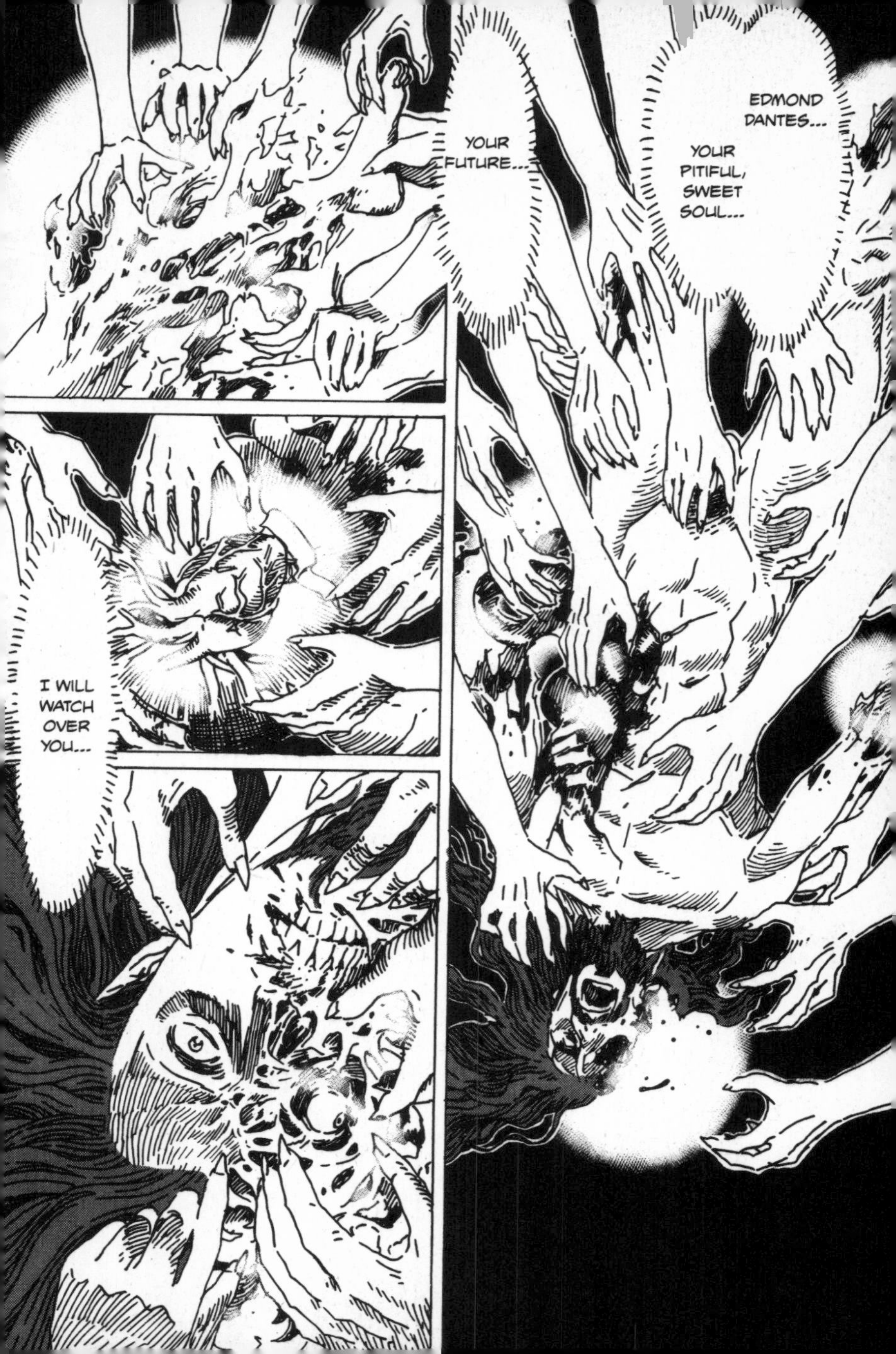
EDMOND DANTES...
YOUR PITIFUL, SWEET SOUL...
YOUR FUTURE...
I WILL WATCH OVER YOU...

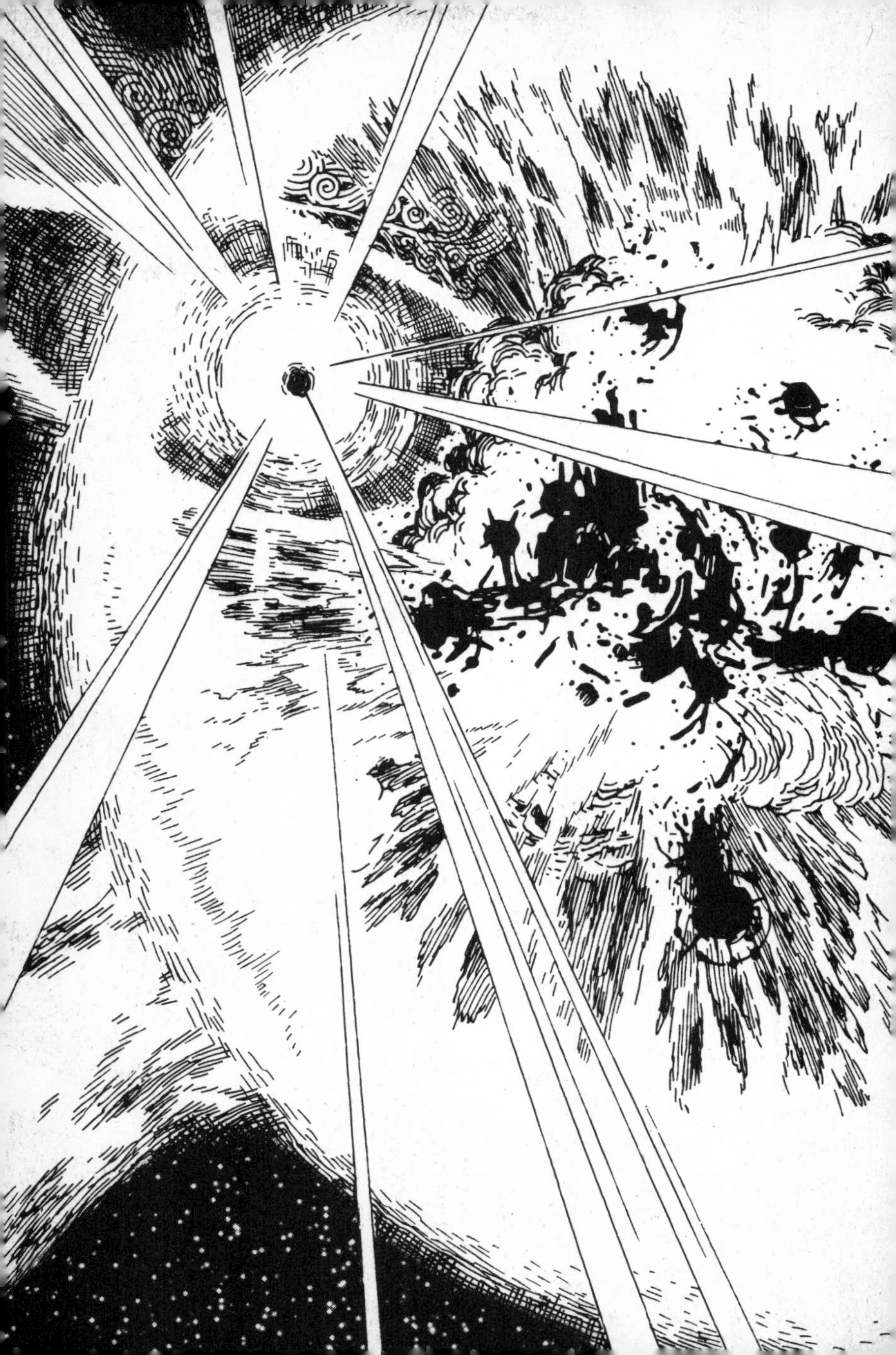

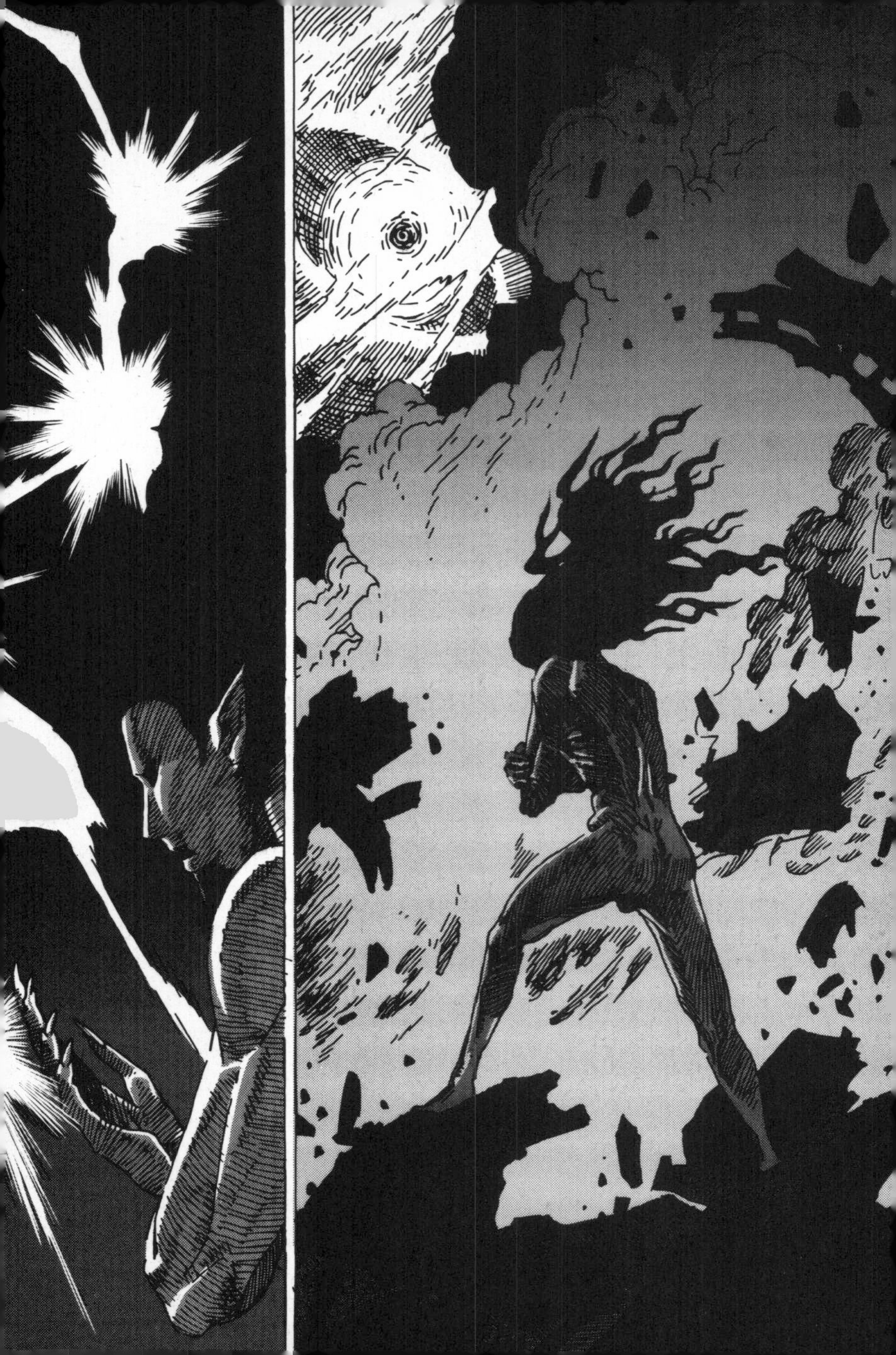

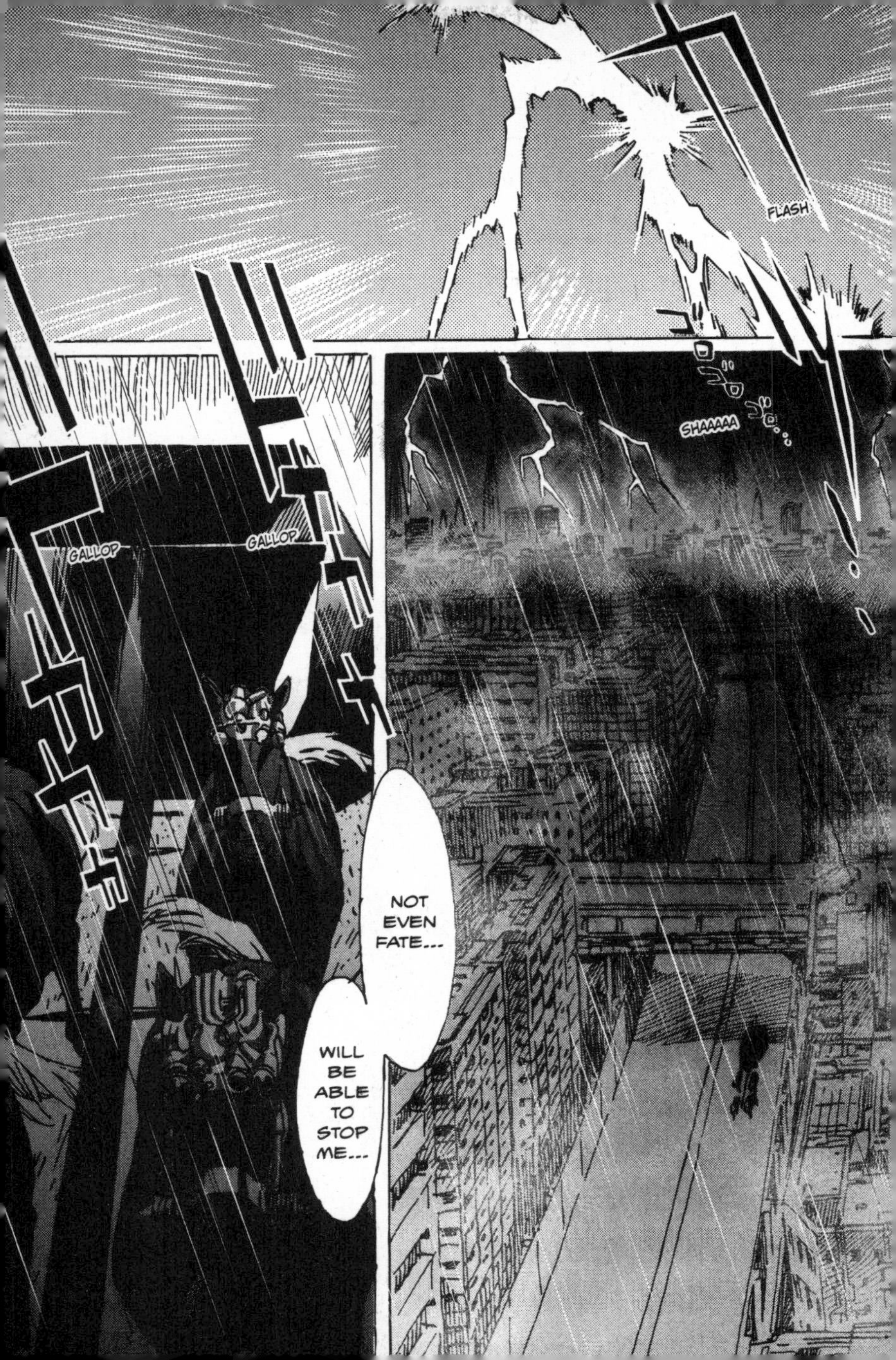
FLASH
SHAAAAA
NOT EVEN FATE...
WILL BE ABLE TO STOP ME...
GALLOP
GALLOP

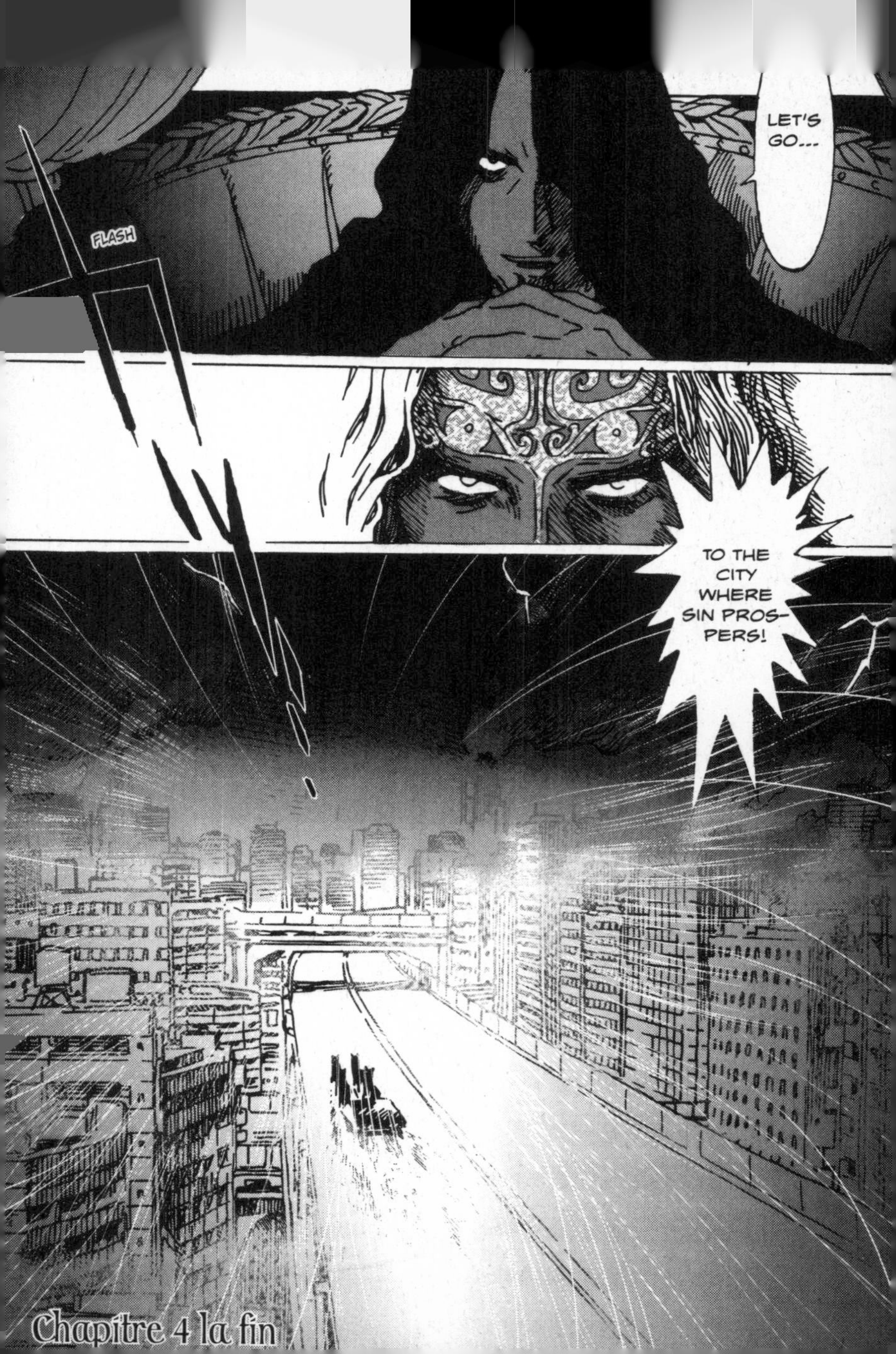
LET'S GO...
FLASH
TO THE CITY WHERE SIN PROS-PERS!
Chapitre 4 la fin

Chapitre 5: The Avenging Angel of the East

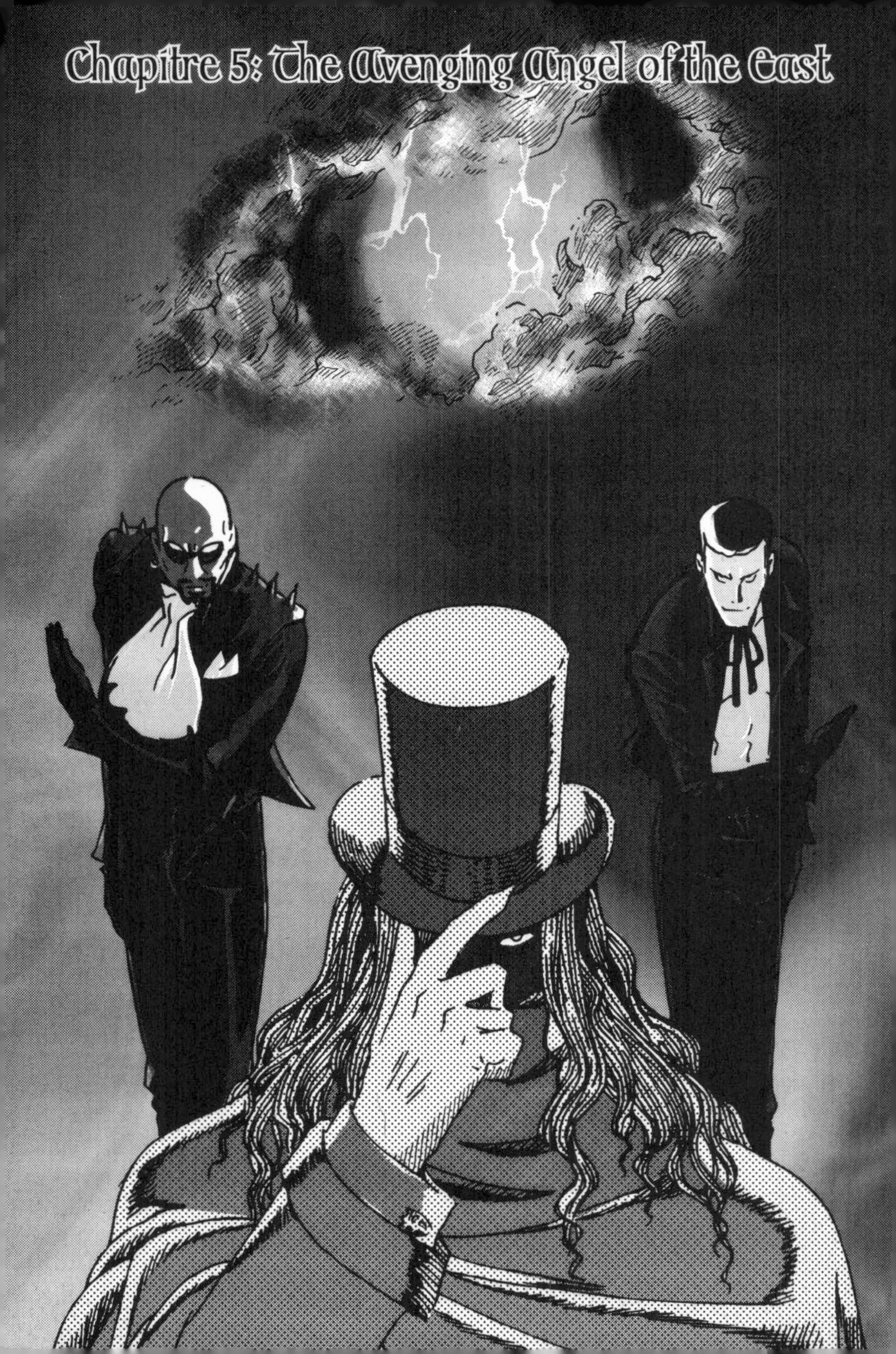

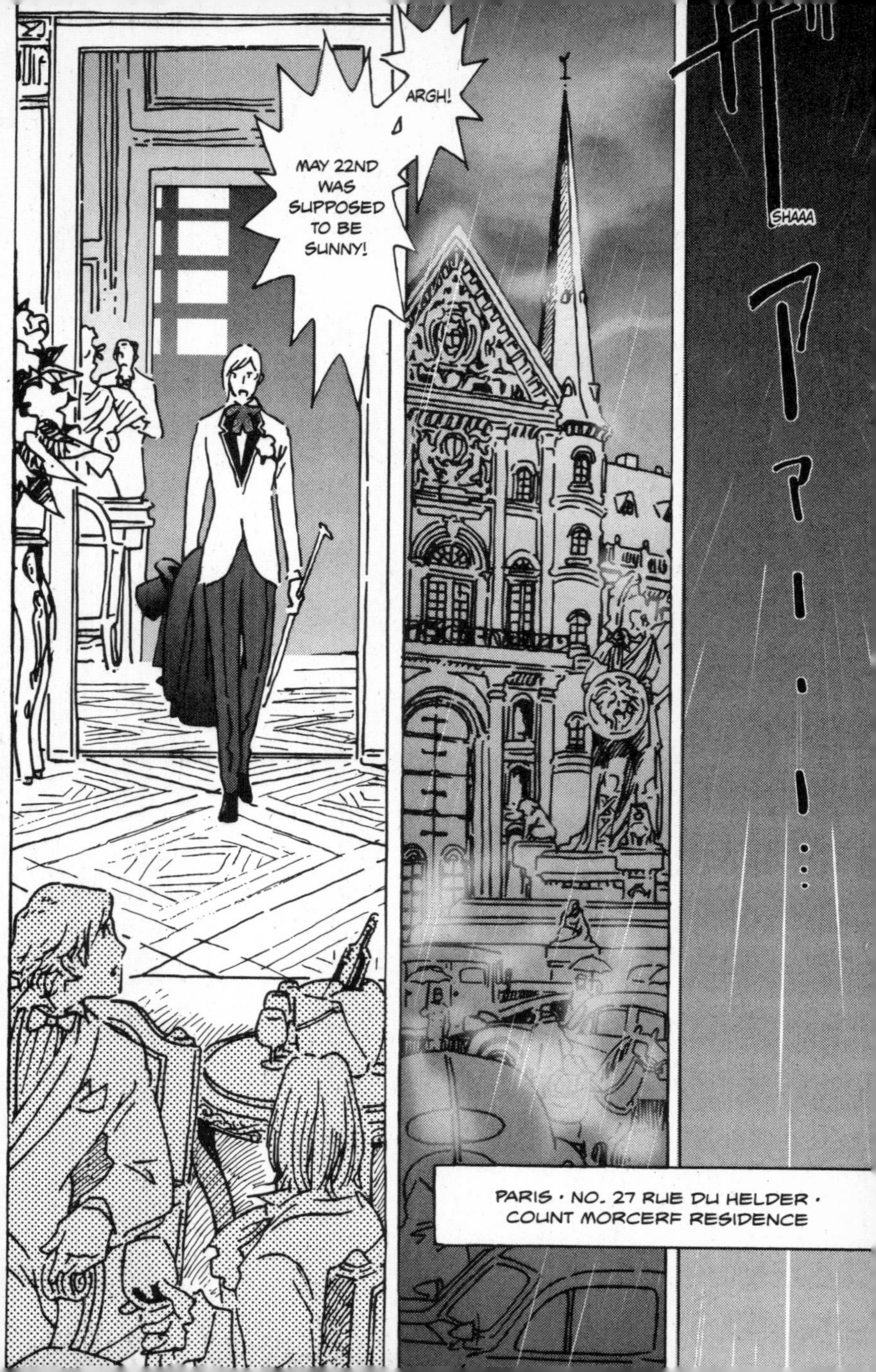
SHAAA
PARIS · NO. 27 RUE DU HELDER ·
COUNT MORCERF RESIDENCE
ARGH!
MAY 22ND WAS SUPPOSED TO BE SUNNY!

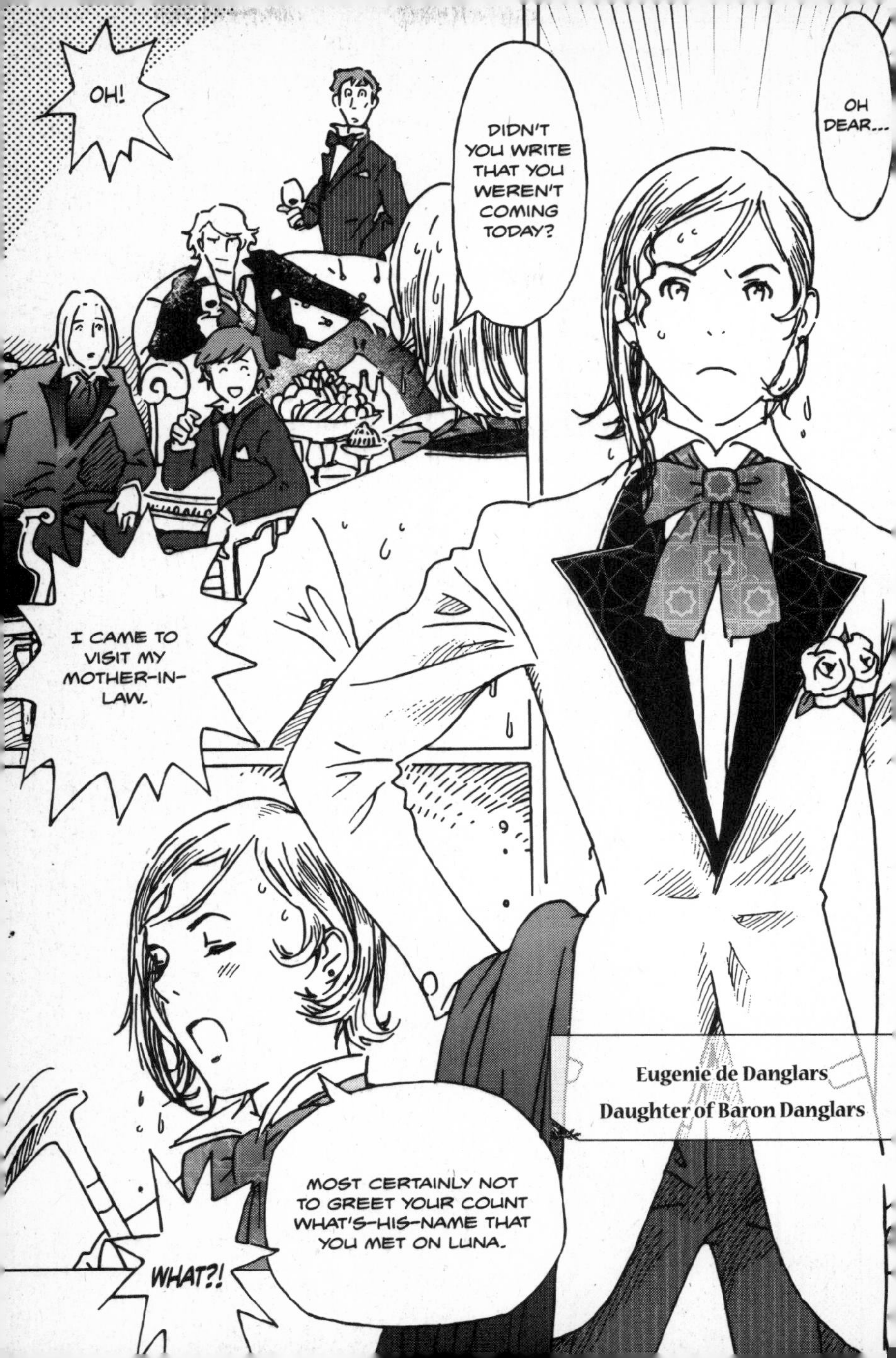
OH DEAR...
DIDN'T YOU WRITE THAT YOU WEREN'T COMING TODAY?
OH!
I CAME TO VISIT MY MOTHER-IN-LAW.
Eugenie de Danglars
Daughter of Baron Danglars
MOST CERTAINLY NOT TO GREET YOUR COUNT WHAT'S-HIS-NAME THAT YOU MET ON LUNA.
WHAT?!

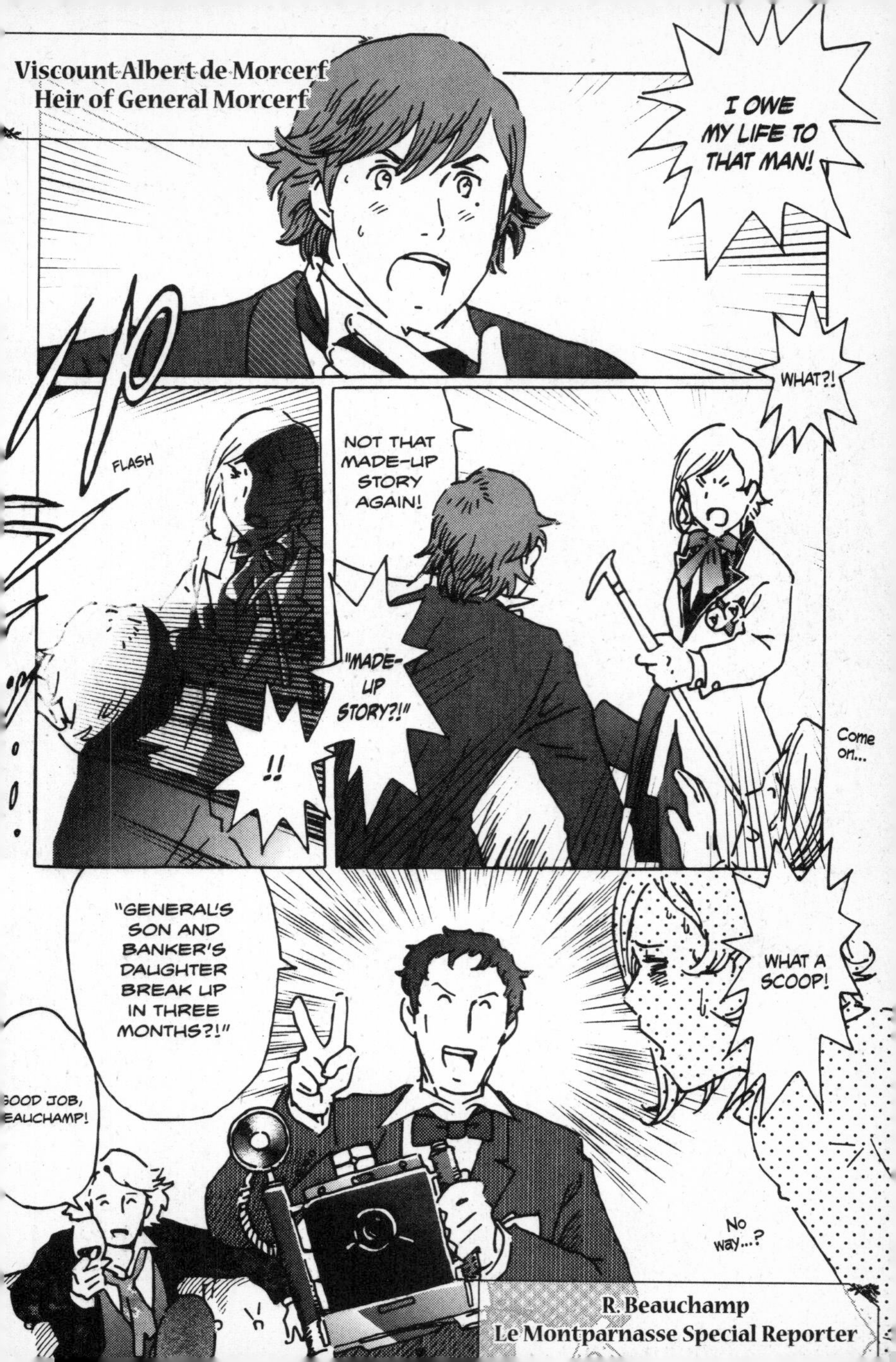
I OWE MY LIFE TO THAT MAN!
Viscount Albert de Morcerf
Heir of General Morcerf
WHAT?!
NOT THAT MADE-UP STORY AGAIN!
Come on...
"MADE-UP STORY?!"
!!
FLASH
WHAT A SCOOP!
"GENERAL'S SON AND BANKER'S DAUGHTER BREAK UP IN THREE MONTHS?!"
No way...?
GOOD JOB, BEAUCHAMP!
R. Beauchamp
Le Montparnasse Special Reporter

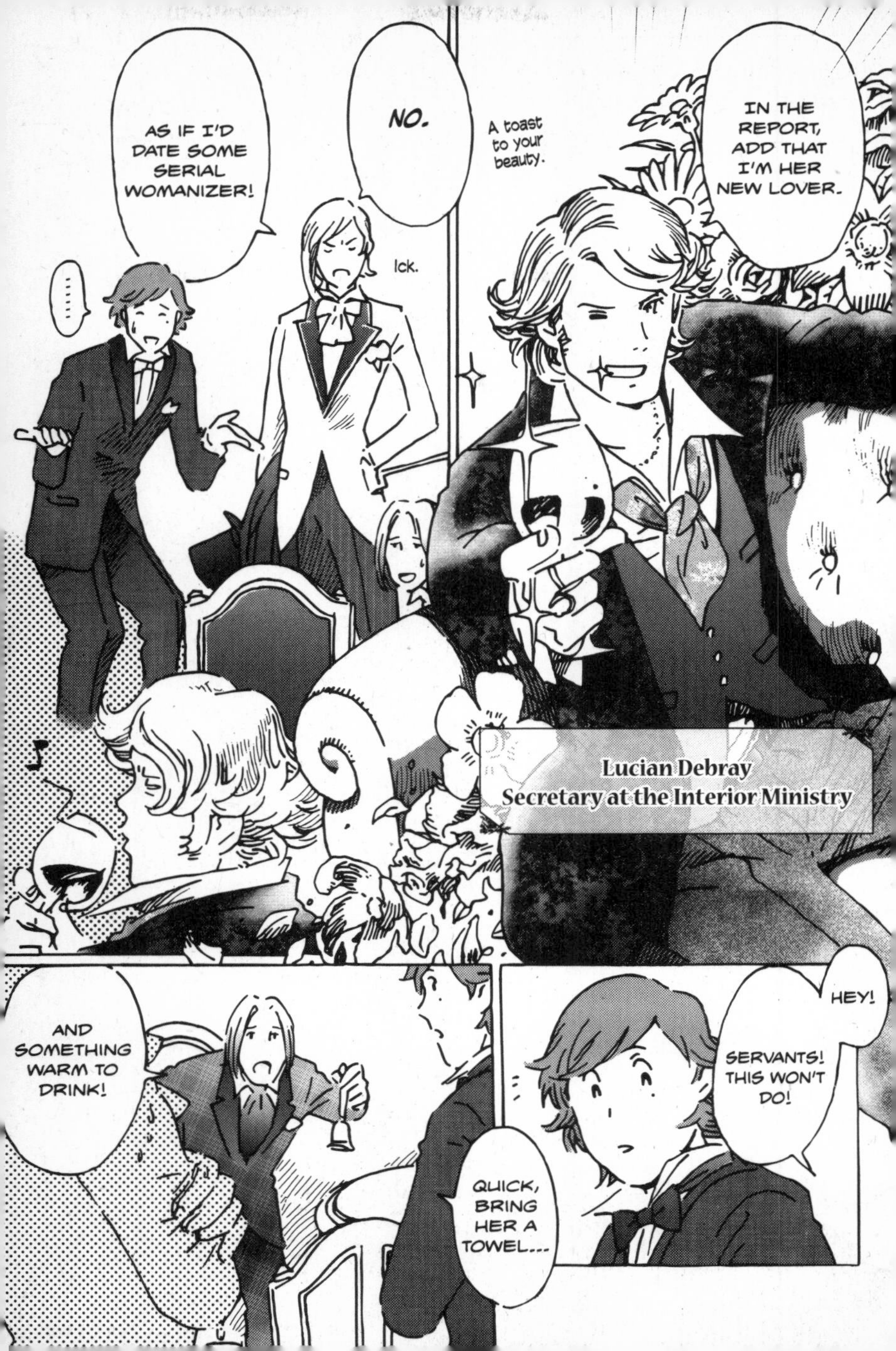
IN THE REPORT, ADD THAT I'M HER NEW LOVER.
A toast to your beauty.
NO.
Ick.
AS IF I'D DATE SOME SERIAL WOMANIZER!
......
Lucian Debray
Secretary at the Interior Ministry
HEY!
SERVANTS! THIS WON'T DO!
QUICK, BRING HER A TOWEL...
AND SOMETHING WARM TO DRINK!

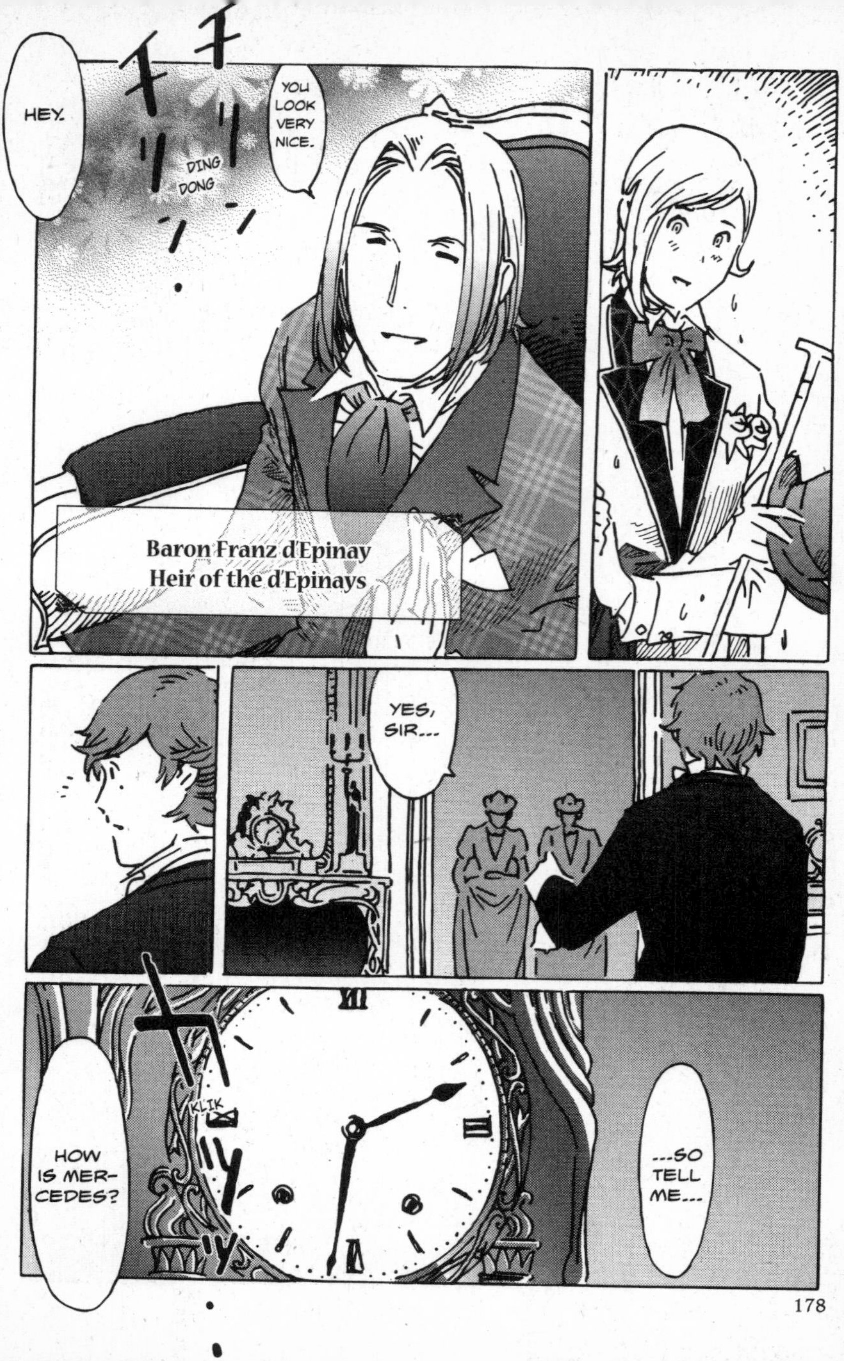
YOU LOOK VERY NICE.
HEY.
DING DONG
Baron Franz d'Epinay
Heir of the d'Epinays
YES, SIR...
...SO TELL ME...
KLIK
HOW IS MER-CEDES?

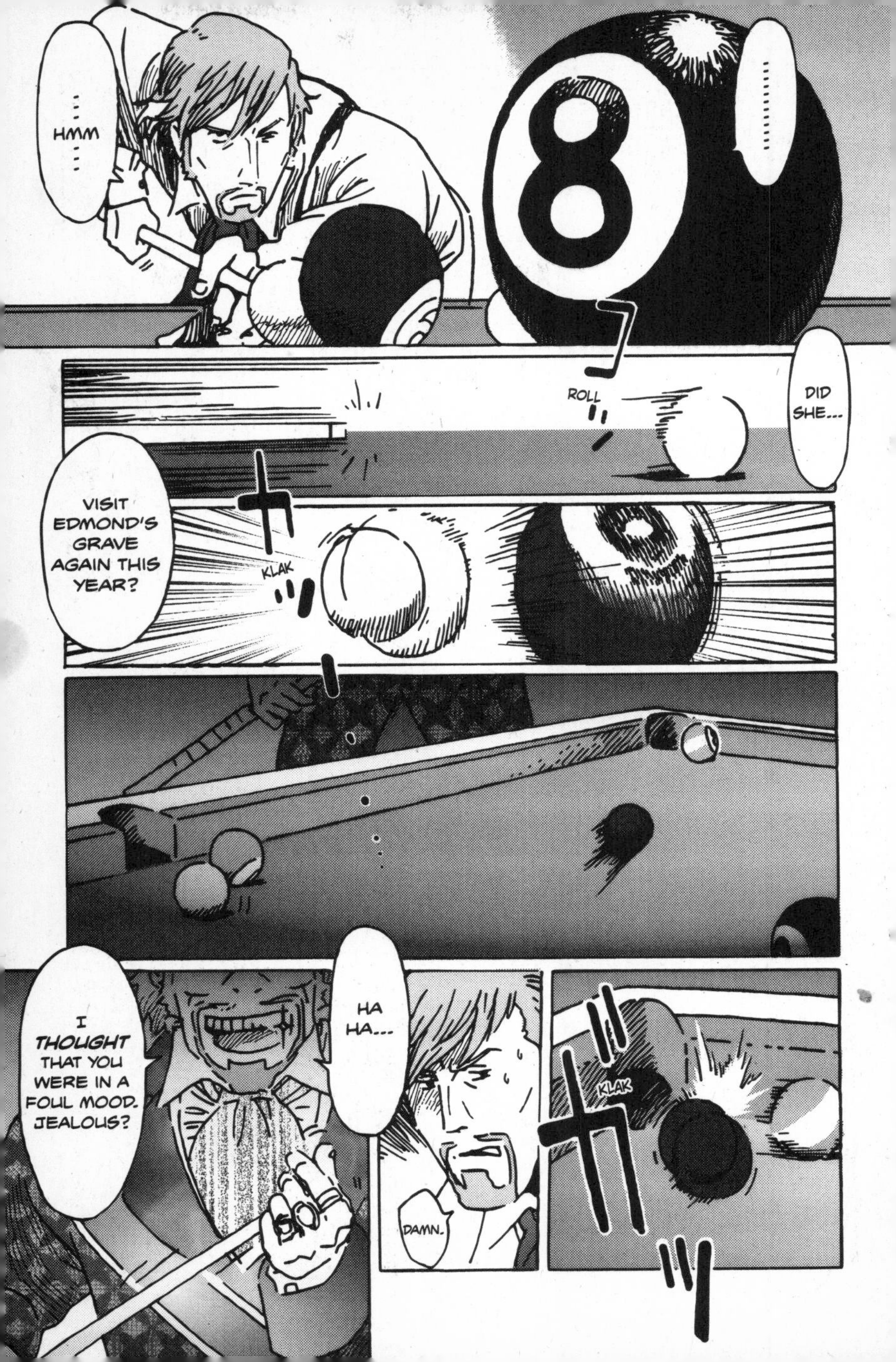
......
......HMM......
DID SHE...
ROLL
VISIT EDMOND'S GRAVE AGAIN THIS YEAR?
KLAK
KLAK
HA HA...
DAMN.
I *THOUGHT* THAT YOU WERE IN A FOUL MOOD. JEALOUS?

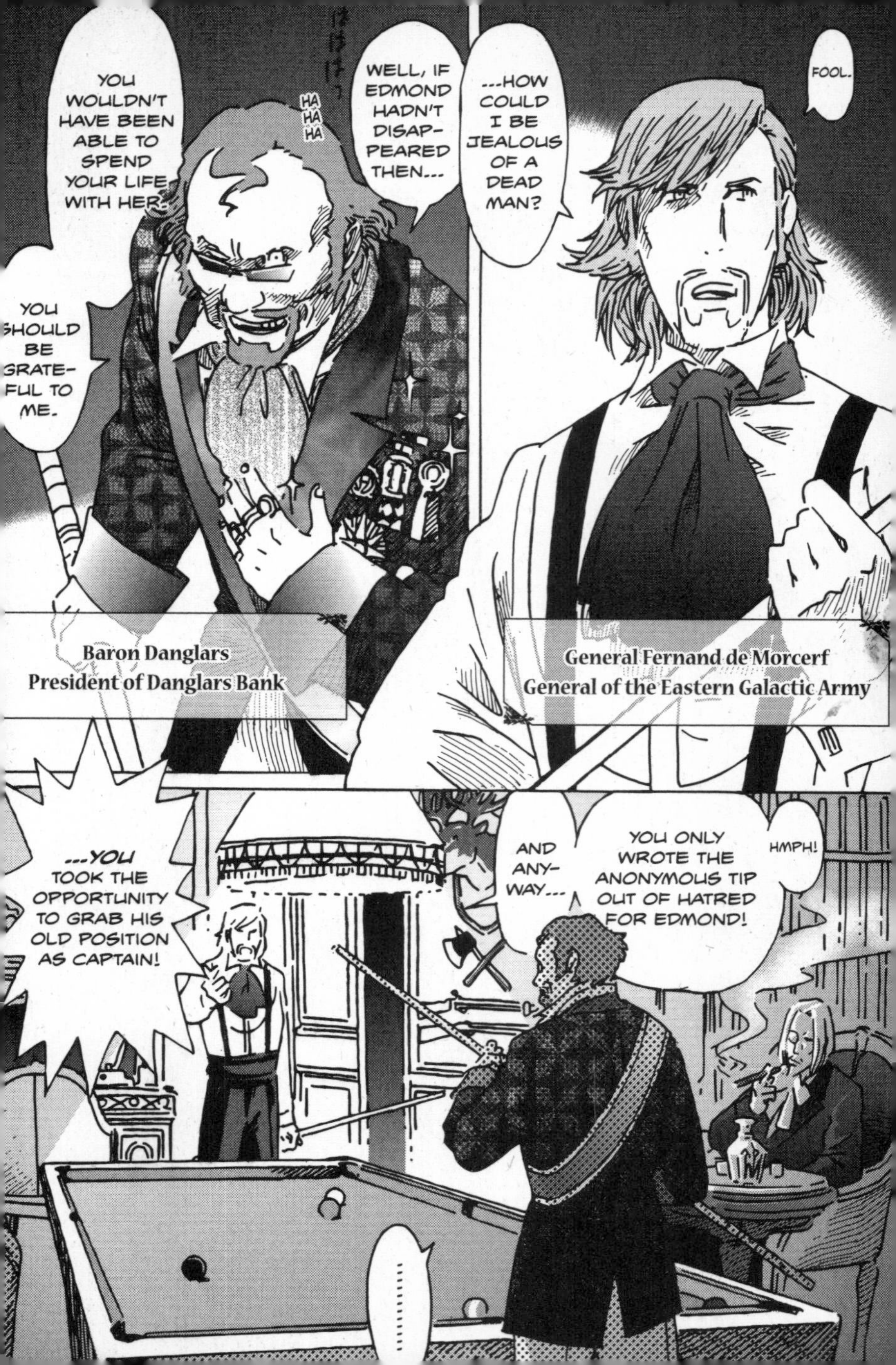
FOOL.
...HOW COULD I BE JEALOUS OF A DEAD MAN?
General Fernand de Morcerf
General of the Eastern Galactic Army
WELL, IF EDMOND HADN'T DISAPPEARED THEN...
HA HA HA
YOU WOULDN'T HAVE BEEN ABLE TO SPEND YOUR LIFE WITH HER.
YOU SHOULD BE GRATEFUL TO ME.
Baron Danglars
President of Danglars Bank
HMPH!
YOU ONLY WROTE THE ANONYMOUS TIP OUT OF HATRED FOR EDMOND!
AND ANYWAY...
...YOU TOOK THE OPPORTUNITY TO GRAB HIS OLD POSITION AS CAPTAIN!
......

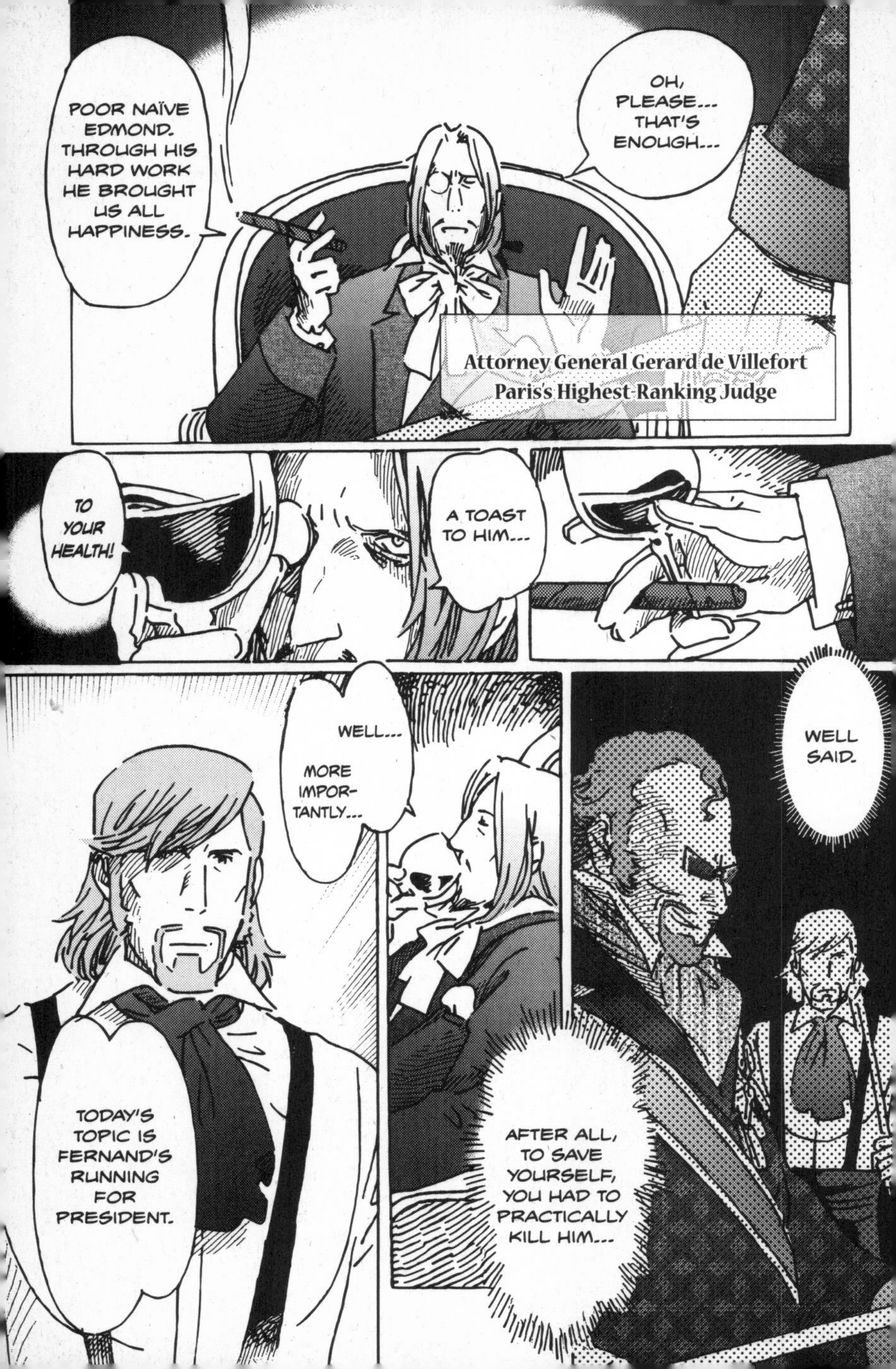
OH, PLEASE... THAT'S ENOUGH...
POOR NAÏVE EDMOND. THROUGH HIS HARD WORK HE BROUGHT US ALL HAPPINESS.
Attorney General Gerard de Villefort
Paris's Highest-Ranking Judge
A TOAST TO HIM...
TO YOUR HEALTH!
WELL SAID.
AFTER ALL, TO SAVE YOURSELF, YOU HAD TO PRACTICALLY KILL HIM...
WELL...
MORE IMPOR-TANTLY...
TODAY'S TOPIC IS FERNAND'S RUNNING FOR PRESIDENT.

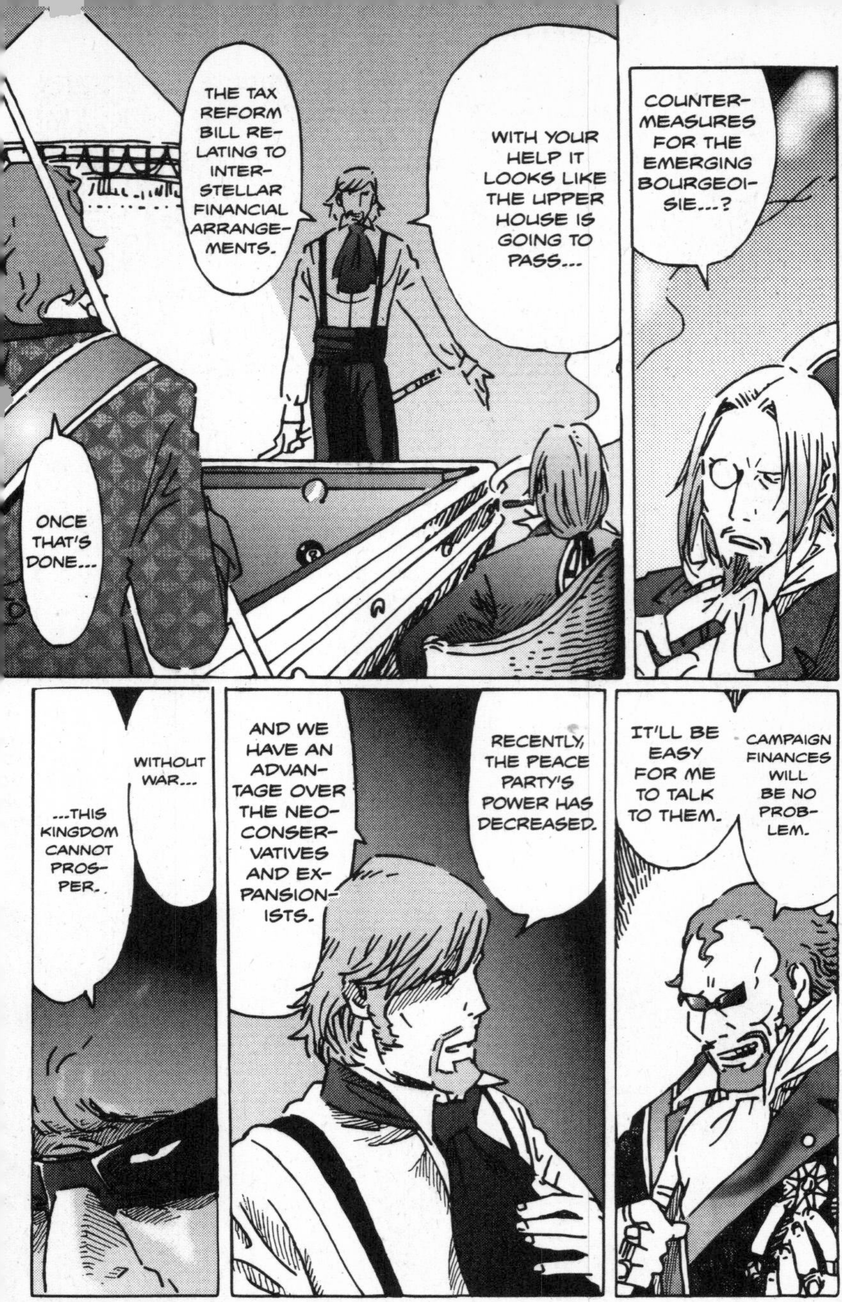
COUNTER-MEASURES FOR THE EMERGING BOURGEOISIE...?
WITH YOUR HELP IT LOOKS LIKE THE UPPER HOUSE IS GOING TO PASS...
THE TAX REFORM BILL RELATING TO INTERSTELLAR FINANCIAL ARRANGEMENTS.
ONCE THAT'S DONE...
CAMPAIGN FINANCES WILL BE NO PROBLEM.
IT'LL BE EASY FOR ME TO TALK TO THEM.
RECENTLY, THE PEACE PARTY'S POWER HAS DECREASED.
AND WE HAVE AN ADVANTAGE OVER THE NEOCONSERVATIVES AND EXPANSIONISTS.
WITHOUT WAR...
...THIS KINGDOM CANNOT PROSPER.

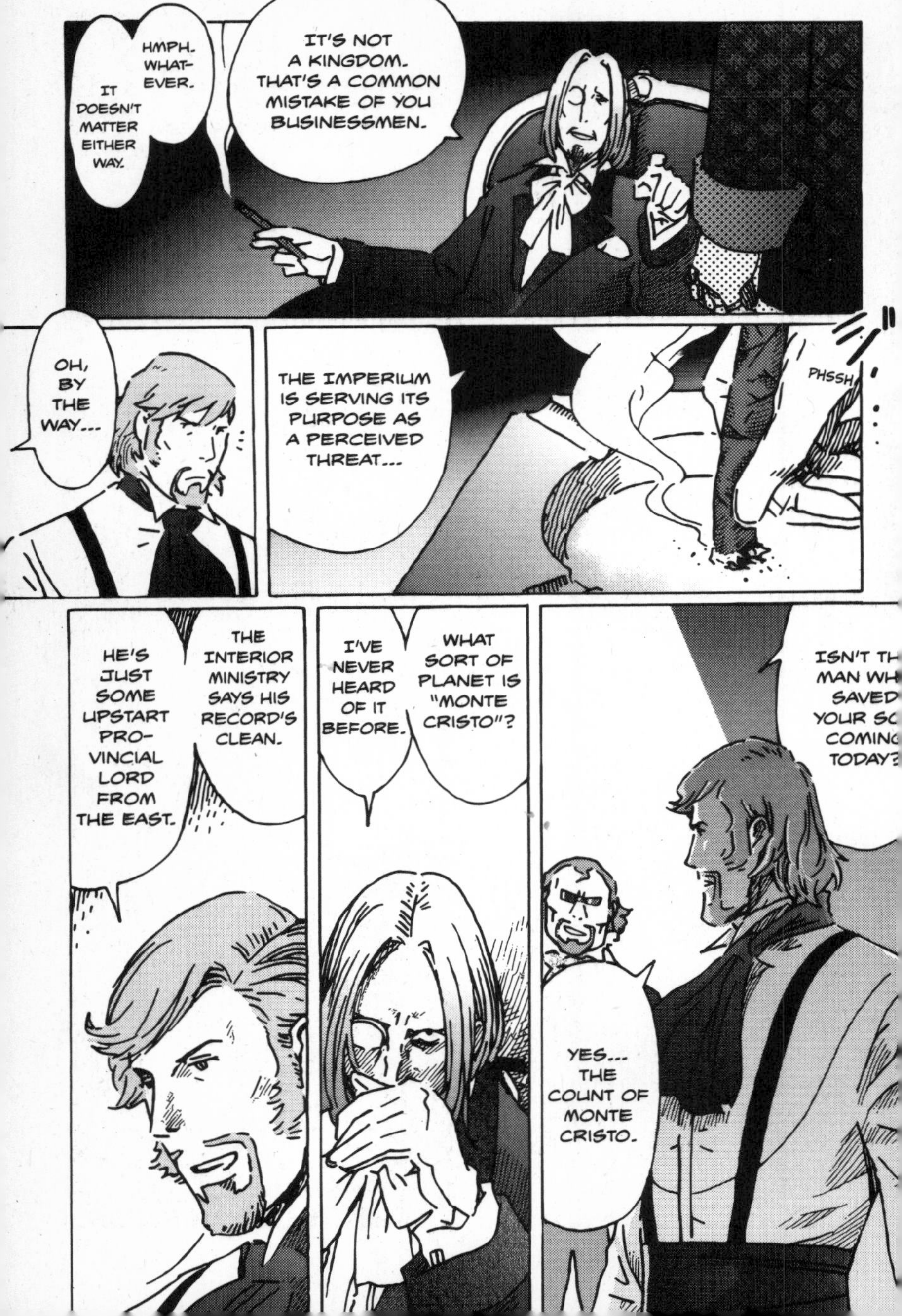
IT'S NOT A KINGDOM. THAT'S A COMMON MISTAKE OF YOU BUSINESSMEN.
HMPH. WHATEVER.
IT DOESN'T MATTER EITHER WAY.
PHSSH
THE IMPERIUM IS SERVING ITS PURPOSE AS A PERCEIVED THREAT...
OH, BY THE WAY...
ISN'T TH MAN WH SAVED YOUR SC COMING TODAY?
YES... THE COUNT OF MONTE CRISTO.
WHAT SORT OF PLANET IS "MONTE CRISTO"?
I'VE NEVER HEARD OF IT BEFORE.
THE INTERIOR MINISTRY SAYS HIS RECORD'S CLEAN.
HE'S JUST SOME UPSTART PROVINCIAL LORD FROM THE EAST.

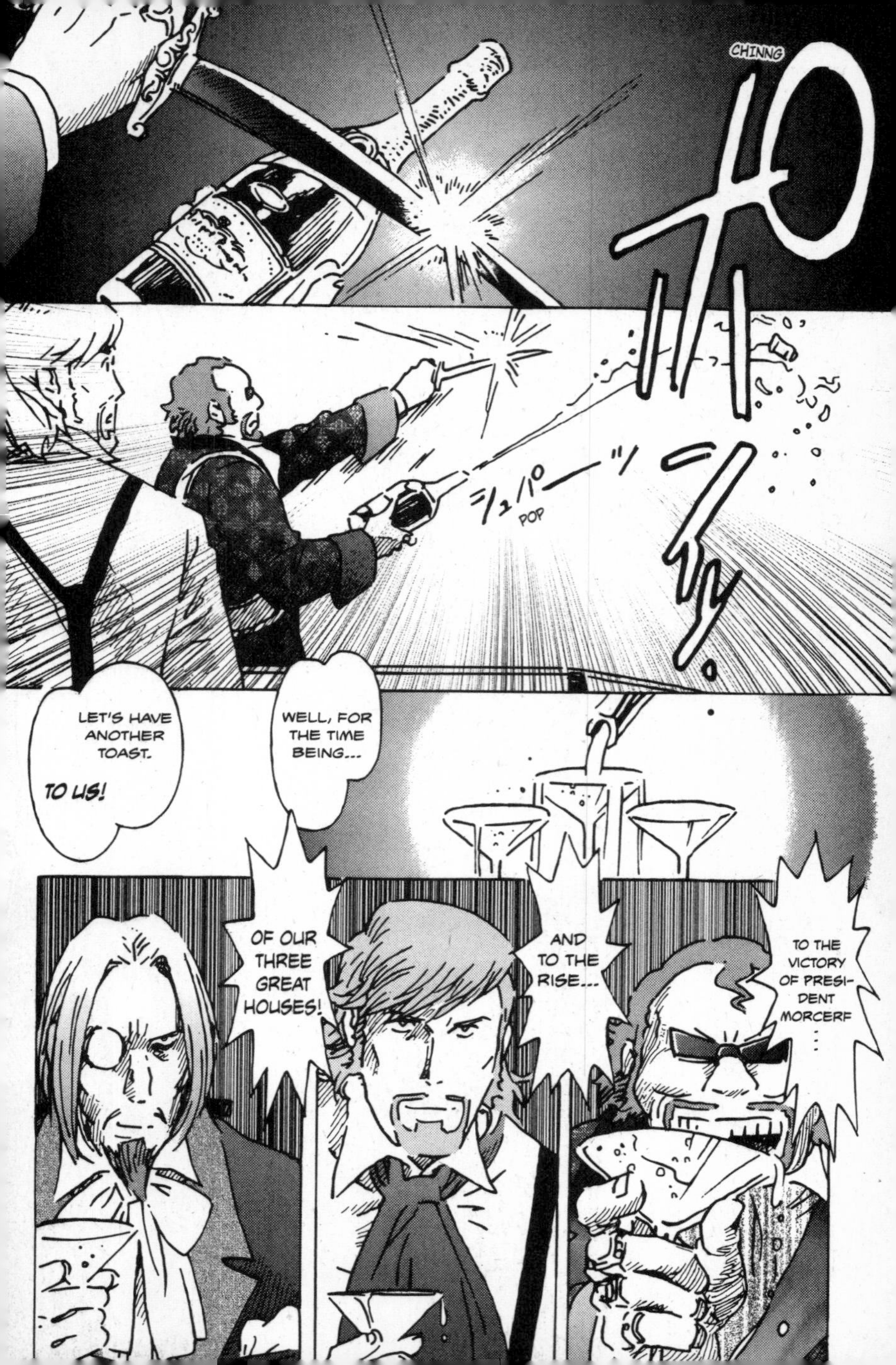
CHINNG
POP
WELL, FOR THE TIME BEING...
LET'S HAVE ANOTHER TOAST.
TO US!
TO THE VICTORY OF PRESI- DENT MORCERF...
AND TO THE RISE...
OF OUR THREE GREAT HOUSES!

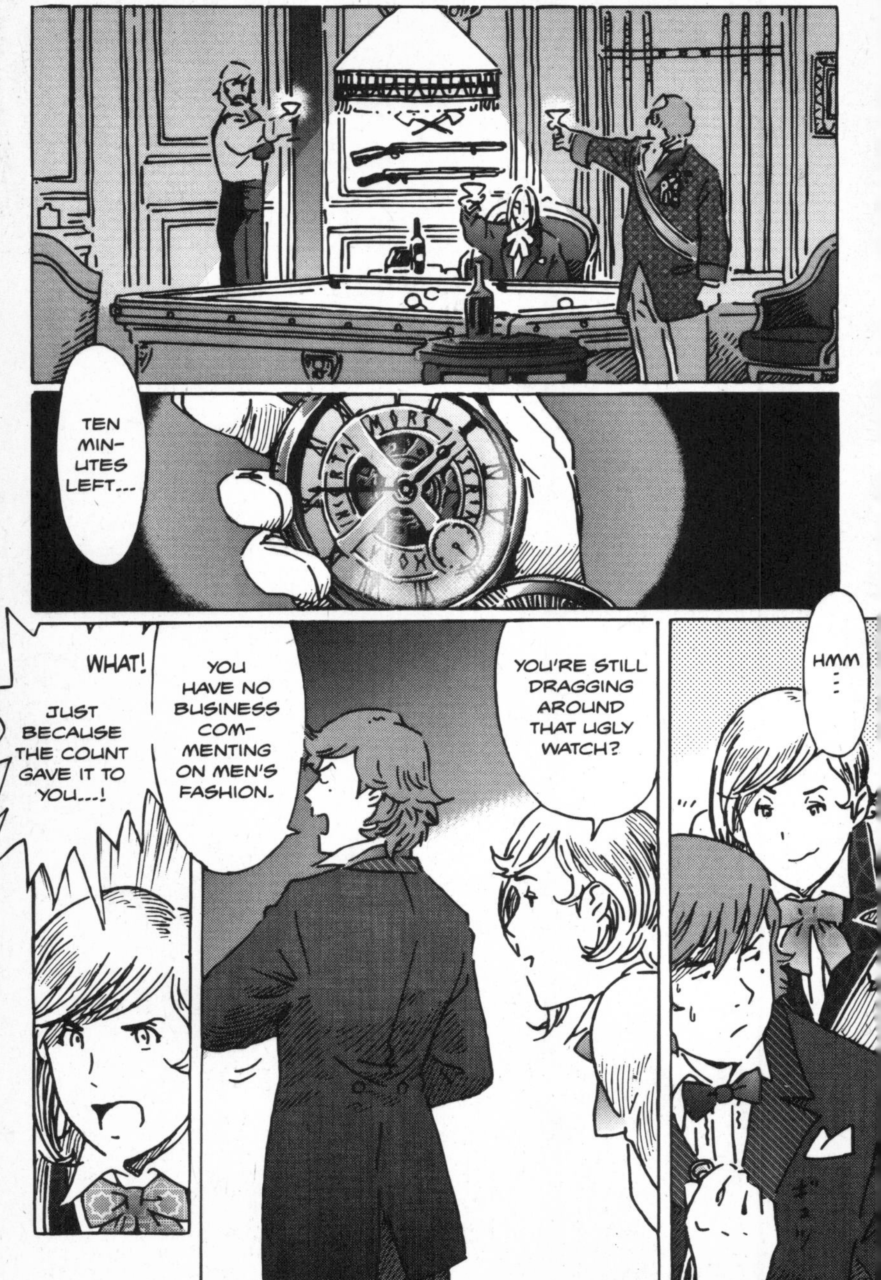
TEN MINUTES LEFT...
HMM...
YOU'RE STILL DRAGGING AROUND THAT UGLY WATCH?
YOU HAVE NO BUSINESS COMMENTING ON MEN'S FASHION.
WHAT!
JUST BECAUSE THE COUNT GAVE IT TO YOU...!

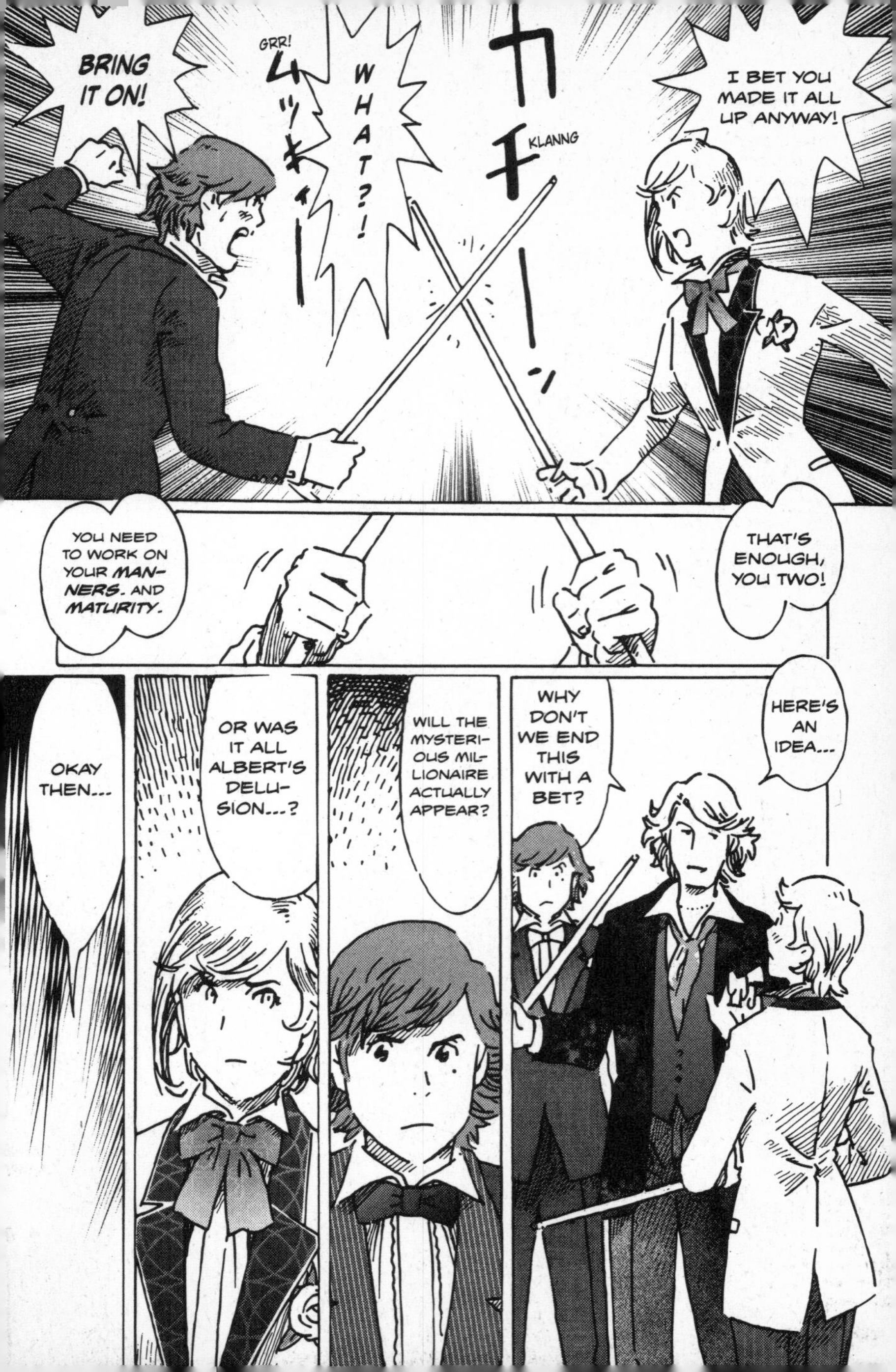
I BET YOU MADE IT ALL UP ANYWAY!
KLANNG
カチーン
WHAT?!
GRR!
ムッキィー
BRING IT ON!
THAT'S ENOUGH, YOU TWO!
YOU NEED TO WORK ON YOUR MANNERS. AND MATURITY.
HERE'S AN IDEA...
WHY DON'T WE END THIS WITH A BET?
WILL THE MYSTERIOUS MILLIONAIRE ACTUALLY APPEAR?
OR WAS IT ALL ALBERT'S DELUSION...?
OKAY THEN...

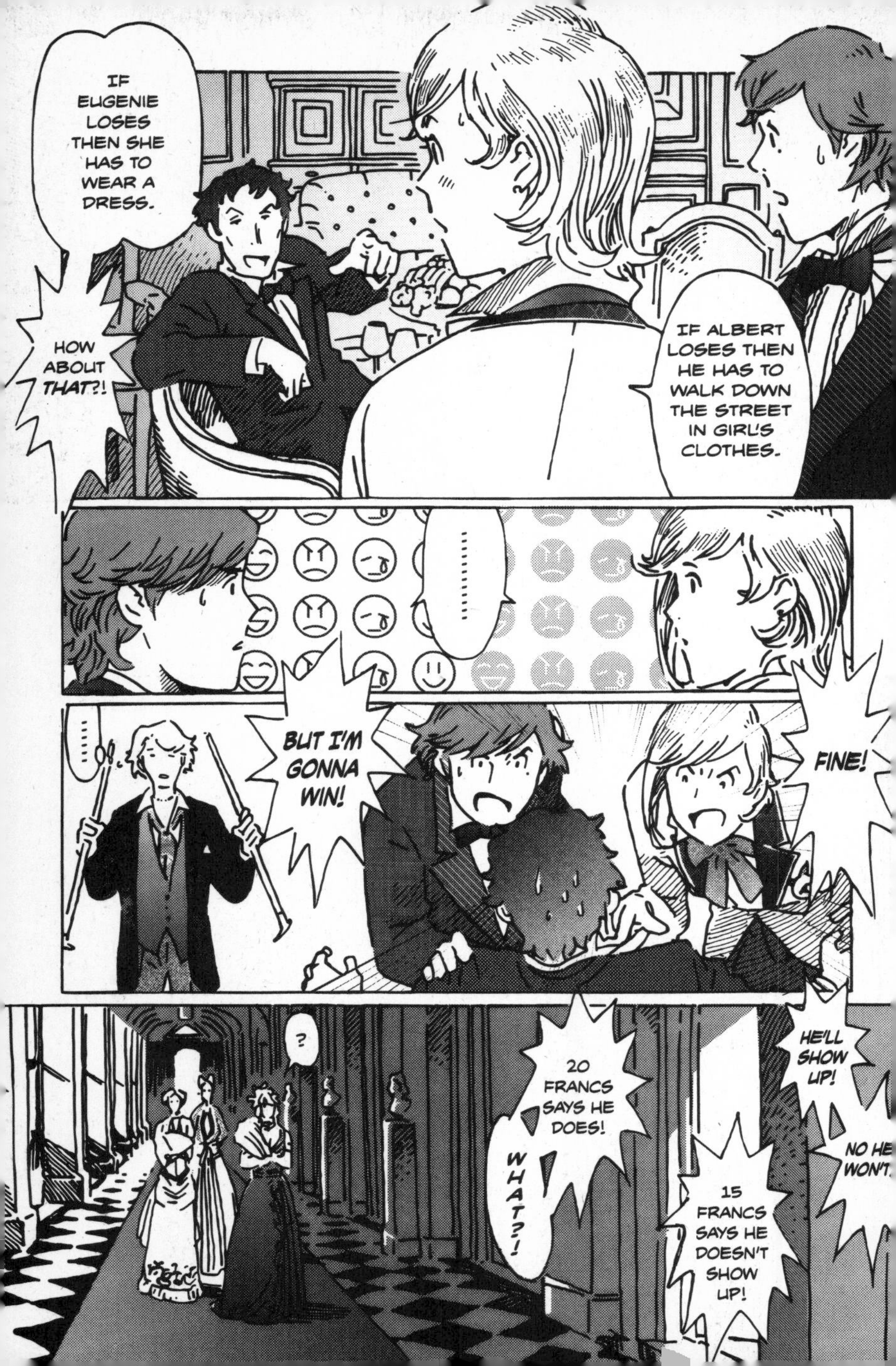
IF ALBERT LOSES THEN HE HAS TO WALK DOWN THE STREET IN GIRL'S CLOTHES.
IF EUGENIE LOSES THEN SHE HAS TO WEAR A DRESS.
HOW ABOUT *THAT*?!
......
FINE!
BUT I'M GONNA WIN!
......
HE'LL SHOW UP!
NO HE WON'T.
15 FRANCS SAYS HE DOESN'T SHOW UP!
20 FRANCS SAYS HE DOES!
WHAT?!
?

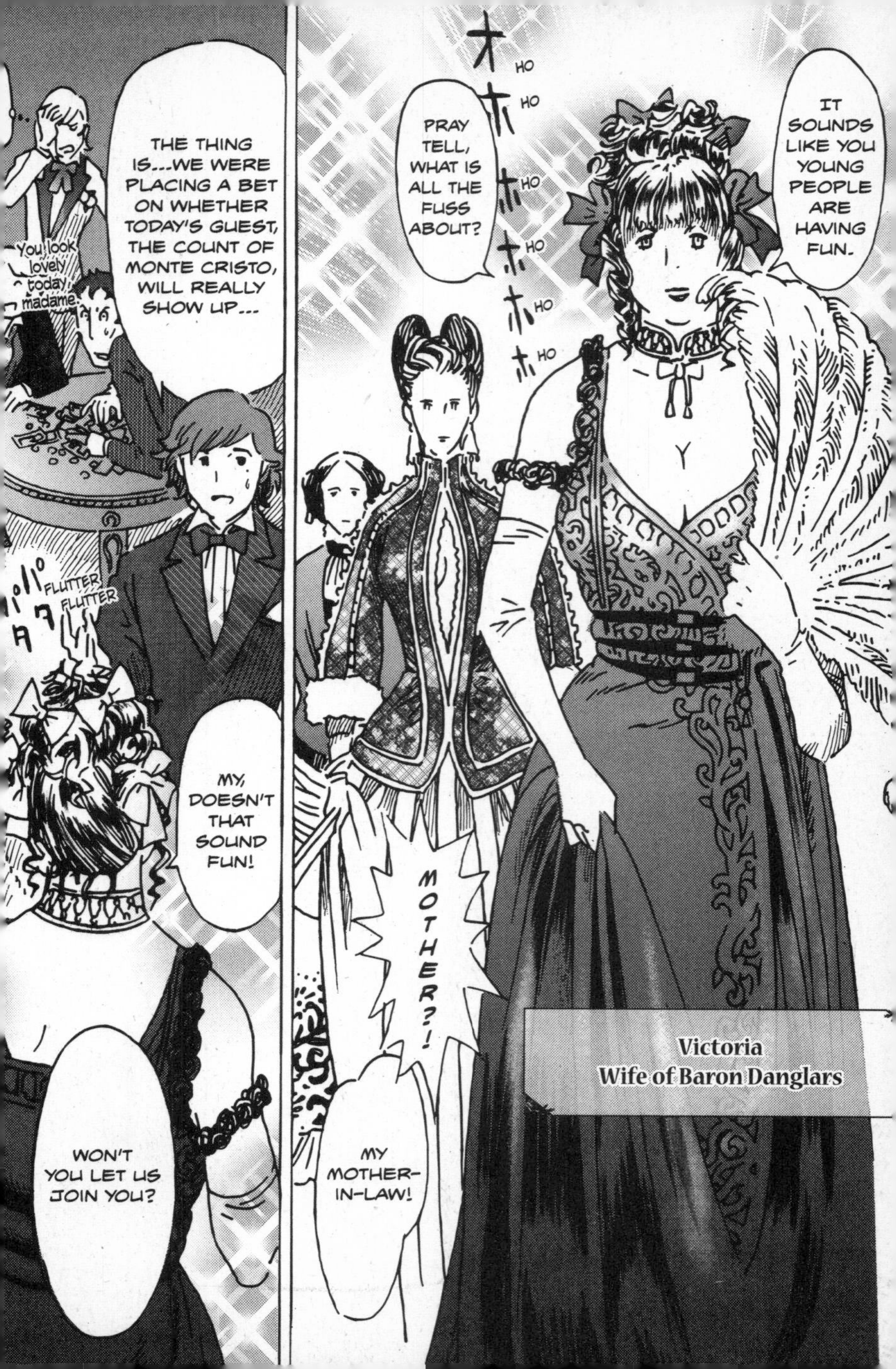
IT SOUNDS LIKE YOU YOUNG PEOPLE ARE HAVING FUN.
HO HO HO HO HO HO
PRAY TELL, WHAT IS ALL THE FUSS ABOUT?
MOTHER?!
MY MOTHER-IN-LAW!
Victoria
Wife of Baron Danglars
THE THING IS...WE WERE PLACING A BET ON WHETHER TODAY'S GUEST, THE COUNT OF MONTE CRISTO, WILL REALLY SHOW UP...
You look lovely today madame.
FLUTTER FLUTTER
MY, DOESN'T THAT SOUND FUN!
WON'T YOU LET US JOIN YOU?

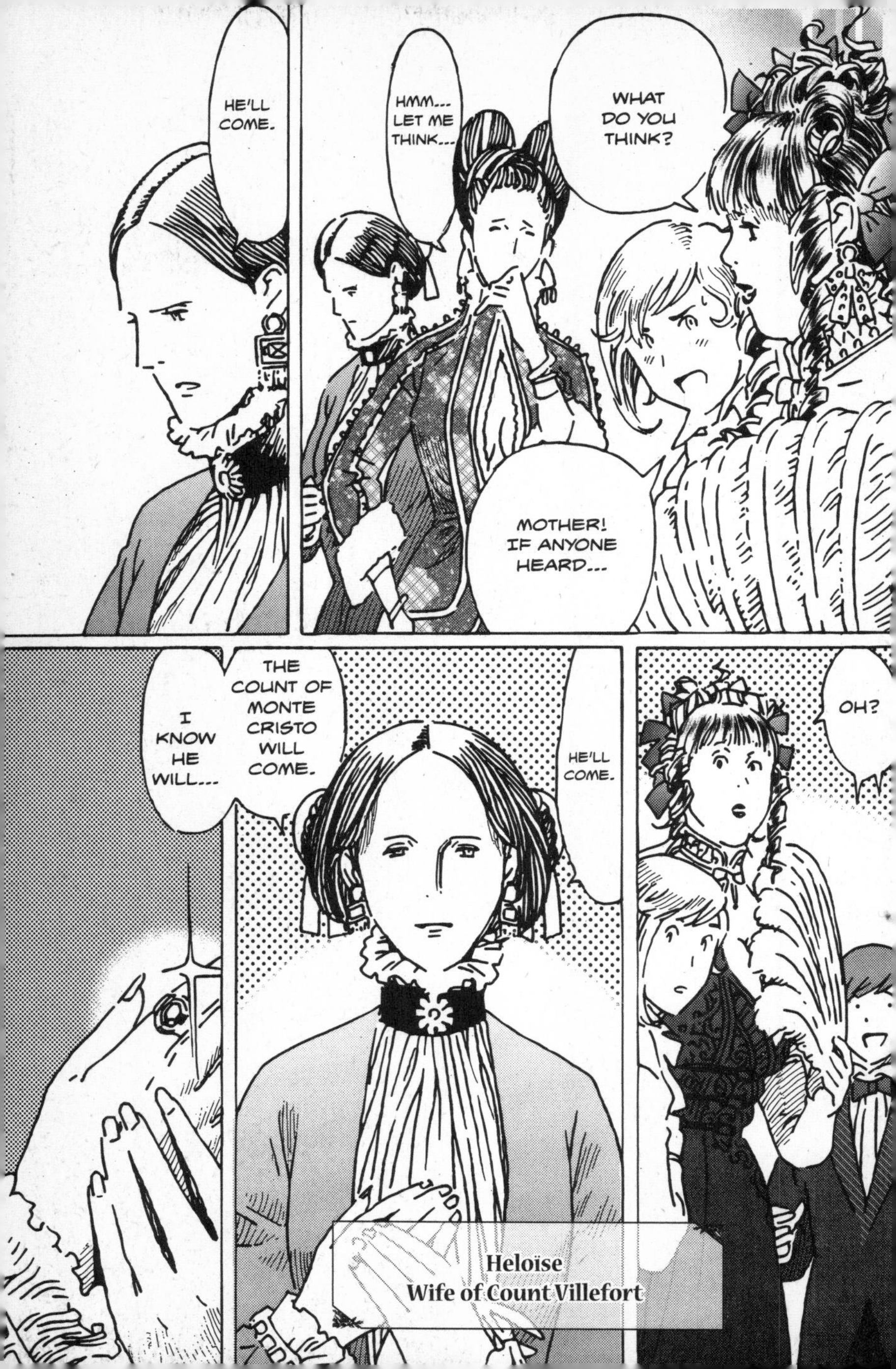
WHAT DO YOU THINK?
HMM... LET ME THINK...
MOTHER! IF ANYONE HEARD...
HE'LL COME.
OH?
HE'LL COME.
THE COUNT OF MONTE CRISTO WILL COME.
I KNOW HE WILL...
Heloïse
Wife of Count Villefort

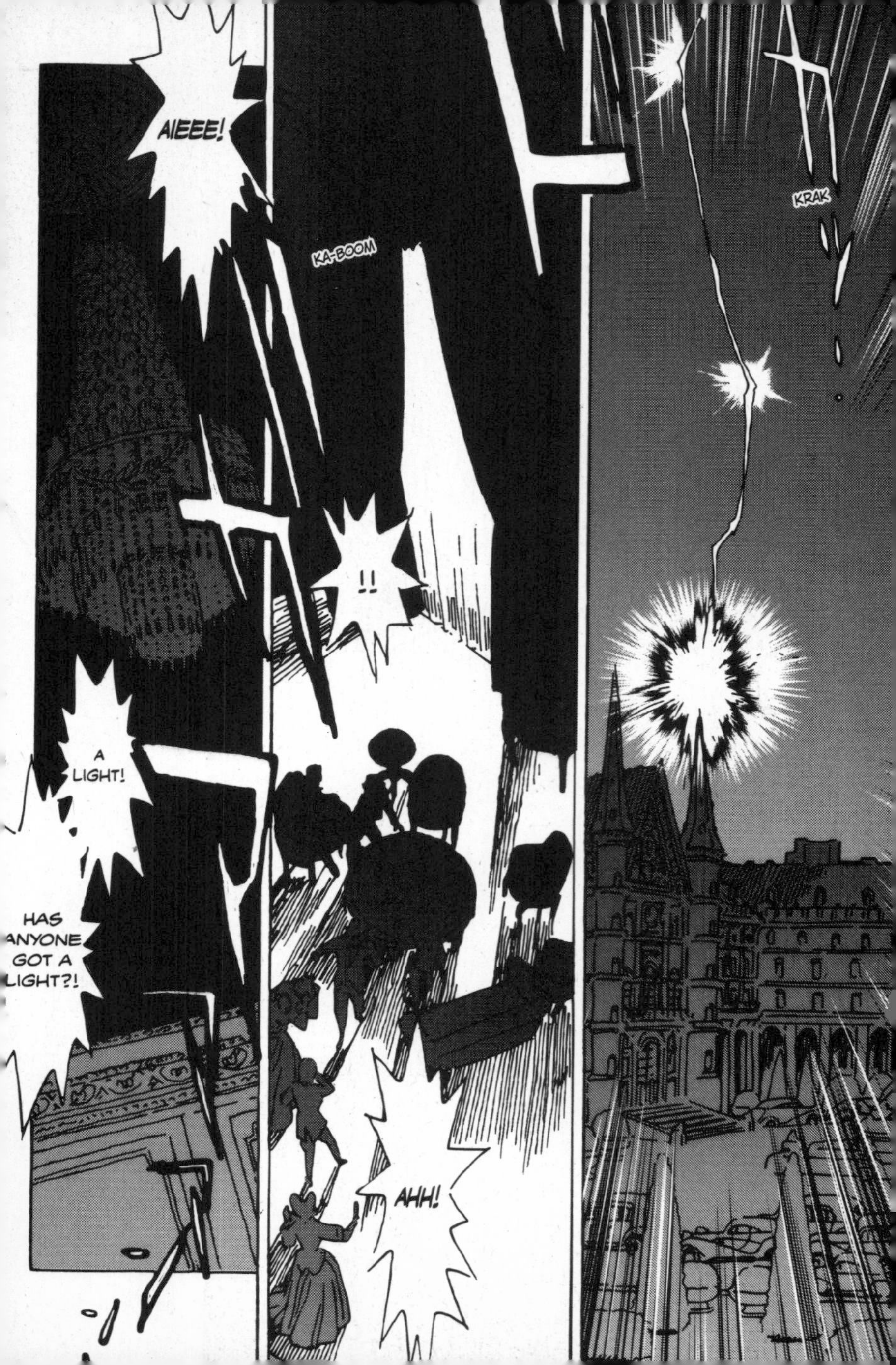
KRAK
KA-BOOM
!!
AHH!
AIEEE!
A LIGHT!
HAS ANYONE GOT A LIGHT?!

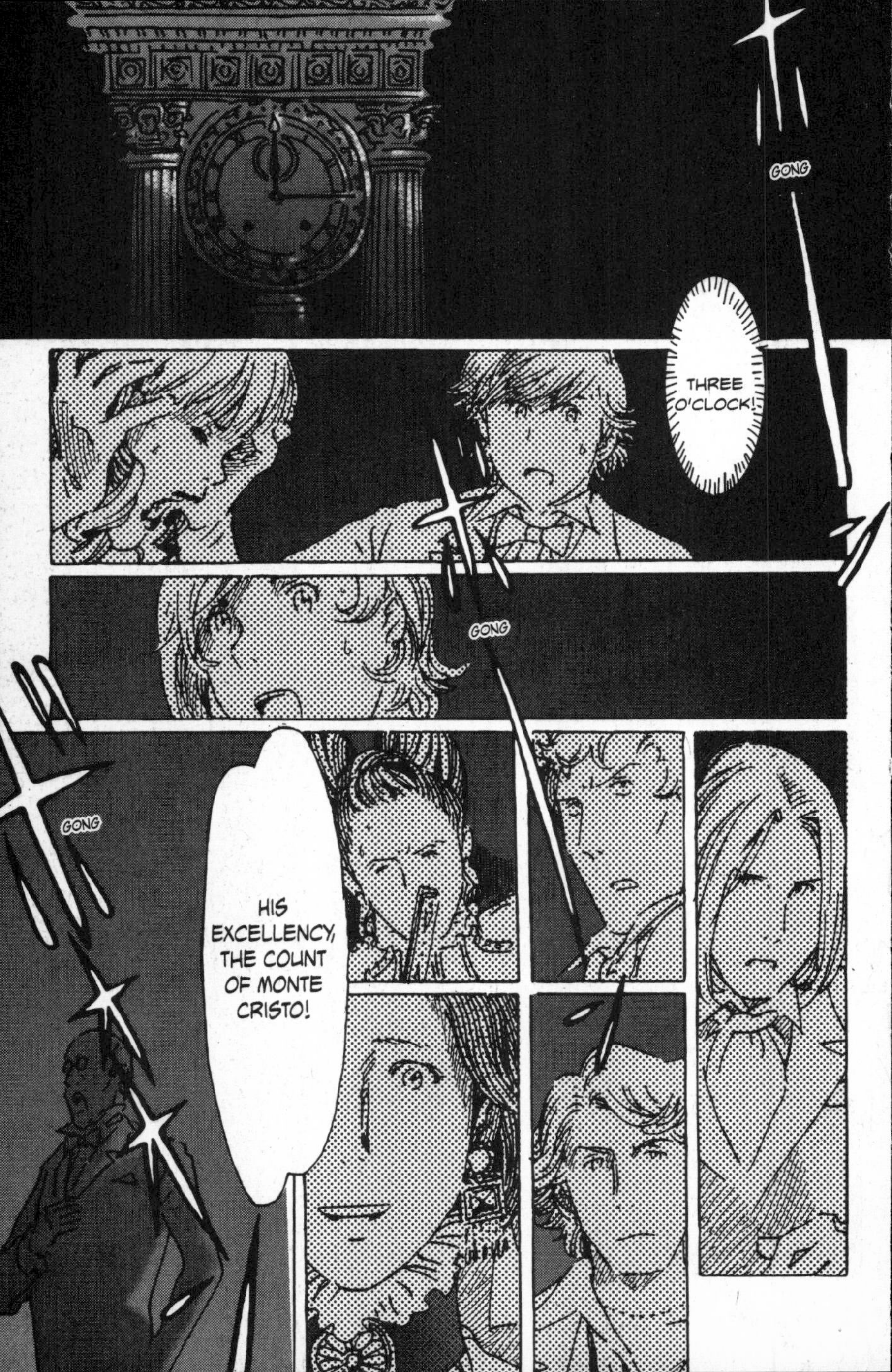
GONG
THREE O'CLOCK!
GONG
GONG
HIS EXCELLENCY, THE COUNT OF MONTE CRISTO!

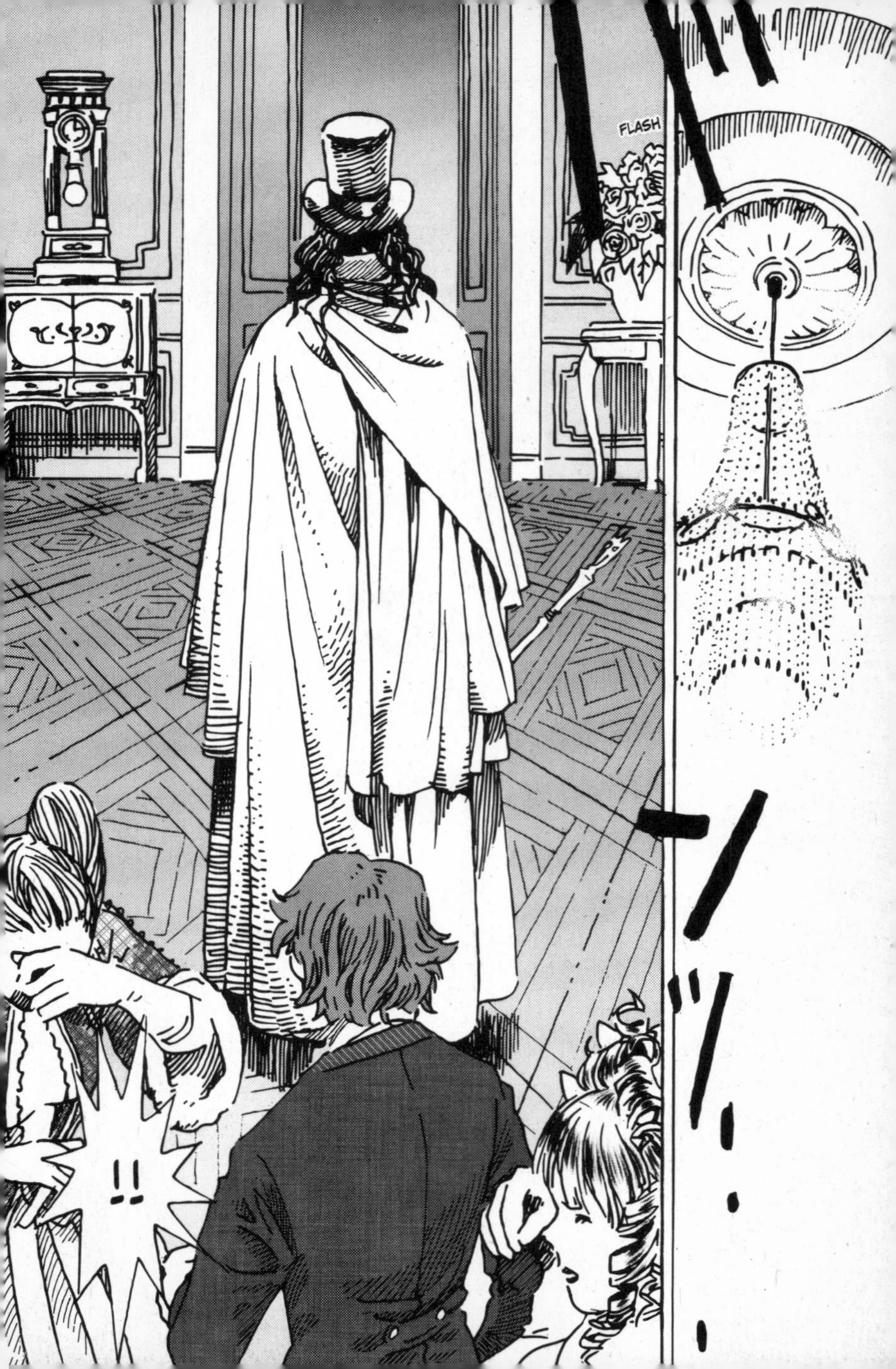
FLASH
!!

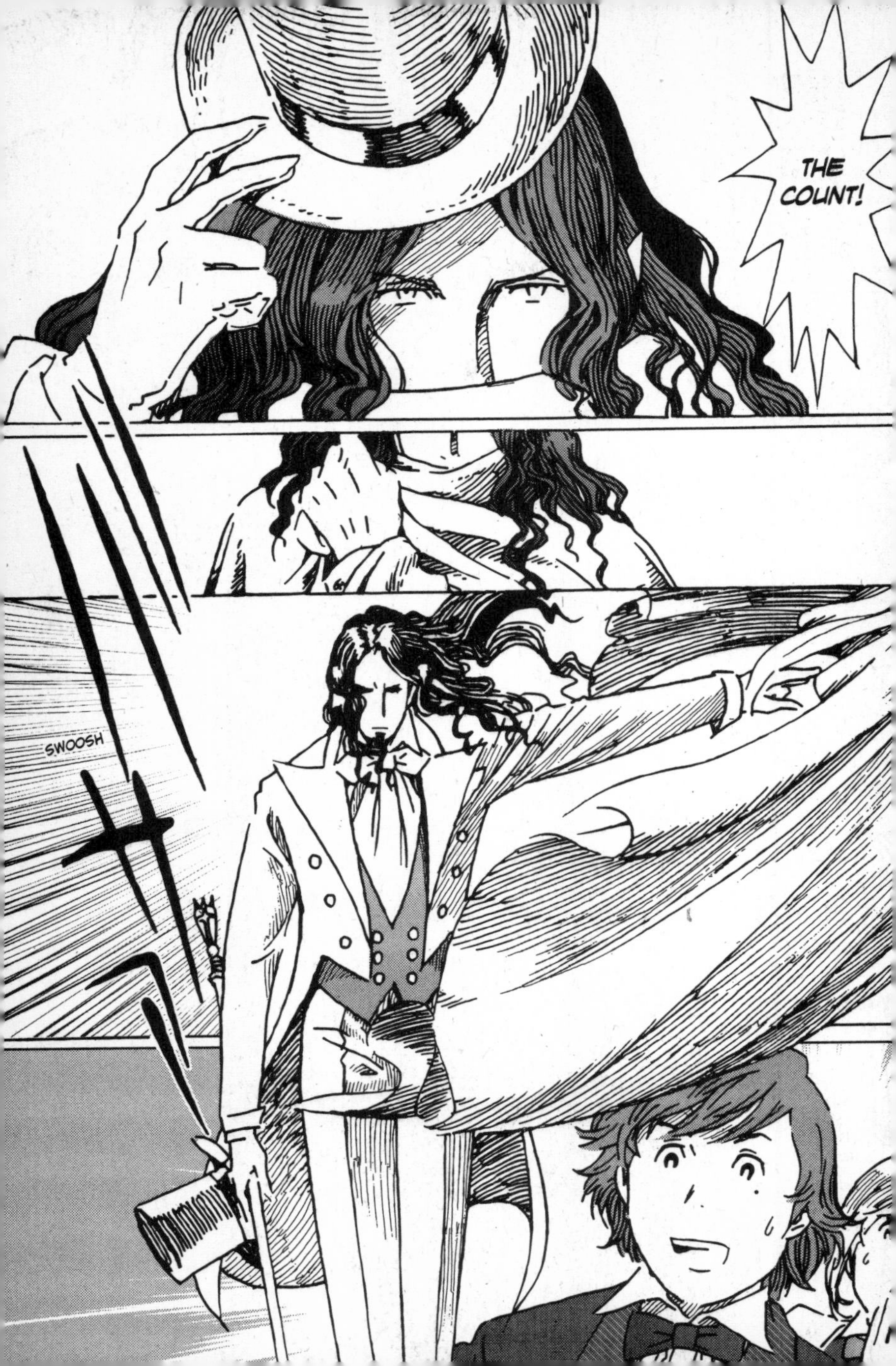
THE COUNT!
SWOOSH

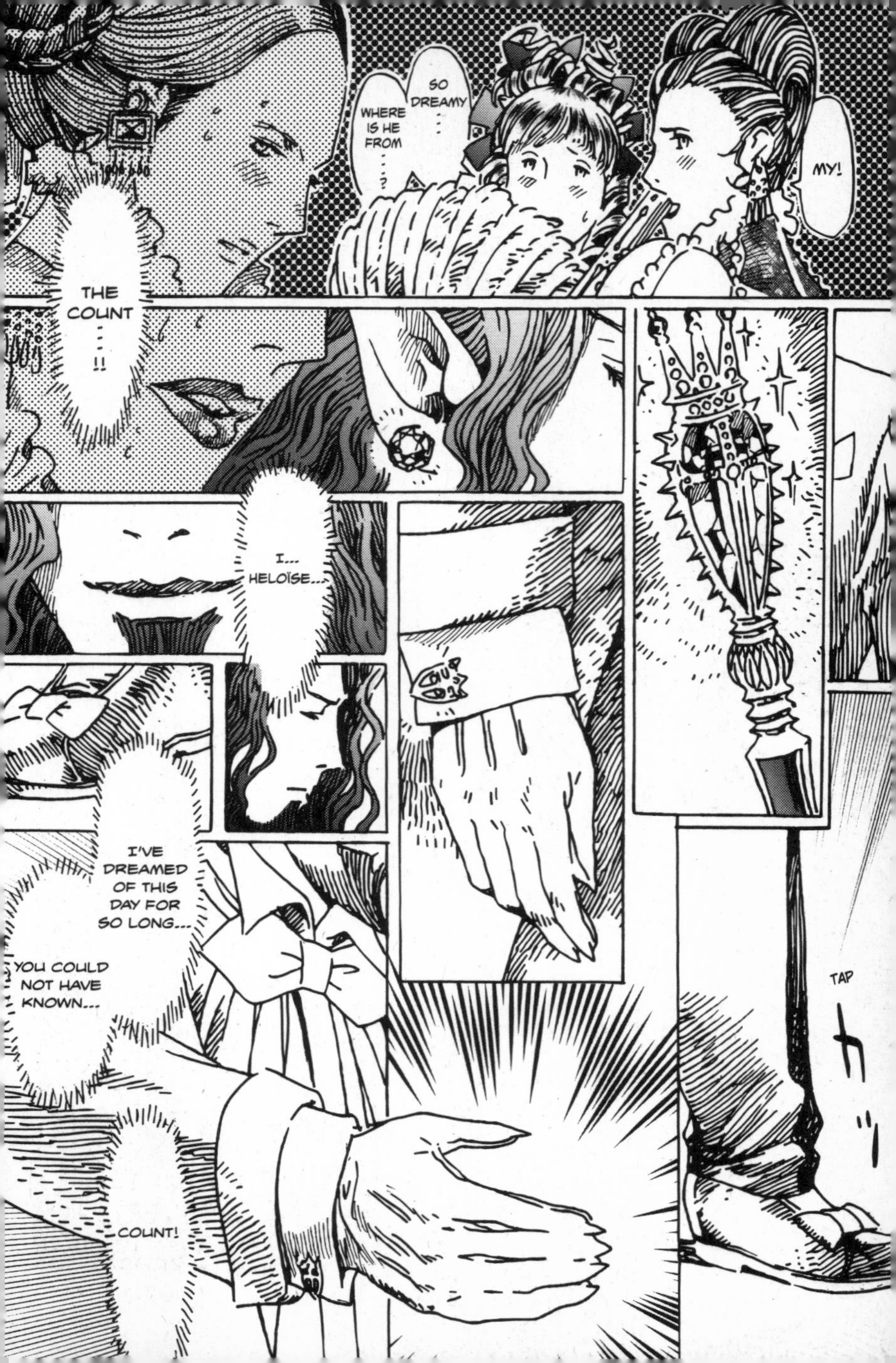
MY!
SO DREAMY...
WHERE IS HE FROM...?
THE COUNT...!!
I... HELOÏSE...
TAP
I'VE DREAMED OF THIS DAY FOR SO LONG...
YOU COULD NOT HAVE KNOWN...
COUNT!

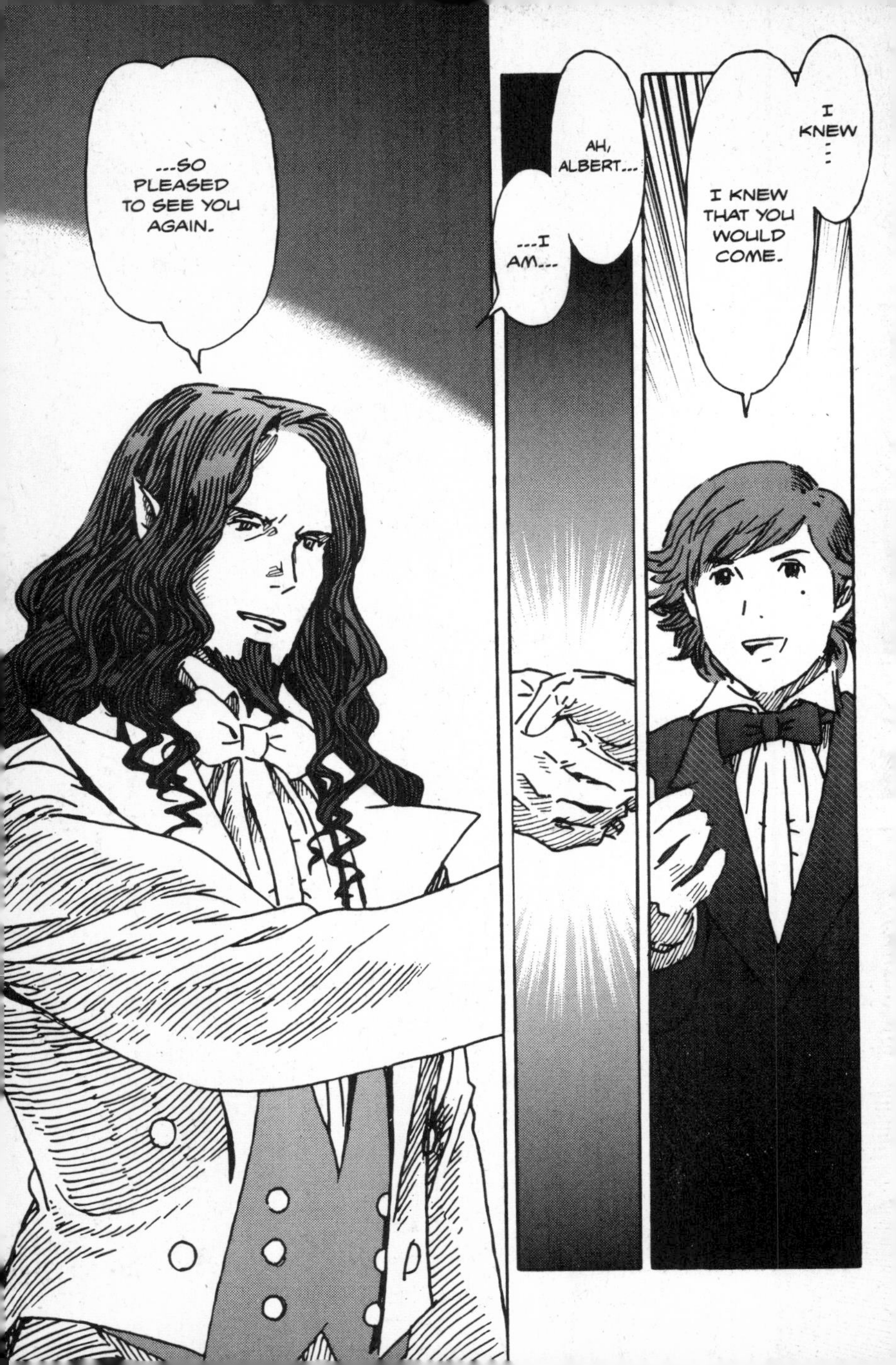
I KNEW...
I KNEW THAT YOU WOULD COME.
AH, ALBERT...
...I AM...
...SO PLEASED TO SEE YOU AGAIN.

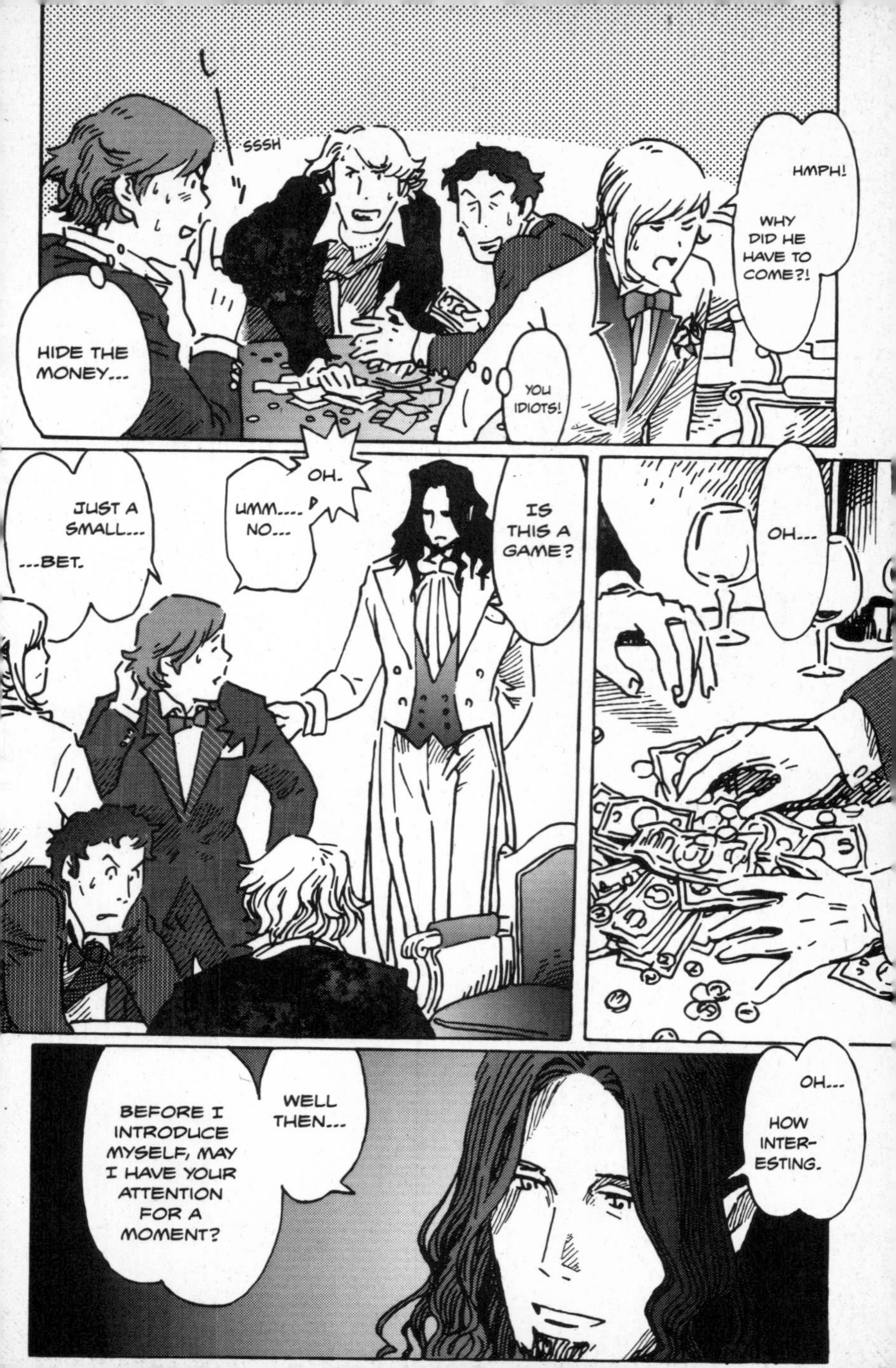
HMPH! WHY DID HE HAVE TO COME?!
SSSH
YOU IDIOTS!
HIDE THE MONEY...
OH...
IS THIS A GAME?
OH.
UMM.... NO...
JUST A SMALL... ...BET.
OH... HOW INTER-ESTING.
WELL THEN...
BEFORE I INTRODUCE MYSELF, MAY I HAVE YOUR ATTENTION FOR A MOMENT?

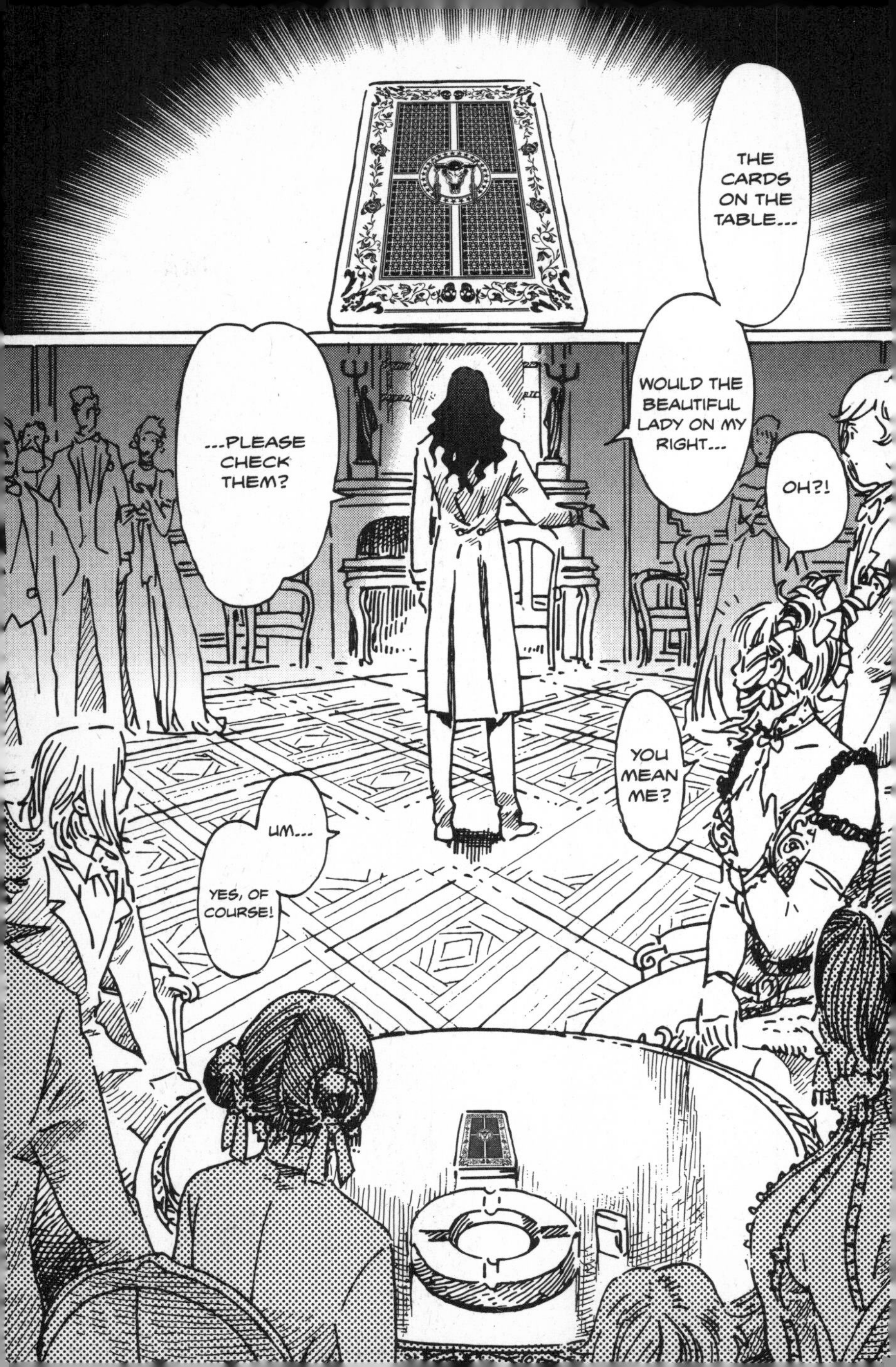
THE CARDS ON THE TABLE...
WOULD THE BEAUTIFUL LADY ON MY RIGHT...
...PLEASE CHECK THEM?
OH?!
YOU MEAN ME?
UM...
YES, OF COURSE!

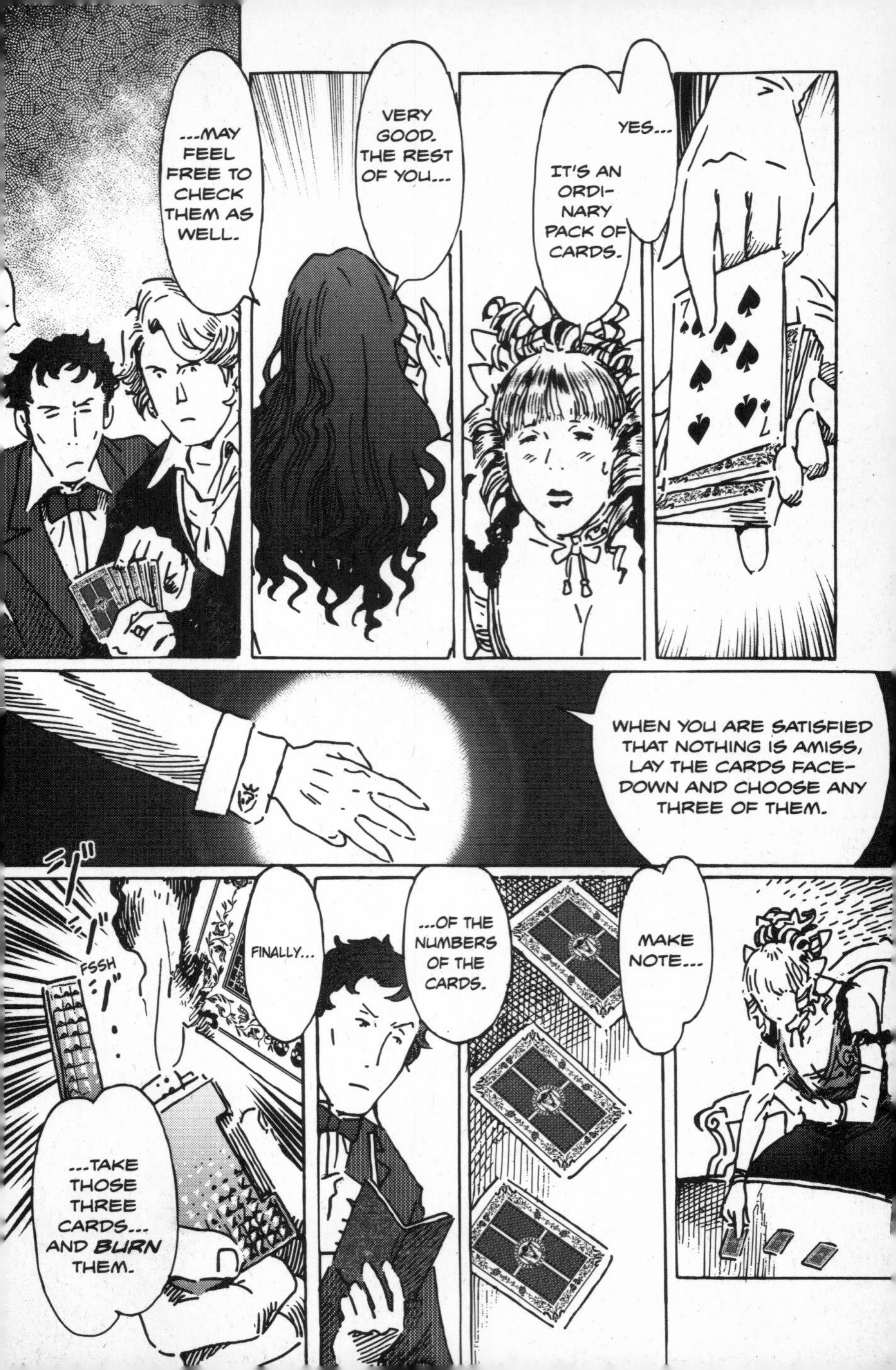
YES...
IT'S AN ORDINARY PACK OF CARDS.
VERY GOOD. THE REST OF YOU...
...MAY FEEL FREE TO CHECK THEM AS WELL.
WHEN YOU ARE SATISFIED THAT NOTHING IS AMISS, LAY THE CARDS FACE-DOWN AND CHOOSE ANY THREE OF THEM.
MAKE NOTE...
...OF THE NUMBERS OF THE CARDS.
FINALLY...
FSSH
...TAKE THOSE THREE CARDS... AND *BURN* THEM.

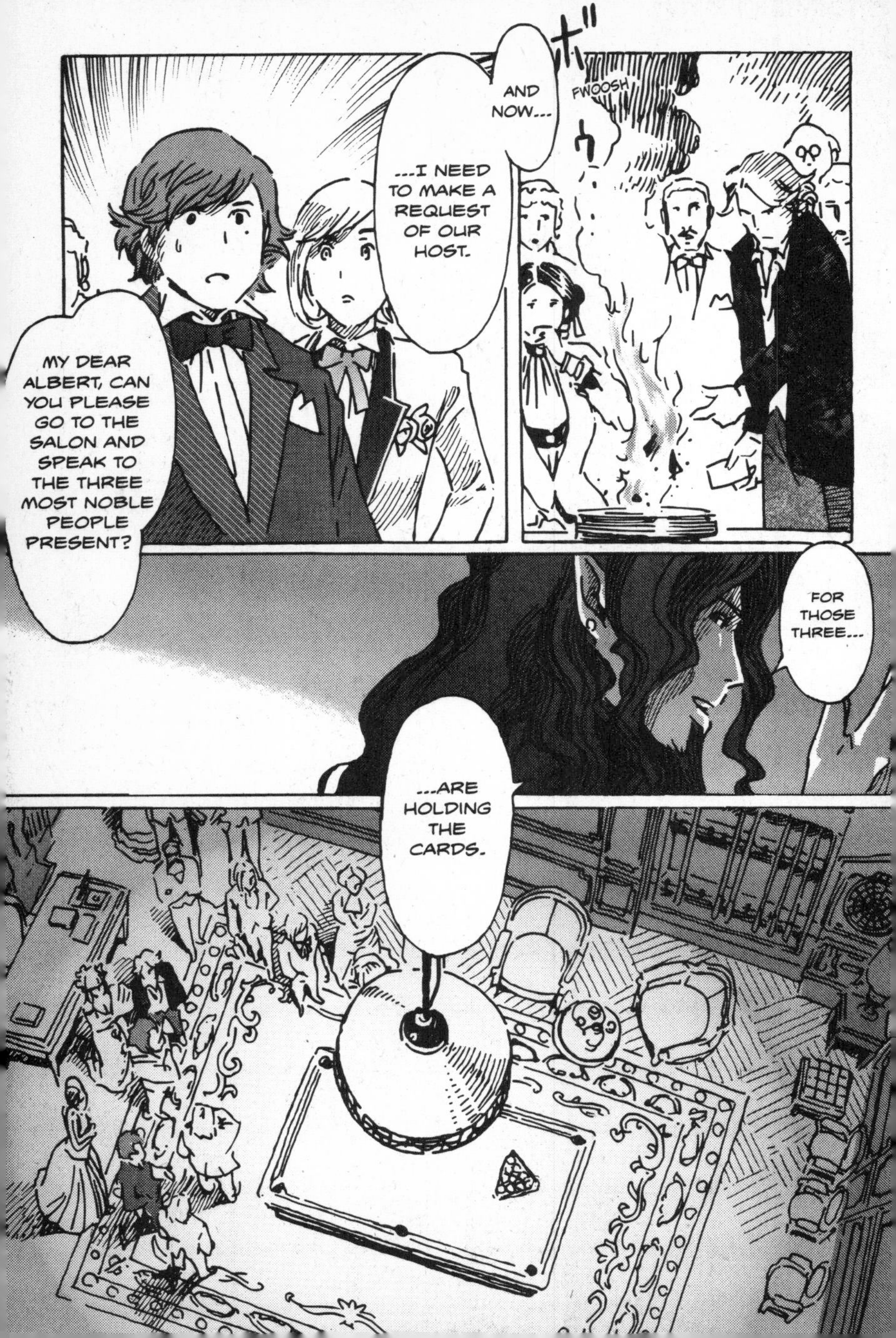
AND NOW...
FWOOSH
...I NEED TO MAKE A REQUEST OF OUR HOST.
MY DEAR ALBERT, CAN YOU PLEASE GO TO THE SALON AND SPEAK TO THE THREE MOST NOBLE PEOPLE PRESENT?
FOR THOSE THREE...
...ARE HOLDING THE CARDS.

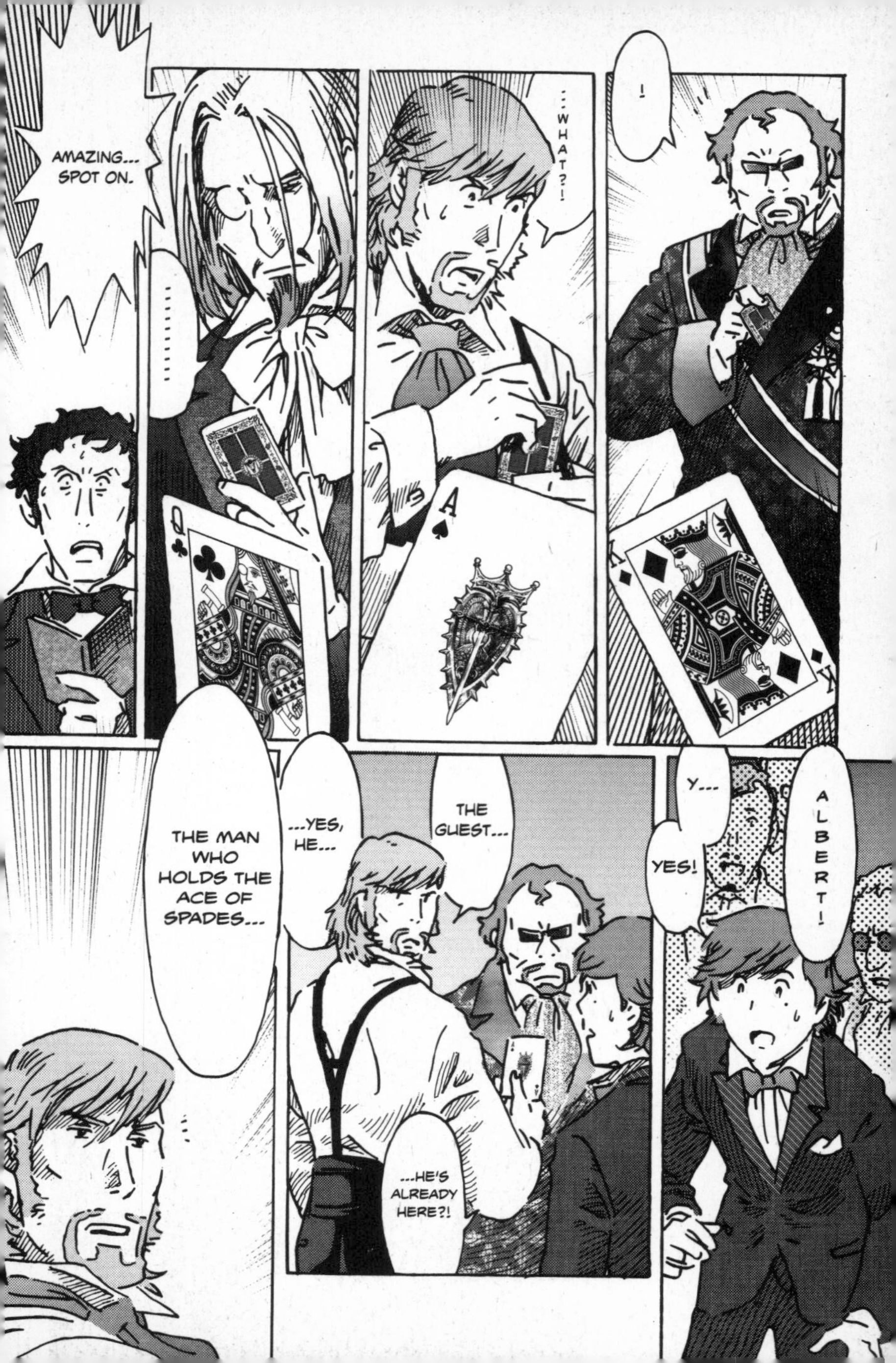
!
...WHAT?!
......
AMAZING... SPOT ON.
ALBERT!
Y...
YES!
THE GUEST...
...YES, HE...
...HE'S ALREADY HERE?!
THE MAN WHO HOLDS THE ACE OF SPADES...
...

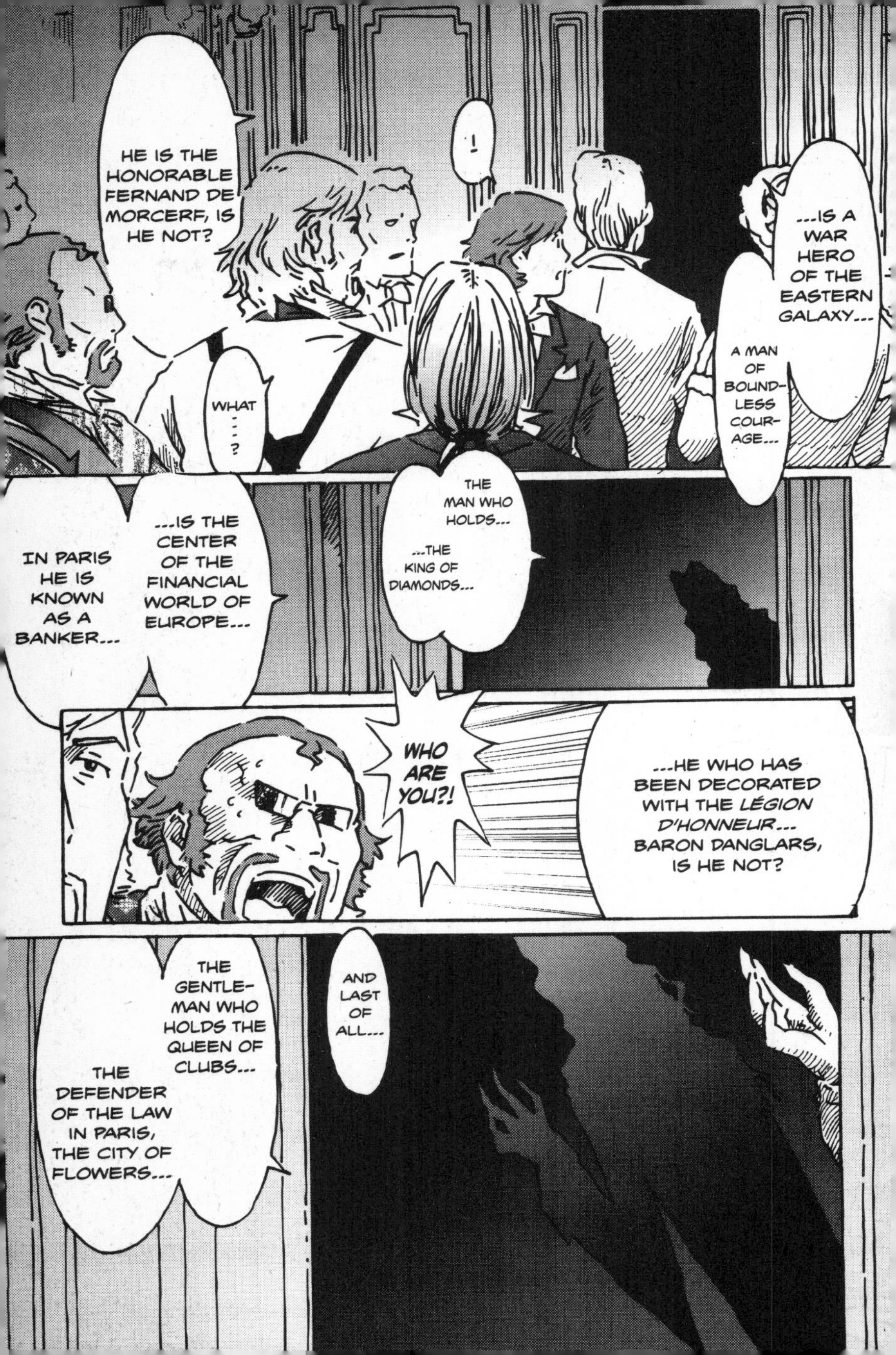

...IS A WAR HERO OF THE EASTERN GALAXY...
A MAN OF BOUNDLESS COURAGE...
!
HE IS THE HONORABLE FERNAND DE MORCERF, IS HE NOT?
WHAT...?
THE MAN WHO HOLDS...
...THE KING OF DIAMONDS...
...IS THE CENTER OF THE FINANCIAL WORLD OF EUROPE...
IN PARIS HE IS KNOWN AS A BANKER...
...HE WHO HAS BEEN DECORATED WITH THE *LÉGION D'HONNEUR*... BARON DANGLARS, IS HE NOT?
WHO ARE YOU?!
AND LAST OF ALL...
THE GENTLEMAN WHO HOLDS THE QUEEN OF CLUBS...
THE DEFENDER OF THE LAW IN PARIS, THE CITY OF FLOWERS...

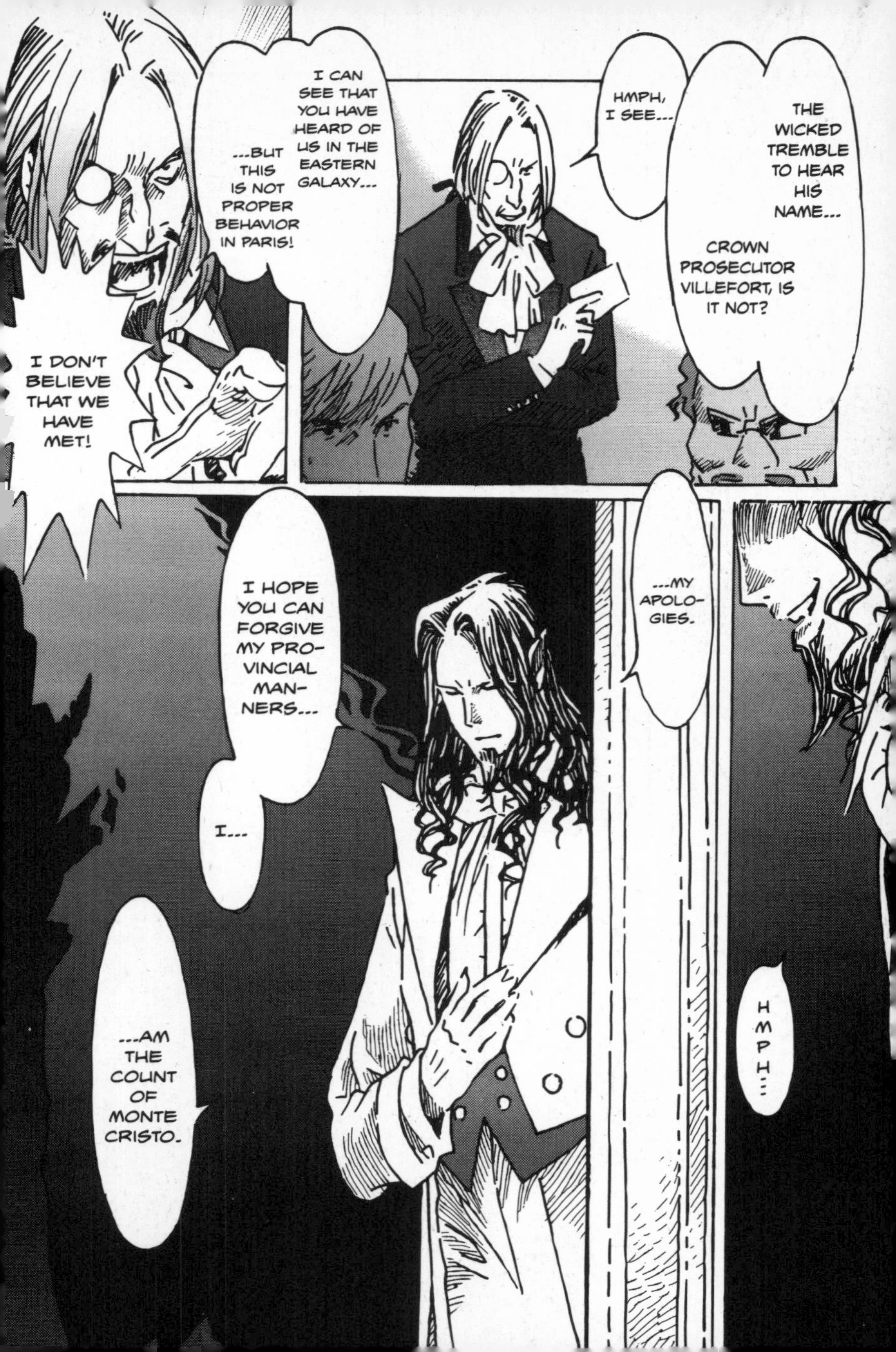
THE WICKED TREMBLE TO HEAR HIS NAME...
CROWN PROSECUTOR VILLEFORT, IS IT NOT?
HMPH, I SEE...
I CAN SEE THAT YOU HAVE HEARD OF US IN THE EASTERN GALAXY...
...BUT THIS IS NOT PROPER BEHAVIOR IN PARIS!
I DON'T BELIEVE THAT WE HAVE MET!
HMPH...
...MY APOLOGIES.
I HOPE YOU CAN FORGIVE MY PROVINCIAL MANNERS...
I...
...AM THE COUNT OF MONTE CRISTO.

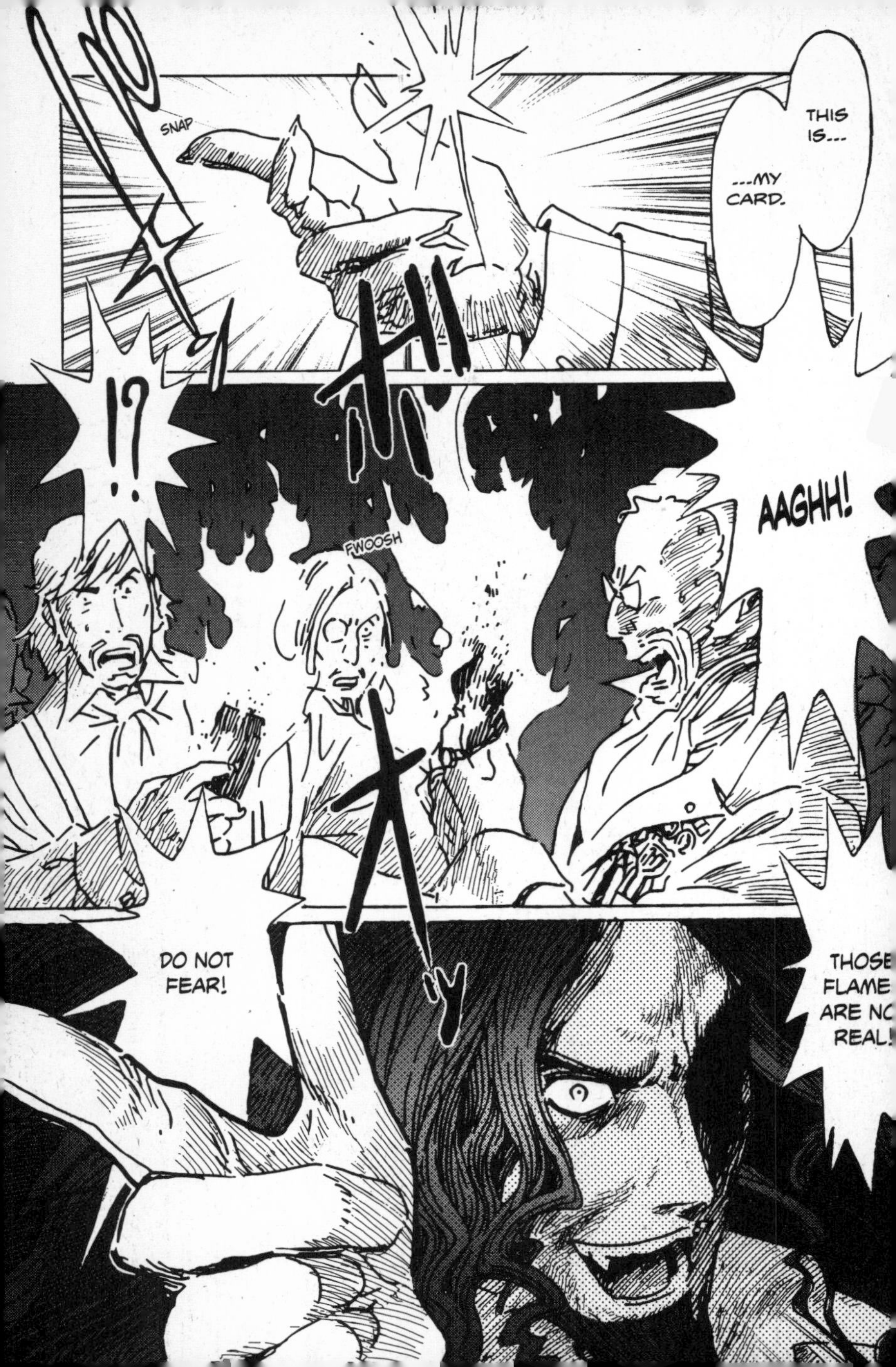
THIS IS...
...MY CARD.
SNAP
AAGHH!
FWOOSH
!?
THOSE FLAME ARE NO REAL!
DO NOT FEAR!

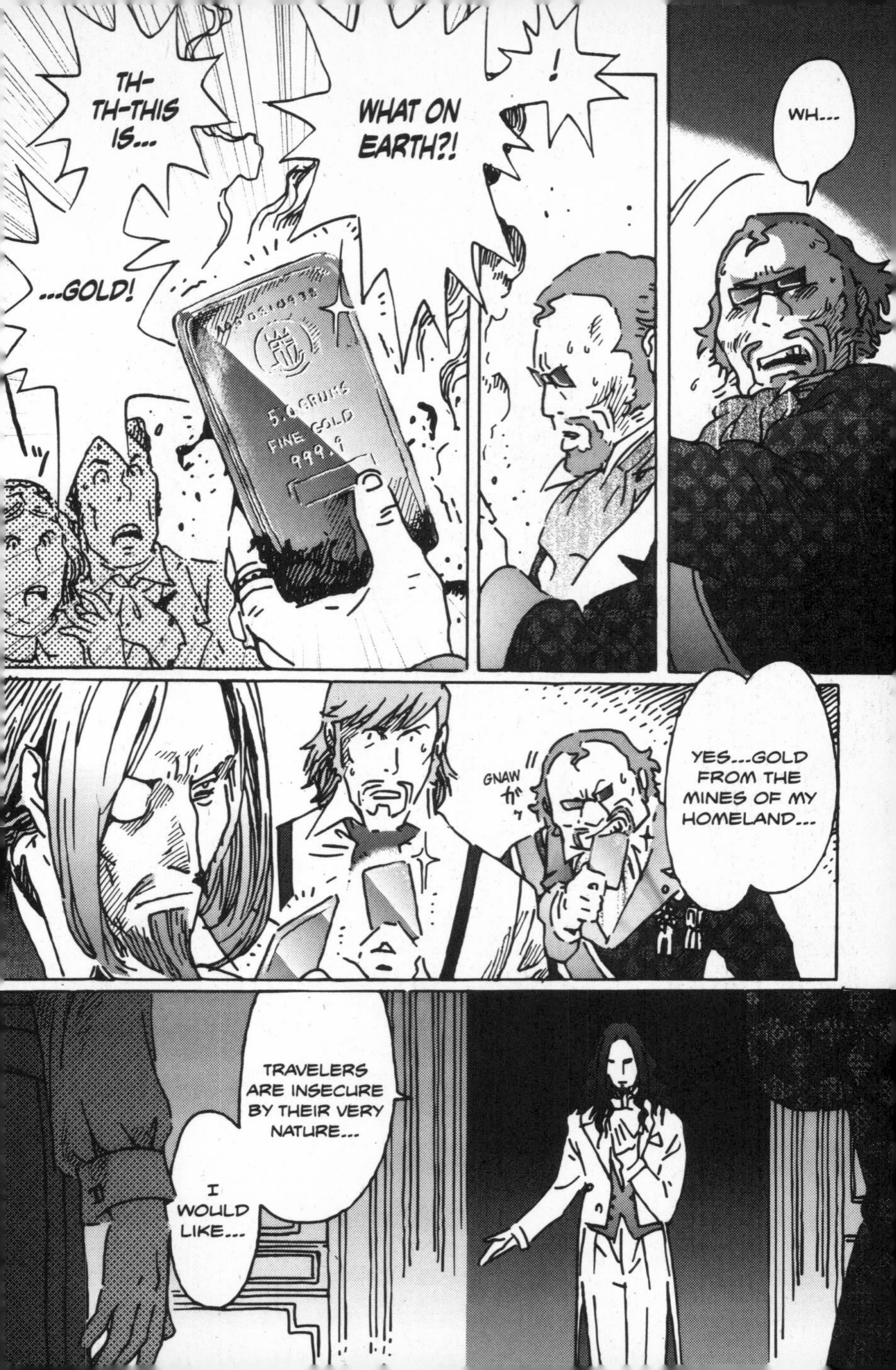
WH...
!
WHAT ON EARTH?!
TH-TH-THIS IS...
...GOLD!
YES...GOLD FROM THE MINES OF MY HOMELAND...
GNAW
ガ
TRAVELERS ARE INSECURE BY THEIR VERY NATURE...
I WOULD LIKE...

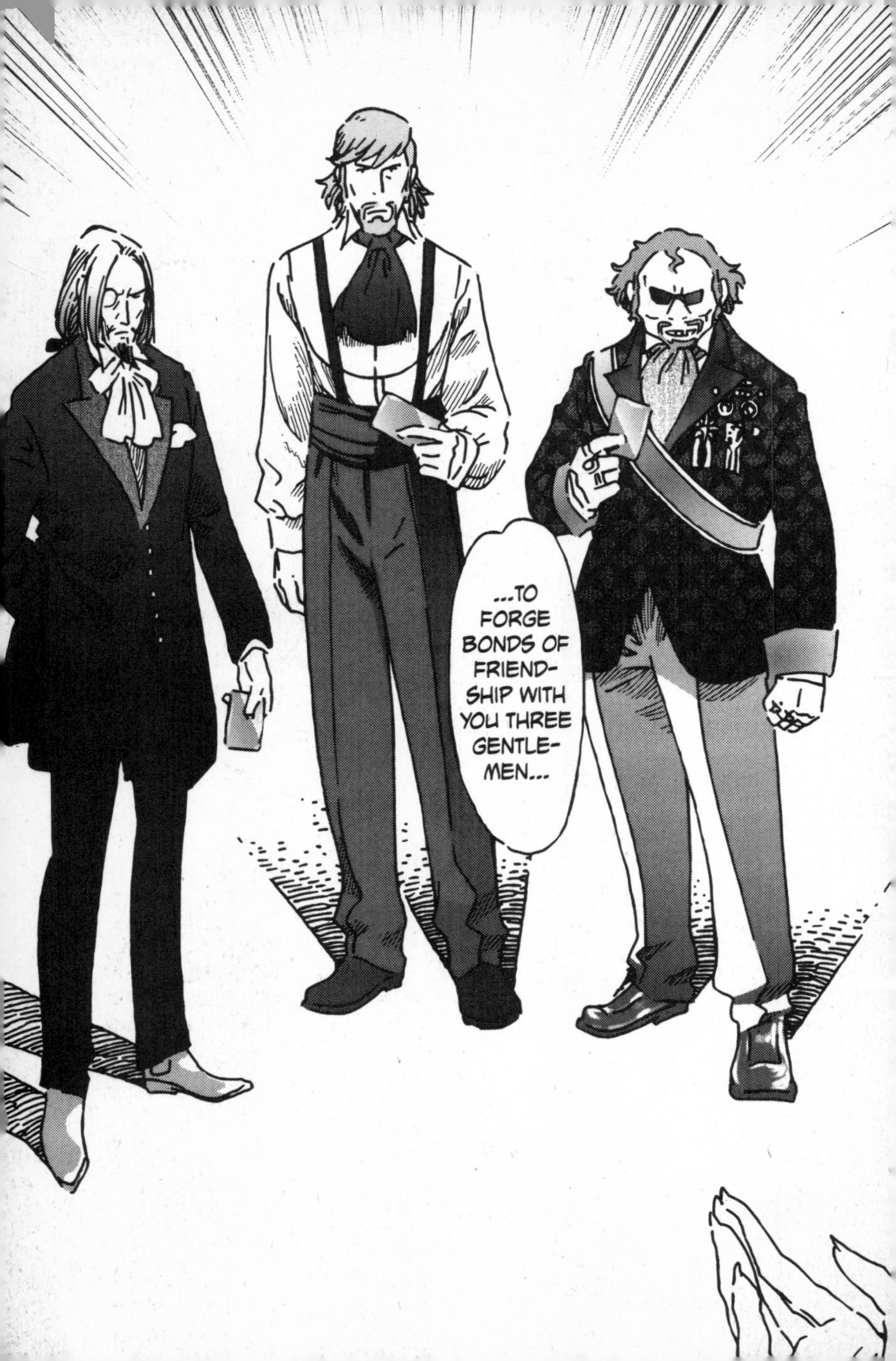
...TO FORGE BONDS OF FRIEND- SHIP WITH YOU THREE GENTLE- MEN...

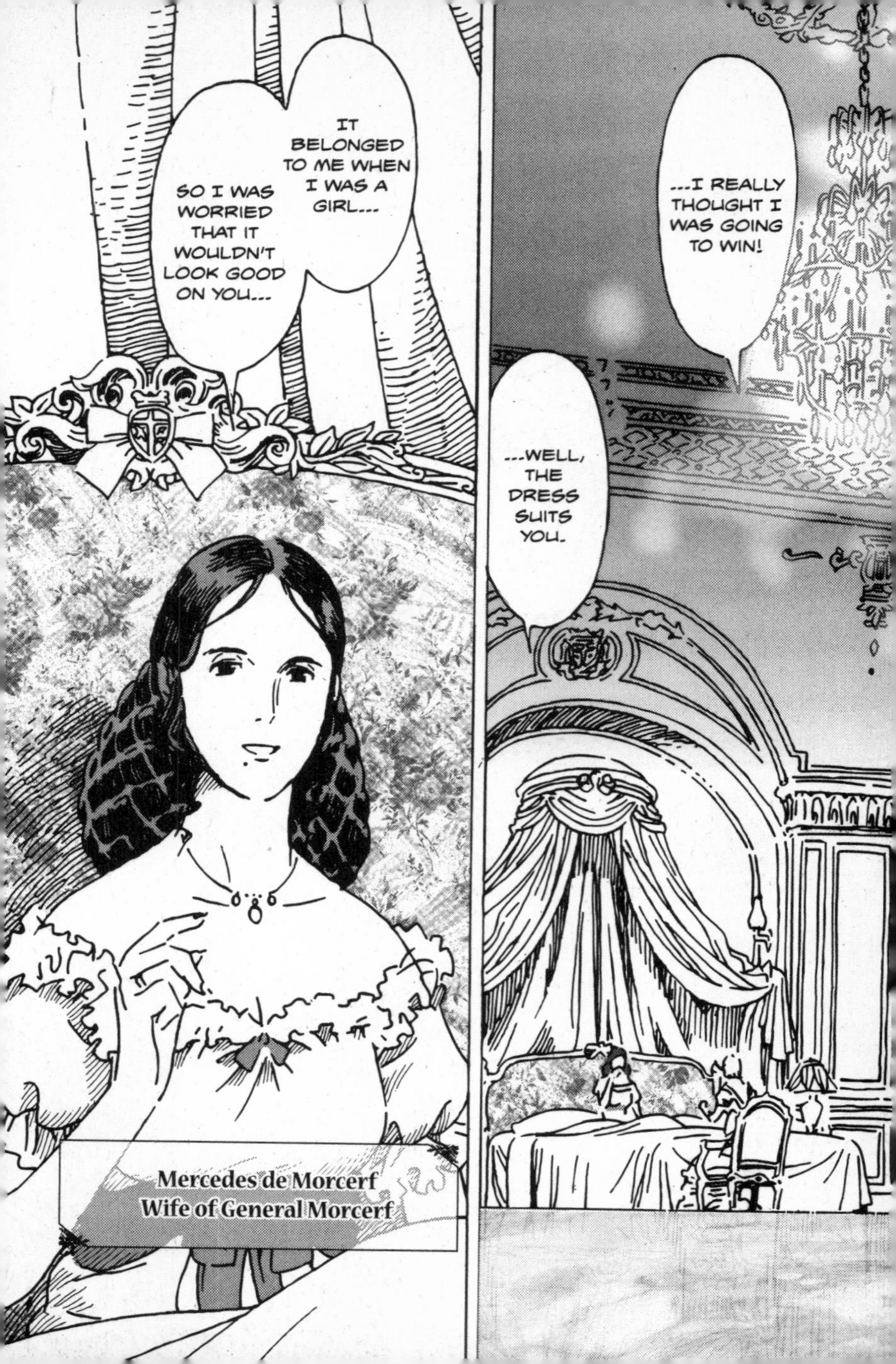
...I REALLY THOUGHT I WAS GOING TO WIN!
...WELL, THE DRESS SUITS YOU.
IT BELONGED TO ME WHEN I WAS A GIRL...
SO I WAS WORRIED THAT IT WOULDN'T LOOK GOOD ON YOU...
Mercedes de Morcerf
Wife of General Morcerf

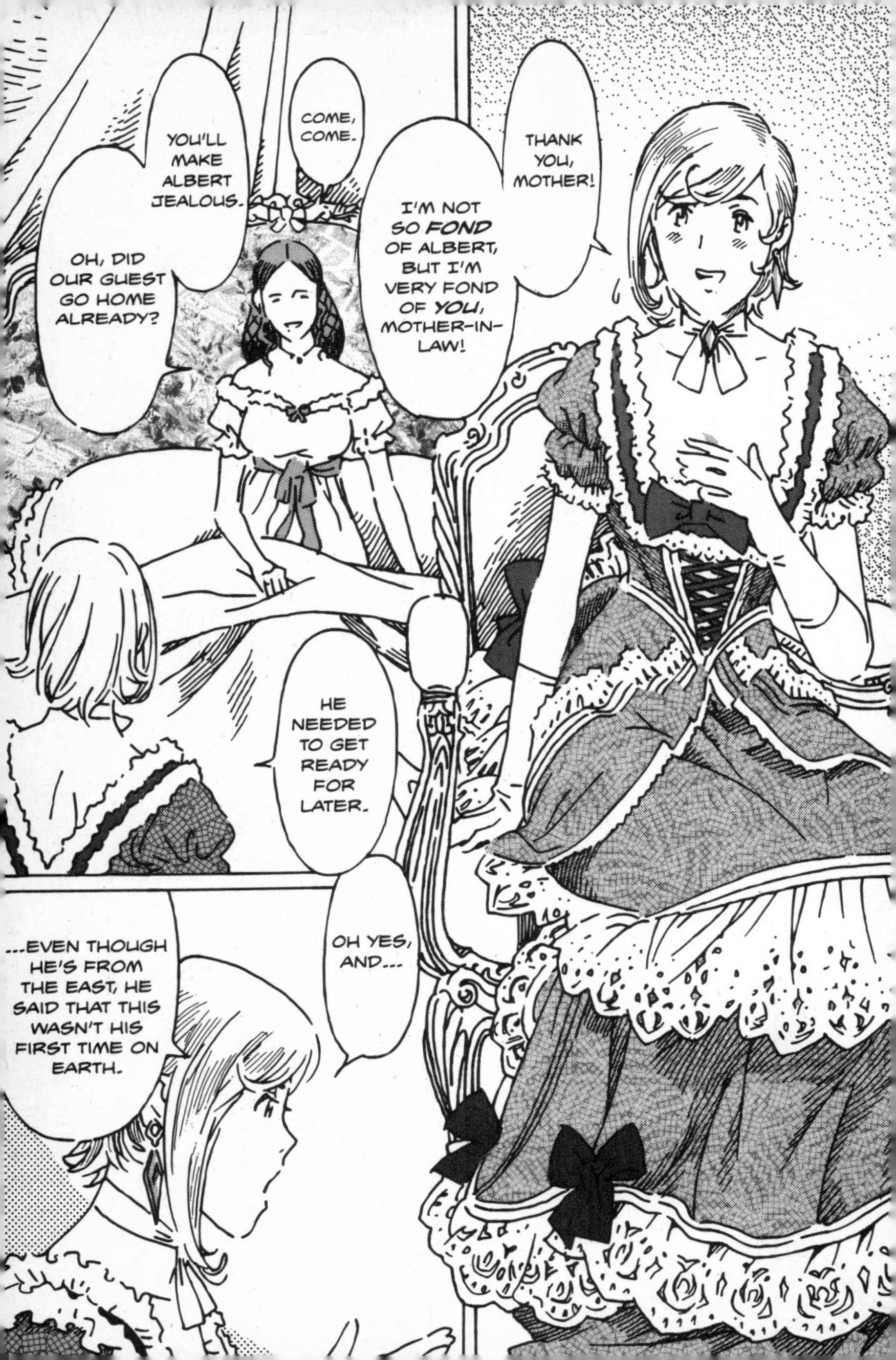
THANK YOU, MOTHER!
I'M NOT SO *FOND* OF ALBERT, BUT I'M VERY FOND OF *YOU*, MOTHER-IN-LAW!
COME, COME.
YOU'LL MAKE ALBERT JEALOUS.
OH, DID OUR GUEST GO HOME ALREADY?
HE NEEDED TO GET READY FOR LATER.
OH YES, AND...
...EVEN THOUGH HE'S FROM THE EAST, HE SAID THAT THIS WASN'T HIS FIRST TIME ON EARTH.

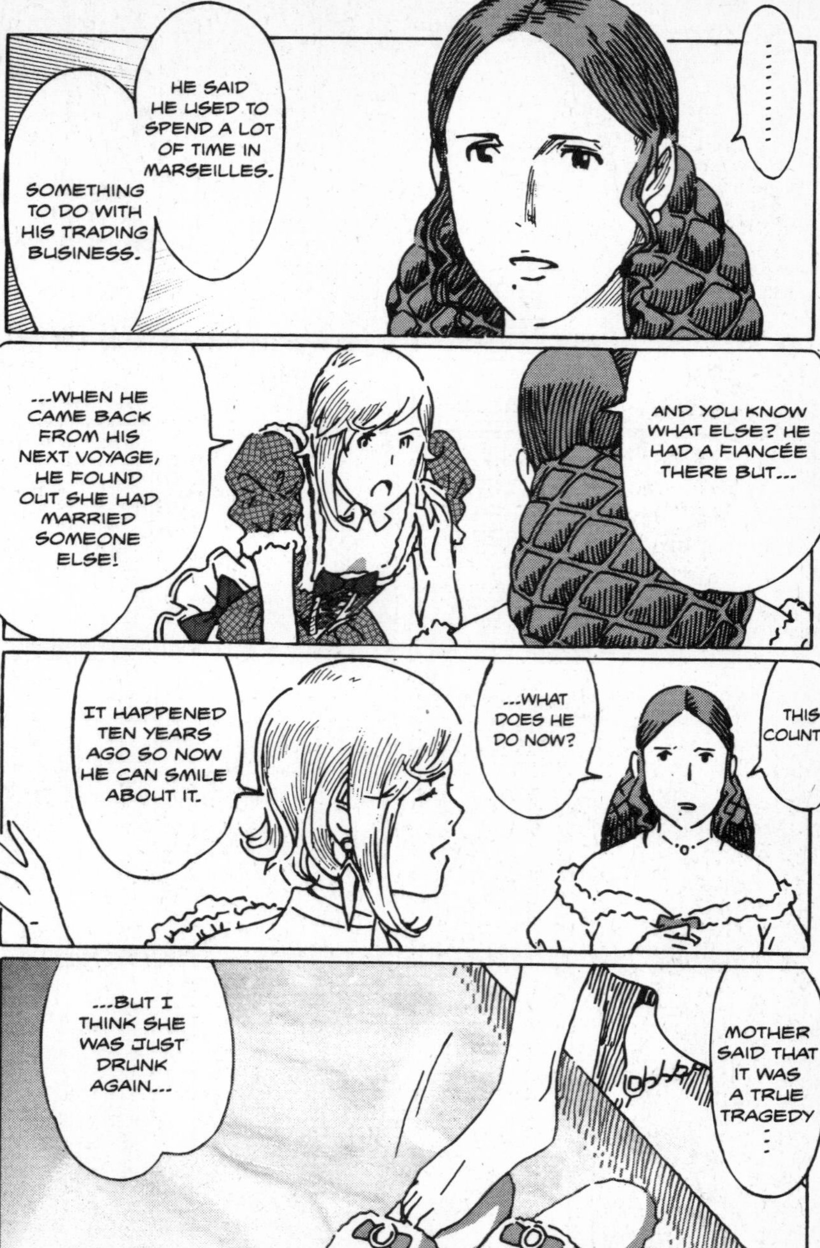
......
HE SAID HE USED TO SPEND A LOT OF TIME IN MARSEILLES.
SOMETHING TO DO WITH HIS TRADING BUSINESS.
AND YOU KNOW WHAT ELSE? HE HAD A FIANCÉE THERE BUT...
...WHEN HE CAME BACK FROM HIS NEXT VOYAGE, HE FOUND OUT SHE HAD MARRIED SOMEONE ELSE!
THIS COUNT...
...WHAT DOES HE DO NOW?
IT HAPPENED TEN YEARS AGO SO NOW HE CAN SMILE ABOUT IT.
MOTHER SAID THAT IT WAS A TRUE TRAGEDY ...
...BUT I THINK SHE WAS JUST DRUNK AGAIN...

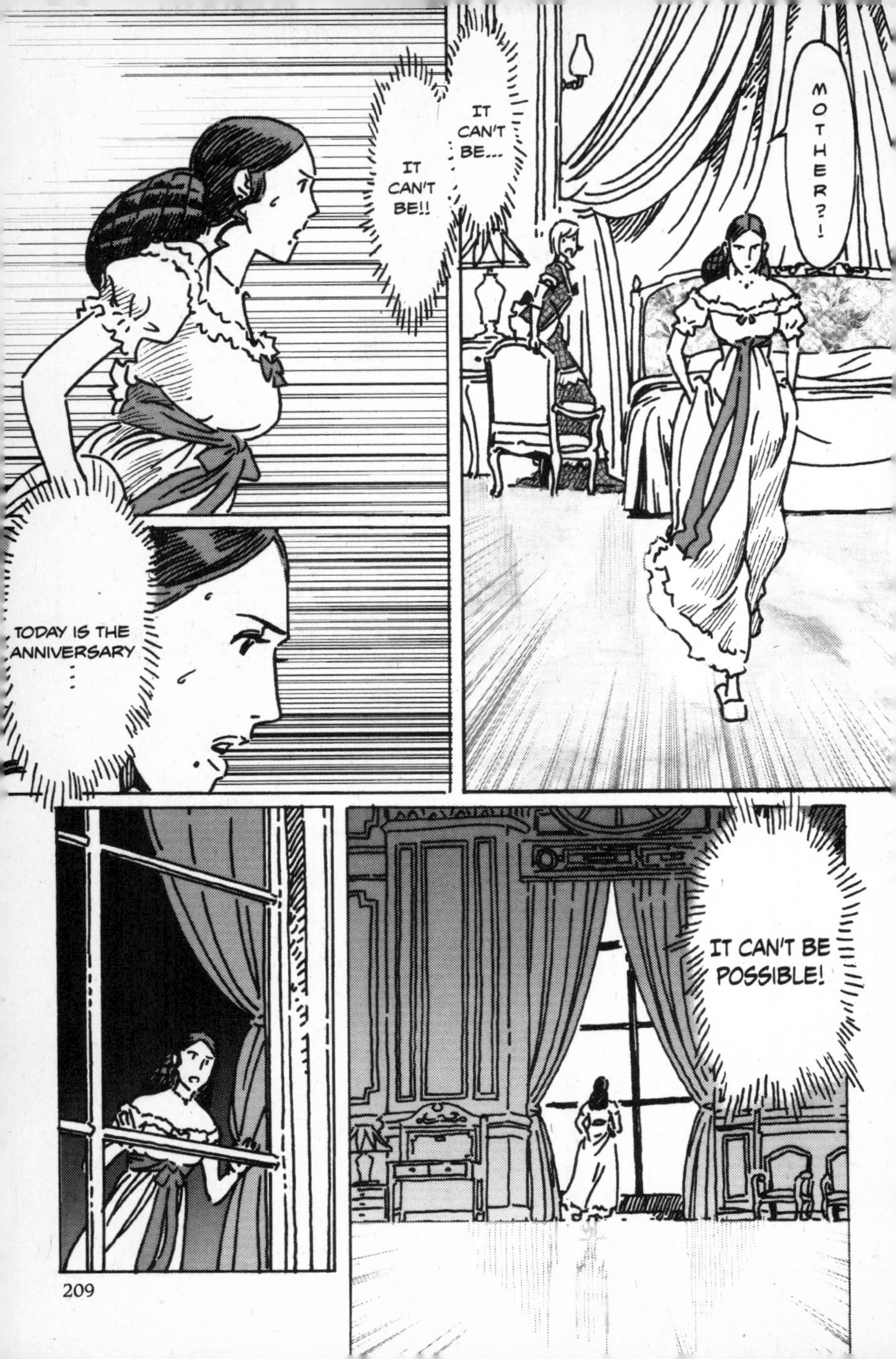
MOTHER?!
IT CAN'T BE...
IT CAN'T BE!!
TODAY IS THE ANNIVERSARY ...
IT CAN'T BE POSSIBLE!

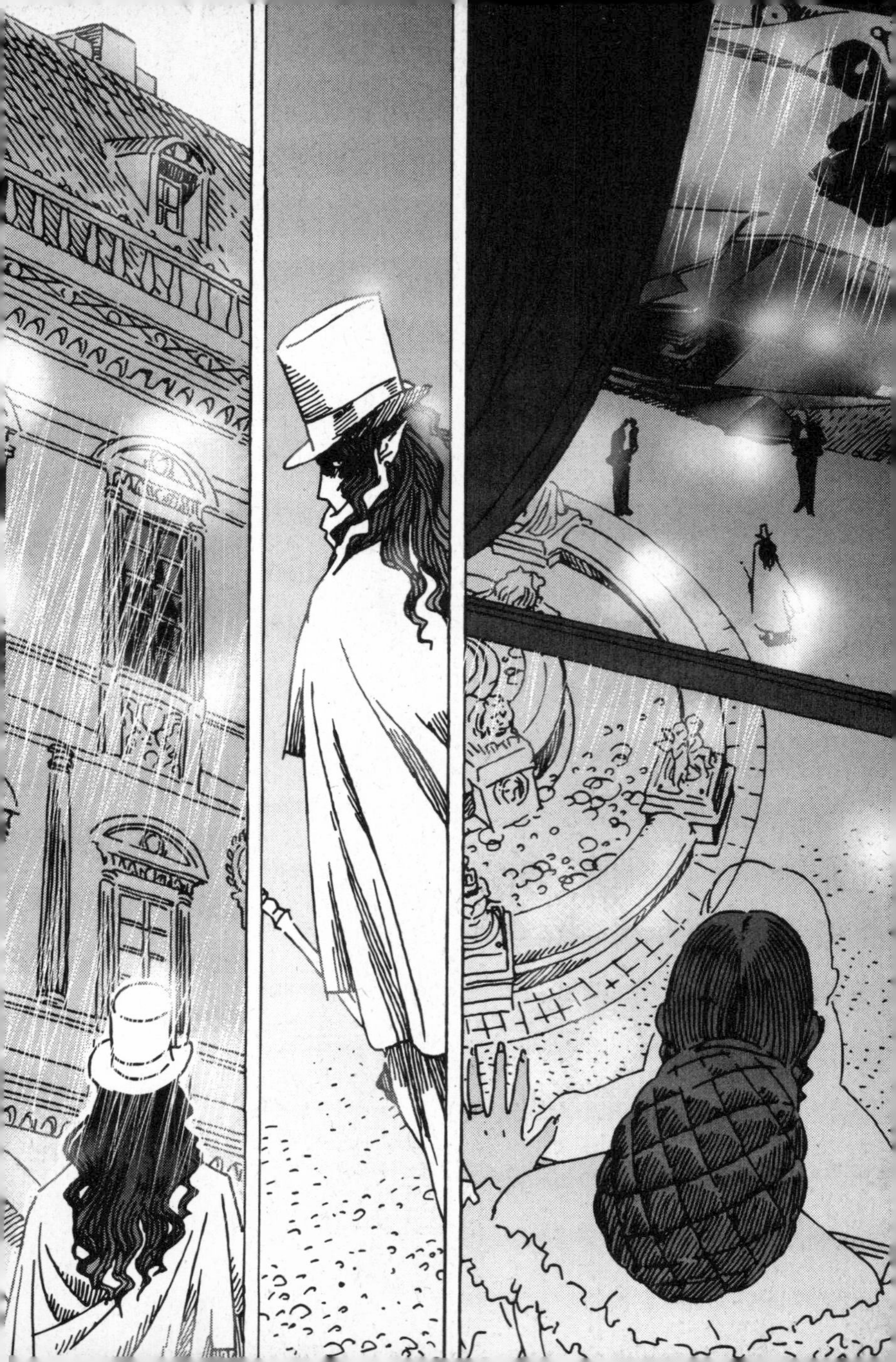

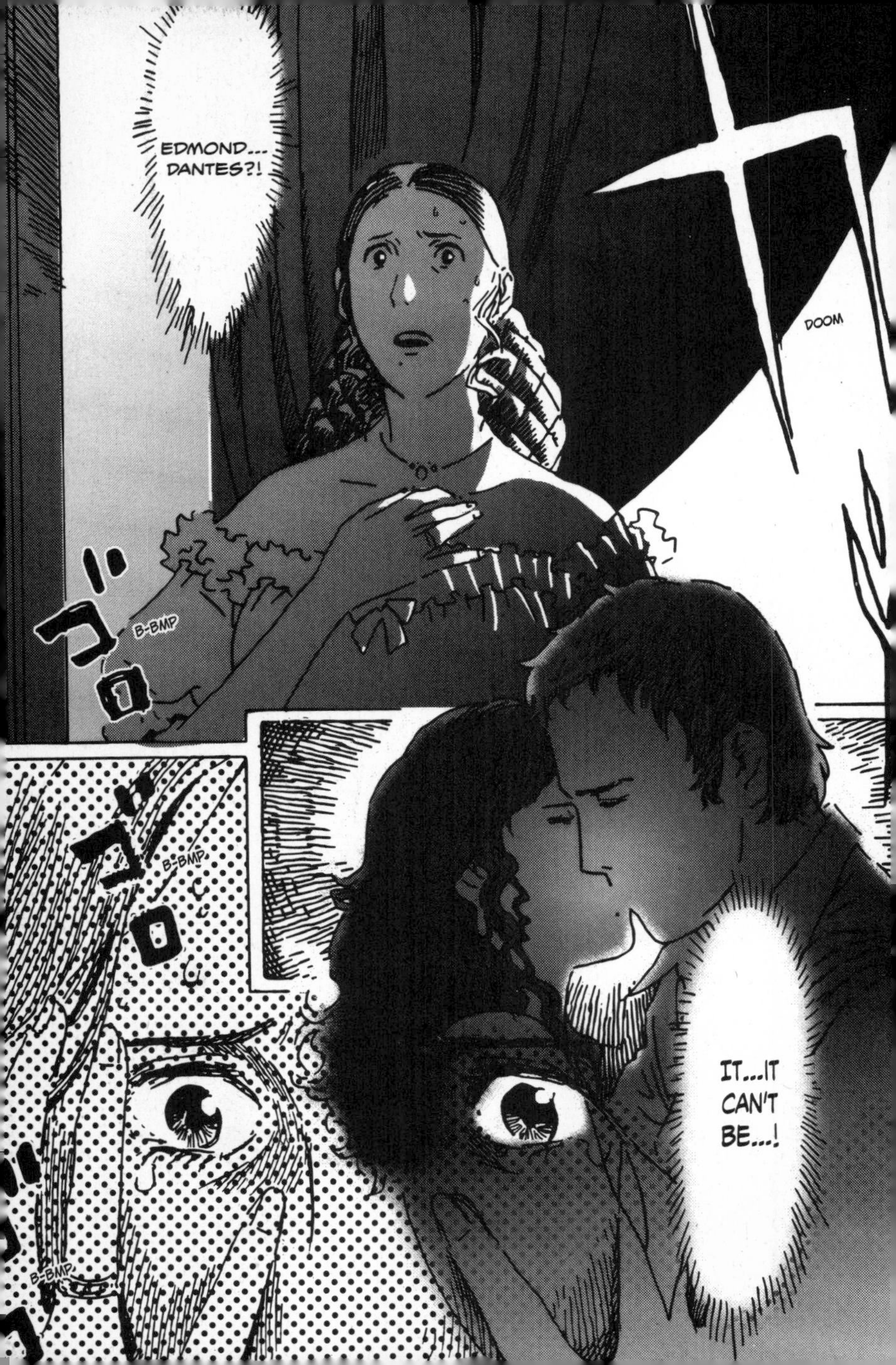
DOOM
EDMOND... DANTES?!
B-BMP
IT...IT CAN'T BE...!
B-BMP
B-BMP

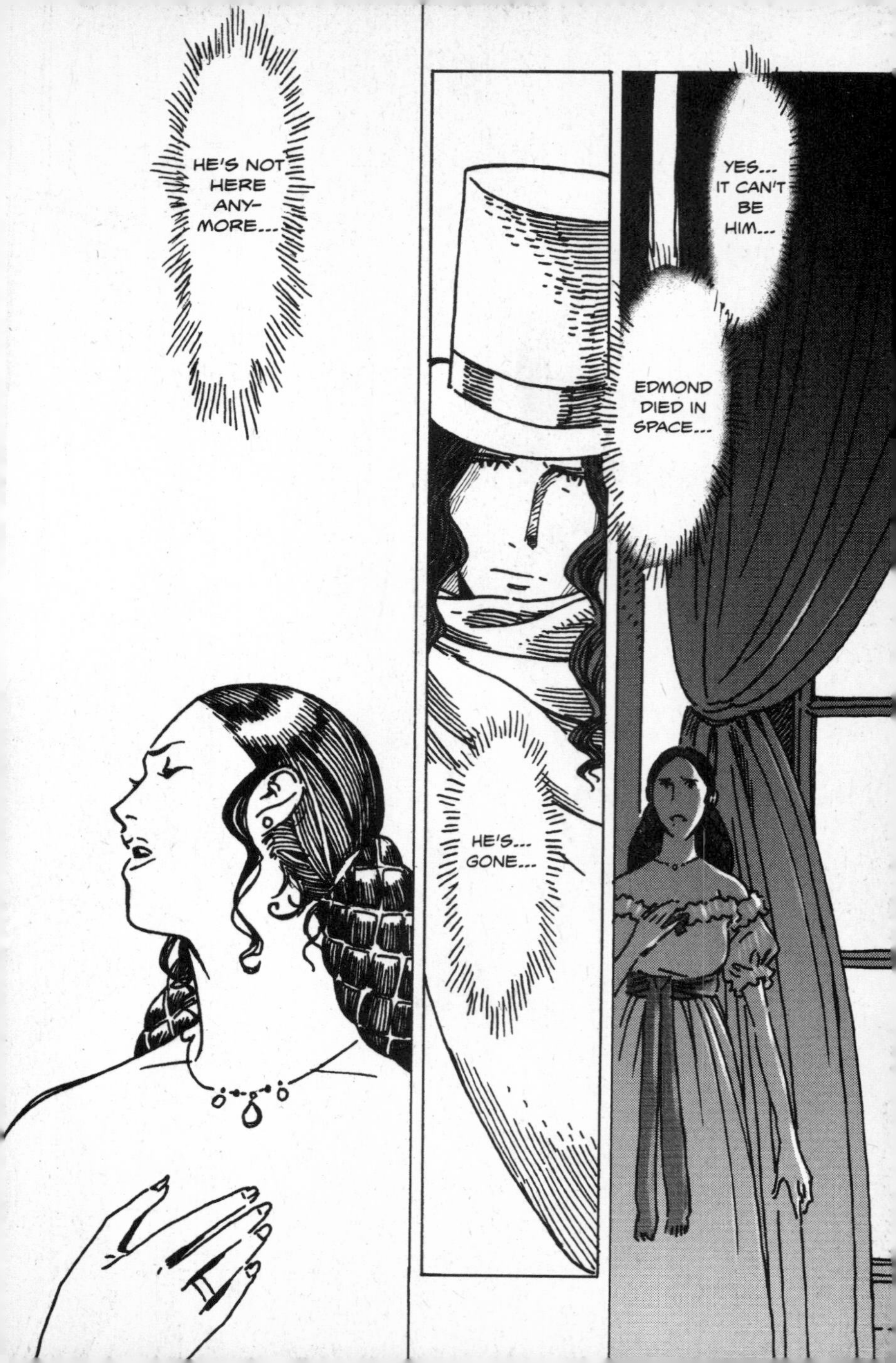
YES... IT CAN'T BE HIM...
EDMOND DIED IN SPACE...
HE'S... GONE...
HE'S NOT HERE ANY-MORE...

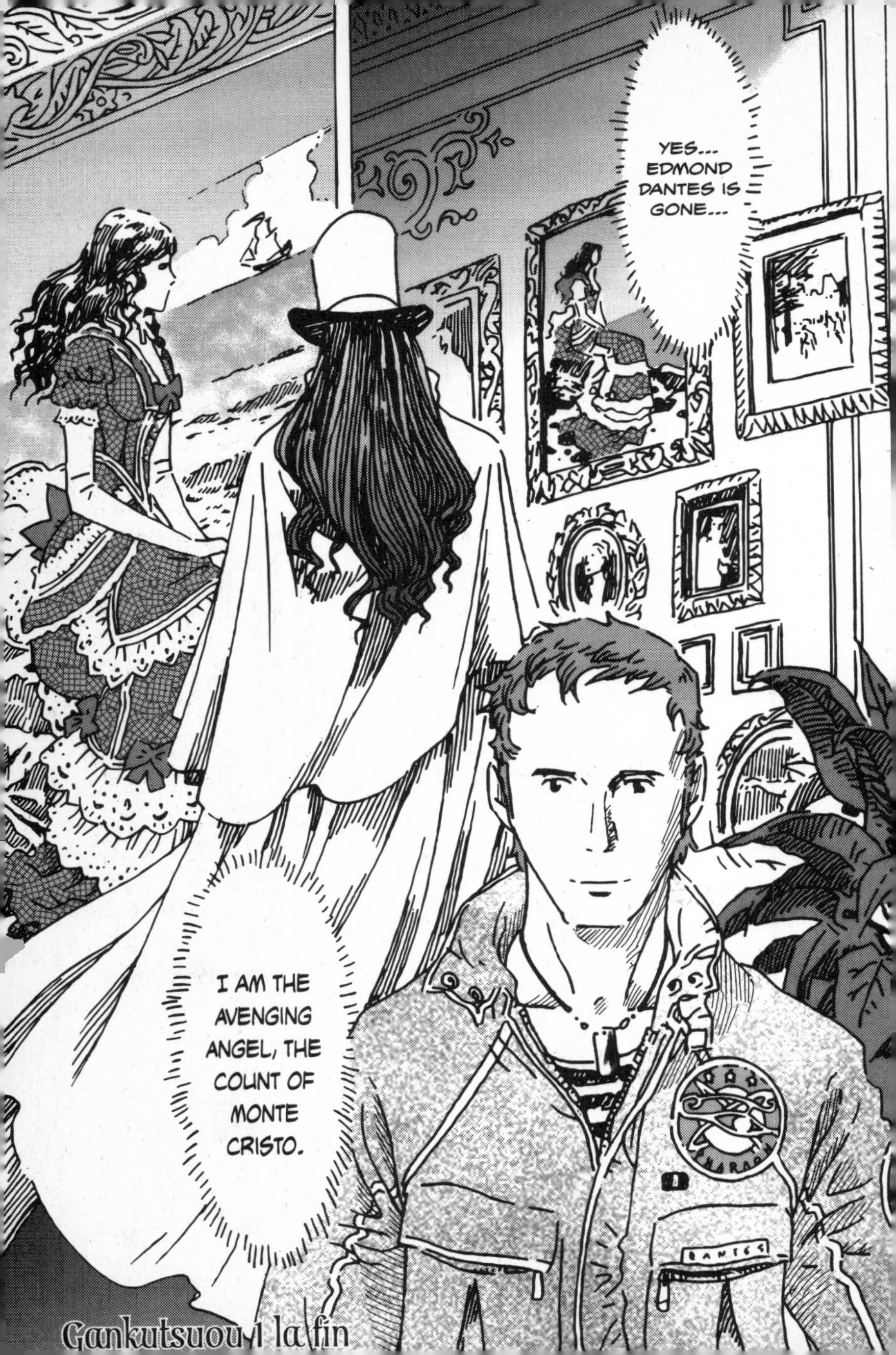
YES... EDMOND DANTES IS GONE...
I AM THE AVENGING ANGEL, THE COUNT OF MONTE CRISTO.
Gankutsuou 1 la fin

One Day with Assistant Furuichi

Furuichi

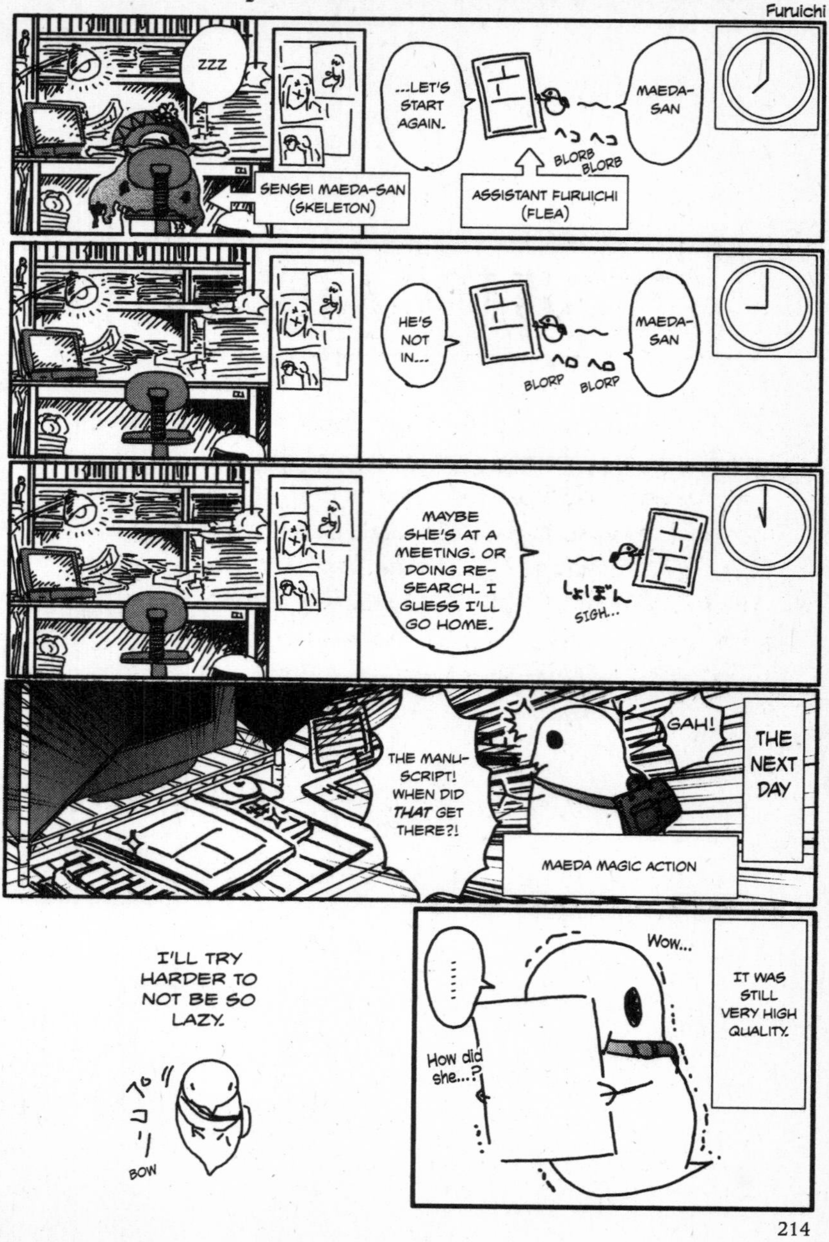
MAEDA-SAN
BLORB BLORB
...LET'S START AGAIN.
ZZZ
ASSISTANT FURUICHI (FLEA)
SENSEI MAEDA-SAN (SKELETON)
MAEDA-SAN
BLORP BLORP
HE'S NOT IN...
しょぼん
SIGH...
MAYBE SHE'S AT A MEETING. OR DOING RE-SEARCH. I GUESS I'LL GO HOME.
THE NEXT DAY
GAH!
MAEDA MAGIC ACTION
THE MANU-SCRIPT! WHEN DID *THAT* GET THERE?!
IT WAS STILL VERY HIGH QUALITY.
Wow...
......
How did she...?
I'LL TRY HARDER TO NOT BE SO LAZY.
BOW

aBOUT THE aUTHORS

Mahiro Maeda is one of the most powerful forces in Japanese animation today, having worked as an animator, a director, and a manga artist. He began his career while a student at university, contributing to such Hayao Miyazaki classics as *Nausicaa of the Valley of the Wind* and *Castle in the Sky*. After having worked for Studio Ghibli and GAINAX, he established GONZO with his friends and went on to direct *Blue Submarine No. 6*, a *Final Fantasy* anime (*FINAL FANTASY: Unlimited*), and his most recent work, *Gankutsuou: The Count of Monte Cristo*.

translation notes

Though *Gankutsuou* was created by a Japanese artist and writer, it is based on Alexandre Dumas's *The Count of Monte Cristo,* a work created in nineteenth-century France. Its science fiction setting thus incorporates many elements of nineteenth-century Europe. Understanding these references will enrich your reading pleasure. Here are notes on some of the allusions to Western culture you'll find in *Gankutsuou: The Count of Monte Cristo.*

Gankutsuou (title)

Japanese for "The King of the Cave." *Gankutsuou* was the Japanese title for Alexandre Dumas's *The Count of Monte Cristo* when it was first translated into Japanese by Kuroiwa Ruikô in 1901-1902. It is also the name for the *Gankutsuou* anime, manga, and Japanese novel series.

Moccoletti, page 9

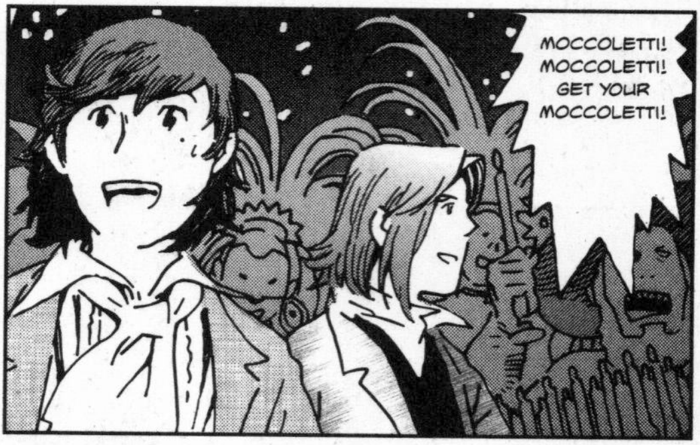
MOCCOLETTI! MOCCOLETTI! GET YOUR MOCCOLETTI!

Italian for "candles." In the Roman Carnival, on which Luna's Carnival is based, there is the tradition of the *Festa dei Moccoletti* (festival of candles). To quote from the original *Count of Monte Cristo*: "The moccoli, or moccoletti, are candles which vary in size from the pascal taper to the rushlight, and which give to each actor in the great final scene of the Carnival two very serious problems to grapple with–first, how to keep his own moccoletto alight; and secondly, how to extinguish the moccoletti of others. The moccoletto is like life: man has found but one means of transmitting it, and that one comes from God. But he has discovered a thousand means of taking it away, and the devil has somewhat aided him."

Countess G___, page 20

Initialing names and places was common in nineteenth-century novels. This was done to create a feeling of verisimilitude while avoiding obvious references to real people, which might cause a scandal, as is the case here with Countess G___. It was also done with locations so the author didn't have to worry about consistency issues or getting the facts straight.

Lucia, page 25

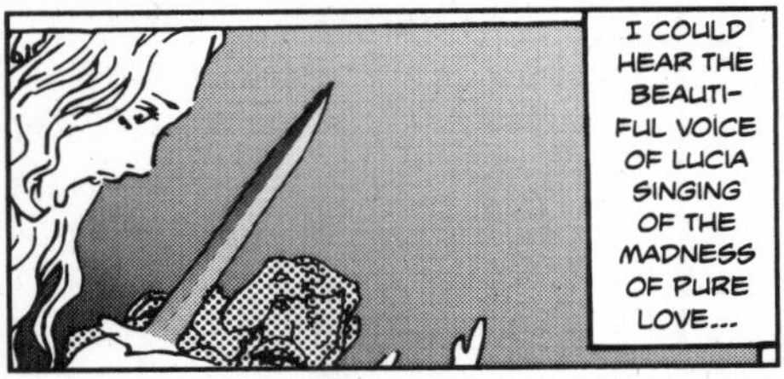
I COULD HEAR THE BEAUTI-FUL VOICE OF LUCIA SINGING OF THE MADNESS OF PURE LOVE...

Lucia di Lammermoor is an Italian opera written in 1835 by Gaetano Donizetti. It is a tragic opera based on Sir Walter Scott's historical novel, "The Bride of Lammermoor." One of the well-known pieces from this opera is Lucia's "mad scene," a technically demanding piece for opera singers.

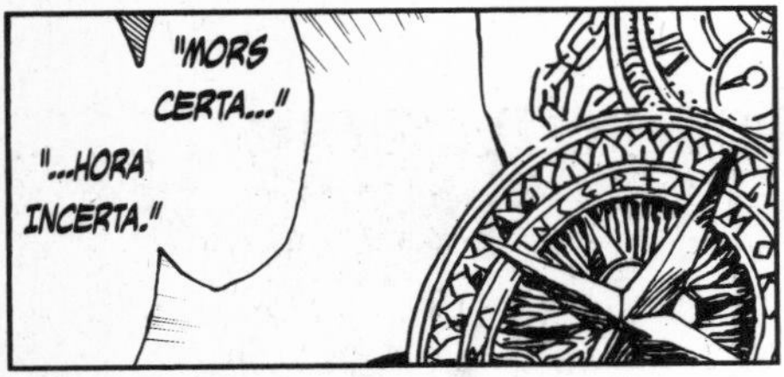
"MORS CERTA..."
"...HORA INCERTA."

Mors Certa, Hora Incerta, page 32

A Latin saying meaning "Death is certain, the hour is not."

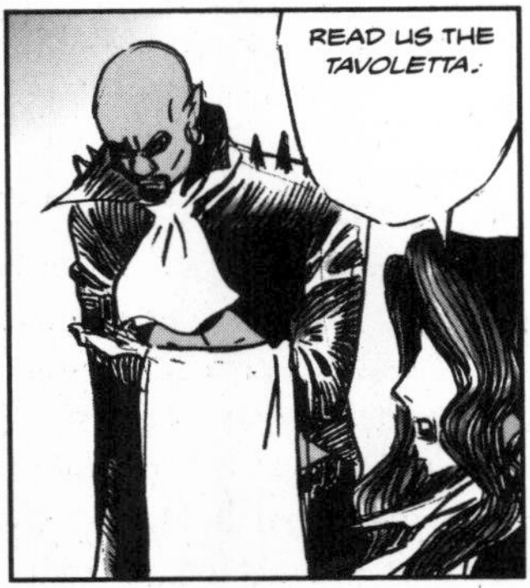
READ US THE TAVOLETTA.

Tavoletta, page 63

Italian for "schedule."

Rue du Faubourg, page 99

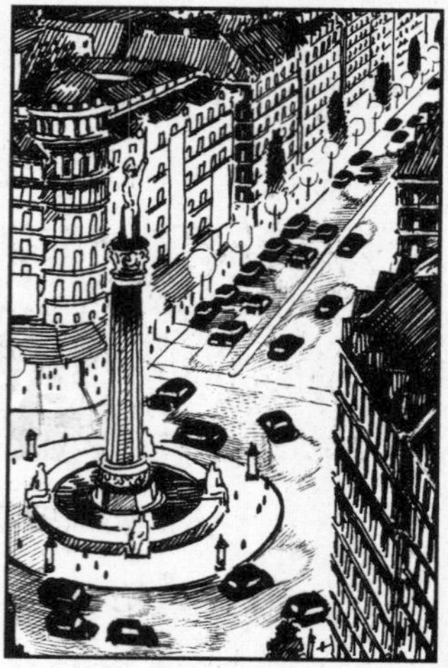

The Rue du Faubourg St. Honoré, although as not as famous as other streets in Paris like the Champs-Élysées, is known for being one of the most fashionable streets of the city. Several famous fashion labels have stores along this street, including the flagship store of Hermès. A family that could afford to live on this street would have to be very wealthy.

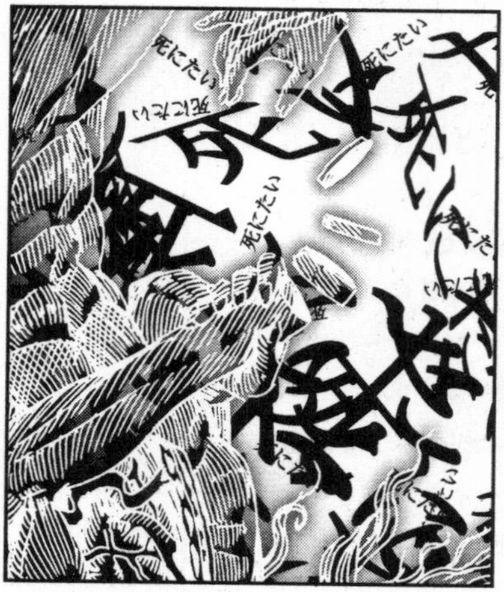
死にたい
死にたい
死にたい

Background Text, pages 154-155

The background text is the Japanese phrase *shinitai* repeated over and over, literally meaning "I want to die."

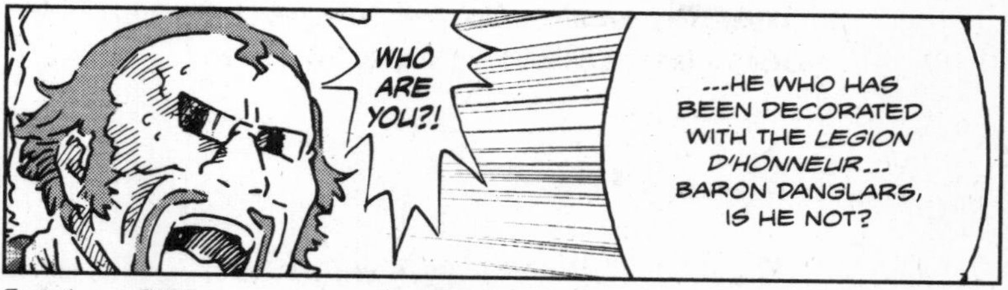
...HE WHO HAS BEEN DECORATED WITH THE *LEGION D'HONNEUR*... BARON DANGLARS, IS HE NOT?
WHO ARE YOU?!

Légion d'Honneur, page 201

The *Légion d'Honneur* ("Legion of Honor") is a French order established by Napoleon Bonaparte to commend civilians and soldiers for their contribution to the country. It is a world-renowned honor and the highest honor in France.

TOMARE! [STOP!]

You are going the wrong way!

Manga is a completely different type of reading experience.

To start at the *beginning*, go to the *end*!

That's right! Authentic manga is read the traditional Japanese way—from right to left. Exactly the *opposite* of how American books are read. It's easy to follow: Just go to the other end of the book, and read each page—and each panel—from right side to left side, starting at the top right. Now you're experiencing manga as it was meant to be.